U•X•L *Encyclopedia of*
Native American Tribes

THIRD EDITION

U•X•L Encyclopedia of

Native American Tribes

THIRD EDITION

VOLUME 3

SOUTHWEST

Laurie J. Edwards, Editor

U·X·L
A part of Gale, Cengage Learning

GALE
CENGAGE Learning·

Detroit • New York • San Francisco • New Haven, Conn • Waterville, Maine • London

U•X•L Encyclopedia of Native American Tribes, 3rd Edition

Laurie J. Edwards

Project Editors: Shelly Dickey, Terri Schell

Rights Acquisition and Management: Leitha Etheridge-Sims

Composition: Evi Abou-El-Seoud

Manufacturing: Wendy Blurton

Imaging: John Watkins

Product Design: Kristine Julien

© 2012 Gale, Cengage Learning

For product information and technology assistance, contact us at **Gale Customer Support, 1-800-877-4253.**
For permission to use material from this text or product, submit all requests online at **www.cengage.com/permissions.**
Further permissions questions can be emailed to **permission request@cengage.com**

Cover photographs reproduced by permission of Sky City, ©Buddy Mays/Alamy; Pottery art sale, ©Geomphotography/Alamy.

While every effort has been made to ensure the reliability of the information presented in this publication, Gale, a part of Cengage Learning, does not guarantee the accuracy of the data contained herein. Gale accepts no payment for listing; and inclusion in the publication of any organization, agency, institution, publication, service, or individual does not imply endorsement of the editors or publisher. Errors brought to the attention of the publisher and verified to the satisfaction of the publisher will be corrected in future editions.

LIBRARY OF CONGRESS CATALOGING-IN-PUBLICATION DATA

U•X•L Encyclopedia of Native American Tribes / Laurie J. Edwards ; Shelly Dickey, Terri Schell, project editors. -- 3rd ed.
    5 v. . cm.
    Includes bibliographical references and index.
    ISBN 978-1-4144-9092-2 (set) -- ISBN 978-1-4144-9093-9 (v. 1) -- ISBN 978-1-4144-9094-6 (v.2) -- ISBN 978-1-4144-9095-3 (v.3) -- ISBN 978-1-4144-9096-0 (v. 4) -- ISBN 978-1-4144-9097-7 (v. 5),
    1. Indians of North America--Encyclopedias, Juvenile. 2. Indians of North America--Encyclopedias. I. Edwards, Laurie J. II. Dickey, Shelly. III. Schell, Terri, 1968-

E76.2.U85 2012
970.004'97003--dc23   2011048142

Gale
27500 Drake Rd.
Farmington Hills, MI, 48331-3535

978-1-4144-9092-2 (set)   1-4144-9092-5 (set)
978-1-4144-9093-9 (v. 1)   1-4144-9093-3 (v. 1)
978-1-4144-9094-6 (v. 2)   1-4144-9094-1 (v. 2)
978-1-4144-9095-3 (v. 3)   1-4144-9095-X (v. 3)
978-1-4144-9096-0 (v. 4)   1-4144-9096-8 (v. 4)
978-1-4144-9097-7 (v. 5)   1-4144-9097-6 (v. 5)

This title is also available as an e-book.
ISBN 13: 978-1-4144-9098-4 ISBN 10: 1-4144-9098-4
Contact your Gale, a part of Cengage Learning, sales representative for ordering information.

Printed in U.S.A.
1 2 3 4 5 6 7 16 15 14 13 12

Contents

Tribes Alphabetically

First numeral signifies volume number. The numeral after the colon signifies page number. For example, 3:871 means Volume 3, page 871.

Reader's Guide

Long before the Vikings, Spaniards, and Portuguese made land-fall on North American shores, the continent already had a rich history of human settlement. The *U•X•L Encyclopedia of Native American Tribes, 3rd Edition* opens up for students the array of tribal ways in the United States and Canada past and present. Included in these volumes, readers will find the stories of:

- the well-known nineteenth century Lakota hunting the buffalo on the Great Plains
- the contemporary Inuit of the Arctic, who in 1999 won their battle for Nunavut, a vast, self-governing territory in Canada
- the Haida of the Pacific Northwest, whose totem poles have become a familiar adornment of the landscape
- the Anasazi in the Southwest, who were building spectacular cities long before Europeans arrived
- the Mohawk men in the Northeast who made such a name for themselves as ironworkers on skyscrapers and bridges that they have long been in demand for such projects as the Golden Gate Bridge
- the Yahi of California, who became extinct when their last member, Ishi, died in 1916.

The *U•X•L Encyclopedia of Native American Tribes, 3rd Edition* presents 106 tribes, confederacies, and Native American groups. Among the tribes included are large and well-known nations, smaller communities with their own fascinating stories, and prehistoric peoples. The tribes are grouped in the ten major geographical/cultural areas of North America in which tribes shared environmental and cultural connections. The ten sections, each beginning with an introductory essay on the geographical area and the shared history and culture within it, are arranged in the volumes as follows:

- Volume 1: Northeast and Subarctic
- Volume 2: Southeast and Great Plains
- Volume 3: Southwest
- Volume 4: California and Plateau
- Volume 5: Great Basin, Pacific Northwest, and Arctic

The *U•X•L Encyclopedia of Native American Tribes, 3rd Edition* provides the history of each of the tribes featured and a fascinating look at their ways of life: how families lived in centuries past and today, what people ate and wore, what their homes were like, how they worshiped, celebrated, governed themselves, and much more. A student can learn in depth about one tribe or compare aspects of many tribes. Each detailed entry is presented in consistent rubrics that allow for easy access and comparison, as follows:

- History
- Religion
- Language
- Government
- Economy
- Daily Life
- Arts
- Customs
- Current Tribal Issues
- Notable People

Each entry begins with vital data on the tribe: name, location, population, language family, origins and group affiliations. A locator map follows, showing the traditional homelands and contemporary communities of the group; regional and migration maps throughout aid in locating the many groups at different times in history. Brief timelines in each entry chronicle important dates of the tribe's history, while an overall timeline at the beginning of all the volumes outlines key events in history pertinent to all Native Americans. Other sidebars present recipes, oral literature or stories, language keys, and background material on the tribe. Color photographs and illustrations, further reading sections, a thorough subject index, and a glossary are special features that make the volumes easy, fun, and informative to use.

A note on terminology

Throughout the *U•X•L Encyclopedia of Native American Tribes, 3rd Edition* various terms are used for Native North Americans, such as *Indian, American Indian, Native,* and *aboriginal.* The Native peoples of the Americas have the unfortunate distinction of having been given the wrong name by the Europeans who first arrived on the continent, mistakenly thinking they had arrived in India. The search for a single name, however, has never been entirely successful. The best way to characterize Native North Americans is by recognizing their specific tribal or community identities. In compiling this book, every effort has been made to keep Native tribal and community identities distinct, but by necessity, inclusive terminology is often used. We do not wish to offend anyone, but rather than favor one term for Native North American people, the editors have used a variety of terminology, trying always to use the most appropriate term in the particular context.

Europeans also had a hand in giving names to tribes, often misunderstanding their languages and the relations between different Native communities. Most tribes have their own names for themselves, and many have succeeded in gaining public acceptance of traditional names. The Inuit, for example, objected to the name Eskimo, which means "eaters of raw meat," and in time their name for themselves was accepted. In the interest of clarity the editors of this book have used the currently accepted terms, while acknowledging the traditional ones or the outmoded ones at the beginning of each entry.

The term *tribe* is not accepted by all Native groups. The people living in North America before the Europeans arrived had many different ways of organizing themselves politically and relating to other groups around them—from complex confederacies and powerful unified nations to isolated villages with little need for political structure. Groups divided, absorbed each other, intermarried, allied, and dissolved. The epidemics and wars that came with non-Native expansion into North America created a demographic catastrophe to many Native groups and greatly affected tribal affiliations. Although in modern times there are actual rules about what comprise a tribe (federal requirements for recognition of tribes are specific, complicated, and often difficult to fulfill), the hundreds of groups living in the Americas in early times did not have any one way of categorizing themselves. Thus, some Native American peoples today find the word *tribe* misleading. In a study of Native peoples, it can also be an elusive defining term. But in facing the challenges of maintaining traditions and heritage in modern times, tribal or community identity is acutely important to many Native Americans. Tremendous efforts have been undertaken to preserve native languages, oral traditions, religions, ceremonies, and traditional arts and economies—the things that, put together, make a tribe a cultural and political unit.

Comments and suggestions

In this third edition of the *U•X•L Encyclopedia of Native American Tribes* we have presented in-depth information on 106 of the hundreds of tribes of North America. While every attempt was made to include a wide representation of groups, many historically important and interesting tribes are not covered in these volumes. We welcome your suggestions for tribes to be featured in future editions, as well as any other comments you may have on this set. Please write: Editors, *U•X•L Encyclopedia of Native American Tribes, 3rd Edition,* U•X•L 27500 Drake Road, Farmington Hills, Michigan 48331-3535; call toll-free 1-800-877-4253; or fax 248-699-8097; or send e-mail via http://www.gale.com.

Words to Know

Aboriginal: Native, or relating to the first or earliest group living in a particular area.

Activism: Taking action for or against a controversial issue; political and social activists may organize or take part in protest demonstrations, rallies, petitioning the government, sit-ins, civil disobedience, and many other forms of activities that draw attention to an issue and/or challenge the authorities to make a change.

Adobe: A brick or other building material made from sun-dried mud, a mixture of clay, sand, and sometimes ashes, rocks, or straw.

Alaska Native Claims Settlement Act (ANCSA): An act of Congress passed in 1971 that gave Alaska Natives 44 million acres of land and $962.5 million. In exchange, Alaska Natives gave up all claim to other lands in Alaska. The ANCSA also resulted in the formation of 12 regional corporations in Alaska in charge of Native communities' economic development and land use.

Allotment: The practice of dividing and distributing land into individual lots. In 1887 the U.S. Congress passed the General Allotment Act (also known as the Dawes Act), which divided Indian reservations into privately owned parcels (pieces) of land. Under allotment, tribes could no longer own their own lands in common (as a group) in the traditional ways. Instead the head of a family received a lot, generally 160 acres. Land not alloted was sold to non-Natives.

American Indian Movement (AIM): An activist movement founded in 1966 to aggressively press for Indian rights. The movement was formed to improve federal, state, and local social services to Native Americans in urban neighborhoods. AIM sought the reorganization of the Bureau of Indian Affairs to make it more responsive to Native American needs and fought for the return of Indian lands illegally taken from them.

Anthropology: The study of human beings in terms of their populations, culture, social relations, ethnic characteristics, customs, and adaptation to their environment.

Archaeology: The study of the remains of past human life, such as fossil relics, artifacts, and monuments, in order to understand earlier human cultures.

Arctic: Relating to the area surrounding the North Pole.

Assimilate: To absorb, or to be absorbed, into the dominant society (those in power, or in the majority). U.S. assimilation policies were directed at causing Native Americans to become like European-Americans in terms of jobs and economics, religion, customs, language, education, family life, and dress.

Band: A small, loosely organized social group composed of several families. In Canada, the word band originally referred to a social unit of nomadic (those who moved from place to place) hunting peoples, but now refers to a community of Indians registered with the government.

Boarding school: A live-in school.

Breechcloth: A garment with front and back flaps that hangs from the waist. Breechcloths were one of the most common articles of clothing worn by many Native American men and sometimes women in pre-European/American settlement times.

Bureau of Indian Affairs (BIA): The U.S. government agency that oversees tribal lands, education, and other aspects of Indian life.

Census: A count of the population.

Ceremony: A special act or set of acts (such as a wedding or a funeral) performed by members of a group on important occasions, usually organized according to the group's traditions and beliefs.

Clan: A group of related house groups and families that trace back to a common ancestor or a common symbol or totem, usually an animal such as the bear or the turtle. The clan forms the basic social and political unit for many Indian societies.

Colonialism: A state or nation's control over a foreign territory.

Colonize: To establish a group of people from a mother country or state in a foreign territory; the colonists set up a community that remains tied to the mother county.

Confederacy: A group of people, states, or nations joined together for mutual support or for a special purpose.

Convert: To cause a person or group to change their beliefs or practices. A convert (noun) is a person who has been converted to a new belief or practice.

Coup: A feat of bravery, especially the touching of an enemy's body during battle without causing or receiving injury. To "count coup" is to count the number of such feats of bravery.

Cradleboard: A board or frame on which an infant was bound or wrapped by some Native American peoples. It was used as a portable carrier or for carrying an infant on the back.

Creation stories: Sacred myths or stories that explain how Earth and its beings were created.

Culture: The set of beliefs, social habits, and ways of surviving in the environment that are held by a particular social group.

Dentalium: Dentalia (plural) are the tooth-like shells that some tribes used as money. The shells were rubbed smooth and strung like beads on strands of animal skin.

Depletion: Decreasing the amount of something; depletion of resources such as animals or minerals through overuse reduces essential elements from the environment.

Dialect: A local variety of a particular language, with unique differences in words, grammar, and pronunciation.

Economy: The way a group obtains, produces, and distributes the goods it needs; the overall system by which it supports itself and accumulates its wealth.

Ecosystem: The overall way that a community and its surrounding environment function together in nature.

Epidemic: The rapid spread of a disease so that many people in an area have it at the same time.

Ethnic group: A group of people who are classed according to certain aspects of their common background, usually by tribal, racial, national, cultural, and language origins.

Extended family: A family group that includes close relatives such as mother, father, and children, plus grandparents, aunts, and uncles, and cousins.

Fast: To go without food.

Federally recognized tribes: Tribes with which the U.S. government maintains official relations as established by treaty, executive order, or act of Congress.

Fetish: An object believed to have magical or spiritual power.

First Nations: One of Canada's terms for its Indian nations.

Five Civilized Tribes: A name given to the Cherokee, Choctaw, Chickasaw, Creek, and Seminole during the mid-1800s. The tribes were given this name by non-Natives because they had democratic constitutional governments, a high literacy rate (many people who could read and write), and ran effective schools.

Formal education: Structured learning that takes place in a school or college under the supervision of trained teachers.

Ghost Dance: A revitalization (renewal or rebirth) movement that arose in the 1870s after many tribes moved to reservations and were being encouraged to give up their traditional beliefs. Many Native Americans hoped that, if they performed it earnestly, the Ghost Dance would bring back traditional Native lifestyles and values, and that the buffalo and Indian ancestors would return to the Earth as in the days before the white settlers.

Great Basin: An elevated region in the western United States in which all water drains toward the center. The Great Basin covers part of Nevada, California, Colorado, Utah, Oregon, and Wyoming.

Guardian spirit: A sacred power, usually embodied in an animal such as a hawk, deer, or turtle, that reveals itself to an individual, offering help throughout the person's lifetime in important matters such as hunting or healing the sick.

Haudenosaunee: The name of the people often called Iroquois or Five Nations. It means "People of the Longhouse."

Head flattening: A practice in which a baby was placed in a cradle, and a padded board was tied to its forehead to mold the head into a desired shape. Sometimes the effect of flattening the back of the head was achieved by binding the infant tightly to a cradleboard.

Immunity: Resistance to disease; the ability to be exposed to a disease with less chance of getting it, and less severe effects if infected.

Indian Territory: An area in present-day Kansas and Oklahoma where the U.S. government once planned to move all Indians, and, eventually, to allow them to run their own province or state. In 1880 nearly one-third of all U.S. Indians lived there, but with the formation of the state of Oklahoma in 1906, the promise of an Indian state dissolved.

Indigenous: Native, or first, in a specific area. Native Americans are often referred to as indigenous peoples of North America.

Intermarriage: Marriage between people of different groups, as between a Native American and a non-Native, or between people from two different tribes.

Kachina: A group of spirits celebrated by the Pueblo Indians; the word also refers to dolls made in the image of kachina spirits.

Kiva: Among the Pueblo, a circular (sometimes rectangular) underground room used for religious ceremonies.

Lacrosse: A game of Native American origin in which players use a long stick with a webbed pouch at the end for catching and throwing a ball.

Language family: A group of languages that are different from one another but are related. These languages share similar words, sounds, or word structures. The languages are alike either because they have borrowed words from each other or because they originally came from the same parent language.

Legend: A story or folktale that tells about people or events in the past.

Life expectancy: The average number of years a person may expect to live.

Linguistics: The study of human speech and language.

Literacy: The state of being able to read and write.

Loincloth: See "Breechcloth".

Longhouse: A large, long building in which several families live together; usually found among Northwest Coast and Iroquois peoples.

Long Walk of the Navajo: The enforced 300-mile walk of the Navajo people in 1864, when they were being removed from their homelands to the Bosque Redondo Reservation in New Mexico.

Manifest Destiny: A belief held by many Americans in the nineteenth century that the destiny of the United States was to expand its territory and extend its political, social, and economic influences throughout North America.

Matrilineal: Tracing family relations through the mother; in a matrilineal society, names and inheritances are passed down through the mother's side of the family.

Medicine bundle: A pouch in which were kept sacred objects believed to have powers that would protect and aid an individual, a clan or family, or a community.

Midewiwin Society: The Medicine Lodge Religion, whose main purpose was to prolong life. The society taught morality, proper conduct, and a knowledge of plants and herbs for healing.

Migration: Movement from one place to another. The migrations of Native peoples were often done by the group, with whole nations moving from one area to another.

Mission: An organized effort by a religious group to spread its beliefs to other parts of the world; mission refers either to the project of spreading a belief system or to the building(s)—such as a church—in which this takes place.

Missionary: Someone sent to a foreign land to convert its people to a particular religion.

Mission school: A school established by missionaries to teach people religious beliefs as well as other subjects.

Moiety: One of the two parts that a tribe or community divided into based on kinship.

Myth: A story passed down through generations, often involving supernatural beings. Myths often express religious beliefs or the values of people. They may attempt to explain how the Earth and its beings were created, or why things are. They are not always meant to be taken as factual.

Natural resources: The sources of supplies provided by the environment for survival and enrichment, such as animals to be hunted, land for farming, minerals, and timber.

Neophyte: Beginner; often used to mean a new convert to a religion.

Nomadic: Traveling and relocating often, usually in search of food and other resources or a better climate.

Nunavut: A new territory in Canada as of April 1, 1999, with the status of a province and a Inuit majority. It is a huge area, covering most of Canada north of the treeline. Nunavut means "Our Land" in Inukitut (the Inuit language).

Oral literature: Oral traditions that are written down after enjoying a long life in spoken form among a people.

Oral traditions: History, mythology, folklore, and other foundations of a culture that have been passed by spoken word, often in the form of stories, from generation to generation within a culture group.

Parent language: A language that is the common structure of two or more languages that came into being at a later time.

Parfleche: A case or a pouch made from tanned animal hide.

Patrilineal: Tracing family relations through the father; in a patrilineal society, names and inheritances are passed down through the father's side of the family.

Per capita income: The average personal income per person.

Petroglyph: A carving or engraving on rock; a common form of ancient art.

Peyote: A substance obtained from cactus that some Indian groups used as part of their religious practice. After eating the substance, which stimulates the nervous system, a person may go into a trance state and see visions. The Peyote Religion features the use of this substance.

Pictograph: A simple picture representing a historical event.

Policy: The overall plan or course of action issued by the government, establishing how it will handle certain situations or people and what its goals are.

Post-European contact: Relating to the time and state of Native Americans and their lands after the Europeans arrived. Depending on the part of the country in which they lived, Native groups experienced contact at differing times in the history of white expansion into the West.

Potlatch: A feast or ceremony, commonly held among Northwest Coast groups; also called a "giveaway." During a potlatch goods are given to guests to show the host's generosity and wealth. Potlatches are used to celebrate major life events such as birth, death, or marriage.

Powwow: A celebration at which the main activity is traditional singing and dancing. In modern times, the singers and dancers at powwows came from many different tribes.

Province: A district or division of a country (like a state in the United States).

Raiding: Entering into another tribe or community's territory, usually by stealth or force, and stealing their livestock and supplies.

Ranchería: Spanish term for a small farm.

Ratify: To approve or confirm. In the United States, the U.S. Senate ratified treaties with the Indians.

Red Power: A term used to describe the Native American activism movement of the 1960s, in which people from many tribes came together to protest the injustices of American policies toward Native Americans.

Removal Act: An act passed by the U.S. Congress in 1830 that directed all Indians to be moved to Indian Territory, west of the Mississippi River.

Removal Period: The time, mostly between 1830 and 1860, when most Indians of the eastern United States were forced to leave their homelands and relocate west of the Mississippi River.

Repatriation: To return something to its place of origin. A law passed in the 1990s says that all bones and grave goods (items that are buried with a body) should be returned to the descendants. Many Native American tribes have used that law to claim bones and other objects belonging to their ancestors. Museums and archaeological digs must return these items to the tribes.

Reservation: Land set aside by the U.S. government for the use of a group or groups of Indians.

Reserve: In Canada, lands set aside for specific Indian bands. Reserve means in Canada approximately what reservation means in the United States.

Revitalization: The feeling or movement in which something seems to come back to life after having been quiet or inactive for a period of time.

Ritual: A formal act that is performed in basically the same way each time; rituals are often performed as part of a ceremony.

Rural: Having to do with the country; opposite of urban.

Sachem: The chief of a confederation of tribes.

Shaman: A priest or medicine person in many Native American groups who understands and works with supernatural matters. Shamans traditionally performed in rituals and were expected to cure the sick, see the future, and obtain supernatural help with hunting and other economic activities.

Smallpox: A very contagious disease that spread across North America and killed many thousands of Indians. Survivors had skin that was badly scarred.

Sovereign: Self-governing or independent. A sovereign nation makes its own laws and rules.

Sun Dance: A renewal and purification ceremony performed by many Plains Indians such as the Sioux and Cheyenne. A striking aspect of the ceremony was the personal sacrifice made by some men. They undertook self-torture in order to gain a vision that might provide spiritual insight beneficial to the community.

Sweat lodge: An airtight hut containing hot stones that were sprinkled with water to make them steam. A person remained inside until he or she was perspiring. The person then usually rushed out and plunged into a cold stream. This treatment was used before a ceremony or for the healing of physical or spiritual ailments. Sweat lodge is also the name of a sacred Native American ceremony involving the building of the lodge and the pouring of water on stones, usually by a medicine person, accompanied by praying and singing. The ceremony has many purposes, including spiritual cleansing and healing.

Taboo: A forbidden object or action. Many Indians believe that the sacred order of the world must be maintained if one is to avoid illness or other misfortunes. This is accomplished, in part, by observing a large assortment of taboos.

Termination: The policy of the U.S. government during the 1950s and 1960s to end the relationships set up by treaties with Indian nations.

Toloache: A substance obtained from a plant called jimsonweed. When consumed, the drug causes a person to go into a trance and see visions. It is used in some religious ceremonies.

Totem: An object that serves as an emblem or represents a family or clan, usually in the form of an animal, bird, fish, plant, or other natural object. A totem pole is a pillar built in front of the homes of Natives in the Northwest. It is painted and carved with a series of totems that show the family background and either mythical or historical events.

Trail of Tears: A series of forced marches of Native Americans of the Southeast in the 1830s, causing the deaths of thousands. The marches were the result of the U.S. government's removal policy, which ordered Native Americans to be moved to Indian Territory.

Treaty: An agreement between two parties or two nations, signed by both, usually defining the benefits to both parties that will result from one side giving up title to a territory of land.

Tribe: A group of Natives who share a name, language, culture, and ancestors; in Canada, called a band.

Tribelet: A community within an organization of communities in which one main settlement was surrounded by a few minor outlying settlements.

Trickster: A common culture hero in Indian myth and legend. tricksters generally have supernatural powers that can be used to do good or harm, and stories about them take into account the different forces of the universe, such as good and evil or night and day. The Trickster takes different forms among various groups; for example, Coyote in the Southwest; Ikhtomi Spider in the High Plains, and Jay or Wolverine in Canada.

Trust: A relationship between two parties (or groups) in which one is responsible for acting in the other's best interests. The U.S. government has a trust relationship with tribal nations. Many tribes do not own their lands outright; according to treaty, the government owns the land "in trust" and tribes are given the use of it.

Unemployment rate: The percentage of the population that is looking for work but unable to find any. (People who have quit looking for work are not included in unemployment rates.)

Urban: Having to do with cities and towns; the opposite of rural.

Values: The ideals that a community of people shares.

Vision quest: A sacred ceremony in which a person (often a teenage boy) goes off alone and fasts, living without food or water for a period of days. During that time he hopes to learn about his spiritual side and to have a vision of a guardian spirit who will give him help and strength throughout his life.

Wampum: Small cylinder-shaped beads cut from shells. Long strings of wampum were used for many different purposes. Indians believed that the exchange of wampum and other goods established a friendship, not just a profit-making relationship.

Wampum belt: A broad woven belt of wampum used to record history, treaties among the tribes, or treaties with colonists or governments.

Weir: A barricade used to funnel fish toward people who wait to catch them.

Timeline

25,000–11,000 BCE Groups of hunters cross from Asia to Alaska on the Bering Sea Land Bridge, which was formed when lands now under the waters of the Bering Strait were exposed for periods of time, according to scientists.

1400 BCE Along the lower Mississippi, people of the Poverty Point culture are constructing large burial mounds and living in planned communities.

500 BCE The Adena people build villages with burial mounds in the Midwest.

100 BCE Hopewell societies construct massive earthen mounds for burying their dead and possibly other religious purposes.

100 BCE–400 CE In the Early Basketmaker period, the Anasazi use baskets as containers and cooking pots; they live in caves.

1 CE: Small, permanent villages of the Hohokam tradition emerge in the southwest.

400–700 In the Modified Basketmaker period, Anasazi communities emerge in the Four Corners region of the Southwest. They learn to make pottery in which they can boil beans. They live in underground pits and begin to use bows and arrows. The Anasazi eventually design communities in large multi-roomed apartment buildings, some with more than 1,200 rooms.

700 CE The Mississippian culture begins.

700–1050 The Developmental Pueblo period begins. The Anasazi move into pueblo-type homes above the ground and develop irrigation methods. A great cultural center is established at Chaco Canyon. Anasazi influence spreads to other areas of the Southwest.

800–950 The early Pecos build pit houses.

900 The Mississippian mound-building groups form complex political and social systems, and participate in long-distance trade and an elaborate and widespread religion.

984 The Vikings under Erik the Red first encounter the Inuit of Greenland.

1000–1350 The Iroquois Confederacy is formed among the Mohawk, Oneida, Onondaga, Cayuga, and Seneca nations. The Five Nations of the Haudenosaunee are, from this time, governed by chiefs from the 49 families who were present at the origin of the confederation.

1040 Pueblos (towns) are flourishing in New Mexico's Chaco Canyon. The pueblos are connected by an extensive road system that stretches many miles across the desert.

1050–1300 In the Classic Pueblo period, Pueblo architecture reaches its height with the building of fabulous cliff dwellings; Acoma Pueblo is a well-established city.

1200 The great city of Cahokia in the Mississippi River Valley flourishes.

1250 Zuñi Pueblo is an important trading center for Native peoples from California, Mexico, and the American Southwest.

1300–1700 During the Regressive Pueblo period, the Anasazi influence declines. The people leave their northern homelands, heading south to mix with other cultures.

1350 Moundville, in present-day Alabama, one of the largest ceremonial centers of the Mound Builders, thrives. With twenty great mounds and a village, it is probably the center of a chiefdom that includes several other related communities.

1400s Two tribes unite to start the Wendat Confederacy.

1494 Christopher Columbus begins the enslavement of American Indians, capturing over 500 Taino of San Salvador and sending them to Spain to be sold.

1503 French explorer Jacques Cartier begins trading with Native Americans along the East Coast.

1524 The Abenaki and Narragansett, among other Eastern tribes, encounter the expedition of Giovanni da Verrazano.

1533 Spaniards led by Nuño de Guzmán enter Yaqui territory.

1534 French explorer Jacques Cartier meets the Micmac on the Gaspé Peninsula, beginning a long association between the French and the Micmac.

1539–43 The Spanish treasure hunter Hernando de Soto becomes the first European to make contact with Mississippian cultures; De Soto and Spaniard Francisco Coronado traverse the Southeast and Southwest, bringing with them disease epidemics that kill thousands of Native Americans.

1540 Hernando de Alarcón first encounters the Yuman.

1570 The Spanish attempt to establish a mission in Powhatan territory, but are driven away or killed by the Natives.

1576 British explorer Martin Frobisher first comes into contact with the central Inuit of northern Canada.

1579 Sir Francis Drake encounters the Coast Miwok.

1590 The Micmac force Iroquoian-speaking Natives to leave the Gaspé Peninsula; as a result, the Micmac dominate the fur trade with the French.

1591 Spanish colonization of Pueblo land begins.

1598 Juan de Oñate sets up a Spanish colony and builds San Geronimo Mission at Taos Pueblo. He brings 7000 head of livestock, among them horses.

1602 Spanish explorer Sebastián Vizcaíno encounters the Ohlone.

1607 The British colonists of the Virginia Company arrive in Powhatan territory.

1609 The fur trade begins when British explorer Henry Hudson, sailing for the Netherlands, opens trade in New Netherland (present-day New York) with several Northeast tribes, including the Delaware.

1615 Ottawa meet Samuel de Champlain at Georgian Bay.

1621 Chief Massasoit allies with Pilgrims.

1622 Frenchman Étienne Brûlé encounters the Ojibway at present-day Sault Sainte Marie.

1634–37 An army of Puritans, Pilgrims, Mohican, and Narragansett attacks and sets fire to the Pequot fort, killing as many as 700 Pequot men, women, and children; Massacre at Mystic ends Pequot War and nearly destroys the tribe.

1648–51 The Iroquois, having exhausted the fur supply in their area, attack other tribes in order to get a new supply. The Beaver Wars begin, and many Northeast tribes are forced to move west toward the Great Lakes area.

mid-1600s The Miami encounter Europeans and provide scouts to guide Father Jacques Marquette and Louis Joliet to the Mississippi River.

1651 Colonists establish first Indian reservation near Richmond, Virginia, for what is left of the Powhatans.

1675–76 The Great Swamp Fight during King Philip's War nearly wipes out the tribe and the loss of life and land ends a way of life for New England tribes.

1680 The Hopi, Jemez, Acoma, and other Pueblo groups force the Spanish out of New Mexico in the Pueblo Revolt.

1682 Robert de la Salle's expedition descends the Mississippi River into Natchez territory.

1687 Father Eusebio Francisco Kino begins missionary work among the Tohono O'odham and establishes the first of twenty-eight missions in Yuman territory.

1692 The Spanish begin their reconquest of Pueblo land; Pecos make peace with Spaniards, in spite of protests from some tribe members.

1700 Pierre-Charles le Sueur encounters the Sioux.

1709 John Lawson discovers and writes about the "Hatteras Indians."

1729 French governor Sieur d' Etchéparre demands Natchez land for a plantation; Natchez revolt begins.

1731 The French destroy the Natchez, the last Mississippian culture. Most survivors are sold into slavery in the Caribbean.

1741 Danish-born Russian explorer Vitus Bering sees buildings on Kayak Island that likely belong to the Chugach; he is the first European to reach the Inuit of Alaska.

1760–63 The Delaware Prophet tells Native Americans in the Northeast that they must drive Europeans out of North America and return to the customs of their ancestors. His message influences Ottawa leader Pontiac, who uses it to unite many tribes against the British.

1761 The Potawatomi switch allegiance from the French to the British; they later help the British by attacking American settlers during the American Revolution.

1763 By the Treaty of Paris, France gives Great Britain the Canadian Maritime provinces, including Micmac territory.

1763 England issues the Proclamation of 1763, which assigns all lands west of the Appalachian Mountains to Native Americans, while colonists are allowed to settle all land to the east. The document respects the aboriginal land rights of Native Americans. It is not popular with colonists who want to move onto Indian lands and becomes one of the conflicts between England and the colonies leading to the American Revolution.

1769 The Spanish build their first mission in California. There will be 23 Spanish missions in California, which are used to convert Native Californians to Christianity, but also reduces them to slave labor.

1769–83 Samuel Hearne and Alexander Mackenzie are the first European explorers to penetrate Alaskan Athabascan territory, looking for furs and a route to the Pacific Ocean. Russian fur traders are not far behind.

c. 1770 Horses, brought to the continent by the Spanish in the sixteenth century, spread onto the Great Plains and lead to the development of a new High Plains Culture.

1776 Most Mohawk tribes side with the British during the Revolutionary War under the leadership of Thayendanégea, also known as Joseph Brant.

1778 The Delaware sign the first formal treaty with the United States, guaranteeing their land and allowing them to be the fourteenth state; the treaty is never ratified.

1778 The treaty-making period begins when the first of 370 treaties between Indian nations and the U.S. government is signed.

1786 The first federal Indian reservations are established.

1789 The Spanish establish a post at Nootka Sound on Vancouver Island, the first permanent European establishment in the territory of the Pacific Northwest Coast tribes; Spain and Great Britain vie for control of the area during the Nootka Sound Controversy.

1791 In the greatest Native American defeat of the U.S. Army, the Miami win against General Arthur St. Clair.

1792 Explorer George Vancouver enters Puget Sound; Robert Gray, John Boit and George Vancouver are the first to mention the Chinook.

1805 The Lewis and Clark expedition ecounter the Flathead, Nez Percé, Yakama, Shoshone, Umatilla, Siletz, and are the first to reach Chinook territory by land.

1811 Shawnee settlement of Prophet's Town is destroyed in the Battle of Tippecanoe.

1813 Chief Tecumseh is killed fighting the Americans at Battle of the Thames in the War of 1812.

1816 Violence erupts during a Métis protest over the Pemmican Proclamation of 1814, and twenty-one Hudson's Bay Company employees are killed.

1817 The First Seminole War occurs when soldiers from neighboring states invade Seminole lands in Florida looking for runaway slaves.

1821 Sequoyah's method for writing the Cherokee language is officially approved by tribal leaders.

1827 The Cherokee adopt a written constitution.

1830 The removal period begins when the U.S. Congress passes the Indian Removal Act. Over the course of the next thirty years many tribes from the Northeast and Southeast are removed to Indian Territory in present-day Oklahoma and Kansas, often forcibly and at great expense in human lives.

1831 Some Seneca and Cayuga move to Indian Territory (now Oklahoma) as part of the U.S. government's plan to move Native Americans westward. Other Iroquois groups stand firm until the government's policy is overturned in 1842.

1832 The U.S. government attempts relocation of the Seminole to Indian Territory in Oklahoma, leading to the Second Seminole War.

1838 The Cherokee leave their homeland on a forced journey known as the Trail of Tears.

1846–48 Mexican-American War is fought; San Juan lands become part of U.S. territory.

1847 Another Pueblo rebellion leads to the assassination of the American territorial governor. In retaliation U.S. troops destroy the mission at Taos Pueblo, killing 150 Taos Indians.

1848 Mexico gives northern Arizona and northern New Mexico lands to the United States. Warfare between the Apache people and the U.S. Army begins.

1850 New Mexico is declared a U.S. territory.

1851 Gold Rush begins at Gold Bluff, prompting settlers to take over Native American lands. As emigration of Europeans to the West increases, eleven Plains tribes sign the Treaty of Fort Laramie, which promises annual payments to the tribes for their land.

1851 Early reservations are created in California to protect the Native population from the violence of U.S. citizens. These reservations are inadequate and serve only a small portion of the Native Californians, while others endure continued violence and hardship.

1854 The Treaty of Medicine Creek is signed, and the Nisqually give up much of their land; the treaty also gives Puyallup lands to the U.S. government and the tribe is sent to a reservation.

1858 Prospectors flood into Washoe lands after the Comstock lode is discovered.

1859 American surveyors map out a reservation on the Gila River for the Pima and Maricopa Indians. It includes fields, but no water.

1861 Cochise is arrested on a false charge, and the Apache Wars begin.

1864 At least 130 Southern Arapaho and Cheyenne—many of them women and children—are killed by U.S. Army troops during the Sand Creek Massacre.

1864 The devastating Long Walk, a forced removal from their homelands, leads the Navajo to a harsh exile at Bosque Redondo.

1867 The United States buys Alaska from Russia for $7.2 million.

1870 The First Ghost Dance Movement begins when Wodzibwob, a Paiute, learns in a vision that a great earthquake will swallow the Earth, and that all Indians will be spared or resurrected within three days of the disaster, returning their world to its state before the Europeans arrived.

1870–90 The Peyote Religion spreads throughout the Great Plains. Peyote (obtained from a cactus plant) brings on a dreamlike feeling that followers believe brings them closer to the spirit world. Tribes develop their own ceremonies, songs, and symbolism, and vow to be trustworthy, honorable, and community-oriented and to follow the Peyote Road.

1871 British Columbia becomes part of Canada; reserve land is set aside for the Nuu-chah-nulth.

1874–75 The Comanche make their last stand; Quanah Parker and his followers are the last to surrender and be placed on a reservation.

1875 The U.S. Army forces the Yavapai and Apache to march to the San Carlos Apache Reservation; 115 die along the way.

1876 The Northern Cheyenne join with the Sioux in defeating General George Custer at the Battle of Little Bighorn.

1876 The Indian Act in Canada establishes an Indian reserve system, in which reserves were governed by voluntary elected band councils. The Act does not recognize Canadian Indians' right to self-government. With the passage of the act, Canadian peoples in Canada are divided into three groups: status Indian, treaty Indian, and non-status Indian. The categories affect the benefits and rights Indians are given by the government.

1877 During the Nez Percé War, Chief Joseph and his people try fleeing to Canada, but are captured by U.S. Army troops.

1879 The Ute kill thirteen U.S. soldiers and ten Indian agency officials, including Nathan Meeker, in a conflict that becomes known as the "Meeker Massacre."

1880s The buffalo on the Great Plains are slaughtered until there are almost none left. Without adequate supplies of buffalo for food, the Plains Indians cannot survive. Many move to reservations.

1884 The Canadian government bans potlatches. The elaborate gift-giving ceremonies have long been a vital part of Pacific Northwest Indian culture.

1886 The final surrender of Geronimo's band marks the end of Apache military resistance to American settlement.

1887 The General Allotment Act (also known as the Dawes Act), is passed by Congress. The act calls for the allotment (parceling out) of tribal lands. Tribes are no longer to own their lands in common in the traditional way. Instead the land is to be assigned to individuals. The head of a family receives 160 acres, and other family members get smaller pieces of land. All Indian lands that are not alloted are sold to settlers.

1888 Ranchers and amateur archaeologists Richard Wetherill and Charlie Mason discover ancient cliff dwellings of the Pueblo people.

1889 The Oklahoma Land Runs open Indian Territory to non-Natives. (Indian Territory had been set aside solely for Indian use.) At noon on April 22, an estimated 50,000 people line up at the boundaries of Indian Territory. They claim two million acres of land. By nightfall, tent cities, banks, and stores are doing business there.

1890 The Second Ghost Dance movement is initiated by Wovoka, a Paiute. It includes many Paiute traditions. In some versions the dance is performed in order to help bring back to Earth many dead ancestors and exterminated game. Ghost Dance practitioners hope the rituals in the movement will restore Indians to their formal state, before the arrival of the non-Native settlers.

1896 Discovery of gold brings hordes of miners and settlers to Alaska.

1897 Oil is discovered beneath Osage land.

1907 With the creation of the state of Oklahoma, the government abolishes the Cherokee tribal government and school system, and the dream of a Native American commonwealth dissolves.

1912 The Alaska Native Brotherhood is formed to promote civil rights issues, such as the right to vote, access to public education, and civil rights in public places. The organization also fights court battles to win land rights.

1916 Ishi, the last Yahi, dies of tuberculosis.

1920 The Canadian government amends the Indian Act to allow for compulsory, or forced, enfranchisement, the process by which Indians have to give up their tribal loyalties to become Canadian citizens. Only 250 Indians had voluntarily become enfranchised between 1857 and 1920.

1924 Congress passes legislation conferring U.S. citizenship on all American Indians. This act does not take away rights that Native Americans had by treaty or the Constitution.

1928 Lewis Meriam is hired to investigate the status of Indian economies, health, and education, and the federal administration of Indian affairs. His report describes the terrible conditions under which Indians are forced to live, listing problems with health care, education, poverty, malnutrition, and land ownership.

1934 U.S. Congress passes the Indian Reorganization Act (IRA), which ends allotment policies and restores some land to Native Americans. The IRA encourages tribes to govern themselves and set up tribal economic corporations, but with the government overseeing their decisions. The IRA also provides more funding to the reservations. Many tribes form tribal governments and adopt constitutions.

1940 Newly opened Grand Coulee Dam floods Spokane land and stops the salmon from running.

1941–45 Navajo Code Talkers send and receive secret messages in their Native language, making a major contribution to the U.S. war effort during World War II.

1942 As hostilities leading to World War II grow, the Iroquois exercise their powers as an independent nation to declare war on Germany, Italy, and Japan.

1946 The Indian Lands Commission (ICC) is created to decide land claims filed by Indian nations. Many tribes expect the ICC to return lost lands, but the ICC chooses to award money instead, and at the value of the land at the time it was lost.

1951 A new Indian Act in Canada reduces the power of the Indian Affairs Office, makes it easier for Indians to gain the right to vote, and helps Indian children enter public schools. It also removes the ban on potlatch and Sun Dance ceremonies.

1954–62 The U.S. Congress carries out its termination policy. At the same time laws are passed giving states and local governments control over tribal members, taking away the tribes' authority to govern themselves. Under the policy of termination, Native Americans lose their special privileges and are treated the same as other U.S. citizens. The tribes that are terminated face extreme poverty and the threat of loss of their community and traditions. By 1961 the government begins rethinking this policy because of the damage it is causing.

1955 The Indian Health Service (IHS) assumes responsibility for Native American health care. The IHS operates hospitals, health centers, health stations, clinics, and community service centers.

1958 Alaska becomes a state; 104 million acres of Native land are taken.

1960 The queen of England approves a law giving status Indians the right to vote in Canada.

1964 The Great Alaska Earthquake and tsunami destroys several Alutiiq villages.

1965 Under the new U.S. government policy, the Self-Determination policy, federal aid to reservations is given directly to Indian tribes and not funneled through the Bureau of Indian Affairs.

1968 Three Ojibway—Dennis Banks, George Mitchell, and Clyde Bellecourt—found the American Indian Movement (AIM) in Minneapolis, Minnesota, to raise public awareness about treaties the federal and state governments violated.

1969 Eighty-nine Native Americans land on Alcatraz Island, a former penitentiary in San Francisco Bay in California. The group calling itself "Indians of All Tribes," claims possession of the island under an 1868 treaty that gave Indians the right to unused federal property on Indian land. Indians of All Tribes occupies the island for 19 months while negotiating with federal officials. They do not win their claim to the island but draw public attention to their cause.

1971 Quebec government unveils plans for the James Bay I hydroelectric project. Cree and Inuit protest the action in Quebec courts.

1971 The Alaska Native Claims Settlement Act (ANCSA) is signed into law. With the act, Alaska Natives give up any claim to nine-tenths of Alaska. In return they are given $962 million and clear title to 44 million acres of land.

1972 Five hundred Native Americans arrive in Washington, D.C., on a march called the Trail of Broken Treaties to protest the government's policies toward Native Americans. The protestors occupy the Bureau of Indian Affairs building for a week, causing considerable damage. They present the government with a list of reforms, but the administration rejects their demands.

1973 After a dispute over Oglala Sioux (Lakota) tribal chair Robert Wilson and his strong-arm tactics at Pine Ridge Reservation, AIM leaders are called in. Wilson's supporters and local authorities arm themselves against protestors, who are also armed, and a ten-week siege begins in which hundreds of federal marshals and Federal Bureau of Investigation (FBI) agents surround the Indian protestors. Two Native American men are shot and killed.

1974 After strong protests and "fish-ins" bring attention to the restrictions on Native American fishing rights in the Pacific Northwest, the U.S. Supreme Court restores Native fishing rights in the case *Department of Game of Washington v. Puyallup Tribe et al.*

1978 U.S. Congress passes legislation called the Tribally Controlled Community College Assistance Act, providing support for tribal colleges, schools of higher education designed to help Native American students achieve academic success and eventually transfer to four-year colleges and universities. Tribal colleges also work with tribal elders and cultural leaders to record languages, oral traditions, and arts in an effort to preserve cultural traditions.

1978 The American Indian Religious Freedom Act is signed. Its stated purpose is to "protect and preserve for American Indians their inherent right of freedom to believe, express, and exercise their traditional religions."

1978 The Bureau of Indian Affairs publishes regulations for the new Federal Acknowledgement Program. This program is responsible for producing a set of "procedures for establishing that an American Indian group exists as an Indian tribe." Many tribes will later discover that these requirements are complicated and difficult to establish.

1982 Canada constitutionally recognizes aboriginal peoples in its new Constitution and Charter of Rights and Freedoms. The Constitution officially divides Canada's aboriginal nations into three designations: the Indian, the Inuit, and the Métis peoples. Native groups feel that the new Constitution does not adequately protect their rights, nor does it give them the right to govern themselves.

1988 The Federal Indian Gambling Regulatory Act of 1988 allows any tribe recognized by the U.S. government to engage in gambling activities. With proceeds from gaming casinos, some tribes pay for health care, support of the elderly and sick, housing, and other improvements, while other tribes buy back homelands, establish scholarship funds, and create new jobs.

1990 Two important acts are passed by U.S. Congress. The Native American Languages Act is designed to preserve, protect, and promote the practice and development of Indian languages. The Graves Protection and Repatriation Act provides for the protection of American Indian grave sites and the repatriation (return) of Indian remains and cultural artifacts to tribes.

1992 Canadians vote against a new Constitution (the Charlotte-town Accord) that contains provisions for aboriginal self-government.

1995 The Iroquois request that all sacred masks and remains of their dead be returned to the tribe; the Smithsonian Institution is the first museum to comply with this request.

1999 A new territory called Nunavut enters the federation of Canada. Nunavut is comprised of vast areas taken from the Northwest Territories and is populated by an Inuit majority. The largest Native land claim in Canadian history, Nunavut is one-fifth of the landmass of Canada, or the size of the combined states of Alaska and Texas. Meaning "Our Land" in the Inukitut (Inuit) language, Nunavut will be primarily governed by the Inuit.

2003 The first official Comanche dictionary is published, compiled entirely by the Comanche people.

2004 Southern Cheyenne Peace Chief W. Richard West Jr. becomes director of the newly opened National Museum of the American Indian in Washington, D.C.

2006 The United Nations censures the United States for reclaiming 60 million acres (90%) of Western Shoshone lands. The federal government uses parts of the land for military testing, open-pit gold mining and nuclear waste disposal. The Shoshone, who have used it for cattle grazing since the Treaty of Ruby Valley in 1863, have repeatedly had their livestock confiscated and fines imposed.

2011 The government gives the Fort Sill Apache 30 acres for a reservation in Deming, New Mexico.

2011 Tacoma Power gives the Skokomish 1,000 acres of land and $11 million.

Makah
Skokomish Duwamish
Puyallup
Nisqually Umatilla
Chinook

Siletz

Yurok
Chilula
Hupa   Modoc
          Pit River   Northern Paiute
Cahto Maidu
Pomo
          Washoe
Miwok
Costanoan
          Kawaiisu
          Yahi and Yana

Chumash

          Cahuilla
          Luiseño

Lake   Spokane
Colville   Salish   Blackfoot
           Flathead

Yakama   Nez
         Percé   Nakota

                                Crow

                    Northern
                    Shoshone
          Western
          Shoshone   Arapaho
                    Eastern
                    Shoshone

                         Ute

Southern Paiute

                    San Carlos
               Anasazi
               Navajo   Pueblo
          Hopi   Jemez
Mohave Apache   San Juan

Yuman   White Mountain   Zuñi
              Yaqui
Tohono O'odham   Acoma

          Pima
               Chiricahua

Lakot

Northern
Cheyenne   Arik

                Pawnee

Southern
Cheyenne

Jicarilla
Taos   Kiowa

                Ki
                Ap

          Pecos   Comanche

PACIFIC
OCEAN

N

California
Great Basin
Great Plains
Northeast
Pacific Northwest
Plateau
Southeast
Southwest

Abenaki

Menominee

Mohawk

Sauk

Iroquois

Fox

Narraganset

Dakota

Wyandot

Pequot

Potawatomi

Wampanoag

Delaware

Hopewell

Miami

Powhatan

Missouri

Shawnee

Mississippian
(Mound Builders)

Osage

Lumbee

Cherokee

Quapaw

Chickasaw

Caddo

Creek

Choctaw

Natchez

Seminole

ATLANTIC
OCEAN

Gulf of Mexico

0   100   200 mi

0   100 200 km

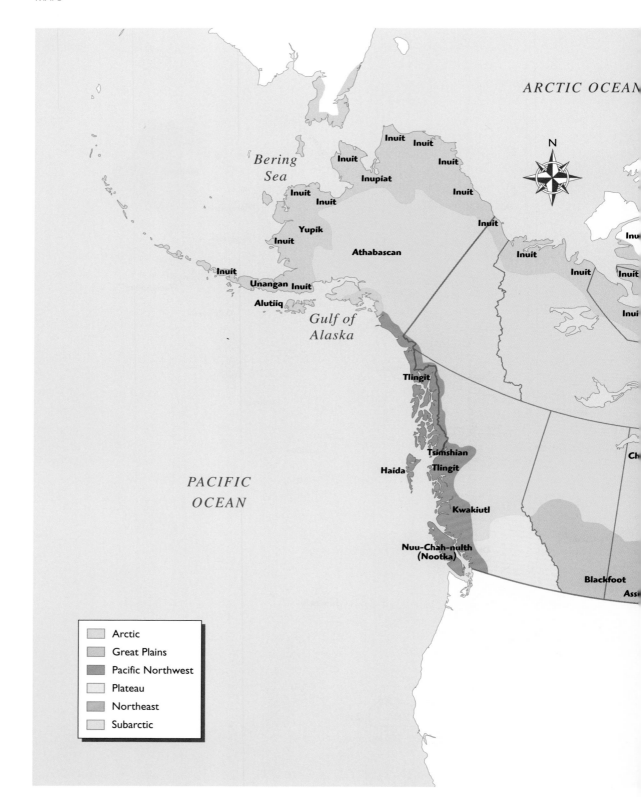

ARCTIC OCEAN

Bering Sea

N

Inuit **Inuit**

Inuit **Inuit**

Inupiat

Inuit

Inuit **Inuit**

Inuit

Inuit

Yupik

Inuit

Athabascan

Inuit

Inu

Inuit **Inuit**

Inui

Inuit

Inuit

Unangan **Inuit**

Alutiiq

Gulf of Alaska

Tlingit

PACIFIC OCEAN

Tsimshian

Haida **Tlingit**

Ch

Kwakiutl

Nuu-Chah-nulth (Nootka)

Blackfoot

Assi

	Arctic
	Great Plains
	Pacific Northwest
	Plateau
	Northeast
	Subarctic

Baffin
Bay

Inuit

Inuit

it

Inuit

Inuit

Inuit

Inuit

Labrador
Sea

Inuit

Inuit

Inuit

Inuit

Inuit

Inuit

Inuit

Inuit

Hudson
Bay

Innu

Cree

Micmac

ATLANTIC
OCEAN

is

Ojibwa

Algonkin

Ottawa

Huron

Wyandotte

0	250	500 mi
0	250	500 km

Southwest

Southwest

The origins of the Southwest Indians are far-reaching, spanning two continents and many centuries. The term "Southwest Indians" refers to North American Native groups living in the American Southwest (present-day Arizona, New Mexico, Utah, Colorado, Nevada, and Texas) and in the region that is now northern Mexico. These groups include, among others, the Hopi and Zuñi—Pueblo Indians of Arizona whose roots and language can be traced to Mexico and Central America—and the Navajo and Apache peoples—Athabaskan speakers from the Northeast who began migrating to the Southwest around 1000 CE. The Southwest Indians are well known for their farming techniques (these are said to have originated in Mexico); their permanent, multistoried settlements; and their crafts, including distinctive painted pottery, basketry, and woven items.

Early history

Evidence of early Southwest Indian settlement may date back as far as ten thousand years. The Cochise (pronounced *koh-CHEES*) cultures most likely developed in present-day Arizona and New Mexico around 5000 BCE. In this mostly arid (dry) environment, these prehistoric societies constantly adapted their economic practices, social patterns, and living arrangements to meet the prevailing conditions. Moving with the change in seasons, they built homes among cliffs, in caves, and along desert valleys. By gathering many different types of plants, the Cochise people are believed to have paved the way for extensive agricultural development by later peoples in the region.

Ancient Native cultures and traditions Four agricultural cultures—the Hohokam, the Mogollon, the Patayan, and the Anasazi—dominated the prehistoric Southwest.

The Hohokam Small permanent villages appeared in the Southwest around 1 CE, marking a shift in the region's nomadic (wandering) hunting and gathering lifestyle. In the Sonoran Desert of present-day south-central

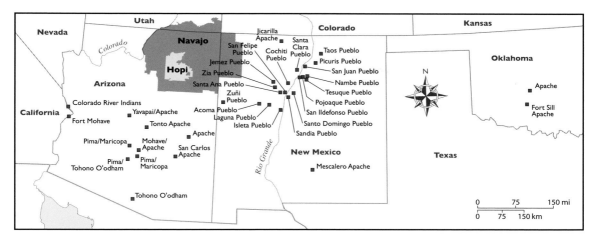

A map of some of the contemporary Native American communities in the Southwest region of the United States. MAP BY XNR PRODUCTIONS. CENGAGE LEARNING, GALE. REPRODUCED BY PERMISSION OF GALE, A PART OF CENGAGE LEARNING.

Arizona, the Hohokam culture emerged. Originally from Mexico, the Hohokam were hunters and gatherers who turned to agriculture around 300 CE. Over the next two hundred years, they developed massive irrigation systems to water the rugged terrain surrounding the Gila and Salt Rivers in present-day central Arizona. The Hohokam are said to be ancestors of the Pima and Tohono O'odham peoples (see entries).

The Mogollon Around the year 200 CE in present-day southern New Mexico, eastern Arizona, and parts of Mexico, the Mogollon people developed small villages of semi-underground, earth-covered pithouses. The Anasazi (see entry) would subsequently modify the Mogollon concept of the villages, creating what are now called pueblos (pronounced *PWEB-lowz*)—small towns made up of multistoried stone or adobe (earthen brick) buildings that often housed many families. The Mogollon people developed systems for farming in a dry climate and established themselves as the foremost potters of their time. Some people of the modern Western Pueblos are believed to be descended from the Mogollon.

The Patayan The Patayan—contemporaries of the Mogollon (they lived at about the same time) and inhabitants of a vast stretch of land in what is now the state of Arizona—were among the first pottery producers in the Southwest. Their homes were small and made of wood or stone. The Patayan people hunted and farmed, growing squash and corn with the help of irrigation. Their culture is thought to have dominated the lower Colorado River region for some 1,500 years.

The ruins of an Anasazi kiva at Pueblo del Arroyo, Chaco Canyon, New Mexico. © NORTH WIND PICTURE ARCHIVES.

The Anasazi An agricultural group called the Anasazi (pronounced *on-uh-SAH-zee*; sometimes referred to as "Ancient Ones") emerged around 400 CE in the Four Corners region of present-day Arizona, New Mexico, Utah, and Colorado. They eventually designed their communities in large, multiroomed, apartment-style buildings—some with more than 1,200 rooms. Though well known for their expertise in farming, the Anasazi were also skilled potters credited with refining the pottery-making techniques first developed by the Mogollon. (The works of both cultures were distinguished by their black-on-white geometric designs.) Modern Pueblos (see entries) of Arizona and New Mexico are descended from the Anasazi.

By about 900 CE, the Anasazi inhabited multistoried cliff dwellings on the Colorado Plateau. Over the next three hundred years, large trading towns—possibly as many as two hundred of them—flourished in the Southwest, especially in a region of present-day northern New Mexico known as Chaco Canyon. Some pueblos had hundreds of rooms. Among the largest were Pueblo Bonito and Chetro Ketl. The pueblos of Chaco Canyon were connected by an extensive road system that stretched many miles across the desert. Archaeological finds from the area indicate that the Natives of Central America, the U.S. Southwest, and the Pacific Coast region engaged in trade with one another.

Aztlán

Around the year 900 CE, long before European contact, the area that is now the southwestern United States and northern Mexico was called Aztlán. Aztlán was named by the Aztecs, builders of a powerful empire that stretched throughout the central highlands of Mexico. In spite of the desertlike conditions that exist in the Southwest, many agricultural communities grew throughout Aztlán. Southwestern farmers developed a variety of innovative irrigation and drainage systems to conserve the scarce rainfall in the region. Agriculture served as an advanced and effective food source for this dry territory.

Aztlán communities consisted of multistory villages (later named *pueblos*) and large ceremonial centers. The ceremonial centers resembled *kivas,* the round underground chambers found among the present-day Hopi in Arizona and the Pueblo in eastern New Mexico.

The Aztec empire expanded and prospered for several centuries until the Spanish arrived in the New World around the turn of the sixteenth century. Aztlán continued to exist under Spanish control until 1821, when Mexico won its independence from Spain. The region was then subject to Mexican rule until the end of the Mexican-American War (1846-48; a war fought between the United States and Mexico in which Mexico lost about one-half of its national territory to the United States), when the U.S. government took over the northern part of Aztlán in 1848.

The tides turn

By the thirteenth century, Athabaskan-speaking Navajo and Apache (see entries) groups had migrated south (most likely from territory that is now part of Canada) and had begun trading with the Pueblo Indians. Their cultures and worldviews blended.

A severe drought then struck the region that is now the southwestern United States (probably between 1275 and 1300). As a result, Southwestern peoples left their once-thriving towns in search of water. Many settled in villages along the Colorado and Rio Grande rivers. Hunting and gathering became increasingly important throughout the Southwest during this time.

European contact

Native nations in the United States were transformed radically by the arrival of Europeans between 1500 and 1700. Age-old cultures, customs, traditions, and political systems were disrupted and suppressed, but not entirely lost, under European dominance.

Spanish reach the New World Southwest Indian contact with whites probably began with the arrival of Spanish explorer Cabeza de Vaca (c. 1490–1557) in 1535. He entered present-day New Mexico and reported back to Spain on the land, the food resources, and, above all, the people he encountered. Five years later another Spanish explorer, Francisco Vásquez de Coronado (c. 1510–1554), traveled into territory that is now part of Arizona and New Mexico, possibly going as far east as present-day Oklahoma. Coronado was searching for the legendary Seven Cities of Cíbola, which were believed to contain great wealth.

Present-day New Mexico had ninety-eight pueblo villages when the Spanish arrived. The Pueblo people had similar cultures, but they spoke four distinct languages: Zuñi, Keres, Tiwa, and Tewa. Coronado came into contact with several Pueblo peoples, including the Hopi.

Ruins of the Pecos Mission Church stand at Pecos Pueblo, New Mexico. © NORTH WIND PICTURE ARCHIVES.

Colonizers and missionaries Spanish colonization began in the Southwest in the late 1500s when Spanish expeditions entered what is now eastern New Mexico. Although they were driven back at first by Pueblo and Apache Indians, by 1598, they had established a Spanish colony at San Juan Pueblo (see entry) in northern New Mexico.

Spanish arrival in the Southwest had a major and lasting impact on the lives of the region's Native populations. Showing no respect for the people's rights or customs, the Europeans simply took over, snatching ancestral lands away, forbidding the Native people to practice their traditional ceremonies and rituals, and making them slaves on the ranches and farms of the Spanish upper class. By 1628, Spanish missionaries had established a solid presence in the region. Their efforts to convert the people to Christianity further fractured the Native communities' ties to the past.

The effects of introduced diseases The populations in the Hopi villages along the Colorado River dropped dramatically because many people died of the diseases brought by Spanish explorers. An estimated ten pueblos were abandoned between 1519 and 1650. Evidence indicates that illness decimated the population at various intervals between the late 1530s and 1598. Spiraling death rates seemed to correspond to uncontrolled outbreaks of smallpox, measles, and the plague that hit the region during these decades. (Experts speculate that between 1500 and 1700 European diseases reduced Native populations in the Northeast, Southeast, and Southwest to less than one-tenth of their original numbers.) By the early 1600s, most Hopi had retreated to their present villages in northern Arizona. There the Spanish tried to rule and spread Christianity, but the Hopi resisted.

The Pueblo uprising In 1680, Popé (c. 1630–1692), a Pueblo spiritual leader, organized a successful rebellion against the Spanish. The Spanish and their Native allies fled, moving on to present-day El Paso, Texas. Popé claimed that the spirits told him to drive away the Spanish and help the Pueblo return to their traditional life. Spanish military forces eventually regained control, and by 1696, many Pueblo people had left their villages to join the Navajo bands that had moved farther north. The Pueblo who remained under Spanish rule were forced to convert to Catholicism, the dominant Christian religion in Spain.

The Comanche move south During the early 1700s, the Comanche moved south to New Mexico from present-day Wyoming. They soon acquired horses from the Spanish. By the mid-1700s, the Comanche had gained control of the horse and gun trade on the southern Plains and had established themselves as the most powerful bison-hunting tribe in the area.

The Spanish wangled trade deals with the Comanche, using bribes and threats of war to achieve their goals. Conflicts arose as a large number of Comanche and Pueblo allied themselves with the Spanish against the horse- and sheep-raiding Apache and Navajo bands. Pueblo villagers migrated to El Paso, following the Spanish retreat down the Rio Grande. Tensions continued throughout the early 1800s during the period of rule by the Mexican Republic.

Pressures increase in the 1800s

The U.S. settlers who streamed into the Southwest after the United States won the territory from Mexico in 1848 met strong opposition from the Native peoples. The American military tried to subdue Native uprisings throughout the Southwest, destroying the people's land, livestock, and even whole communities in the process. Outbreaks of violence crossed tribal lines as various Native peoples rebelled against U.S. policies.

Taos Pueblo revolt The Taos Pueblo (see entry), angered by the conduct of the United States during the Mexican-American War, attacked and killed the U.S. governor of New Mexico in 1847. American troops retaliated, attacking the Taos Pueblo and killing approximately 165 people.

Navajo resistance to U.S. influence For more than two hundred years, the Navajo spent considerable time and effort dealing with the Spanish. At the end of the Mexican-American War in 1848, American settlers poured into California and New Mexico. The Navajo—the largest Native nation in the United States at that time—were one of the first tribes in the American Southwest to confront the U.S. government in a prolonged struggle for their rights.

Cattle raids lead to trouble Cattle, sheep, and horses had been introduced to the Native peoples of the Southwest during the period of European domination. By the 1800s, the Navajo had built up large herds of these animals by raiding the Spanish and other tribes. Even after the American victory in the war with Mexico, the Navajo people continued their raids, storming U.S. settlements in present-day New Mexico. These actions led to conflict between the Navajo and the U.S. Army.

Fighting ensued. Many Navajo cornfields were burned, fruit trees were destroyed, sheep were slaughtered, and communities were ruined. The Navajo managed to resist for seventeen years, but, facing starvation in 1863 and 1864, they finally surrendered.

Long Walk of the Navajo The Navajo people's unsuccessful attack on Fort Defiance, an American base located in the middle of their territory, sealed their fate, resulting in their final defeat in 1864. The tribe was subsequently forced to march 800 miles (1,300 kilometers) to a 40-square-mile (65-square-kilometer) reserve at Fort Sumner, New Mexico. Two thousand people died along the way from starvation and exposure (lack of shelter). The nine thousand survivors found themselves on land that lacked water and had poor soil. The nearest available wood was 5 to 18 miles (8 to 29 kilometers) away. Hordes of grasshoppers swept the area. The Navajo called the reservation *Hweeldi,* meaning "prison."

The Navajo were expected to farm this drought-ravaged land. The U.S. government did little to help the tribe until a Santa Fe newspaper wrote about the terrible conditions on the reserve. As a result, federal officials allowed the Navajo to return to a small portion (10 percent) of their original homeland. In later years, more land was added as the Navajo population grew.

Reservations in New Mexico

In 1861, General James Carleton (1814–1873) of the U.S. Army formed reservations in New Mexico. Carleton planned to gather the Apache and Navajo together "little by little onto a Reservation away from the haunts and hills and hiding places of their own county, and there be kind to them: there teach their children how to read and write; teach them the art of peace; teach them the truths of Christianity." Carleton and others like him promoted the idea of assimilation, arguing that the education of Natives to the ways of Euro-American people was right, just, and necessary. He proposed a plan under which Native peoples would "acquire new habits, new ideas, new modes of life: the old Indians will die off … the young ones will take their places … and thus, little by little, they will become a happy and contented people." Despite Carleton's stated intentions of applying his assimilation policy gently, he killed many Indians while trying to force them onto reservations. Thousands more died in the harsh conditions they encountered on the reservations.

Cochise and the Apache Wars Around the time of the ill-fated Navajo uprising, Cochise (c. 1812–1874), an Apache warrior, led his people in a series of conflicts known as the Apache Wars (1863–72). From his stronghold in the Dragoon Mountains (located in southern Arizona), Cochise led an effective campaign against U.S. and Mexican forces. In 1871, he opposed efforts to relocate his people to a reservation in New Mexico. A year later, the Apache leader finally agreed to end the tribe's attacks on the U.S. Army. This peace agreement hinged on the federal government's promise of reservation land for the Apache in eastern Arizona.

The twentieth century

The 1920s was a key decade in Native American history. In response to pressure applied by reformers who wished to see conditions improved for Native Americans throughout the country, U.S. secretary of the interior Hubert Work (1860–1942) appointed the Committee of One Hundred to investigate American Indian policies. The committee, which met in 1923, recommended increasing funding for Native health care, public education, scholarships, and legal action to rule on Native land claims.

Pueblo Lands Act

When the United States took over the American Southwest from Mexico in 1848, the Pueblo were the only Southwest tribe who had citizenship in Mexico. As Mexican citizens, they were automatically granted U.S. citizenship. As citizens, however, the Pueblo peoples did not receive the same rights and protections granted to federally recognized Native American nations. As a result, much Pueblo land—the finest farmland in the Southwest—was lost.

The Pueblo asked for—and then sued for—Native American status, which they gained in 1916. By that time, though, they had already been forced to surrender some of their best lands, including important religious sites. The All Indian Pueblo Council, a loose federation of Pueblo representatives, organized delegates from all the pueblos to rally for rights to their old lands. The resulting Pueblo Lands Act of 1924 restored Pueblo lands, but the battle was not over. In the early 2000s, the Pueblo continued the fight to obtain and keep their water rights. Not until a decade later were some of those rights returned by the U.S. courts; in some cases pueblos also received monetary awards to assist them in securing their water supplies, managing their groundwater, constructing waterworks, and improving water quality.

Hopi-Navajo Joint Use Area When the Navajo began settling on Hopi lands in the nineteenth century, frequent disputes arose between the two tribes. It soon became clear that the conflict would not be settled without outside intervention, so U.S. courts created a Joint Use Area—1.8 million acres to be shared between the Hopi and the Navajo. Under the terms of the joint use agreement, only a portion of the Hopi reservation was held for the exclusive use of the Hopi, and by 1973, clashes again erupted between the Hopi and the Navajo over ownership of the area.

The next year, U.S. Congress passed the Hopi and Navajo Relocation Act, which divided the Joint Use Area between the two nations and provided $16 million to compensate (repay) eight hundred Navajo families who were required to relocate. Even after the settlement, though, tensions between the Hopi and the Navajo continued to exist.

The dawn of the twenty-first century

In spite of the disruptive effects of European colonization and U.S. law on Native populations, the spirit of the Southwest Indians has not been broken. Their Native identities, though influenced by the ideas and practices of invading forces, remain whole and intact. Southwest Native efforts in the late twentieth and early twenty-first centuries have focused mainly on countering the negative impact of Euro-American influence and preserving their traditional Native languages and culture.

BOOKS

Colwell-Chanthaphonh, Chip. *Living Histories: Native Americans and Southwestern Archaeology.* Walnut Creek, CA: AltaMira Press, 2011.

Doherty, Craig A., and Katherine M. Doherty. *Southwest Indians.* Minneapolis, MN: Chelsea House, 2007.

Dwyer, Helen, ed. *Peoples of the Southwest, West, and North.* Redding, CT: Brown Bear Books, 2009.

Eaton, William M. *Odyssey of the Pueblo Indians: An Introduction to Pueblo Indian Petroglyphs, Pictographs and Kiva Art Murals in the Southwest.* Paducah, KY: Turner Publishing Company, 2001.

Glowacki, Donna M., and Scott Van Keuren. *Religious Transformation in the Late Pre-Hispanic Pueblo World.* Tucson: University of Arizona Press, 2012.

Griffin-Pierce, Trudy. *Native Peoples of the Southwest.* Santa Fe: University of New Mexico Press, 2000.

Griffin-Pierce, Trudy. *The Columbia Guide to American Indians of the Southwest.* New York: Columbia University Press, 2010.

Indians of the Southwest. Chicago: World Book, 2009.

Kuiper, Kathleen, ed. *American Indians of California, the Great Basin, and the Southwest.* New York: Rosen Educational Services, 2012.

Marshall, Ann, ed. *Home: Native People in the Southwest.* Phoenix, AZ: Heard Museum, 2005.

McDaniel, Melissa. *Southwest Indians.* Chicago: Heinemann Library, 2012.

Munson, Marit. *The Archaeology of Art in the American Southwest.* Walnut Creek, CA: AltaMira Press, 2011.

Nottage, James H. *Generations: The Helen Cox Kersting Collection of Southwestern Cultural Arts.* Indianapolis, IN: Eiteljorg Museum of American Indians and Western Art, 2010.

Ortiz, Alfonso, ed. *Handbook of American Indians.* Vols. 9–10. *The Southwest.* Washington, DC: Smithsonian Institution, 1978–83.

Page, Jake, and Susanne Page. *Indian Arts of the Southwest.* Tucson, AZ: Rio Nuevo Publishers, 2008.

Perritano, John. *Spanish Missions.* New York: Children's Press, 2010.

Stuart, David E. *The Ancient Southwest: Chaco Canyon, Bandelier, and Mesa Verde.* Albuquerque: University of New Mexico Press, 2009.

Waldman, Carl, ed. *Encyclopedia of Native American Tribes.* New York: Facts on File, 2006.

Walker, Clifford J. *Gone the Way of the Earth: Indian Slave Trade in the Old Southwest.* 3rd ed. Barstow, CA: Mojave River Valley Museum Association, 2009.

Wyborny, Sheila. *North American Indians: Native Americans of the Southwest.* San Diego: KidHaven Press, 2004.

WEB SITES

"The Greater Southwest." *Southwestern Archaeology, Inc.* http://www.swanet.org/ (accessed on July 20, 2011).

"Southwestern United States Rock Art Gallery." *Arch Net.* http://net.indra.com/-dheyser/rockart.html (accessed on July 20, 2011).

"Trading Posts in the American Southwest." *Southwest Crossroads.* http://southwestcrossroads.org/record.php?num=742&hl=chiricahua:: apache (accessed on July 20, 2011).

"Words & Place—Native Literature from the American Southwest." *University of Arizona.* http://wordsandplace.arizona.edu/kane.html (accessed on December 1, 2011).

Anasazi (Hisatsinom)

Name

Anasazi (pronounced *on-uh-SAH-zee*) is a Navajo word meaning "enemy ancestors." Some Pueblo peoples find this term offensive and prefer to translate the name as "ancient ones." Others choose to call them the Ancient Pueblo People, or Ancestral Pueblos, although the Navajos do not like these terms. In the early twenty-first century, the Hopi use the word "Hisatsinom" to refer to this ancient tribe.

Location

The Anasazi once lived in the Four Corners area of the United States where Utah, Colorado, Arizona, and New Mexico meet. These are hot, dry areas of steep canyons and the high, flat hilltops the Spanish called *mesas* (meaning "tables"). Large numbers of Anasazi were located in three major areas: Mesa Verde (pronounced *MAY-sah VUR-dee* or *VAIR-day*, meaning "green table"), Colorado; Chaco Canyon, New Mexico; and Kayenta, Arizona. The best-known Anasazi settlement is the one at Mesa Verde, stretching more than 150 miles (241 kilometers) from the Colorado River in Utah east to the Animas River in Colorado.

Population

Between the years 1000 and 1200 CE, there may have been as many as 100,000 ancient peoples, including the Anasazi, the Mogollon, the Hohokam, and other trading partners who have since disappeared.

Language family

Uto-Aztecan.

Origins and group affiliations

The main theory on Anasazi origin is that the group's ancestors were part of the migration from Asia during the last Ice Age, which occurred about twenty thousand years ago. These ancient peoples may have reached what is now Mesa Verde, Colorado, some ten thousand years ago. Along with the

Traditional Anasazi Communities

Anasazi lands: 750–1150 CE

The Anasazi lived for 400 years in the "Four Corners" area, where Utah, Colorado, Arizona, and New Mexico meet.

A map of traditional Anasazi communities. MAP BY XNR PRODUCTIONS. CENGAGE LEARNING, GALE. REPRODUCED BY PERMISSION OF GALE, A PART OF CENGAGE LEARNING.

Mogollon, the Hohokam, and the Patayan, the Anasazi became one of four major civilizations of farming peoples who lived in the Four Corners area of what is now the American Southwest.

For centuries the Anasazi have been a great American mystery. Many unanswered questions remain about the people and their culture. Why did they suddenly move from the fertile valleys and mesa tops of their homeland to dangerous cliff alcoves? Why, less than one hundred years later, did they abandon those cliffs altogether, mix with other cultures, and disappear as a separate people? How could they have become master builders without the aid of horses, other pack animals, or wheels? How did they manage to construct the wide boulevards that connect their villages and their huge, reddish-gold sandstone homes? What is known about these ancient peoples is actually a compilation of theories put together by archaeologists, people who collect and study the remains of past civilizations.

HISTORY

Ancient Basketmakers

The earliest Anasazi people were referred to as "Basketmakers." They wandered the Southwest for thousands of years. Theirs was an extremely hard life, one marked by a constant search for water and food, without the benefit of bows and arrows for hunting. The people apparently lived in shallow caves for a few days at a time and then moved on. The development of watertight baskets made a big difference in their way of life. Baskets could be used to hold, carry, and even cook food (when filled with water and hot rocks).

About two thousand years ago, the Basketmakers learned how to grow corn and squash, and thus they settled down to farm. They lived in more permanent homes, usually pits that were partially underground.

About 550 years later, the Basketmakers lived in or near three major areas: Mesa Verde, Chaco Canyon, and Kayenta. The Anasazi learned from their neighbors, the Mogollon, how to make a primitive type of undecorated pottery that allowed them to cook over a fire. This enabled them to prepare beans, which must be boiled for a long time to make them tender. As a result, beans became a staple crop.

Great building phase begins

At the beginning of the Developmental Pueblo period (700–1050), the Anasazi began to build the huge homes for which they will always be remembered. Over the next four hundred years, their civilization flourished. Chaco Canyon in northern New Mexico became the heart of the Anasazi culture. It formed the hub of a vast trading network that may have extended all the way to the Pacific Coast. By 1050, more than five thousand inhabitants had settled the Chaco Canyon area.

Important Dates

100 BCE–400 CE: In the Early Basketmaker period, the Anasazi use baskets as containers and cooking pots; they live in caves.

400–700: In the Modified Basketmaker period, the Anasazi learn to make pottery in which they can boil beans. They live in underground pits and begin to use bows and arrows.

700–1050: The Developmental Pueblo period begins. The Anasazi move into pueblo-type homes above the ground and develop irrigation methods. A great cultural center is established at Chaco Canyon. Anasazi influence spreads to other areas of the Southwest.

1050–1300: In the Classic Pueblo period, Pueblo architecture reaches its height with the building of fabulous cliff dwellings.

1300–1700: During the Regressive Pueblo period, the Anasazi influence declines. The people leave their northern homelands, heading south to mix with other cultures.

1700–present: Once the Historic Pueblo period begins, the Spaniards, Mexicans, and Americans take over Anasazi lands. Some modern Pueblo tribes carry on Anasazi traditions.

1888: Ranchers and amateur archaeologists Richard Wetherill and Charlie Mason discover ancient cliff dwellings.

A drawing shows a restoration of Pueblo Bonito. © NORTH WIND/NORTH WIND PICTURE ARCHIVES. ALL RIGHTS RESERVED.

An extensive network of wide roads (more than 400 miles, or 640 kilometers) connected other communities to Chaco Canyon. At points along the roads, the Anasazi set up signal stations and maintained fires to communicate with and guide travelers. Traders from faraway places journeyed along the roads, exchanging a variety of exotic goods—macaw feathers from Mexico, seashells from the Sea of Cortez, and turquoise from eastern New Mexico.

The Anasazi built twelve large pueblos in the valley of Chaco Canyon, but the greatest of all was Pueblo Bonito. (*Pueblo* is the Spanish word for city or village.) It is a D-shaped, four-story complex of six hundred to eight hundred rooms and is considered the jewel in the crown of Anasazi architecture. Pueblo was large enough to hold one thousand people. Some of its rooms appear to have been used for storage of surplus crops, luxury items, and art treasures. Until 1882, Pueblo Bonito (though no longer inhabited) held the title of "the world's largest apartment house"; that year, a larger one was constructed in New York City.

Also during the Developmental Pueblo period, the Anasazi people also moved from remote areas and small villages into apartment-style buildings in Mesa Verde, Colorado, and Kayenta, Arizona.

Cliff dwellings

Between 1050 and 1300, the Anasazi were at the height of their architectural genius. Then, for reasons that remain unclear, they began to move down from the tops of mesas and build dwellings under the edges of cliffs. These huge dwellings were very difficult to reach; ladders were often required to get from one level to another. Perhaps the people built them this way for protection against invaders. They also constructed lookout towers around the same time, which lends support to this theory. Another possibility is that the population was growing so large that the Anasazi needed to free up land for farming. Either way, archaeological evidence indicates that the civilization began to wane around this time.

A drawing imagines a restored Anasazi cliff dwelling and masonry tower. © NORTH WIND PICTURE ARCHIVES.

Many reasons have been given for the decline of the Anasazi. Tree ring studies show that a one-hundred-year drought began during the Classic Pueblo period of 1050 to 1300, causing crop failures and food shortages. Other studies indicate that the people may have cut down trees to build houses, leaving no wood for fires and ruining the top soil in the process. Perhaps the Anasazi fled from enemy raids or left because they could not agree among themselves how to distribute dwindling food supplies. Whatever the reason, by 1300, less than one hundred years after their settlement, the cliff dwellings were abandoned, and the Anasazi had left the region forever.

Hohokam, Mogollon, and Patayan Cultures

In addition to the Anasazi, three other early farming cultures dominated the Southwest: the Mogollon, the Hohokam, and the Patayan. A major difference among the groups was the irrigation technique they employed to farm in regions where water tended to be scarce. The Anasazi used several different methods, depending on where they lived. Some sought out ditches that collected rainwater, then built dams along the ditches to divert the water to nearby crops. Others conserved water by planting their gardens on hillside terraces (ridges), thereby taking advantage of the natural flow of water from upper to lower levels.

Mogollon culture

The Mogollon were mountain people who farmed the valleys of east-central Arizona and west-central New Mexico. Their small villages of earth-covered houses appeared in the Southwest around 200 CE. As the earliest of the agricultural groups in the region, the Mogollon were fortunate enough to have a relatively abundant water supply. They planted their crops along the many streams in their homeland. This group is best known for its pottery, which depicted humans, animals, and insects outlined and painted in black over white clay. The Mogollon culture survived until about 1300 CE and may be the ancestors of the present-day western Pueblo (see entry). The Hohokam and Anasazi cultures

adopted or refined some of the Mongollon practices, including the construction of semi-underground, earth-covered pit houses.

Hohokam culture

The name Hohokam comes from a Pima (see entry) word for "those who have gone before." The Hohokam migrated from Mexico around 300 BCE and established their villages along the Gila and Salt rivers in central Arizona. Their greatest accomplishment was the development of an ingenious irrigation system that improved farm yields: a series of canals that channeled the rivers' floodwaters directly to their dry fields. The Hohokam culture is believed to have faded around 1450 CE. Its people may have been the ancestors of the present-day Tohono O'odham (see entry) and the Pima.

Patayan culture

The Patayan people lived in present-day Arizona along the lower Colorado River and in the nearby desert beginning in 200 CE. Like the Hohokam, the Patayan took advantage of the annual flooding of nearby rivers to irrigate their fields. That same flooding swept away most of the remains of their culture, so not much is known about the Patayan people or their traditions. The Hualapai people who came after them gave them the name "Patayan," which means "the old people."

The Anasazi moved in a roundabout way and joined the Hohokam, the Mogollon, and other peoples on the Colorado and upper Rio Grande rivers. The Anasazi intermarried with those peoples, mixed their customs with those of their hosts, and ceased to exist as a separate people.

The Hopi, Zuñi, Rio Grande Pueblo, and Acoma Pueblo (see entries) are thought to be the descendants of the Anasazi.

Cowboys find Anasazi ruins

In the winter of 1888, two cowboys named Richard Wetherill and Charlie Mason were retrieving stray cattle in Colorado when they spied an amazing sight in the distance: a row of huge sandstone houses in an area where they had never seen any people. Wetherill later named the discovery "Cliff Palace." Cliff Palace was once a village housing more than two hundred people.

Later that same day, the explorers discovered "Spruce Tree House." The next morning, they found a third village with a tall four-story tower; they named the village "Square Tower House." Over the next few years, Wetherill and Mason discovered more than 182 sites in all.

Wetherill and Mason were not expert archaeologists. At first, they hoped to make money from their find, selling the remains of the ancient culture to curiosity seekers. Wetherill later decided that it would be in the best interest of scientific discovery if complete collections of artifacts were sold to museums. Over the next several years, Wetherill made many more interesting discoveries. (See "Burial.") Archaeologists who came after Wetherill proposed different theories about the "ancient ones." Research continues to shed new light on the many mysteries of the ancient Anasazi. Their influence and history permeate the modern Southwest.

RELIGION

Old beliefs seen in modern Pueblo practices

Although Anasazi religious beliefs are generally unknown, archaeologists have discovered rooms called *kivas* that were apparently constructed around 750 CE. These chambers were actually former pit houses of the early Anasazi. When the people moved above ground, they retained the pit houses for use as spiritual centers, usually for the male members. The kivas were utilized for ceremonial and religious purposes in much the same way they continue to be used in modern times among Pueblo tribes.

Anasazi kivas were deeper than those of the Mogollon people. Each one was supported by about six columns, contained a hole in the roof for entry, and featured benches along the inside wall. In the floor of the kiva was a small, cup-shaped hole called a *sipapu,* which was believed to be a gateway to and from the spiritual world.

The *Kachina* religion practiced by modern-day Pueblo people may have begun with the Anasazi. Kachina were said to be reincarnated (reborn after death) ancestors who served as messengers between the people and their gods. The term *kachina* also refers to (1) the dolls that represent Pueblo Indians' ancestral spirits and (2) the masked dancers who perform at agricultural ceremonies. Kachina masks dating back many hundreds of years have been unearthed from various Anasazi sites.

Influences from distant civilizations

Strong evidence exists that the Anasazi had contact with distant civilizations, including the Aztec and Mayan peoples of Mexico, and they may have shared some religious beliefs with them. Petroglyphs (paintings or carvings on rock) at Chaco Canyon are similar to those found in Mexico and parts of South America. For example, a spiral symbol that appears on Anasazi petroglyphs may represent a serpent in a coiled position, like the Mayan *Quetzalcoatl* (pronounced *KWET-sahl-koh-WAH-tuhl*), or feathered serpent, a nature god.

The Mayan and Aztec cultures also sacrificed humans to the sun god. Although it has not been proven that the Anasazi sacrificed humans for religious reasons, evidence indicates they may have eaten humans, a practice called cannibalism. (See "Current Tribal Issues.")

LANGUAGE

Because the Ancient Pueblo people disappeared, no evidence was left behind to show what language, or languages, they spoke. Some scholars believe they may have spoken Nahuatl (pronounced *nah-WAH-tuhl*), an Aztec language. Nahuatl is a branch of the Uto-Aztecan language spoken today by some of the Pueblo peoples in central Mexico. Diverse languages among the present Pueblo peoples indicate that their ancestors may have had a complex and far-reaching interaction with outsiders. Pueblo languages show the influence of Numic peoples in the West (such as the Paiute; see entry) and Plains Indians in the East.

GOVERNMENT

It was long believed that all people in Anasazi society were considered equal. This assumption was based in part on archaeological evidence, which showed that no palaces or special buildings were set aside for wealthy and powerful people. However, opinions changed after Richard Wetherill's 1897 discovery of a mummified body of a woman he nicknamed "Princess." Pictographs had been painted above her grave. The lavish and careful burial of Princess, along with the pictographs, seems to indicate that she may have been a member of Anasazi royalty.

Belief in the existence of an Anasazi royal line was further supported by Peruvian scientist Guido Lombardi in 1998. Dr. Lombardi also based his theory on mummies. Archaeologists had long assumed that the bodies of the Anasazi dead had mummified naturally over time—a direct result of the area's climate. However, Lombardi contended that mummification was done on purpose. It was not performed on all Anasazi dead—only on certain special persons.

ECONOMY

Early Pueblo people were hunter-gatherers, but by 1500 BCE, they had begun growing corn. Agricultural knowledge may have come to them from Mexico. About two thousand years ago, they may have begun dry farming. This type of farming uses only natural sources for irrigating crops—melting snow, rain, and groundwater. During this time, the people probably did not plant crops but harvested those that grew naturally.

In later centuries, farming became a main source of food. The Ancestral Pueblo farmed wherever rainfall was sufficient for crops, often on mesa tops, in canyons, or on grasslands. Some communities built reservoirs and dams. They stored surplus crops for times of drought. Although they farmed extensively in some areas, they still hunted and gathered wild plants.

Items found in Anasazi ruins show that they traded with people who lived far from their homelands. Goods came from the Gulf of Mexico, the Great Plains, and the Pacific Coast. Seashells came from California; copper bells came from Mexico. Studies from the late twentieth and early twenty-first centuries show the Anasazi imported from distant areas huge logs for building. During the Developmental Pueblo period, the Anasazi traded with their southern neighbors, who were cotton growers.

DAILY LIFE

Buildings

The Anasazi are often associated with unusual and startling cliff dwellings such as Cliff Palace and Spruce Tree House at Mesa Verde, but cliff dwellings existed for only a brief period of Anasazi history. More typical were

A view of Anasazi ruins at Mesa Verde National Park. © NATIONAL PARK SERVICE/MARTHA SMITH.

blocks of rooms on mesa tops or underground pit houses clustered together to form communities. Pit houses often had egg-shaped or bottle-shaped storage bins dug into the floors, and the walls were covered with stone slabs or plaster. Occasionally, they built larger buildings, about 25 or 30 feet (7.5 to 9 meters) in diameter, perhaps for ceremonies or other gatherings.

In the eighth century, the Anasazi began to build *jacals* (houses) above ground. Setting poles upright in the earth to form the outline of a house, they wove sticks among the poles. They constructed roofs the same way and added a thick coating of mud to weatherproof the top and sides of the house. Jacals had central fire pits, usually lined with stone, and some were also faced with stone.

Sometime before 1000 CE, the Anasazi began using sandstone for masonry, replacing the traditional pole and mud construction of homes. These beautiful sandstone buildings were strong enough to support rafters and adobe roofs (pronounced *uh-DOE-bee*; a sun-dried mud made of a mixture of clay, sand, and sometimes ashes, rocks, or straw). They were expertly made, some standing as high as three stories and containing more than fifty rooms. The apartment-like rooms were often built around a central courtyard or plaza that contained several kivas.

The Classic Pueblo period Near the end of the twelfth century, the Anasazi abandoned the mesa tops, relocating to crevices in cliffs, where they built fabulous structures such as Cliff Palace, the largest dwelling at Mesa Verde. It contained 217 rooms and 23 kivas. The rooms were low and narrow, stacked as high as four stories. The average size of a living room measured 6 feet by 8 feet (2 meters by 2.5 meters) and was only about 5 feet 6 inches (1.5 meters) high.

Life in the cliff dwellings was likely very demanding. Farmers had to climb up or down from the crevices in the cliffs to work their fields on the mesas, a task that required some agility. Accidents were apparently common; crutches have been found among Anasazi ruins.

Food

Domestic routine was a central and time-consuming part of Anasazi life. It included fetching and boiling water, grinding corn into powder with a mano (a hard smooth stone), and gathering and storing beans and piñon nuts. Crops were limited to what could thrive in the dry climate. The Anasazi grew beans, corn, and squash, but they also continued to hunt and gather. They collected timber and nuts from the surrounding forests, fish from nearby rivers, and fowl and berries from the valley floors. By the late 600s, the Anasazi were using the bow and arrow for hunting. Before that, they had used the *atlatl* (pronounced *AHT-lah-tuhl*; dart thrower). The group also domesticated (tamed) several animals, including dogs and turkeys.

With spears and atlatl and later with bows and arrows, the men hunted large game. Mule deer, elk, black bear, squirrel, pronghorn (antelope), and birds provided most of their meat. Women gathered sunflower seeds, tansy mustard seeds, rice grass, amaranth (an edible flower), and herbs. They cooked their food by dropping hot stones into water, using baskets lined with pitch to make them waterproof.

Clothing and adornment

In the summer months, the Anasazi wore little more than apronlike coverings tied around the waist. In the winter, they added robes and blankets of turkey feathers or rabbit skin. They obtained cotton in trade (some southern Anasazi also grew it) and wove it to make clothing and blankets, which they then painted or dyed with juices from plants and berries. They used fabric to create socks, kilts, shirts, and robes. In addition to cotton, the Anasazi also wove plant fibers, human hair, and animal hair.

Sandals made from plant fibers were an absolute necessity. They protected people's feet from the rugged terrain during farming and made it more comfortable to travel by foot in pursuit of wild game or wood for building and burning. Other footwear included moccasins and possibly snowshoes. In the winter, they kept their feet warm with matted fiber from juniper bark. This fiber was also used for diapers and menstrual pads.

Both sexes wore jewelry, most of it studded with shells and turquoise from faraway places. Necklaces, earrings, armbands, hair combs, and pins were popular. They made these from bone, shell, coral, jet (coal), and slate. Jewelry may have denoted social status. The Classic Pueblo period was a time of tremendous artistic growth. Archaeologists have discovered various decorative items, including feather robes, girdles, belts, and wooden necklaces and earrings.

ARTS

Baskets and pottery

Anasazi artistic traditions are recognized far and wide. In addition to their architectural prowess, the people are known for their distinctive basketry and pottery. Some scholars believe that, in Anasazi culture, men were weavers and women were potters.

Anasazi ceramics fall into several different categories. The earliest pottery, first made around 600 CE, was known as the White Ware style. It was actually gray in color because they did not have kilns (heated enclosures that dry or "fire" the freshly shaped clayware). Pottery fired over open fires will not "take" colors, so it turns gray.

During the Classic period, Anasazi pottery reached its artistic height. The style for which the group is most famous is the black-on-white style, common in Chaco Canyon and the Mesa Verde region. It consisted of black geometric designs on a white background. Black paint was produced from plant juices and ground-up minerals. The people in Kayenta, Arizona, produced the red ware style, also known as "polychrome ware" for its many colors. Designs were very distinctive, with broad lines and solid triangles. Some pottery motifs resembled basket patterns.

Anasazi Diaspora

Many people wonder what happened to the Anasazi. Did they migrate to other places or join other tribes? Did they starve, or were they captured or slaughtered? Or did they just vanish one day? This Navajo (see entry) tale is one of the stories about the Anasazi disappearance.

"*Shi cheii,* My Grandfather, where did the Anasazi people go?"

"*Shi'tsoi,* My Grandson, the Anasazi had to leave the land long before *Dinéh,* the Navajo people, came into the Fourth World."

"But Grandfather, their villages are still here. Please tell me the story of the people who disappeared."

"Yes, My Grandson, those ancient ones were blessed in many ways. They were taught by the spirits ways to live productive and holy lives. They lived and enjoyed the blessings. They built great cities, they made beautiful pottery, they had fields of golden corn. They needed nothing beyond that. But they became lazy. This offended the spirits."

"How?"

"They chose to live easy lives instead of living by the rules they were taught to maintain holiness."

"What were those rules?"

"They were to recognize the gods. To pay them homage. To observe ceremonies. To celebrate seasons. To celebrate births and other stages of life. Special healers were appointed and given power to remove illness and restore harmony. But the healers decided to perform this ceremony for everyone, regardless of their health and age. Four times they were warned not to abuse the ceremony. Four times, they chose not to listen."

"And …?"

"On the fifth day, the great wind rose out of the canyon walls and roared throughout the land. People were lifted out of their homes, out of their villages, out of the canyons and valleys. They were scattered throughout this land never to come together again. The buildings were left standing to remind us for all time what will happen if we choose to forget our history, our stories, and above all, our relation to our mother, the earth."

SOURCE: Begay, Shonto. *Navajo Visions and Voices Across the Mesa.* New York: Scholastic Inc., 1995.

The Anasazi were also known for their basketry. They made baskets by twisting plant materials into coils, then winding these coils one layer on top of another. Splints—often dyed red or black with juices from plants and berries—held the layers of the basket together. Many baskets had elaborate, textured designs. The Anasazi coated baskets with pitch (a black, sticky substance from piñon pine) to waterproof them. Baskets served many purposes, from cooking food and carrying water to storage and even burial.

Rock art

Although the Anasazi left behind no written literature, they did produce thousands of petroglyphs and pictographs, and their oral histories no doubt helped to shape today's Hopi, Zuñi, and Rio Grande Pueblo cultures. Ancient rock art painted or chipped into the sandstone cliffs consists of spirals that may have been used as calendars. The sun strikes them differently at certain times of the year. Several sites, such as the Sun Dagger at Chaco Canyon, seem to indicate that the people were knowledgeable about astronomy, especially the seasons and the lunar cycles.

Modern Pueblo people say some of the spirals depict the people's travels; other designs show clans and family groups. Drawings of animals and corn plants can also be seen. The ages of these petroglyphs range from 3000 BCE on; other groups, such as the early Ute and Navajo peoples, continued the tradition.

CUSTOMS

Pastimes

Excavations have revealed that the Anasazi may have played games using small disks. They also smoked tubular-shaped pipes and carved flower blossoms from pieces of wood.

Moving on

Although agriculture changed the Anasazi way of life, the people did not remain in one area for long periods of time. Anasazi tradition is marked by a pattern of settling and then abandoning their communities. Some researchers speculate that the Anasazi stayed in one place until the resources had been depleted, then searched for a new area to live. Others suggest the migrations may have been a result of drought or of conflicts, either external or within the group.

Warlike or peaceful?

It was long thought that the Anasazi were a peaceful people, until Richard Wetherill's "Cave 7" was rediscovered in 1990. This site had apparently been the scene of a bloody massacre more than 1,500 years ago, a battle that involved stabbings, poison darts, beatings with blunt instruments, scalping, and possibly even torture.

Head flattening

Like their Mexican trading partners, the early Anasazi adopted the practice of flattening the heads of infants. They strapped babies' heads to hard boards that flattened their naturally soft skulls over time. Some Native groups considered a flat head attractive.

Burial

What is known about Anasazi burial practices has been learned by digging up burial sites. In 1893, Wetherill discovered a number of basketry containers filled with skeletons. The people he discovered had no pottery; used the *atlatl* (dart thrower) rather than bow and arrow; made baskets of yucca, willow, and squawbrush; were apparently taller than the cliff-dwelling Anasazi; and had flattened skulls. Although Wetherill thought they were a different people, it is now known that these were the early Anasazi.

When Cliff Palace was excavated, archaeologists found that the entire area in front of the settlement had been used as a trash or refuse area. In addition to discovering food fragments, broken tools, and worn-out clothing, archaeologists determined that this section was used as a burial place for the dead, who were wrapped in yucca-fiber mats, rabbit-fur robes, or turkey-feather blankets.

Other sites have revealed bodies buried with items to take to the next world, including new sandals, jewelry, and food. Tools, baskets, weapons, and ceremonial objects have also been found in some graves. The dead were buried fully clothed in a bent position. At some sites, the bodies of children have been found buried beneath the floors of homes, whereas the bodies of older people were buried some distance away.

CURRENT TRIBAL ISSUES

Archaeologists have been examining Anasazi relics for more than one hundred years and are still coming up with theories to resolve unanswered questions about the culture. In 1998, *Discover* magazine reported on a controversial theory that some Anasazi may have been cannibals. While excavating at Cowboy Wash in Colorado, archaeologists discovered piles of human bones—bones that they maintain show evidence of the Anasazi people's cannibalistic activity. It is possible that drought caused starvation, which led a desperate people to survive by consuming human flesh. Another theory suggests that, when several groups were competing for scarce resources, the Anasazi tried to frighten others away by openly engaging in cannibalism.

Studies published in 2007 by geochemist Nathan English indicated that the logs the Ancient Puebloans used to build their homes came from areas about 60 miles (100 kilometers) away. English developed a test to determine the exact location where wood originates. The roofs of the twelve large houses in the Chaco Canyon contain about 200,000 wooden beams. The dwellings rise to five stories high and contain hundreds of rooms. No one yet knows how these ancient people moved all these logs, some weighing 600 pounds (275 kilograms), such a great distance.

Preservation of archaeological sites is an ongoing concern. At Grand Gulch Primitive Area in Utah, the collection of Anasazi specimens is disappearing as visitors help themselves to souvenirs. Conservation groups have worked to have Grand Gulch and other areas designated as protected wilderness areas to help cut down on the thefts. Many of the cliff dwellings of the Anasazi are preserved at Mesa Verde National Park in southwestern Colorado and at Chaco Culture National Historic Park in New Mexico, home of Pueblo Bonito, the largest Anasazi pueblo. Some present-day Native nations consider it a violation of their culture when mining companies and even archaeologists unearth artifacts and burial sites.

Canyons of the Ancients National Monument in southwestern Colorado contain more than six thousand recorded archaeological sites. In 2000, President Bill Clinton (1946–; served 1993–2001) signed a proclamation designating the area a national monument. Despite this, by 2010, approximately 80 percent of the monument had been leased for oil and gas development. Although the companies were warned to minimize damage to the site, many people fear that the drilling, pipelines, and construction will damage the already fragile ancient monument.

BOOKS

Arnold, Caroline, and Richard R. Hewett. *The Ancient Cliff Dwellers of Mesa Verde.* New York: Clarion Books, 2000.

Childs, Craig. *House of Rain: Tracking a Vanished Civilization across the American Southwest.* 2nd ed. New York: Back Bay Books, 2008.

Feldman, George Franklin. *Cannibalism, Headhunting, and Human Sacrifice in North America: A History Forgotten.* Chambersburg, PA: Alan C. Hood & Co., 2008.

Joseph, Frank. *Advanced Civilizations of Prehistoric America: The Lost Kingdoms of the Adena, Hopewell, Mississippians, and Anasazi.* Rochester, VT: Bear, 2010.

Lourie, Peter. *The Lost World of the Anasazi: Exploring the Mysteries of Chaco Canyon.* Honesdale, PA: Boyds Mills Press, 2007.

Noble, David Grant, ed. *In Search of Chaco: New Approaches to an Archaeological Enigma.* Santa Fe, NM: School of American Research Press, 2004.

Roberts, David. *Sandstone Spine: Seeking the Anasazi on the First Traverse of the Comb Ridge.* Seattle, WA: Mountaineers Books, 2006.

Sullivan, Cathie, and Gordon Sullivan. *Roadside Guide to Indian Ruins & Rock Art of the Southwest.* Englewood, CO: Westcliffe Publishers, 2006.

PERIODICALS

Dold, Catherine. "American Cannibal." *Discover* 19, no. 2 (February 1998): 64.

Phillips, Jeff. "Grand Gulch: On the Trail of Utah's Secret Kivas." *Sunset* 200, no. 5 (May 1998): 131.

Siegel, Lee. "Mummies Might Have Been Made by Anasazi." *Salt Lake Tribune,* April 2, 1998.

Trivedi, Bijal P. "Ancient Timbers Reveal Secrets of Anasazi Builders." *National Geographic Today,* September 28, 2001. Available online at http://news.nationalgeographic.com/news/2001/09/0928_TVchaco.html (accessed on June 29, 2007).

WEB SITES

"Anasazi Heritage Center: Ancestral Pueblos." *Bureau of Land Management Colorado.* http://www.co.blm.gov/ahc/anasazi.htm (accessed on July 13, 2011).

"The Anasazi or 'Ancient Pueblo.'" *Northern Arizona University.* http://www.cpluhna.nau.edu/People/anasazi.htm (accessed on July 20, 2011).

"Anasazi: The Ancient Ones." *Manitou Cliff Dwellings Museum.* http://www.cliffdwellingsmuseum.com/anasazi.htm (accessed on July 20, 2011).

Burns, Samuel. "Indian Ruins of AZ and NM" (video). *University of Illinois.* http://www.vimeo.com/9385727 (accessed on July 20, 2011).

Cordell, Linda. "Anasazi." *Scholastic.* http://www2.scholastic.com/browse/article.jsp?id=5042 (accessed on July 20, 2011).

Hurst, Winston. "Anasazi." *Utah History to Go: State of Utah.* http://historytogo.utah.gov/utah_chapters/american_indians/anasazi.html (accessed on July 20, 2011).

Sharp, Jay W. "The Anasazi: The People of the Mountains, Mesas, and Grasslands." *Desert USA.* http://www.desertusa.com/ind1/du_peo_ana.html (accessed on July 20, 2011).

Skopec, Eric. "What Mystery?" *Anasazi Adventure.* http://www.anasaziadventure.com/what_mystery.pdf (accessed on July 20, 2011).

Stewart, Kenneth. "Kivas." *Scholastic.* http://www2.scholastic.com/browse/article.jsp?id=5052 (accessed on July 20, 2011).

Apache

For more information on Apache groups, please see Chiricahua Apache, San Carlos Apache, and White Mountain Apache entries.

Name

Apache (pronounced *uh-PATCH-ee*) comes from the Yuma word meaning "fighting-men" or the Zuñi word *apachu,* meaning "enemy." The Apache call themselves *Inde* or *Ndé,* meaning "people."

Location

The Apache once lived in a vast region stretching from what is now central Arizona to central Texas, and from northern Mexico to the high plains of southeastern Colorado. In the early 2000s, about 37,500 Apache resided on nine reservations in Arizona, New Mexico, and Oklahoma. The remaining Apache were scattered throughout the United States.

Population

At the end of the 1600s, there were an estimated 5,000 Apache. In the 1990 U.S. Census, 53,330 people identified themselves as Apache. In 2000, that number had risen to 57,199, and a total of 96,833 people claimed some Apache heritage, making the tribe the seventh largest in the United States. In the 2010 census, 63,193 identified themselves as Apache, with a total of 111,810 people claiming some Apache heritage. According to the Oklahoma Indian Affairs Commission, 2011 enrollment for the Apache Tribe of Oklahoma was 2,263; Fort Sill Apache numbered 650.

Language family

Athabaskan.

Origins and group affiliations

According to European historians, the Apache people made a gradual move from western Canada to the American Southwest between the thirteenth and sixteenth centuries. Apache oral history, however, indicates that their

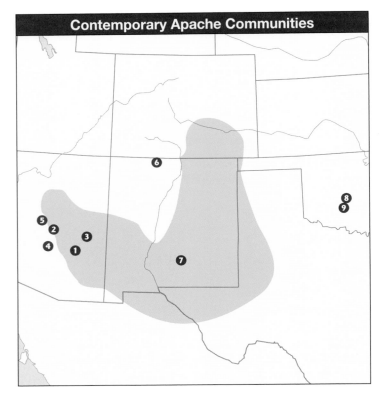

Contemporary Apache Communities

Arizona
1. San Carlos Apache Tribe
2. Tonto Apache Reservation
3. Fort Apache Reservation
4. Fort McDowell Mohave-Apache Indian Community
5. Yavapai-Apache Tribe

New Mexico
6. Jicarilla Apache Tribe
7. Mescalero Apache Tribe

Oklahoma
8. Apache Tribe of Oklahoma
9. Fort Sill Apache Tribe of Oklahoma

Shaded area
Traditional lands of the Apache in present-day Arizona, New Mexico, Texas, northern Mexico, and southeastern Colorado

A map of contemporary Apache communities. MAP BY XNR PRODUCTIONS. CENGAGE LEARNING, GALE. REPRODUCED BY PERMISSION OF GALE, A PART OF CENGAGE LEARNING.

people migrated north, and those who live in the Southwest in modern times were the ones who stayed behind. The Apache were never one unified group, but rather a number of bands who spoke related languages and shared similar customs. Today, the Apache are divided into two groups: Western Apache and Eastern Apache (also known as Plains Apache).

The Eastern Apache include the Chiricahua (pronounced *CHEER-uh-KAH-wuh*), Jicarilla (*hi-kah-REE-yah*), Lipan, Mescalero (*mes-KAH-lair-ro*), and Kiowa (*KYE-o-wah*) Apache peoples. Their descendants now live in New Mexico and Oklahoma. Western Apache include the Cibecue, Coyotero, Northern Tonto, Southern Tonto, San Carlos, and White Mountain Apache. Their descendants now live in Arizona.

Apache oral history states that they once lived beneath the earth's surface. Long ago, they came above ground and found themselves in the American Southwest, their sacred homeland. Apache feel a powerful spiritual tie to their land, a place of majestic mountains, grassy hills, vast deserts, steep canyons, hot springs, and dense forests of pine, sycamore, cottonwood, juniper, and oak. They are a fierce, proud, religious people who wandered the Southwest for centuries before the Europeans came, hunting game and gathering the abundant fruits and nuts there.

HISTORY

Trading and raiding

The Apache were wanderers in a harsh, dry land where temperatures could abruptly change from extremely hot to extremely cold. They often quarreled among themselves and had uneasy relations with their neighbors, especially the Pueblo and Pima tribes (see entries). They sometimes traded with those tribes, but they could also take up their weapons and raid Pueblo and Pima villages.

An illustration depicts Mescalero Apache chief San Juan, medicine man Gorgonio, and war chief Nantzili, circa 1880s. © NORTH WIND PICTURE ARCHIVES.

Important Dates

1540: Spanish gold seekers encounter the Apache for the first time.

1847: The Apache come under American control.

1886: The final surrender of Geronimo's band marks the end of Apache military resistance to American settlement.

1934: The Indian Reorganization Act results in self-government for Apache tribes.

When the Spanish arrived in 1540 bringing guns and horses, the Apache at first happily traded with the Europeans. For more than 300 years, the Spaniards had heard stories about seven lost cities of gold, and they believed Apache land was their hiding place. Relations between the Apache and the Spanish disintegrated after the Spaniards tried to take control of Apache land. The Apache carried out sneak attacks on European settlements, stealing their guns, horses, cattle, and even children. The Spanish, in return, took Apache women and children into slavery.

By 1700, the Comanche tribe (see entry) had acquired horses, which allowed them to leave the Great Plains and travel greater distances than ever before. They entered Apache territory and forced the people out of their hunting grounds. Unable to hunt for buffalo, the Apache carried out more raids against Spanish settlements.

When the Spanish signed a peace treaty with the Comanche in 1786, they employed Comanche and Navajo (see entry) warriors to hunt down the Apache. The Spanish then offered bribes if the Apache people would settle near Spanish missions, stop raiding Spanish livestock, and live peacefully. One by one, Apache groups accepted the terms. Some fled to the mountains, however, and continued to carry out raids against Spanish settlements in what is now Mexico. The Mexican government responded by offering to pay a price for every Apache scalp taken. (For more information, see Chiricahua Apache entry.)

Apache come under U.S. control

In 1821, Mexico won its independence from Spain and gained land in the Southwest that included Apache territory. In 1848, the United States took over part of the region under the terms of the Treaty of Guadalupe-Hidalgo, which settled the Mexican-American War (1846–48; a war fought in the Southwest after which Mexico lost one-half of its land to the United States). In the treaty, U.S. government officials promised Mexico that if any tribes on the new American lands carried out raids in Mexico, America would punish them. Now, instead of the Mexican government, the Apache had a new enemy—the U.S. Army.

American settlers and gold seekers streamed through Apache territory. They did not try to get along with the Apache, as the Spanish had done. Instead, they called out the U.S. Army to subdue the tribe. The Apache put up such a fierce resistance, however, that they were not conquered until the final surrender of the feared and respected Apache leader Geronimo (1829–1909) and his band in 1886. (For more information, see Chiricahua Apache entry.) Newspaper headlines across the nation announced: "Apache War Ended!" The "roving Apache," as one army general called them, were now under the control of the U.S. government.

Some became prisoners of war, shipped first to Florida, then to Alabama, and finally to the Fort Sill Reservation in Oklahoma. Others were placed on reservations in the Southwest. Different Apache groups had various destinies (see Chiricahua Apache, San Carlos Apache, and White Mountain Apache entries).

Geronimo, or Goyathlay, was the leader of the Apache resistance to Mexican and U.S. forces in the mid- to late nineteenth century. © BETTMANN/CORBIS.

RELIGION

The Apache are very religious, and all of their actions are guided by their beliefs. They seek the help and guidance of the gods before hunting, farming, or going to war. The Apache believe in a creator called Usen, or Life Giver, who is the most important of their several gods. Other supernatural spirits include White Painted Woman, the symbol of life, and her children, Child of the Water and Killer of Enemies. The friendly Mountain Spirits are worshiped in special ceremonies led by spiritual leaders called shamans (pronounced *SHAH-munz* or *SHAY-munz*), who could also heal the sick.

Many Apache people converted to the Catholic faith under the influence of Spanish missionaries, but they never abandoned their ancient religion because it is such an important element in their way of life. In the late 1800s, the U.S. government and Christian missionaries tried to suppress the old religion, and rituals like the Sunrise Ceremony became illegal. To keep their traditions alive, the Apache held their

An Apache girl participates in her Sunrise Ceremony, a ritual that ushers young Apache girls into womanhood. © SCOTT WARREN/AURORA PHOTOS.

ceremonies in secret. In 1978, the American Indian Religious Freedom Act passed, and the tribe could once again perform these rituals openly. In the second decade of the 2000s, many Apache still practiced those customs, and it was not uncommon for Apache people to participate in both Christian and traditional religions.

LANGUAGE

The Southwestern Athabaskan language, which is sometimes called Apachean, has seven dialects (varieties): Navajo, Western Apache, Chiricahua, Mescalero, Jicarilla, Lipan, and Kiowa Apache. All Apache dialects differ from one another in some ways, but members of the different groups can still understand one another. Most dialects, especially Western Apache, are spoken in modern times.

When the Spanish came to the New World in the mid-1500s, the Apache easily communicated with them using sign language. Many tribes also found sign language useful for trading with each other.

GOVERNMENT

In early times

For the Apache, the family is the most important unit. Until the twentieth century, the people never had a government body that ruled everyone. Instead, family groups usually acted independently. Apache groups moved about constantly from place to place, and government officials found it hard to find them and reach agreements with them.

From time to time, a number of these family groups came together to make important decisions, such as whether to send out a war party. In those instances, the male heads of each family group formed a council, discussed the problem, and made a decision. Even if they chose to act together, though, the groups were never very large. When faced with threats from the Comanche (see entry), the Spaniards, the Mexicans, or the Americans, the Apache might have a war or raiding party consisting of a maximum of one hundred men (and sometimes women). Although Apache men made decisions about war and whether to move to a new location, women had influence too. The oldest woman in a household acted as leader and was greatly respected.

Western Apache Words

góshé	"dog"
ndeeń	"man"
aidzán	"woman"
ya'ái	"sun"
tú	"water"

On the reservations

After they moved to the reservations, the Apache came under the control of government agents who did not always treat them well. The agents were mainly interested in making Native peoples more like European Americans, and they devoted efforts to getting the Apache and other groups to turn over decision-making power to them. A U.S. Indian Police force oversaw law enforcement, health, and the use of land.

In 1934, the U.S. Congress passed the Indian Reorganization Act. American Indian tribes were given the opportunity to form their own elective tribal councils, a type of government the Apache still use in the twenty-first century.

ECONOMY

Early livelihoods

Prior to the arrival of the Europeans, the Apache carried on a lively trade, especially with the Pueblo and Pima (see entries) tribes. The Apache were very clever at hunting and manufacturing items from buffalo, especially robes and jerky (meat that is cut into long strips and then dried in the sun or cured by exposing it to smoke). In return for these goods, the Apache received corn and beans, gourds, cotton cloth, and minerals from other tribes.

Later the Apache traded with the Spanish, exchanging buffalo hides for grain and cattle, as well as for horses and guns that allowed them to expand their hunting and trading opportunities. Raiding was as natural to them as trading, though, and they often took what they wanted from other tribes and from the Mexicans. Some Apache groups relied on a limited amount of farming for food, but once they had horses, they depended less on farming.

Apaches assemble to receive a ration of beef from Indian agents at San Carlos Reservation in the 1890s. © NORTH WIND PICTURE ARCHIVES.

The U.S. government began moving the Apache onto reservations in the late 1800s. The limits of life on the reservations were a great shock to a people who were accustomed to roaming. The government expected men who were once warriors to turn to farming, and the Apache struggled to do so for a time. Some succeeded, but others did not; the land was of poor quality and there was little water. Some left the reservations to work for wages.

Twentieth-century economy

After 1918, the U.S. government encouraged the Apache to begin raising cattle, and some tribes did so very successfully. Others engaged in processing lumber. When large numbers of Americans began to own cars and travel in the 1950s, many Apache turned to the outdoor recreation business.

In the twenty-first century, the Apache can be found pursuing careers in all the professions, though most of them must leave their communities to do so. Those who live on the reservations face a persistently high level of unemployment. Farming and ranching continue to provide employment for some, and casinos bring in income for many Apache reservations.

DAILY LIFE

Families

Daily life revolved around the extended family, which included mother, father, children, grandparents, cousins, uncles, and aunts, who lived in single-family homes placed close together. Apache women bore few children. There was no word in the Apache language for "cousins," and children considered their cousins to be their brothers and sisters.

Although the Apache had a reputation as warlike, they were gentle and affectionate with their own children and other relatives. Children were taught manners, kindness, endurance, and obedience. They played games to improve their skills and quickness.

Buildings

The Apache usually built single-family homes called wickiups (pronounced *WIK-ee-ups*). These cone- or dome-shaped structures had a framework of poles covered with brush, grass, reed mats, or sometimes skins. A fire pit in the center vented smoke through a hole directly above it. The Kiowa Apache and Jicarilla usually lived in Plains-style tepees covered with hides, although some Jicarilla may have lived in Pueblo-style homes.

Wickiups were easy to put up, take down, and carry to the different camps that Apache bands lived in throughout the year. In very early times, before they acquired horses, they strapped their housing materials to the backs of dogs to carry to the new location.

The Recreation Business

Several Apache tribes have been successful at taking advantage of people's interest in outdoor recreation. For example, many members of the Mescalero Apache find employment at their ski resort, Ski Apache. Others work at the tribal museum and visitor center in Mescalero, Arizona. A large Mescalero enterprise, the Inn of the Mountain Gods in New Mexico, has a gift shop, several restaurants, an eighteen-hole golf course, and a casino. It also offers horseback riding, skeet and trap shooting, and tennis among other activities.

For the Yavapai Apache, whose small reservation has fewer than three hundred acres of land suitable for agriculture, the tourist complex at the Montezuma Castle National Monument, where the tribe owns the seventy-five acres of land surrounding the monument, is an important source of employment and revenue. The Jicarilla Apache operate a ski enterprise, offering equipment rentals and trails for a cross-country ski program during the winter months. The gift shop at the Jicarilla museum provides an outlet for the sale of locally crafted traditional items, including basketry, beadwork, feather work, and finely tanned buckskin leather.

Tourism, especially for events such as tribal fairs and for hunting and fishing, provides jobs and brings money into the local economies at a number of reservations. Trophy and big-game hunting are especially popular on the Jicarilla reservation. Several bands also maintain campgrounds. The Apache are also known as some of the finest professional rodeo performers.

Apache adults and children stand at their wickiup. NATIONAL ARCHIVES AND RECORDS ADMINISTRATION.

Education

Apache children learned by listening to, observing, and imitating their parents. Both boys and girls learned survival skills such as how to run swiftly, how to ride horses (the Apache were outstanding riders), and how to sneak up on enemy villages because these skills might one day save their lives. Games and contests were held for fun, but they also made contestants stronger.

Boys trained for warfare by walking for miles without food and water. They learned to send and read smoke signals and to hunt silently. Girls learned to do household chores because they usually married very young.

Once they were on reservations and under the control of U.S. government agents, Apache children were expected to become "civilized," or more like the settlers. Not long after the 1879 founding of the Carlisle Indian School in Pennsylvania, many Apache children were sent there to live, far from their homeland and families. Government and mission schools were established among the Apache in the 1890s. All of these schools offered instruction only in English.

An Apache family gathers in front of their wickiup, circa 1880s. © NORTH WIND PICTURE ARCHIVES.

In the early 2000s, the majority of the Apache population was under the age of eighteen. Education remains highly regarded, and the Apache take an active role in making decisions about their children's education. This has resulted in some Apache public schools being singled out by the U.S. government as model schools for their bilingual and bicultural programs, especially in the elementary grades.

Food

The Apache were hunter-gatherers. They hunted bison, antelope, deer, elk, cougar, coyote, javelina, mountain sheep, and such birds as quail and wild turkey. Apache religion would not allow the eating of fish or bear. The people believed some animals were unclean—snakes, frogs, prairie dogs, and fish—so they never ate them. Bears resembled people because they sometimes walked on two legs, so most bands did not kill them. Before the men hunted for game, they greased their bodies with animal fat so their human scent would not scare off the prey.

After they acquired horses in the late 1600s, some Apache groups hunted buffalo like their Plains neighbors, but buffalo were not plentiful. The men had to travel great distances to find buffalo, and they sometimes approached the animals by crawling a long way through the underbrush to disguise their scent.

Gathered foods included agave (pronounced *ah-gah-VEE*; a plant with tough, spiny, sword-shaped leaves that grows in hot, dry regions), cactus fruits, pecans, acorns, black walnuts, pine nuts, chokecherries, juniper berries, and raspberries. The climate of the Southwest was not good for farming, and water was scarce. Some Western tribes who were willing to carry water, however, produced limited amounts of corn, beans, pumpkins, and squash.

Clothing and adornment

Apache men wore buckskin breechcloths (garments with front and back flaps that hung from the waist), ponchos (blanket-like cloaks with a hole for the head), and moccasins with attached leggings. Women wore buckskin skirts, similar ponchos, and high bootlike moccasins. These moccasins with their attached leggings protected the Apache from the rough terrain of the deserts, the spikes of spiny cacti, and snakes. Some leggings extended almost to the hip, and the top could be folded over to hold a knife.

Men usually cut their hair shoulder-length and tied a cloth headband across their forehead. They also wore deerskin caps with symbolic decorations. Women wore their hair long.

The Apache acquired cloth and wool through trade with other tribes. At the turn of the twentieth century, they began to wear more American-style clothing, such as white cotton shirts and black vests for men and long-sleeved cotton blouses and full skirts for women. Regalia, or traditional clothing, is worn on important occasions. A girl's puberty ceremony costume generally consists of a two-piece buckskin dress of the highest quality, adorned with fringe, shells, beads, and metal pieces. A shaman's buckskin garment might have feathers, beads, and paint.

Healing practices

The Apache believed that sicknesses were often (but not always) sent by evil spirits to people who had offended them. Such ailments were cured by male or female healers called shamans, who cured with herbs and by dancing and chanting. A suffering person requested the aid of a healer, then sprinkled the healer's head with pollen and offered a gift. The shaman would accept the gift only if he or she decided to take the case. During the healing ceremony, the shaman sprinkled the patient with pollen and performed a ritual involving four dancers. The ceremony would be repeated over four nights.

Sweat baths were sometimes used as a remedy for colds and fever. The Apache also knew practical skills such as how to set broken bones with splints fashioned from cedar bark. Bloodletting—draining blood from a sick person—was also a medical treatment used for headaches and other ailments.

Twentieth-century health problems

Well into the twentieth century, ailing Apache continued to seek the services of shamans, but the kinds of ailments they suffered had changed. The people experienced tremendous health problems associated with malnutrition (poor diet), poverty, and despair. They had incredibly high rates of contagious diseases such as tuberculosis. With the establishment of schools in the early 1900s, the tuberculosis bacteria spread rapidly through the tribe. By 1914, 90 percent of the Jicarilla suffered from tuberculosis. Between 1900 and 1920, one-fourth of the people died. One of the reservation schools had to be converted into a tuberculosis sanatorium (a type of treatment facility) in an attempt to address the crisis. The sanatorium remained open until 1940.

Like other tribes, the Apache have struggled with the effects of alcohol abuse. Alcohol, although long known to the Apache, was not always a destructive force. In times past, the custom of sharing the drink *telapi,* made from fermented corn sprouts, "made people feel good about each other and what they were doing," said an Apache elder. Tribal leaders have attempted to address these health problems through education and by creating jobs to help people from feeling the despair that can come from unemployment.

ARTS

Crafts revival

Many Apache are demonstrating a new pride in traditional crafts as they attempt to survive in the larger American culture while remaining Apache. Basketry and pottery making, which had nearly died out during the 1950s, are now valued skills once again, taught and learned with renewed vigor.

Oral literature

The Apache tell stories about the creation of the universe and the supernatural, but these stories are considered sacred and are kept secret. Other tales about the adventures of Coyote and Big Owl are

The Emergence: How the Apache Came to Earth

Long ago they say. Long ago they made the earth and the sky. There were no people living on the earth then. There were four places under the earth where Red Ants were living. These Red Ants were talking about this country up here on the surface of the earth, and they wanted to come up here. Among them was the Red Ant chief and he talked about coming here. "All right, let's go to this new place above!" all the Ants decided. There was a big cane growing in that place. This grew upwards toward the sky. Then all the Red Ant People started off from the bottom of this cane and traveled up it. When they reached the first joint of the cane they made camp there all night. The next day they traveled on from there, still upwards.

They spent many nights on their way, always making their camp at the joints of the cane. They kept on traveling that way, upwards, and then finally the chief told them to look around this place where they were. So all the people went out and looked around this new country and all of them said that this was a nice place. There were lots of foods growing all around. The chief said, "Bring in all those foods that are good to eat, to our camp." So the people

brought in the different kinds of foods and fruits that were good. They went all over the country for these wild foods. This way they found lots to eat and they found good places to live all over the new land.

After that the chief told the people to look around, and then he sang a song. At every song that he sang all the people were to come together again. Then the chief was singing and in his song he said, "You can go off any place you want to, and when you find a place that is good, then stop there and settle." So this was the first place that people were living, and these were the first people, the Red Ants.

Badger and Porcupine were the first ones on this earth also. Then all kinds of birds started to live on this earth; Eagle and Hawk and all the other kinds. Then God had made man on this earth and everyone was living well. This is the story about how man first became.

SOURCE: Bane, Tithla. *"Hatc'onondai* (The Emergence, or the Emerging Place)." In *Myths and Tales of the White Mountain Apache,* compiled by Grenville Goodwin. New York: American Folklore Society, 1939.

told to instruct young people and to entertain, and some of these stories have been written down.

Coyote is sometimes portrayed as a hero because he taught the Apache how to care for themselves. At other times, Coyote plays the role of a fool, for he frequently makes bad moral decisions and then suffers the consequences. The Apache believe Coyote was responsible for bringing death and darkness into the world.

CUSTOMS

Festivals and ceremonies

The Apache did not have rituals celebrating the harvest, as many other tribes do. Apache ceremonies focused on celebrating important life events such as the naming of an infant, receiving the first pair of moccasins, getting the first haircut, entering puberty, healing by shamans, and asking supernatural beings for power. There might be hundreds of ceremonies celebrating life events each year.

Most rituals involved the use of pollen and the number four. Pollen is a symbol of life, fertility, and beauty. The Apache believe it brings good luck and still use it in some ceremonies. The number four represents the four directions (north, south, east, west), and rituals are often performed four times.

Puberty

Unlike adolescents in many other tribes, Apache boys and girls did not go on vision quests to receive the spiritual guidance some call Power. Instead, Power came to them suddenly and unexpectedly, and this could happen several times throughout a person's life. Without Power, a man could not be a leader, and a woman had no influence.

A girl's coming-of-age was the occasion for a major ceremony, the Sunrise Ceremony, which lasted four days and was hosted by her parents. Part of the ceremony is called the Dance of the Mountain Spirits, in which masked participants pretend to be gods of the mountains. The young girl being honored impersonated White Painted Woman, who is like Mother Earth. Performance of the dance brought good fortune to the entire tribe. During the ceremony, the young girl was attended by an older woman who would be her guide throughout life. After four days of constant singing and dancing, a girl took four days to recover. This puberty ceremony is still observed today, although because of the expenses involved in paying dancers and providing food for the tribe, it may last only a day or two, or several girls may share the same ceremony.

The boy's version of a puberty ceremony was his first four raids on enemy settlements. After he completed them, he was considered an adult.

Courtship and marriage

Young Apache women were supervised to limit their contact with young men, and dances provided rare and welcome opportunities for socializing. A young man's entire family decided on his choice of a bride. Once all his relatives had voiced their approval of his choice, the young man's parents or their representative offered presents to the girl's parents.

If the bride's parents accepted the gift, the couple was often considered married with little or no further ceremony. Author Michael Melody described one simple Apache wedding that he observed: "A basin made of buffalo hide was carried to a secluded place and filled with fresh water. The bride and groom stepped into it, held hands, and awaited the appearance of both sets of parents, who had to acknowledge the matrimony." Afterward, the couple joined a public dance.

Married life

The Apache trace their ancestry through the mother, and married couples set up housekeeping near the wife's parents in a separate wickiup. The Apache believed a marriage would be happier if the wife's mother never spoke to, or even appeared in the presence of, her son-in-law. No such rule applied to the wife's grandmother, who today remains a powerful presence in family life.

A man had to take care of his wife's family, and if she died, he had to marry her sister or unwed cousin. Successful hunters, warriors, or other men who could afford it had more than one wife. In the case of divorce, children remained with the wife's extended family. Modern-day Apache have adopted American marriage customs.

War rituals

Warfare was a major part of the Apache existence until almost 1900. Michael Melody wrote that most Apache battles "were undertaken to avenge deaths of group members, usually killed during raids. The slain warrior's family led the way during battle." The Apache requested the help of the gods prior to battle in a ceremony that included warriors in costume. The dancers acted out the brave deeds they intended to perform. If the warriors were successful, another dance was held in which they acted out their achievements.

War parties might consist of a maximum of one hundred warriors who bravely faced much larger forces. During the late 1800s, Apache warriors took on the U.S. Army. When a cause seemed hopeless, however, warriors would scatter rather than fight to the bitter end.

Death and burial

Death of loved ones was a source of great dread for Apache, who feared they would be haunted by the ghost of the deceased. They painted the face of a corpse red, and they wrapped the body in skins and disposed of it as soon as possible to hasten the spirit's journey to the underworld. They loaded the body onto a horse and took it to a cave or some other secluded area, where they entombed it and sealed the opening. The horse was then killed, and the deceased's house and belongings were destroyed. Survivors did not go near the burial ground, nor did they ever again speak the name of the dead person.

CURRENT TRIBAL ISSUES

Environmental and land issues

On the Fort Sill Apache lands, many people developed lupus and cancer. They believe this is related to the oil drilling on their land. The Mescalero Apache are working to reduce hazardous fuels, clean up their water, and prevent forest fires. A forest fire in 1996 destroyed a large portion of the Jicarilla Apache lands and has adversely affected the wildlife and fish. The Jicarilla tribe is also struggling with problems related to clear-cut logging, overgrazing, erosion, and pollution. On the Fort McDowell and Camp Verde Indian reservations, the quality of the water supply is an ongoing concern.

Many Native nations, including the Hopi, Navajo (see entries), Yavapai, Hualapai, and Apache, have concerns about a proposal to expand the Snowbowl ski resort in the San Francisco Peaks in Arizona's Coconino National Forest. The resort wants to make artificial snow from recycled sewage, but the Native nations object to them cutting down rare alpine

---

Camp Grant Massacre (April 30, 1871)

In 1871, more than five hundred starving Aravaipa Apache requested sanctuary at Fort Grant in Arizona. They asked to grow crops along the creek in their former homeland. Lt. Royal Whitman, officer in charge, agreed they could settle there.

The following month, raids and several deaths were attributed to Native tribes. After cattle were stolen, the Papago (see Tohono O'odham entry), enemies of the Apache, blamed it on the Aravaipa. Tucson residents formed a posse. A large group of Mexicans, Americans, and Papago sneaked into the Aravaipa camp at night. They murdered the sleeping people—eight men and 110 women and children. They sold twenty-eight babies into slavery.

Later that year, all 104 members of the posse were tried. The five-day trial ended with less than twenty minutes of deliberation. The verdict for each person was the same: Not guilty.

More than one hundred years passed before a marker was erected at the site where this massacre occurred.

---

habitat and using wastewater in an area that is sacred to their people. Lawsuits and appeals that alternated decisions both for and against the development prevented construction for several years. When in 2009 the U.S. Supreme Court refused to hear their case, the Native nations attempted to negotiate an agreement with the federal government. An environmental group also introduced a lawsuit, expressing concern about the dangers of using sewer water that would melt and turn into groundwater.

Another issue is the illegal seizure and use of Apache lands over the centuries. The Jicarilla Apache won almost $10 million in a lawsuit for land unfairly taken from them, but the United States will not return any of the land. In 1982, the U.S. Supreme Court ruled that the Jicarilla have the right to impose tribal taxes on minerals extracted from their lands by others. Since that time, though, several court cases involving royalty payments (for example, one against the U.S. Department of the Interior in 2008 and another against a mining company in 2009) have been decided against the Jicarilla.

Crime and poverty

Crime is an ongoing problem on many reservations. Most have few police officers, and federal law enforcement is often slow to respond to cases on the reservation. In 2008, a series of fifteen or more rapes of young girls on Arizona's Fort Apache Reservation was not investigated promptly, nor were other girls warned about the danger. After suspects were arrested, the case was declared closed. The men turned out to be innocent and are suing for false arrest, however, and the real criminal was never caught. To improve situations such as this, President Barack Obama (1961–; served 2009–) in 2010 signed a Tribal Law and Order Act that introduced some law enforcement reforms. The act gives tribal authorities the ability to lengthen prison sentences, which are presently limited to three years, and it gives them access to criminal databases along with strengthening other areas of law enforcement.

Poverty—and what to do about it—is a major issue for many of the people. The Apache have been working hard to resolve this problem. Most reservations have opened casinos, which provide jobs and benefit the economy.

NOTABLE PEOPLE

Jicarilla Apache scholar Veronica E. Velarde Tiller is the author of *Discover Indian Reservations USA, Tiller's Guide to Indian Country: Economic Profiles of American Indian Reservations, The Jicarilla Apache*

Tribe: A History, and other works. Apache-Hopi-Pueblo author Michael Lacapa, who was raised as an Apache, has written award-winning children's books both alone and with his wife, Kathleen, a Mohawk. They coauthored *Less than Half, More than Whole* (1994), about a part-Native child troubled by his mixed heritage. The works of poet and educator Jose Garza (Coahuiltec-Apache) and poet and short-story-writer Lorenzo Baca (Mescalero Apache) appear in *Returning the Gift: Poetry and Prose from the First North American Native Writers' Festival* (1994) and elsewhere.

BOOKS

Ball, Eve, Nora Henn, and Lynda A. Sánchez. *Indeh: An Apache Odyssey.* Reprint. Norman: University of Oklahoma Press, 1988.

Behnke, Alison. *The Apaches.* Minneapolis, MN: Lerner Publications, 2006.

Birchfield, D.L., and Helen Dwyer. *Apache History and Culture.* New York: Gareth Stevens, 2012.

Colwell-Chanthaphonh, Chip. *Massacre at Camp Grant: Forgetting and Remembering Apache History.* Tucson: University of Arizona Press, 2007.

Geronimo. *The Autobiography of Geronimo.* St. Petersburg, FL: Red and Black Publishers, 2011.

Kissock, Heather, and Jordan McGill. *Apache: American Indian Art and Culture.* New York: Weigl Publishers, 2011.

Jastrzembski, Joseph C. *The Apache.* Minneapolis: Chelsea House, 2011.

Jastrzembski, Joseph C. *The Apache Wars: The Final Resistance.* Minneapolis: Chelsea House, 2007.

Melody, Michael E., and Paul Rosier. *The Apache.* Minneapolis: Chelsea House, 2005.

Miller, Raymond H. *North American Indians: The Apache.* San Diego: KidHaven Press, 2005.

Santiago, Mark. *The Jar of Severed Hands: Spanish Deportation of Apache Prisoners of War, 1770–1810.* Norman: University of Oklahoma, 2011.

Stockel, H. Henrietta, with Marian D. Kelley. *Drumbeats from Mescalero: Conversations with Apache Elders, Warriors, and Horseholders.* College Station: Texas A&M University Press, 2011.

Sullivan, George. *Geronimo: Apache Renegade.* New York: Sterling, 2010.

Tiller, Veronica E. Velarde. *Culture and Customs of the Apache Indians.* Santa Barbara, CA: ABC-CLIO, 2011.

PERIODICALS

Bourke, John Gregory. "General Crook in the Indian Country." *The Century Magazine,* March 1891. Available online from http://www.discoverseaz.com/History/General_Crook.html (accessed on July 20, 2011).

WEB SITES

"Apache." *Southwest Crossroads.* http://southwestcrossroads.org/search. php?query=Apache (accessed on July 20, 2011).

"Apache Indian History." *Access Genealogy.* http://www.accessgenealogy.com/ native/tribes/apache/apachehist.htm (accessed on July 15, 2011).

"Apache Indians." *AAA Native Arts.* http://www.aaanativearts.com/apache (accessed on July 15, 2011).

"Apache Nation: Nde Nation." *San Carlos Apache Nation.* http://www. sancarlosapache.com/home.htm (accessed on July 15, 2011).

"Apache Tribal Nation." *Dreams of the Great Earth Changes.* http://www. greatdreams.com/apache/apache-tribe.htm (accessed on July 15, 2011).

Browne, J. Ross. "Adventures in the Apache Country: A Tour through Arizona and Sonora, 1864." *Discover Southeast Arizona.* http://www.discoverseaz. com/History/Browne.html (accessed on July 20, 2011).

Carlin, Dan. "Apache Indian Wars." *Hardcore History* on *You Tube.* Part 1 of 8.Video Series.http://www.youtube.com/watch?v=4xqSTKgUXD0 (accessed on July 20, 2011).

"The Children of Changing Woman." *Peabody Museum of Archaeology and Ethnology.* http://www.peabody.harvard.edu/maria/Cwoman.html (accessed on July 15, 2011).

"Community Page." *Lipan Apache Tribe of Texas.* http://www.lipanapache.org/ Communitypages.html (accessed on July 15, 2011).

Everett, Diana. "Apache Tribe of Oklahoma." *Oklahoma Historical Society.* http:// digital.library.okstate.edu/encyclopedia/entries/A/AP002.html(accessed on July 15, 2011).

Field Division of Education. "Material Culture of the Pima, Papago, and Western Apache." *National Park Service.* http://www.cr.nps.gov/history/ online_books/berkeley/beals1/beals1i.htm (accessed on July 20, 2011).

Goodwin, Grenville. "The Apache Diaries: A Father-Son Journey (excerpts)." *Southwest Crossroads.* http://southwestcrossroads.org/record. php?num=820&hl=chiricahua:: apache (accessed on July 20, 2011).

"Inde (Apache) Literature." *Indigeneous People.* http://www.indigenouspeople. net/apache.htm (accessed on July 20, 2011).

Jicarilla Apache Nation. http://www.jicarillaonline.com/ (accessed on July 15, 2011).

Mescalero Apache Reservation. www.mescaleroapache.com/ (accessed on July 15, 2011).

Moore, R. Edward. "The Texas Apaches." *Texas Indians.* http://www.texasindians. com/ap2.htm (accessed on July 15, 2011).

National Geographic. "Girl's Rite of Passage." YouTube video, 4:40. Posted by "NationalGeographic," May 31, 2007. http://www.youtube.com/watch?v=5B3A bpv0ysM&feature=fvwrel (accessed on July 20, 2011).

"Native Americans and Public Policy." *Native American Guide. The University of Oklahoma: Carl Albert Center Congressional Archive.* http://www.ou.edu/ special/albertctr/archives/Natv.htm (accessed on July 15, 2011).

Redish, Laura, and Orrin Lewis. "Apache Indian Language." *Native American Languages.* http://www.native-languages.org/apache.htm (accessed on July 15, 2011).

Shanklin, M. Trevor, Carla Paciotto, and Greg Prater. "KinderApache Song and Dance Project." *Northern Arizona University.* http://jan.ucc.nau.edu/-jar/TIL_8.html (accessed on July 20, 2011).

"We Shall Remain." *PBS.* http://www.pbs.org/wgbh/amex/weshallremain/ (accessed on July 20, 2011).

Weiser, Kathy. "Apache—The Fiercest Warriors in the Southwest." *Legends of America.* http://www.legendsofamerica.com/na-apache.html (accessed on July 20, 2011).

"Who Were the Lipan and the Kiowa-Apaches?" *Southwest Crossroads.* http://southwestcrossroads.org/record.php?num=522&hl=chiricahua:: apache (accessed on July 20, 2011).

Yavapai-Apache Nation. http://www.yavapai-apache.org/index.html (accessed on July 15, 2011).

Yupanqui, Tika. "Becoming Woman: Apache Female Puberty Sunrise Ceremony." *Webwinds.* http://www.webwinds.com/yupanqui/apachesunrise.htm (accessed on July 20, 2011).

Chiricahua Apache

Name

The name Chiricahua (pronounced *CHEER-uh-KAH-wuh*), or "great mountain," most likely came from the tribe's mountainous homeland in Arizona. Other sources indicate that it means "chatterer," referring to the warriors' way of speaking to one another in code during battle. It has also been translated "grinder" because of their custom of breaking the bones of captured Mexican soldiers. The Apache call themselves *Ndé,* meaning "man" or "person," and the Chiricahua refer to themselves as *Aiaha.* The people have also been called Mimbreños, Coppermine, Warm Springs, Mogollon, Pinery, and Cochise Apache.

Location

The Chiricahua Apache once lived in the rugged mountainous areas of present-day southeastern Arizona, southwestern New Mexico, and northern Mexico. In the early twenty-first century, a little more than one hundred Chiricahua lived on individual plots of land in southwestern Oklahoma, where they organized as the Fort Sill Apache Tribe with headquarters in Apache, Oklahoma. In 2011, the Fort Sill Apache received land for a reservation in Deming, New Mexico. Other Chiricahua intermarried with the Mescalero and Lipan Apache at the Mescalero Reservation in New Mexico and are no longer considered a separate tribe.

Population

In the early to mid-1800s, there were an estimated 2,500 to 3,000 Chiricahua Apache. In 1886, there were just over 500. By 1959, about 91 full-blooded Chiricahua lived at the Mescalero Reservation in New Mexico, but in 1990 only 17 Chiricahua were living in New Mexico. In the 1990 U.S. Census, 739 people identified themselves as Chiricahua, and 103 people identified themselves as Fort Sill Apache. By 2000, the number of people who said they were Chiricahua had increased to 1,155, and 237 said they were Fort Sill Apache. According to 2011 tribal records, the Fort Sill Apache Tribe had 685 members; about one-fourth of them lived near tribal headquarters, but approximately half of the lived outside the state of Oklahoma.

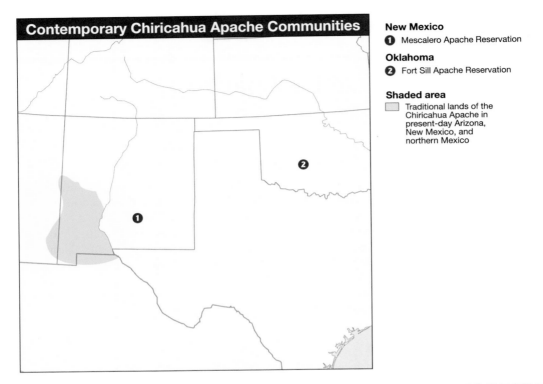

Contemporary Chiricahua Apache Communities

New Mexico
❶ Mescalero Apache Reservation

Oklahoma
❷ Fort Sill Apache Reservation

Shaded area
☐ Traditional lands of the Chiricahua Apache in present-day Arizona, New Mexico, and northern Mexico

A map of contemporary Chiricahua Apache communities. MAP BY XNR PRODUCTIONS. CENGAGE LEARNING, GALE. REPRODUCED BY PERMISSION OF GALE, A PART OF CENGAGE LEARNING.

Language family
Athabaskan.

Origins and group affiliations

The Chiricahua most likely journeyed from western Canada to the American Southwest between the thirteenth and sixteenth centuries. They are divided into three groups: Eastern Chiricahua (who call themselves "red paint people"), Central Chiricahua, and Southern Chiricahua (who are called "enemy people").

Apache groups put up perhaps the fiercest and most long-lasting Native American resistance to the invasion of their homelands by Spanish and European American settlers. Certain Chiricahua men and women became known across America for their leadership of resistance groups. Legendary figures Cochise, Chato, Geronimo, and Victorio were all Chiricahua Apache, and many U.S. Army commanders tried and repeatedly failed to capture them. It was not until the surrender of Geronimo's band in 1886 that Apache armed resistance to American settlement ended.

HISTORY

Chiricahua enemies

The Chiricahua homeland was west of the Rio Grande River and centered on Warm Springs (or Ojo Caliente, which is the Spanish name) in present-day New Mexico. Spanish explorers passed through in the 1500s, but because they did not write about meeting the Chiricahua, some historians believed the Chiricahua were not yet living in the Southwest. Other experts believe the Spanish did not see the remote mountain homes of the Chiricahua, where they may have concealed themselves to avoid attack. They did not stay hidden from the Spanish invaders for long, however.

By the late 1500s, the Spanish were building settlements and missions throughout the Southwest. At first, the Chiricahua were willing to trade with them, but they soon grew unhappy with the newcomers' ways. Spanish soldiers considered Native peoples to be "savages" and took many as slaves. Spanish missionaries tried to turn them away from their religion. All Apache objected to the Spanish attitude, but the Chiricahua people proved to be the bitterest of enemies for the Spanish.

Centuries of battles followed between the Chiricahua and the Spanish. The Chiricahua later battled with the Mexicans, who became independent of Spain in 1821 but inherited Spain's enemies. All sides carried out frequent raids and murders. During the conflicts, the Chiricahua may have learned from the Mexicans the custom of scalping a victim and then replacing his hat. Despite many military expeditions sent to subdue them, the Chiricahua held on to their sacred homeland.

Under American control

In 1848, the United States defeated Mexico, who turned over vast tracts of the Southwest. The land included much of the Apache territory in Arizona and New Mexico. The Apache now had a new and larger enemy than Mexico: the government of the United States. The United States refused to put up with Apache raids and would not allow the bands to hunt on land that American settlers wanted. All the Apache resisted the settlers, but none fought as long or hard as the Chiricahua.

Important Dates

1540: Spanish expeditions cross Apache territory.

1861: Cochise is arrested on a false charge, and the Apache Wars begin.

1872: Cochise signs a treaty with the U.S. government and moves his band to an Arizona reservation.

1874: Cochise dies.

1886: Geronimo and his band surrender.

1913: The majority of surviving Chiricahua resettle on Mescalero Reservation in New Mexico.

1977: Fort Sill (Oklahoma) Apache Tribe receives federal recognition. The people also were awarded $6 million for land they lost while tribal members were imprisoned and for resources taken illegally from their land.

2011: The government gives the Fort Sill Apache 30 acres for a reservation in Deming, New Mexico.

Between the 1850s and 1875, Apache groups were settled on several reservations in Arizona and New Mexico. Then the American government decided that it was too expensive to maintain so many reservations and tried to move all the Apache to two reservations: Mescalero Reservation in New Mexico and the barren San Carlos Reservation in Arizona. The Apache were outraged. Fights broke out, and many fled the reservations. The leaders of the groups that fled became legends.

Cochise and the Apache Wars

Cochise (pronounced *coh-CHEES*; c. 1812–1874), whose name means "hardwood," is one of the best-known Chiricahua leaders and was an early opponent of white settlement in Apache territory. He was not well known when he moved with his people onto a reservation in 1853, but his unjust arrest in 1861 and his subsequent escape from custody, which may have ignited the Apache Wars, brought his name to the attention of Americans all over the southwestern United States and as far east as the nation's capital. A young army officer named Bascom arrested Cochise on a false kidnapping charge. Cochise was taken prisoner with some companions; he escaped, but his people were murdered. The Apache Wars that followed lasted for more than three decades.

Cochise and his father-in-law, Mangas Coloradas (1791–1863), fought many battles with the U.S. military. In 1863, Mangas Coloradas was captured, tortured, and killed. Cochise and his small group of followers held on for another ten years, until Cochise's white friend, Thomas Jeffords (1832–1914), convinced Cochise to end the wars by settling on a reservation in his homeland. After Cochise died in 1874, this agreement dissolved, and the Chiricahua lost their reservation. They were moved to the San Carlos Reservation in Arizona. Unhappy with the area, with the Apache already living there, and with their treatment by U.S. government agents, some Chiricahua escaped. Another decade of fighting began.

Geronimo

Geronimo (pronounced *juh-RON-uh-moe*; 1829–1909) was born in present-day Arizona, and his people often hunted and camped with Cochise's band. He was not a chief, but he was a medicine man and warrior. Geronimo believed, as many Apache did, that to be removed from one's homeland was to die. He battled Mexicans and U.S. settlers to preserve the Apache people.

Geronimo's people called him Goyathlay, "One Who Yawns." When Mexican raiders killed his mother, wife, and three children in 1858, Geronimo vowed vengeance. He carried out deadly raids in Mexican territory and earned the name Geronimo by awed Mexican soldiers. (One story says that the Mexicans may have been crying out in fear to St. Jerome when they saw Geronimo, or they may simply have been mispronouncing his Apache name.) More than once he was caught and returned to the reservation, only to escape again. His raiding and fighting in Mexico lasted until U.S. General George H. Crook's (1829–1890) soldiers captured him in 1886.

The arrest of Apache leader Cochise in 1861 was one of the factors that led to the Apache Wars.

It took an army of thousands of soldiers to finally capture Geronimo and his band; with him at the time of his surrender were thirty-six warriors, women, and children. They were forced to resettle in Florida, where, according to his own account, Geronimo and his men were forced to do hard labor. They did not see their families until the following year, when the prisoners were moved to Alabama. During the imprisonment, many people died, and one of Geronimo's wives returned to New Mexico. Finally, in 1894, the Apache were moved to a reservation at Fort Sill, Oklahoma. Geronimo lived out his years there, raising watermelons and selling his autograph to soldiers and at fairs. He died in 1909 after he fell off his horse into a creek and became ill.

Chato

With Geronimo at the time of an 1881 escape from the San Carlos Reservation was Alfred Chato (c. 1860–1934), known simply as Chato for most of his life. Chato rode with Geronimo and also led his own raiding

The grave of Apache leader Geronimo is at Fort Sill, Oklahoma. © TIM THOMPSON/CORBIS.

parties throughout Arizona and New Mexico, stealing ammunition, killing white settlers, and spreading terror. He was convinced to return to San Carlos along with Geronimo in 1884, and thereafter, his life took a different path from Geronimo's.

Chato adapted to reservation life and learned to farm. He was frequently employed by the U.S. army as a scout and consultant on Native ways. (He later received a medal for his service.) In 1886, when the army commander in charge decided it was time to move the Chiricahua from the San Carlos Reservation and back to the home of their ancestors, Chato went to Washington, D.C., to discuss the move. Washington officials asked Chato to convince the Chiricahua to move to Florida instead, but he refused. On Chato's return trip from Washington, he was arrested and sent to Florida, where Geronimo and his people had already been sent.

Conditions in Florida were very bad. In 1894, Chato and the other Chiricahua moved with Geronimo to Fort Sill, Oklahoma. Although it was not their homeland, at least it was closer to it than Florida had been. Chato was appointed leader of a small village near the reservation and was given a small plot of land for farming. At some point during his stay at Fort Sill, he converted to Christianity. He resumed work for the U.S. Army.

In 1913, Chato again traveled to Washington, this time to ask that his people be allowed to return to their homeland. After long discussions, and in spite of U.S. settlers in New Mexico who voiced their fears that the Chiricahua would begin raiding again, the Apache were offered the opportunity to return to New Mexico.

Chato was respected by both the Native peoples and the white community in New Mexico, where he lived the remainder of his life. He died in an automobile accident in March 1934.

Victorio

Tribal leader Victorio (c. 1820–1880) is not as well known as Geronimo, but he too took on the U.S. Army. In 1879, he was told that his reservation at Warm Springs, New Mexico, would be opened for settlement. Victorio responded: "If you force me and my people to leave [Warm Springs], there will be trouble. Leave us alone, so that we may remain at peace." Fearing he would be taken prisoner, as Geronimo had been, Victorio left the reservation, never to return.

African American soldiers (called Buffalo Soldiers) were sent to capture him, but Victorio eluded them. He was finally trapped by Mexican soldiers, who blasted Victorio's people out of their hiding place with dynamite. Sixty-one warriors and eighteen women and children were killed. Sixty other women and children, including two of his sons, were captured and taken into slavery. Victorio killed himself rather than be taken.

Gouyen

Born into the Warm Springs Apache band about 1857, Gouyen ("Wise-Woman") earned fame by avenging her husband's death. She had survived a Mexican attack on the tribe from which only seventeen people, including Gouyen and her young son, escaped, and she endured the murder of her baby daughter. Later, after her husband was killed by the Comanches (see entry), Gouyen went to the Comanche camp, where the warriors were celebrating with a victory dance. The chief had her husband's scalp hanging from his belt. She pretended to be interested in the chief, and when they were alone, she scalped him and cut off his beaded breechcloth, an apronlike covering that hangs from the waist. She also took his moccasins and gave all of these as gifts to her in-laws.

Chiricahua reservations

In 1913, Geronimo's followers at Fort Sill were given the choice of remaining in Oklahoma and receiving eighty acres of land apiece, or returning to New Mexico—their homeland—to live on the Mescalero Reservation. Eighty-seven chose to remain in Oklahoma, while the remaining 171 returned to New Mexico with Victorio.

The Mescalero Reservation was already home to Mescalero and Lipan Apache. For a time, the Chiricahua kept an isolated area to themselves and held on to their tribal identity. Eventually, they intermarried with the other Apache, and their culture was absorbed into the larger group.

The Fort Sill Chiricahua who received land instead of a reservation lived apart from each other on scattered plots. They likewise intermarried with members of other tribes and with settlers. Over time, their tribal identity has been diluted.

RELIGION

The Chiricahua believed that coyotes, insects, and birds had once been human beings. Nature was central to their beliefs, and religious beliefs were passed down through stories and poetry. White Painted Woman's son destroyed the evil monsters that plagued the people of long ago and made the earth livable again. White Painted Woman is also of central importance to a girl's four-day puberty rites.

In 1881, an Apache medicine man named Nochedelklinne began to preach about a vision he had, in which white men vanished from the earth and dead Apache came back to life. His vision included a dance, which he taught to increasing numbers of Apache. The dance was so lively, and dancers became so enthusiastic performing it, that government officials feared it might start a revolution. Most Indians, though, believed Nochedelklinne's teachings meant they should leave revenge to Usen, the Creator.

Nevertheless, U.S. Army Colonel Eugene Carr (1830–1910) received orders to arrest or kill the medicine man. When Nochedelklinne did not report to Fort Apache as commanded, Carr marched to his encampment, and a gun battle broke out. The Apache scouts accompanying the colonel deserted and fought against the colonel. Geronimo, too, participated in the battle, and his anger against the United States was inflamed when Nochedelklinne as well as his wife and son. The medicine man's religion did not survive long after his death; later, the Ghost Dance religion replaced it.

Christian missionaries from the Reformed Church in America arrived at Fort Sill in 1899 and opened the Apache Mission of the Reformed Church. They set up schools, tended the sick, and conducted religious services. Their success was assured when Geronimo agreed to convert, although he was soon expelled for gambling. This church remains a strong presence at Fort Sill.

Mescalero Apache Words	
chúúné	"dog"
tú	"water"
sháa	"sun"
yidiits;e	"hear"
haadi'a	"sing"
idzúút'i	"leave"

LANGUAGE

Because the Chiricahua had no reservation of their own, their language and culture were largely absorbed into other tribes or into mainstream American culture. Their language almost disappeared. In 1981, estimates indicated that only five Chiricahua speakers still remained at Fort Sill, Oklahoma, and all were more than fifty years old. According to statistics from the Summer Institute of Linguistics (SIL) International in 1990, the population at the Mescalero Reservation included 279 Chiricahua speakers. Within a decade, that number had dropped to 175. A small number also spoke Chiricahua at Fort Sill, although most of those speakers were older adults.

GOVERNMENT

Because the names of many Chiricahua leaders and warriors have become well known, some people think they were chiefs in charge of large groups of followers. The Chiricahua, however, did not have a chief who told them what to do. Each small group had a leader; the people took his advice because he had qualities his followers admired, such as wisdom, bravery, or a convincing way of speaking. Although the leader influenced the band, he did not make major decisions on his own. He always consulted the heads of other families in his group.

After the defeat of Geronimo, the Chiricahua took different paths. Those who went to the Mescalero Reservation at first joined the Mescalero and Lipan Apache in meetings with U.S. government agents who ran the reservations. Later, the government offered tribes on reservations the opportunity to organize and handle their own affairs.

At Mescalero, the three Apache groups accepted the opportunity offered by the federal government and organized as the Mescalero Apache. This entitled them to receive federal recognition. Federally recognized tribes are those with which the U.S. government maintains official relations. The Mescalero Apache formed a tribal council made up of a president, vice president, and eight elected members. The reservation has had strong leaders who have overseen advances in health care, education, and economic independence.

For a long time, the Fort Sill Apache had only an informal business council. The U.S. government terminated (dissolved) many tribes in the 1950s, a move that ended any relationship with the government. Members of the Fort Sill Apache rallied to fight termination by forming a tribal committee. In the 1970s, the Fort Sill Apache formed a new government with elected members and received federal recognition. They are considered a separate Chiricahua tribe, even though there are Chiricahua at the Mescalero Reservation.

ECONOMY

Mescalero Reservation

On the Mescalero Reservation in New Mexico, the people are fortunate to have land on which to develop businesses. Extremely successful timber and tourist operations have been established, including the well-known Inn of the Mountain Gods, a resort, casino, and sports center. The Big Game Hunting Lodge offers hunting for trophy elk as well as bear and wild birds. Ski Apache also attracts many tourists. Grazing land supports a thriving cattle industry. Mescalero Forest Products harvests timber and processes lumber for sale. All of these businesses provide jobs; some also help fund housing, health, education, and social activities. In spite of these economic advances, the Bureau of Indian Affairs reported an unemployment rate of 62 percent on the Mescalero Reservation in 2001, which meant that more than half of the people who wanted to work could not find jobs. By 2011, the unemployment rate had dropped to 18.5 percent, but it was still high compared to the national average.

Fort Sill

Circumstances did not play out so well for the Fort Sill people, who had no reservation. When they moved onto individual plots of land in 1913, the people raised cattle and farmed. In the 1920s and 1930s, oil and gas were found on their land. The U.S. government negotiated on behalf of the Apache with outside companies to lease the land. Many Apache did not speak English well and did not understand the agreements. Their land and their children's land was leased without their consent. Although they were entitled to 12 percent of all the resources taken from their property, most received less than 1 percent.

In the 1940s and 1950s, large-scale farms blossomed in Oklahoma, requiring expensive machinery, and many Fort Sill Chiricahua could not afford to compete. Some left to find work. In the 1970s, the federal government gave aid to the tribe, and the economy improved somewhat. In 1979, the people received $6 million for oil and gas that were taken from their land, which some said was only a small portion of the money they were owed. The Fort Sill Apache started working with the secretary of the interior to foreclose (shut down) on companies who did not pay what they owed.

During the early 2000s, some people leased their land for farming and cattle grazing, and the Fort Sill Apache were exploring other business opportunities. They were working to develop both wind and solar energy, and in 2004, they built a wind farm near the tribal complex. Fort Sill Apache Industries, a contracting business, and the casinos continue to provide jobs along with income to support tribal services.

DAILY LIFE

Buildings

The Chiricahua were wandering mountain dwellers who changed camps often. In the summer, they lived in the highlands where it was cooler, and in the winter, they moved to the lowlands. Their winter encampments often included a sweat lodge for the men. Their basic moveable shelter was a *kuugh'a* (home) made by placing a hides or blankets over a cone-shaped group of poles. Meat hung from the rafters to dry.

Women built the homes, but if they were constructing a more permanent structure, men sometimes helped. These larger dwellings were made of four 8-foot (3-meter) posts set in a square. Crosspieces connected the poles and were covered with brush or grass thatch. The Chiricahua dug a hole for a central fireplace inside and then placedthat dirt around the outside edges of the house to block water from entering. Doorways often faced east, and homes had a covered outdoor area for shade. Brush fences corralled their animals, kept down the wind, and protected the people from wild animals. As they moved from place to place, the Chiricahua took little with them. They used the materials in the new location to make their new homes.

Food

Like other Apache, the Chiricahua were hunter-gatherers. They migrated, following the seasons and readily available crops and game. Men hunted for deer and antelope using deer-head disguises and employing bows and arrows. They also hunted elk, mountain goats, and mountain sheep, but these were scarce. Small boys assisted by hunting cottontail rabbits, squirrels, birds, and opossums. Some animals, such as the badger and wildcat, were hunted only for their skins.

The Apache never ate bugs or anything that lived in water or had scales. They also refused to eat any animals that fed on those things, such as pigs, turkeys, or dogs. At times, the Chiricahua ate rodents, whose diets consisted of plants and seeds. Most Apache tribes did not hunt bear because they stood upright, making them too humanlike, and they ate forbidden foods. The Chiricahua, however, sometimes killed them for grease and fur. When food was scarce, the Apache often raided neighboring tribes.

Women dug roots and harvested plants, berries, and fruits. Fruit from the yucca plant was a favorite food; they also pounded this in water to make suds for shampoo. One of their staple foods was the mescal plant, which is why the Spanish called some Apache people "Mescalero."

Clothing and adornment

Before the coming of Europeans, Chiricahua men and women wore clothing made of tanned animal skins. They usually painted buckskin yellow with mineral paint and decorated it with beadwork and fringe. Because they lived near the Mexican border, the Chiricahua began early to adapt some of the Mexican-style clothing. Most common were white cotton shirts with red trim at the seams for the men and long white cotton breechcloths (garments with front and back flaps that hung from the waist) or baggy Spanish-style pants that they tucked into the tops of their tall boot-like moccasins. At the waist they wore cartridge belts (belts with loops or pockets for carrying ammunition). In the later nineteenth century, they added American-style black vests or jackets.

The women wore poncho-like buckskin blouses with round yokes hung with metal jingles. They often cut designs, such as half-circles or triangles, into the fabric. The deer tail hung from the back of the blouse. Skirts were made so the deer tails hung from the hem. Seams and hems were often fringed.In the late nineteenth century, women adopted American clothing by wearing long-sleeved calico blouses and full skirts of three tiers with a decorative border at the bottom. They tied them with cloth bands around their waists.

Children wore buckskin ponchos held in at the waist with belts, so adults could pick them up quickly in case of danger. As they got older, boys and girls started wearing clothing similar to that of their parents.

Men often wore scarves around their necks and fabric headbands with the tails hanging down in back. Both men and women had necklaces made of shells, turquoise, beads, and even plant roots or seeds. They also wore earrings, bracelets, and rings. They originally made earrings and bracelets from strands of beads, but silver and brass later became popular materials for bracelets, and Spanish coins for rings and tie slides. Both sexes wore unpainted wood charms for personal protection, and men carried leather cases with ornate beadwork.

Healing practices

The Chiricahua were skilled at using herbs for healing. Well into the twentieth century, they prepared a potion for the elderly to help keep their blood thin. They made it from a weed called zagosti, which has been used by modern medical experts to prepare blood thinner for heart patients. The Chiricahua used roots such as the osha, either chewed or ground up in tobacco, for the common cold. They used Apache plume for diarrhea and constipation. Mud baths were also prescribed for many ailments. A hot cloth spread with grease and ashes was sometimes used for such maladies as mumps.

In the early 2000s, the Mescalero Apache operated a hospital and an outpatient program with clinics, as well as dental, laboratory, nutrition, social work, substance abuse, and pharmacy services. The Mescalero Apache MHPIP Project was a partnership between a variety of organizations to increase suicide prevention, substance abuse prevention, and other mental and physical health programs to the reservation and schools.

Why the Bat Has Short Legs

Many tribes tell tales of times long ago when animals lived as people. Those legends, like this one, often explain how an animal developed certain physical features. This Chiricahua Apache story tells how bats ended up with short legs.

Long ago, Killer-of-Enemies vowed to save his people from the terror of monster eagles that roamed the skies and carried off children. Killer-of-Enemies tricked one monster eagle into carrying him up to the eagle nest on the cliff, where he killed the monster eagle and its family. But Killer-of-Enemies did not know how to get down from the cliff. Just then, he saw an old woman approaching. It was Old Woman Bat.

"Grandmother, help me. Take me down," Killer-of-Enemies said. Old Woman Bat looked all around, but did not see him. Killer-of-Enemies called out again, and again, and again. Finally, Old Woman Bat saw him high in the eagle's nest. She came over to the cliff and began to climb.

"What are you doing here?" she asked, when she reached the top.

"Monster eagle carried me up here," he said. "Please take me down."

"Climb in my basket," Old Woman Bat said. Killer of Enemies looked at the burden basket on the old woman's back. Its carrying strap was made of spider's silk.

"That strap is too fine," he said. "It will break and I shall fall."

"Nonsense! I've carried a bighorn sheep in this basket," Old Woman Bat said. "Get in and close your eyes. If you look, we will fall."

Old Woman Bat clambered down the rock, singing a strange song. Her burden basket swayed wildly from side to side. Killer-of-Enemies thought the spider thread would surely break, so he opened his eyes to look.

As soon as Kill-of-Enemies opened his eyes. He and Old Woman Bat crashed down from the cliff. Old Woman Bat landed first and broke her legs. Killer-of-Enemies fell on top of her and was safe. Old Woman Bat's broken legs soon mended but from that day on her legs were short.

SOURCE: "Native American Legends: Why The Bat Has Short Legs." *First People.* http://www.firstpeople.us/FP-Html-Legends/Why_The_Bat_Has_Short_Legs-Apache.html (accessed on July 20, 2011).

Fort Sill has facilities that offer dental and medical services. Health concerns plague many Fort Sill Apache. In addition to diabetes, which is a problem for many Native peoples, the tribe also has high rates of cancer and lupus, which may be related to the oil drilling on their land.

Education

By the time he was confined on the Fort Sill Reservation in 1894, Geronimo realized that the old ways of educating Apache children would no longer work in American society. He encouraged children on the reservation to learn the ways of the "White Eyes." Some Fort Sill children were sent to the Carlisle Indian School in Pennsylvania. Others were taught white ways by Christian missionaries, who set up schools at Fort Sill. At most schools, children were forbidden to speak their native language.

Today, Fort Sill children attend local public schools in the five counties where the Chiricahua own plots of land. The Mescalero Apache School opened in 2003 to offer classes for grades K–12. In addition to its regular curriculum, the school also included courses in forestry and agriculture.

CUSTOMS

Festivals and ceremonies

The Apache Dance for the Mountain Spirits, originally held for every young girl's puberty ceremony, is now an annual event. The Fort Sill Apache host the dance in September, while the Mescalero hold it at their July Ceremonial, a four-day gala event (four is their special number) that pays tribute to young girls who have reached puberty and includes feasting and a rodeo.

Fort Sill Apache keep in touch with other Native nations by hosting rodeos and powwows. A powwow is a celebration at which the main activities are traditional singing and dancing. In modern times the singers and dancers at powwows come from many different tribes. While at Fort Sill, visitors can view the works of famed Chiricahua sculptor Allan Houser at the tribal headquarters.

CURRENT TRIBAL ISSUES

In 2007, the U.S. Environmental Protection Agency awarded $109,000 to the Fort Sill Apache Tribe to enable them to develop an environmental protection program. The tribe has been using the money to decrease illegal dumping, increase recycling, educate the public about environmental concerns, and train staff as certified water operators.

In 2011, the Fort Sill Apache protested the proposed plans for a Jemez Pueblo (see entry) casino. Some of the concerns that they expressed to the Bureau of Indian Affairs were about water and air quality and the impact of increased traffic as well as the Chiricahua historical and cultural ties to the area to be developed. An additional concern is that another gaming facility could draw away business from their own casino.

In November 2011, the U.S. government granted the Fort Sill Apache 30 acres of land near Deming, New Mexico for a reservation. The people had lost their homeland when Geronimo was taken prisoner in the 1880s. Since that time, the Fort Sill Apache had been landless, except for the property where their tribal headquarters is located and 120 acres of farmland.

Also in 2011, the United States killed the terrorist Osama bin Laden. In the news that followed, it was noted that the CIA code name for bin Laden was "Geronimo." Perhaps the name was chosen because, for about a decade, bin Laden eluded the forces sent to capture him; Geronimo, too, evaded U.S. forces for many years. Hearing this code name upset many Native people, however, especially the Chiricahua and descendants

May We Have Peace, *a sculpture by Chiricahua Apache artist Allan Houser, is on display at the Smithsonian National Museum of the American Indian.* © ALEX WONG/STAFF/GETTY IMAGES NEWS/GETTY IMAGES.

of Geronimo. Harlyn Geronimo, the great grandson of the famous Indian leader, called comparing his ancestor with a mass murderer "unpardonable slander," and Jeff Haozous (Houser), the chairperson of the Fort Sill Apache Tribe, asked for formal apology from the U.S. government.

The Mescalero Apache Nation wants to lease its water rights to other communities in the area. In 2011, an act was introduced to Congress that would permit the tribe to lease or transfer their water rights for up to ninety-nine years. If passed, this legislation would provide an ongoing source of income for the nation.

NOTABLE PEOPLE

Allan Houser (1914–1994) was a Chiricahua Apache sculptor who has been acclaimed throughout the world for his six decades of work in wood, marble, stone, and bronze. In April 1994, he presented an 11-foot (3-meter) bronze sculpture entitled "May We Have Peace" to then first lady Hillary Rodham Clinton (1947–) in Washington, D.C., as a gift from the American Indians to all people. Houser's work is on view in museums all over the world, and he received many awards during his lifetime, including the Prix de West Award in 1993 for a bronze sculpture titled "Smoke Signals," now a part of the permanent collection of the National Cowboy Hall of Fame. In 1992, he became the first Native person to win the National Medal of the Arts.

Lozen (c. 1840s–1886), the sister of Chiricahua war leader Victorio, is the most famous of the Apache War Women. Although they were few in number, their accomplishments were significant, especially at a time when women everywhere enjoyed little freedom. Lozen was a medicine woman and an accomplished horsewoman whose advice and guidance was sought by both men and women of her band. She rode to battle with Victorio and later with Geronimo, with whom she was photographed several times. Along with Geronimo, she was taken as a prisoner to Florida. She died, probably of tuberculosis, in 1886.

BOOKS

Aleshire, Peter. *Fox and the Whirlwind: General George Crook and Geronimo, a Paired Biography.* Victoria, British Columbia, Canada: Castle Books, 2009.

Aleshire, Peter. *Warrior Woman: The Story of Lozen, Apache Warrior and Shaman.* New York: St. Martin's Press, 2001.

Browner, Tara, ed. *Music of the First Nations: Tradition and Innovation in Native North America.* Urbana: University of Illinois Press, 2009.

Geronimo. *The Autobiography of Geronimo.* St. Petersburg, FL: Red and Black Publishers, 2011.

Griffin-Pierce, Trudy. *Chiricahua Apache Enduring Power: Naiche's Puberty Ceremony Paintings.* Tuscaloosa: University Alabama Press, 2007.

Jastrzembski, Joseph C. *The Apache.* Minneapolis: Chelsea House, 2011.

Katanski, Amelia V. *Learning to Write "Indian": The Boarding-School Experience and American Indian Literature.* Norman: University of Oklahoma Press, 2007.

Opler, Morris Edward. *Myths and Tales of the Chiricahua Apache Indians.* Charleston, SC: Kessinger Publishing, 2011.

Rielly, Edward J. *Legends of American Indian Resistance.* Westport, CT: Greenwood, 2011.

Shapard, Bud. *Chief Loco: Apache Peacemaker.* Norman: University of Oklahoma Press, c. 2010.

St. John, Rachel. *Line in the Sand: A History of the Western U.S.-Mexico Border.* Princeton University Press, 2011.

Stockel, H. Henrietta. *Chiricahua Apache Women and Children: Safekeepers of the Heritage.* Austin: Texas A&M University Press, 2000.

Stockel, H. Henrietta. *Drumbeats from Mescalero: Conversations with Apache Elders, Warriors, and Horseholders.* Charleston, SC: TAMU Press, 2011.

Sweeney, Edwin R. *From Cochise to Geronimo: The Chiricahua Apaches, 1874–1886.* Norman: University of Oklahoma Press, 2010.

PERIODICALS

Wagner, Dennis. "Stolen Artifacts Shatter Ancient Culture." *The Arizona Republic,* November 12, 2006.

WEB SITES

Ball, Eve. "The Vengeance of Gouyen." *Southwest Crossroads.* http://southwestcrossroads.org/record.php?num=386 (accessed on July 20, 2011).

Boyer, Ruth McDonald, and Narcissus Duffy Gayton. "Apache Mothers and Daughters: Four Generations of a Family. Remembrances of an Apache Elder Woman." *Southwest Crossroads.* http://southwestcrossroads.org/record.php?num=825&hl=Apache (accessed on July 20, 2011).

"The Children of Changing Woman." *Peabody Museum of Archaeology and Ethnology.* http://www.peabody.harvard.edu/maria/Cwoman.html (accessed on July 20, 2011).

Chihuahua, Eugene. "The Odyssey Ends." *Southwest Crossroads.* http://southwestcrossroads.org/record.php?num=537&hl=Apache (accessed on July 20, 2011).

Chiricahua Apache Prisoner of War Committee. "Native American Prisoners of War: Chiricahua Apaches 1886–1914." *Mescalero Apache Tribe of New Mexico.* http://www.chiricahua-apache.com/ (accessed on July 20, 2011).

"Chiricahua Indian History." *Access Genealogy.* http://www.accessgenealogy.com/native/tribes/apache/chiricahua.htm (accessed on July 20, 2011).

Davis, Britton. "A Conference with General Crook." *Southwest Crossroads.* http://southwestcrossroads.org/record.php?num=538&hl=Apache (accessed on July 20, 2011).

Fort Sill Apache Tribe. http://www.fortsillapache.com (accessed on July 20, 2011).

"Geronimo, His Own Story: A Prisoner of War." *From Revolution to Reconstruction.* http://www.let.rug.nl/usa/B/geronimo/geroni17.htm (accessed on July 20, 2011).

Gordon, Raymond G., Jr. ed. "Apache, Mescalera-Chiricahua" *Ethnologue: Languages of the World,* 15th edition. Dallas, TX: SIL International, 2005–09. http://www.ethnologue.com/%5C/15/show_language.asp?code=apm (accessed on December 1, 2011).

Jozhe, Benedict. "A Brief History of the Fort Sill Apache Tribe." *Oklahoma Historical Society.* http://digital.library.okstate.edu/Chronicles/v039/v039p427.pdf (accessed on July 20, 2011).

"Massai, Chiricahua Apache." *Discover Southeast Arizona.* http://www.discoverseaz.com/History/Massai.html (accessed on July 20, 2011).

National Museum of the American Indian. "Chiricahua Apache Prisoners of War." May 8, 2008. Video. *MeFeedia.* http://www.mefeedia.com/watch/28123349 (accessed on July 20, 2011).

"Nde Nation." *Chiricahua: Apache Nation.* http://www.chiricahuaapache.org/ (accessed on July 20, 2011).

Weiser, Kathy. "Victorio—Fighting for Ancestral Lands." *Legends of America.* http://www.legendsofamerica.com/na-victorio.html (accessed on July 20, 2011).

San Carlos Apache

Name

The name San Carlos Apache (pronounced *sahn CAR-los uh-PATCH-ee*) refers to the area where the tribe lives, along the San Carlos River in Arizona.

Location

The Apache who make up the San Carlos Apache tribe descended from members of many Apache groups. The traditional Apache homeland included a vast region stretching from what is now central Arizona to central Texas, and from northern Mexico to the high plains of southeastern Colorado. The modern-day San Carlos Apache live on the San Carlos Indian Reservation, which covers 1.8 million acres in Gila, Graham, and Pinal counties in central Arizona. The reservation is located about 20 miles (30 kilometers) southeast of Globe and 100 miles (160 kilometers) east of Phoenix, Arizona.

Population

In 1930, there were 3,000 San Carlos Apache. In the 1990 U.S. Census, 32,912 people identified themselves as Apache; of that number, 2,300 said they were San Carlos Apache. The San Carlos Indian Reservation claimed an enrollment of 10,500. In 2000, the census indicated that a total of 57,199 Apache lived in the United States and, of those, 9,867 of those were San Carlos Apache. By 2010, the census counted a total of 63,193 Apache living in the United States.

Language family

Athabaskan.

Origins and group affiliations

Most historians believe the Apache made a gradual move from western Canada to the American Southwest between the thirteenth and sixteenth centuries. The Apaches themselves, however, say they originated in the Southwest and migrated north. According to their oral history, those who live in the Southwest today were people who stayed behind. The Apaches were never one unified group, but rather a number of bands who spoke

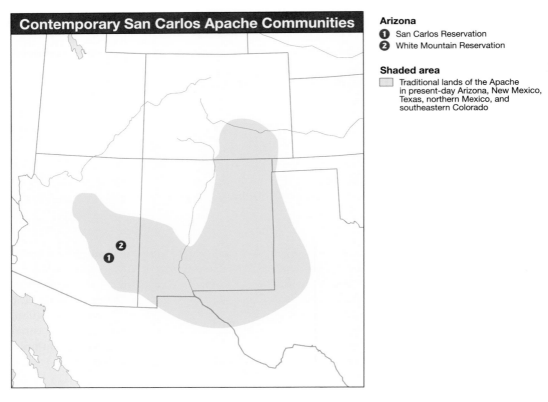

Contemporary San Carlos Apache Communities

Arizona
1 San Carlos Reservation
2 White Mountain Reservation

Shaded area
Traditional lands of the Apache in present-day Arizona, New Mexico, Texas, northern Mexico, and southeastern Colorado

A map of contemporary San Carlos Apache communities. MAP BY XNR PRODUCTIONS. CENGAGE LEARNING, GALE. REPRODUCED BY PERMISSION OF GALE, A PART OF CENGAGE LEARNING.

similar languages and shared similar customs. The people who now make up the San Carlos Apache tribe descended from the Aravaipa, Chiricahua (see entry), Coyotero, Mimbreño, Mogollon, Pinaleno, and Tonto Apache peoples.

The U.S. government established the San Carlos Indian Reservation in 1871 to hold members of many Apache groups and stop their raiding of American and Mexican settlements. The confining nature of reservation life caused considerable unrest among the Apache, who were used to living in small family groups. The trouble was compounded by persistent poverty, pressure to give up their native ways, and mismanagement of the fragile Arizona landscape where they lived. The San Carlos Apache have yet to overcome these problems, but some advancements have been made in recent years.

HISTORY

San Carlos Indian Reservation established

In 1848, the United States took over Apache lands from Mexico. The American government soon made it clear that it would not tolerate Apache raids or allow Natives to hunt on land claimed by settlers. (See Apache and Chiricahua Apache entries.) Following years of resistance by Apache groups, some were moved in 1871 to a new site, Arizona's White Mountain-San Carlos Indian Reservation, located at the place where the Gila River joined the San Carlos River.

Life on this reservation was brutal. The scorching heat, frequent dust storms, clouds of bugs, and lack of water meant that crops, other than cacti, could not grow. Many people became sick, and hundreds died. Neighboring ranchers used Apache property and stole their cattle and wood. In addition, the San Carlos Apache did not receive the rations they had been promised. The Indian agent assigned to the reservation, J.C. Tiffany, in 1882 was convicted of fraud and larceny, but for years before that, the people on the San Carlos reservation went hungry.

Escapes from San Carlos

In 1877, Victorio and Loco, chiefs of the Warm Springs Apache, fled with others from the San Carlos Reservation. They fought the U.S. army, and soldiers took them back to San Carlos in 1878. Victorio, who refused to go, continued to battle but also tried to negotiate with government forces during the next two years. After being pursued by scouts and Buffalo Soldiers (African American troops), Victorio led his followers into Mexico, where Mexican soldiers scalped him and most of his party. Seventy-eight scalps were paraded through town, including sixteen belonging to women and children. The Mexicans took the survivors of Victorio's party as slaves.

Between 1881 and 1884, other starving Chiricahua people left the San Carlos Reservation to head into the mountains of Mexico. They returned to the reservation but went out again when their hunger became too great. John Gregory Bourke, a member of U.S. General George Crook's staff, once said sarcastically about the Chiricahua's struggle for survival:

> A difference of opinion soon arose with the agent as to what constituted a ration, the wicked Indians laboring under the delusion that it was enough food to keep the recipient from starving to death. … To the credit of the agent it must be said that he made a praise-worthy but

ineffectual effort to alleviate the pangs of hunger by a liberal distribution of hymn-books among his wards. The perverse Chiricahuas, not being able to digest works of that nature … made up their minds to sally out from San Carlos and take refuge in the more hospitable wilderness of the Sierra Madre.

In 1885, more leaders living on the San Carlos reservation, among them Geronimo (1829–1909) and Naiche (c. 1857–1919), led more than one hundred of their people off the reservation. Apache scouts tracked them down, and U.S. troops killed or captured them. Both Naiche and Geronimo said they had left the reservation because they feared they would be arrested and hanged for crimes they had not committed.

Broken promises

Almost four hundred people were taken to St. Augustine, Florida, where they joined other Chiricahua who had been rounded up five months before. Although Geronimo and Naiche had been promised they could stay with their families, the government separated them and some of the other men from theirs. Fifteen men were sent to Fort Pickens, Florida. The rest went to Fort Marion in St. Augustine, Florida. The children were sent to the Carlisle Indian School in Pennsylvania.

Those were not the only terms of surrender that were ignored. The prisoners were forced to labor at the fort even though they had been promised otherwise. Told they would be released after two years, some people were not freed until 1914, nearly thirty years later.

Move to Alabama

Rather than freeing the Chiricahua at Fort Marion, the government moved them to an old army fort, Mount Vernon Barracks, in Mobile, Alabama. For people used to the hot, dry Arizona, the humidity and mosquitoes were a difficult adjustment. Unlike the soldiers who had netting to protect them as they slept, the Chiricahua were exposed to the mosquitoes. Many people got malaria, and babies died. Schoolchildren who were dying of tuberculosis were sent home, and others caught their sickness. In 1889, statistics showed that, of the 498 Apaches imprisoned in 1886, 119 had died: 49 deaths occurred at St. Augustine, 30 at the Carlisle Indian School, and 50 at Mt. Vernon, Alabama.

In spite of their hardships and losses, the people tried to keep their customs alive. They passed along their oral history to the children, followed their usual marriage customs, performed the Puberty Ceremonies, and sent their boys on vision quests. Some men joined the army for the small amount of pay it provided.

Resettlement of the Chiricahua

Although reports in 1890 stressed the need to move the Apache to another place, several years passed before Congress passed legislation that would remove them to Indian Territory in Oklahoma. In 1894, the people were moved to Fort Sill. There they were told they could make their homes around the fort, but the settlers in the area opposed that.

To ease the tension, the government put the San Carlos Apache on nearby land that had belonged to the Comanche and Kiowa-Apache. They freed eighty-four of the prisoners and gave them allotment lands around present-day Apache, Oklahoma. Although the parcels were supposed to be 160 acres, everyone received less than the promised amount of land. Most received fewer than 80 acres. The plots were scattered, so the people were unable to stay together. Some believed that was deliberate on the part of the government to keep them apart and prevent an uprising.

Important Dates

1848: Mexico gives northern Arizona and northern New Mexico lands to United States. Warfare between the Apache people and the U.S. Army begins.

1871: The United States establishes White Mountain-San Carlos Indian Reservation to hold captured Apache.

1897: The White Mountain-San Carlos Indian Reservation is divided and renamed the Fort Apache and San Carlos Reservations.

1972: A U.S. Executive Order increases the size of the reservation.

1990: The Apache Survival Coalition is formed to oppose the building of a telescope atop Mt. Graham, a sacred site of the San Carlos Apache.

1994: A telescope on Mt. Graham is dedicated.

1994: The Apache Gold Casino opens.

1995: The San Carlos Apache Culture Center opens.

Although some of the San Carlos Apache settled in Oklahoma, many of them longed for their original Southwest homelands. They joined the Mescalero Apache on their reservation in New Mexico.

In 1897, the White Mountain-San Carlos Indian Reservation was divided into the San Carlos Indian Reservation and the Fort Apache Reservation (where the White Mountain Apache now live; see entry). From the beginning, government officials ran the San Carlos Reservation. They expected the Apache to become farmers, a way of life that was totally alien to the people. Although the land was beautiful, much of it was desert—dry and not at all suited for agricultural use.

Slowly, the Apache adapted to their new lives, but it was not long before their land was found to be rich in mineral resources. Between

The building of the Coolidge Dam in 1928 created San Carlos Lake on the reservation. © ANDERS RYMAN/CORBIS.

1872 and 1902, the U.S. government took away reservation land five times at the urging of white business owners. Copper and silver mines were opened, and the San Carlos Apache found their reservation reduced to about one-third of its original size.

Coolidge Dam construction

Construction of the Coolidge Dam across the Gila River changed the lives of the San Carlos Apache. The dam stretches across the portion of the Gila River that runs through southeast-central Arizona, forming San Carlos Lake (now a popular fishing and water sports center). Completed in 1928, the dam was intended to help farmers in the region by sending much-needed water their way. When backed-up waters flooded San Carlos in 1929, headquarters were then moved upstream on the San Carlos River to the village of Rice (later renamed San Carlos).

RELIGION

Traditional beliefs

Although many modern-day San Carlos Apache are Christian, some people still retain traditional Apache beliefs. They have also adopted features of other Southwestern religions. Apaches believe that Ussen, the Creator, sent the Ga'an to teach the people how to walk in the Holy Life Way. Important principles include kindness, charity, respect for others (even in hunting and warfare), and living in harmony with the earth and with others.

Ga'an (mountain spirits or crown dancers) bring blessings and ward off evil. Four men, their bodies painted with black and white animal, lightning, and mountain motifs, represent the four directions. A clown, painted gray, dances with them. These five dancers perform at the Sunrise Dances for girls' initiation into womanhood.

Controversy over Coronado National Forest

Like many Native peoples, the San Carlos Apache have long considered their religious beliefs to be a private matter—one not to be discussed with outsiders. It was not widely known, then, that members of the tribe still traveled to Mt. Graham in the Coronado National Forest in Arizona to conduct dances in honor of the mountain spirits. The mountain also provided special herbs for traditional ceremonies, and burials once took place there. Mt. Graham, one of the Pinaleno Mountains, was taken from the Natives by government order in 1873, but it is still considered sacred (see "Festivals and ceremonies"). San Carlos Apache priests were forced to openly discuss their beliefs after the University of Arizona announced in the early 1980s that it would build multiple telescopes there.

The university's plan generated considerable controversy both as an issue of religious freedom and as an environmental issue. It pitted nonreligious Apache people against traditional Apache, and Natives and environmentalists against astronomers, politicians, and the Roman Catholic Church. In 1990, the Apache Survival Coalition was formed to save the sacred mountain. Although the group failed in this effort—a telescope was erected and dedicated there in 1994—the group remains active in the struggle for the religious freedom and rights of the San Carlos Apache.

Apache Words

gidi	"cat"
chaa	"beaver"
piishii	"nighthawk"
nnee	"people"
nadä'	"corn"
dlö'	"bird"

LANGUAGE

Government schools built around the turn of the twentieth century routinely punished children for speaking their Native languages on the reservation, but the Apache have managed to retain their language. Many fear that it may soon be lost as the American culture takes over and Apache people intermarry with non-Natives.

GOVERNMENT

The San Carlos Apache tribe is run democratically (by the people) according to a constitution. An elected tribal council has a chairperson, vice chairperson, and nine representatives from five districts. A secretary and treasurer are appointed. In 1993, the tribe started the San Carlos Elders Cultural Advisory Council (ECAC). This group advises the tribal council and works to preserve Apache culture.

In the 1990s, the San Carlos Reservation had a prolonged period of political instability that included accusations of secret meetings and deals, which lead to protests, demonstrations, and even takeovers. The ECAC, whose members range from mid-forties to late nineties, helped to provide direction. Their guidance is respected, although sometimes during this period their counsel was ignored; clashes occurred between those who wanted to make money and those who wanted to preserve the land and traditional values. In most cases, however, the council is seen as a source of wisdom, and the elder members of the council mentor the younger members to ensure that their heritage is passed on to future generations.

ECONOMY

Land-based economy

After enduring years of poverty as the people adjusted to life on the reservation, the economy at San Carlos improved when cattle were introduced around 1930. Overgrazing occurred, however, and cattle monies declined. At the turn of the twenty-first century, San Carlos cattle operations were the tribe's third-largest source of money, generating about $1 million in sales annually.

One-third of the tribe's land is forest or woodland, and timber operations are another source of income. Arizona is one of only three places in the world where the rare peridot (a transparent yellowish-green mineral) gemstones can be found, and the San Carlos tribe earns money from mining it.

The San Carlos Apache have been haunted by poverty and lack of opportunity, and their standard of living remains well below the national level. In recent years, though, the San Carlos tribe has placed a high priority on the development of agriculture. Irrigation facilities are being modernized, and an Agricultural Development Committee was formed to guide the process. Alfalfa (a haylike plant) and jojoba beans (pronounced *huh-HOBE-uh*; edible seeds that are also prized for their thick moisturizing liquid center) are promising crops.

Government and recreation as employers

Recreation yields a significant amount of money for the tribe. San Carlos Lake, the state's largest body of water, offers fishing opportunities, but from time to time the lake dries up completely. Hunters pay fees to track big and small game like elk, bighorn sheep, antelope, and migratory birds. Campgrounds, boat ramps, stores, tackle shops, and warm- and cold-water fisheries are available to tourists. Visitors are also permitted to observe Apache ceremonies while in the area.

The Apache Gold Casino, which includes a hotel, restaurant, a recreational vehicle park, and a pavilion for car shows, rodeos, powwows, and concerts, opened in 1996 and is a big moneymaker for the tribe. The government is a major employer of San Carlos Apache. It operates health, education, and other services on the reservation and provides jobs for members of the tribe. Despite these enterprises, reservation members still contend with poverty and high unemployment.

A sign welcomes visitors to the Apache Gold Casino and Resort, which is owned by the local Apache tribe. © ANDERS RYMAN/CORBIS.

Life in the Carlisle Indian School

The children from Fort Marion (see "History") in Florida were taken from their parents and sent to the Carlisle Indian School in Pennsylvania. There, the head of the school, Captain Richard Henry Pratt, was determined to "kill the Indian" in the students. Asa Daklugie, who was to be chief to his people, told of his arrival at the school.

> The next day the torture began. The first thing they did was cut our hair. I had taken my knife from one of my long braids and wrapped it in my blankets, so I didn't lose it. But I lost my hair. And without it how would Ussen [see "Religion"] recognize me when I went to the Happy Place [afterlife]?
>
> … While we were bathing our breech-clouts were taken, and we were ordered to put on trousers. We'd lost our hair and we'd lost our clothes; with the two we'd lost our identity as Indians. Greater punishment could hardly have been devised. That's what I thought till they marched us into a room and our interpreter ordered us to line up with our backs to the wall. I went to the head of the line because that's where a chief belongs.
>
> Then a man went down it. Starting with me he began: "Asa, Benjamin, Charles, Daniel, Eli, Frank." Frank was Mangus' son. So he became Frank Mangus and I became Asa Daklugie. … I've always hated that name. It was forced on me as though I was an animal."

SOURCE: Daklugie, Asa, quoted in Eve Ball. *Indeh, an Apache Odyssey.* Reprint. Norman: University of Oklahoma Press, 1988, p. 144.

DAILY LIFE

Education

Children received a traditional education from their parents. At early ages, they helped with adult chores and learned their responsibilities. When the San Carlos Apache were taken prisoner and sent to Florida in the 1880s, their children were sent to the Carlisle Indian School in Pennsylvania. The purpose of the school was to rid the children of their Apache culture and train them to become American citizens.

In 1900, the U.S. government opened a boarding school on the San Carlos reservation. Children were taken from their families and forced to attend the school, where they were not allowed to speak their Native language or practice their traditional religion. The experiment proved to be a failure and left many Apache with a long-standing resentment toward U. S. schools and their style of education. This has contributed to low levels of educational attainment on the reservation.

Apache leaders are trying to address these critical educational issues. They encourage higher education by offering scholarships to college; they also offer GED programs and job training for adults. The reservation houses a library, and the tribe was proud to announce the opening of its cultural center in 1995. Located in Peridot, Arizona, the center tells the story of the Apache people in their own words and offers educational programs in cooperation with Arizona schools and other groups.

Healing practices

In modern times, some San Carlos Apache still place their trust in medicine men, who journey to Mt. Graham to look for healing herbs that can only be found there and to learn healing techniques from the mountain spirits.

The U.S. Public Health Service operates a hospital on the reservation, but the tribe is in process of taking over the management of the facility. They intend to combine traditional healing with modern medicine to deal with many of the health challenges of the community. The San Carlos Apache tribe faces serious health problems, including alcoholism (and the illnesses that result from it), obesity, diabetes, and high rates of infant death and teenage suicide.

ARTS

Basketry

The Apache tribe is known for its outstanding basket makers and artists. San Carlos Apache Cultural Center contains an arts and crafts guild where visitors can buy many traditional crafts such as burden baskets, beaded moccasins, and leatherwork as well as artwork by many Apache artists.

The first Fort Sill Apache to be born free, Allan Houser (1914–1994; Allan C. Haozous), became a renowned sculptor. He first exhibited his work in the late 1960s, and collectors bought his pieces. From the 1970s until he died in 1994, he created almost one thousand sculptures in bronze, stone, and wood. After nearly fifty solo exhibitions in

Securing Fire

Many tribes tell tales of Coyote, who is a trick-ster. Sometimes he uses his skills to harm others, but in this San Carlos Apache story, he triumphs, and people get fire. The legend also explains how animals came to have certain physical features.

They say long ago there was no fire. The people ate their food uncooked. There were only two men who had fire. They [the San Carlos People] could see it in the tops of a very tall pine tree which stood there.

Coyote proposed that a large com-pany of people be invited to come together for a dance. He also sug-gested that a letter be sent to those who had fire asking them to bring some as they wished. to gamble with the guessing game.

Coyote told his companions to tie dry grass around his tail. When it was day-break Coyote danced by himself. "I will dance over the fire," he said. "Your tail is afire," they called to him. "Why do you say my tail is burning?" he asked. "Your tail is burning," they called to him again. He went around the fire four times and then jumped over them. He ran away with the fire. Those who owned the fire ran after him and put

out what fire they found. They caught Coyote after he had run a long distance and pulled out his nose so it is long and spread his mouth apart so it is wide.

Then another man was running away beyond with the fire. It was Night Hawk. They caught him after a long chase. They pushed the crown of his head down hard and spread his mouth open.

Another person was running with the fire. It was Turkey Buzzard. They caught him a long distance away and pulled the hair out of his head. He had given the fire to Humming Bird. A large mountain was standing in the distance. Fire was coming out from the top of this mountain. The people had been without fire but came to have plenty of it because of Coyote. The fire went inside of the trees and became plentiful.

SOURCE: Goddard, Pliny Earle. "Securing Fire (Second Version)." In *Anthropological Papers of the American Museum of Natural History, Vol. XXIV, Part I: Myths and Tales from the San Carlos Apache.* New York: The American Museum of Natural History, 1918. Available online at: http://digitallibrary.amnh.org/dspace/bitstream/2246/164/1/A024a01.pdf (accessed on July 20, 2011).

countries around the world, he earned an international reputation for his award-winning work. Houser passed his talent on to his two sons, Philip (1941–) and Bob (1943–) Haozous, who both became artists like their father.

CUSTOMS

Festivals and ceremonies

The San Carlos Indian Reservation hosts the annual Holy Ground Ceremony. The building of telescopes on Apache sacred land sparked a renewed interest in this traditional religious practice. For decades since then, runners have carried prayers from the San Carlos Apache Reservation to a sacred site at the top of Dzil Nchaa Sian (Mount Graham), a distance of two hundred miles. The four-day event begins with a sweat lodge and a blessing. A special holy water ceremony is held at the end to remember previous runners who have died. People of all ages take part in the event, and many runners who participated as youngsters now bring their own children.

The tribe also celebrates the coming-of-age of its young women in a Sunrise Ceremony, formerly called the Changing Woman Ceremony. (For more information on the Sunrise Ceremony, see Apache entry.)

The casino sponsors several powwows a year that are open to tourists. Powwows are celebrations that include traditional singing and dancing. The Mt. Turnbull Rodeo and the All-Indian Rodeo Fair are annual events. On June 18, the San Carlos Apache hold Independence Day festivities that celebrate their culture.

CURRENT TRIBAL ISSUES

The San Carlos Apache are currently engaged in efforts to reverse the trends of alcoholism, suicide, crime, and violence that plague their people. According to experts, serious problems like these often result from decades of poverty and high unemployment. Many homes lack electricity and indoor plumbing. Disputes between the tribe and mining companies over rights to Arizona's scarce water supplies are also a nagging issue.

Until 1998, the reservation had three dumping sites, but when a new landfill opened and the tribe offered curbside pickup, many people did not want to pay. Instead, they dumped their trash illegally. Fourteen different dumpsites were discovered, some as large as six acres. To deal with the problem, the tribe set up stations where people could take their trash. That helped stop the illegal dumping, but officials worried that the existing dumps could pollute the groundwater. They obtained a grant from the Environmental Protection Agency (EPA) to clean up the sites. They hauled away junked cars and refrigerators, which can leak dangerous chemicals. Police and game rangers also began enforcing the no-dumping policies.

Another major problem facing the San Carlos people is the looting of the eight-hundred-year-old ruins. Looters today have access to modern equipment like Global Positioning Systems (GPS), enabling them to locate artifacts more easily. As a result, relics are disappearing from tribal lands in great numbers. With 1.8 million acres to cover and only a handful of enforcement officers, the government has little chance of catching the thieves. The damage amateur archaeologists inflict on the ancient sites is very great; many areas are pockmarked with holes, and important pieces of history are lost forever. Even worse for most tribes is the violation of graves; grave robbers care more about profit than the spiritual and scientific losses they cause.

NOTABLE PEOPLE

Evalena Henry (1939–) is a San Carlos Apache known for her award-winning baskets. In 2001, she became an NEA (National Endowment for the Arts) National Heritage Fellow. Henry's works are on display at the Heard Museum in Phoenix and are held by art collectors all over the world. Her goal is to pass on her basketmaking methods to future generations.

Painter, sculptor, and teacher Allan Houser (see "Arts") inspired others to become artists. He received many awards for his work, including the National Medal for the Arts in 1982. His sons, Philip and Bob Haozous, followed in their father's footsteps by becoming sculptors.

Mildred Cleghorn (1910–1997; also known as *Eh-Ohn* and *Lay-a-Bet*), the first chairperson of the San Carlos Apache, was a doll maker and leader in preserving the Apache culture. In 1996, she filed a lawsuit on behalf of more than 300,000 Native people who had reason to believe that the Bureau of Indian Affairs had mismanaged their money held in trust.

BOOKS

Geronimo. *The Autobiography of Geronimo.* St. Petersburg, FL: Red and Black Publishers, 2011.

Goddard, Pliny Earle. *Myths and Tales from the San Carlos Apache.* Whitefish, MT: Kessinger Publishing, 2006.

———. *San Carlos Apache Texts.* Kila, MN: Kessinger Publishing, 2006.

Jastrzembski, Joseph C. *The Apache.* Minneapolis: Chelsea House, 2011.

McKanna, Jr., Clare V. *Court-martial of Apache Kid: The Renegade of Renegades.* Lubbock: Texas Tech University Press, 2009.

Nickens, Paul and Kathleen. *Old San Carlos.* Charleston, SC: Arcadia Publishing, 2008.

Record, Ian W. *Big Sycamore Stands Alone: The Western Apaches, Aravaipa, and the Struggle for Place.* Norman: University of Oklahoma Press, 2008.

Samuels, David W. *Putting a Song on Top of It: Expression and Identity on the San Carlos Apache Reservation.* Tucson: University of Arizona Press, 2006.

Shapard, Bud. *Chief Loco: Apache Peacemaker.* Norman: University of Oklahoma Press, 2010.

Sterngass, Jon. *Geronimo.* New York: Chelsea House, 2010.

PERIODICALS

Martin, Evelyn. "The Last Mountain (Mount Graham in Arizona)." *American Forests* 99, no. 3–4 (March–April 1993): 44.

Warshall, Peter. "The Heart of Genuine Sadness: Astronomers, Politicians, and Federal Employees Desecrate the Holiest Mountain of the San Carlos Apache." *Whole Earth* 91 (Winter 1997): 30.

WEB SITES

Berry, John. "Mildred Cleghorn." *First Nations Cumulative Index.* http://www.dickshovel.com/elders.html#Mildred (accessed on July 20, 2011).

Center for American Indian Economic Development. "The San Carlos Apache Indian Reservation." *Northern Arizona University.* http://www.cba.nau.edu/caied/tribepages/SanCarlos.asp (accessed on July 20, 2011).

"The Children of Changing Woman." *Peabody Museum of Archaeology and Ethnology.* http://www.peabody.harvard.edu/maria/Cwoman.html (accessed on July 20, 2011).

Chiricahua Apache Prisoner of War Committee. "Other Chiricahua Apaches Escape San Carlos (1881–1885)." *Mescalero Apache Tribe of New Mexico.* http://www.chiricahua-apache.com/chiricahua-apache-pow-history/who-are-the-chiricahua-apaches/chiricahua-apaches-and-the-san-carlos-indian-reservation/ (accessed on July 20, 2011).

Goodwin, Grenville and Neil. "The Apache Diaries: A Father-Son Journey (excerpts)." *Southwest Crossroads.* http://southwestcrossroads.org/record.php?num=820 (accessed on July 20, 2011).

Machula, Paul R. "East Central Arizona History." *Zybtarizona.* http://zybtarizona.com/ (accessed on July 20, 2011).

San Carlos Apache Cultural Center. http://www.sancarlosapache.com/home.htm (accessed on July 20, 2011).

"San Carlos Apache Sunrise Dance." *World News Network.* http://wn.com/San_Carlos_Apache_Sunrise_Dance (accessed on July 20, 2011).

"Unconquered: Allan Houser and the Legacy of One Apache Family." *Oklahoma History Center.* http://www.okhistory.org/unconquered/index.html (accessed on July 20, 2011).

Weiser, Kathy. "Nana—Oldest Apache Warrior." *Legends of America.* http://www.legendsofamerica.com/na-nana.html (accessed on July 20, 2011).

White Mountain Apache

Name

The name White Mountain Apache refers to the White Mountain region of Arizona where the tribe resides. The people, who were part of the Coyoteros, have also been called the Sierra Blanca Apache, a Spanish version of their name. The Apache refer to themselves as *Ndeé*, or "the people," and the White Mountain Apache go by *Shis-Inday*, or "People of the Woods," a name that may have arisen because they spent the winter in the forests of the Sierra Madre.

Location

The White Mountain Apache homeland in east-central Arizona once stretched from the Pinaleno Mountains to the south to the White Mountains to the north. Presently the tribe lives on the Fort Apache Reservation, which covers 1.7 million acres in Arizona's Navajo, Apache, and Gila counties. Their largest city is Whiteriver.

Population

In 1850, there were an estimated 1,400 to 1,500 White Mountain Apache. In the 1990 U.S. Census, 9,700 people identified themselves as White Mountain Apache. In 2000, that number had increased to 12,377, and 10,686 of those people lived on the Fort Apache reservation. By 2011, tribal enrollment had grown to almost 15,000.

Language family

Athabaskan.

Origins and group affiliations

Most historians believe the Apache people made a gradual move from western Canada to the American Southwest between the thirteenth and sixteenth centuries. The Apache themselves, however, tell a different story. They say they originated in the Southwest, and some of their people moved north. According to their oral history, present-day Apaches belong the group of

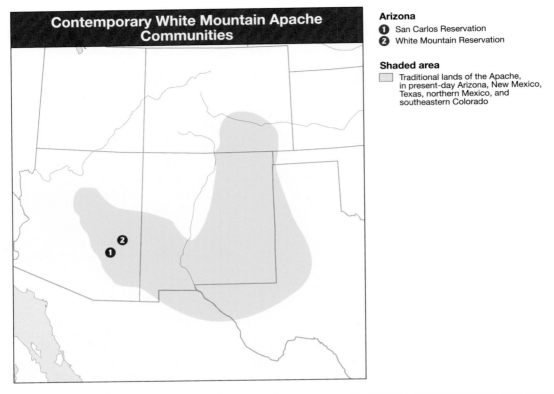

A map of contemporary White Mountain Apache communities. MAP BY XNR PRODUCTIONS. CENGAGE LEARNING, GALE. REPRODUCED BY PERMISSION OF GALE, A PART OF CENGAGE LEARNING.

people who did not migrate north. The Apaches were never one unified group, but rather a number of different bands who spoke similar languages and shared similar customs. Settlers referred to the Apache people as Western or Eastern Apache. Those called White Mountain Apache are descendants of the easternmost group of Western Apache. The White Mountain people most likely learned agricultural techniques from the Navajo or Pueblo (see entries). The name White Mountain Apache now is applied to all peoples who live on the Fort Apache Reservation. Some of the original groups who settled there were the Arivaipa, Tsiltaden or Chilion, Chiricahua (see entry), Coyotero, Mimbreño, and Mogollon.

The White Mountain Apache differed from other Apache groups for two main reasons: they farmed, and they interacted more with other tribes, which led to significant changes in their culture. The White Mountain people served as scouts for the U.S. Army to help round up other Apache groups—including the group led by Chiricahua Apache warrior Geronimo (1829–1909)—who refused to move to reservations. In August 1998, *Newsweek* called the White Mountain Apache one of five Native North American "tribes to watch" because of their astonishing economic successes.

HISTORY

Cooperative relations with United States

The land belonging to the White Mountain Apache ended up in U.S. hands in 1853, when the Gadsden Purchase, a land deal with Mexico, was sealed. Although the tribe continued the longstanding Apache custom of raiding Mexican settlements for food, they avoided confronting the U.S. Army. In fact, they aided the army by providing scouts and fighters. When American forces established Camp Ord on White Mountain Apache land to protect Arizona settlers, the people did not object. Camp Ord later became Fort Apache Reservation.

Old Fort Apache has been preserved as a museum and is on the National Register of Historic Places. © ANDERS RYMAN/CORBIS.

Important Dates

1853: The United States acquires White Mountain Apache land in the Gadsden Purchase.

Early 1870s: The White Mountain Apache move to reservation land.

1897: The White Mountain–San Carlos Indian Reservation is divided into two reservations. The White Mountain Apache are given their own reservation (now called Fort Apache Reservation).

1938: The White Mountain Apache constitution is ratified, and a tribal council is elected.

In 1874, the U.S. government adopted a peace policy and began to place all Native nations on reservations. General George Crook (1829–1890) and his White Mountain Apache scouts tracked down every hostile band. Without the Indian scouts, this feat might have proved impossible. The White Mountain people believed that their traditional way of life was over. They cooperated with the government's reservation policy and moved to the White Mountain–San Carlos Indian Reservation, established in 1871.

In 1897, the White Mountain–San Carlos Indian Reservation was divided into the San Carlos Indian Reservation and the Fort Apache Reservation. The White Mountain Apache were a more unified group than the Chiricahua who were confined to San Carlos, but they did have to abandon most of their old ways in order to survive. While under military supervision at Fort Apache, they learned to farm, build irrigation dams, and tend livestock. Armed with this knowledge, they were able to create a strong economy over the course of the twentieth century. The population has grown tremendously, thanks to better health care and improvements in sanitation and housing. More than 13,500 people were enrolled in the Fort Apache tribe in the early 2000s; about 1,500 were from other tribes, mainly Navajo.

LANGUAGE

In the late 1990s, approximately 75 percent of the White Mountain people spoke Apache in their homes. According to a study done by the White Mountain Apache language scholar Bernadette Adley-SantaMaria, 95 percent of the tribe over age forty spoke Apache, but only 28 percent of those under thirty used the language. About 10 percent of the tribe, mostly the young, spoke only English. Although everyone questioned agreed that learning their language and culture is important, the decrease in language skills among the younger generations reflects the impact of cultural change.

GOVERNMENT

The Apache were divided into small local groups that governed themselves. White Mountain groups were often named after the location of their farmland. They had chiefs who organized food-gathering, farming projects, and interactions with other local groups.

In 1934, the U.S. government passed the Indian Reorganization Act, which encouraged Native American communities to govern themselves and set up tribal economic corporations. The White Mountain Apache adopted a constitution in 1938 and formed a tribal council consisting of a chairperson, a vice chairperson, and nine members elected from four voting districts. All members serve four-year terms. Tribal headquarters is in Whiteriver, Arizona. Although Apache communities had never tried this type of government before, it worked well throughout the rest of the century.

The tribe also has a legal office that assists the tribal attorney and the general council. The legal department advises the chairperson and other council members, while the tribal attorney handles lawsuits necessary to enforce tribal laws or to fight for tribal rights.

ECONOMY

Before 1918

The White Mountain Apache lived in a region of deserts and watered valleys. About 75 percent of the food economy was based on hunting and gathering; the rest came from gardening. When families left their fields and moved back to winter quarters, the men of the tribe took to raiding (stealing) livestock, including horses, which they used mostly for food.

On the reservation in the early 1900s, the people of Fort Apache earned wages by working for whites. They cut hay for U.S. Cavalry horses stabled at Fort Apache. They also leased land to U.S. cattle ranchers, then worked for them.

Twentieth century

After 1918, the U.S. government supplied the reservations with cattle. Fort Apache residents received four hundred head of cattle, and the cattle-raising business took off. As of 1998, the tribe boasted a herd of fifteen thousand purebred whiteface cattle. They ran a feedlot and feed store as well as a nine-hundred-acre farm to grow alfalfa. They also owned and managed the Alchesay Fish Hatchery.

A 2002 forest fire destroyed thousands of acres of forest and strained the White Mountain Apache's lumber business. © AP IMAGES/ MATT YORK.

Since 1934, the White Mountain Apache Tribal Council has overseen the building of a strong economy on the Fort Apache Reservation. The council is responsible for an 800,000-acre (324,000-hectare) forest, which supports a substantial lumber business. The tribe owned and operated the Fort Apache Timber Company in Whiteriver, Arizona. During the late 1990s, they employed about four hundred Apache workers and had an annual income of approximately $30 million. In the summer of 2002, a wildfire destroyed hundreds of thousands of acres of forest, 60 percent of it on tribal lands. Another fire in 2004 damaged a smaller area, as did a blaze in 2011; it will take the tribe decades to restore the areas to pre-fire condition. Meanwhile, it must rely on other businesses to generate much-needed income.

Twenty-first century

In addition to several stores and gas stations, the tribe owns a hotel, a recreational vehicle park, and other tourist attractions, such as Kinishba archaeological ruins with petroglyphs (ancient picture writing), Geronimo's Cave, and Old Fort Apache. The Hon-Dah (which means "Welcome") Home Center received grants in 2003 to build public housing, provide scholarships, organize job fairs, and teach residents financial skills. Some tribal members work in these enterprises. Others are employed by the Apache Aerospace Company to build helicopters or Apache Materials to manufacture earth-friendly construction materials.

Tourists in White Mountain Apache country are entertained at a large complex of operations that includes hunting, fishing, winter sports, and water sports. Big-game hunting draws wealthy people and celebrities, and the Hon-Dah Resort-Casino is also a big attraction. The tribe owns the White Mountain Apache Motel and Restaurant, the Sunrise Park Ski Resort, and the Sunrise Park Resort and Spa. These contributes both job and tourist dollars to the local economy.

Over the years, various members of the tribe have made a name for themselves in the field of firefighting. White Mountain Apache people are in demand all over the western United States as forest firefighting specialists. The Apache 8, a group of women firefighters, has been combating blazes around the country for three decades. Formerly open only to women, the group is now open to both genders.

DAILY LIFE

Food

Farming supplied about one-fourth of the White Mountain tribe's food. They set up summer camps along streams and constructed dams and channels to irrigate their small fields. They grew limited amounts of corn, beans, pumpkins, and squash. Once the seeds were planted, the women moved out across the land in gathering groups, collecting such foods as acorns, mescal (pronounced *MESS-kal*; a type of small cactus), and berries. The men left to hunt for deer, elk, mountain sheep and goats, and pronghorn (antelope). They did not eat birds but hunted them for their feathers. (Eagle feathers were especially prized.) Fish were considered unclean, so they were not eaten.

Education

In early times Boys played until they were about five and girls until about age seven. Until that time, mothers trained both sexes. Mothers recited oral history and taught them prayers. Children learned to be respectful. If they were not, their mothers splashed water in their faces. Girls looked after younger children and learned to cook, chop wood, build a wickiup (see "Buildings" in Apache entry), sew, carry water, and butcher animals. They also learned to use weapons. Although most women did not accompany war parties, if their people were attacked, they fought alongside the men.

Boys rose before dawn to bathe in the creek, even if it was iced over, and then ran up a hill without stopping and without breathing through their mouths. To prove they had done it, they filled their mouths with water, which they spit out when they returned. Strength and physical endurance was important to hunting and war, so they practiced dodging, tracking, horseback riding, and walking silently. Grandfathers taught boys tribal rituals and how to make weapons. Boys helped their fathers hunt and care for horses. As soon as they could handle a bow, they shot small animals. By age fourteen or fifteen, they hunted with adults.

Modern schooling In the twenty-first century, many children of the White Mountain Apache tribe are educated at public schools in Whiteriver. Others attend schools run by the Bureau of Indian Affairs or a Lutheran school on the reservation. A branch of the Northland Pioneer College also operates in Whiteriver. Many White Mountain Apache students go on to college.

Old Fort Apache preserves culture Old Fort Apache, now owned and preserved by the tribe, is on the National Register of Historic Places. Visitors to the fort can learn about Apache culture and history at the Heritage Museum and at various archaeological sites.

Healing practices

The ancient Apache people believed in the power of supernatural spirits. Some spirits were said to be benevolent (kind or good), but evil witches were thought to cause sickness, insanity, and even death. Suspected witches were still feared by some tribes at the end of the twentieth century. According to Native tradition, witches could make people sick by poisoning them, by thinking evil thoughts, or by "shooting" victims with a piece of wood or charcoal, a pebble, a bead, or an arrowhead. A victim of witchcraft could either seek treatment through a ceremony conducted by a medicine man, or shaman (pronounced *SHAH-mun* or *SHAY-mun*), or do nothing and allow the condition to get worse.

Traditional White Mountain healing ceremonies were performed at night. Before beginning, the shaman was given a piece of shell with an eagle feather attached to it; white shells were used for female patients, and turquoise shells were used for males. If the ceremonies worked, the witch died and the victim recovered.

Releasing the Deer

Native Americans believed that everything on the earth was put here by the Creator to be shared with all. They did not understand the European concept of land ownership or acquiring goods or food when others were needy. No one in the tribe would go hungry, because everyone shared what they had. Adults often told stories to teach a moral. In this White Mountain Apache tale, a greedy man loses all that he tried to hoard.

> Ganisk'ide was the only one who owned deer. He was the only one who brought them home and who ate their flesh. He gave none of the meat to the people who lived near him.
>
> Ravens, who were then people, proposed that they make a puppy and desert it. They did this; they moved away and left a puppy lying there. When the children of Ganisk'ide went where the people had moved away, they found the puppy. They took it up and carried it home.
>
> Ganisk'ide told the children to throw the puppy away, but when they objected, he told them to try the dog's eyes by holding fire in front of them. When they brought the fire near the dog's eyes it cried, "gai gai gai." "It is a real dog," Ganisk'ide said. "You may take him behind the stone door where the deer are enclosed and let him eat the entrails."
>
> When the children had taken the dog behind this door he became a man again. He moved the stone to one side and the deer that were inside ran out. Ganisk'ide called to his wife from the doorway to touch the nostrils of the deer.... She touched each of the deer on the nose as they ran by her and they received the sense of smell. They ran away from her.
>
> "You said it was a dog," he said to his children with whom he was angry, "but he turned them out for us." The deer scattered all over the earth.

SOURCE: Goddard, Pliny Earle. *Anthropological Papers of the American Museum of Natural History, Vol. XXIV, Part II: Myths and Tales from the White Mountain Apache.* New York: The American Museum of Natural History, 1919. Available online from http://digitallibrary.amnh.org/dspace/bitstream/2246/169/1/A024a02.pdf (accessed on July 20, 2011).

Modern-day White Mountain Apache seek the assistance of shamans and health care professionals at an Indian Health Service hospital in Whiteriver. If more specialized care is needed, a helicopter can airlift patients to Phoenix, Arizona. The reservation also offers mental health and substance abuse services, and an outpatient and emergency care clinic is available in Cibecue.

ARTS

Basketry is important to the White Mountain Apaches, and their baskets, especially burden baskets, are collected by people around the country. Basket making is a traditional art that has been kept alive because baskets play an important role in ceremonies. They are also symbolic: the opening represents a person's birth into the world, and the basket itself stands for a person's life and world. Designs on the basket show the landscape the person inhabits.

CUSTOMS

Birth and childhood

The Apache had a variety of ceremonies related to the stages of life. Four days after birth, a baby was placed in a cradleboard during a Cradleboard Ceremony. Each cradleboard was made especially for the child, and boys' and girls' cradleboards were decorated differently. Until the infant's neck and spine were strong, the baby did not stay in the cradleboard all the time. After the first month or so, it remained in its *tosch* (cradle) constantly. Babies had their earlobes pierced to be sure they would hear and obey important instructions.

When babies took their first steps, the First Moccasins Ceremony was held. Every spring, children received haircuts, which were an occasion for celebration.

Puberty

The most important celebration, the Sunrise Ceremony, honored girls reaching puberty. Four days of sacred rituals, songs, and dances imbued them with the physical and spiritual power of White Painted Woman and marked their passage to womanhood.

Around age sixteen, boys had to join the men on four raids. If those were successful, they became warriors. After that, they were considered men and could marry.

Festivals and ceremonies

The White Mountain Apache held a ceremony after returning from a raid. If a woman chose to participate in the ceremonial dancing, the successful raider had to give her one of the animals he had captured.

Some of the rich culture of the Apache people faded during the twentieth century, but the White Mountain people are working to restore some key traditions, including the Girls' Puberty Ceremony. During this major annual event, young girls perform the Sunrise Dance to receive special blessings.

The Crown Dance is also an important part of the traditional White Mountain Apache culture. Performed by men whose bodies are painted with designs, it is a healing dance. The participants wear headdresses shaped like crowns, bedecked with eagle feathers.

Another tradition of the White Mountain Apache is the Hoop Dance, which was originally practiced by medicine men. The moving hoops enabled them to see visions of the future and evoke healing. The hoop also symbolizes the circle of life from birth to death and can be used for blessing, healing, or protection.

CURRENT TRIBAL ISSUES

Problems still exist for the White Mountain Apache on the reservation. Many people are out of work, and much of the available housing is poor. School attendance is low, while alcoholism, drug use, and teen suicide rates are high. However, the White Mountain Apache are taking renewed pride in their language and tradition. Experts feel that the outlook for the tribe is improving. Income from the casino and other businesses helps funds social services.

The tribe won a lawsuit against the state of New Mexico in 1982, giving it control over the fish and game on the tribal lands. Since then, the White Mountain Apache have developed one of the most respected wildlife conservation departments in the world. In 2000, the tribe received an award for its efforts in establishing the White Mountain Apache Wildlife and Outdoor Recreation Program. The tribe hired a full-time staff of workers in addition to part-time people during the warmer months. It sells recreational and hunting permits to make money to sustain the program. By 2011, the area had one of the richest wildlife habitats in the state, and the tribe, with the help of its partners, had succeeded in bringing the Apache trout back from near extinction.

In 2006, the White Mountain Apache joined several other tribes including the Navajo and Hopi (see entries) in a lawsuit against the Forest Service. At issue was a proposal by Arizona Snowbowl, a ski resort, to use wastewater to make snow. The tribes hoped to halt the desecration of places they consider sacred. The judge ruled against them, leading many Native Americans to question whether the Religious Freedom and Restoration Act of 1993 truly does protect their religious rights.

In exchange for a $200-million, state-funded drinking water project on their reservation, which will include a dam, reservoir, treatment plant, and delivery pipelines, the White Mountain Apache have agreed to drop several pending lawsuits against the government. This project is compensation for the government's clear-cutting of trees and plants on thousands of acres of reservation land that increased the water flow into the Salt River. The state channeled that additional water to major cities such as Phoenix and Scottsdale.

In the summer of 2011, a wildfire raged out of control, damaging a portion of the White Mountain and San Carlos Reservations. Firefighters worked to bulldoze land and clear brush to prevent the fire from reaching Dzil Ligai (White Mountain, or Mount Baldy), a holy place for many Native peoples. The White Mountain Apache are still struggling to recover from the 2002 wildfires that destroyed about 475,000 acres of forest (see "Economy"). Although much of the acreage appeared to be saved from this fire, the ash and residue created air and water quality hazards.

BOOKS

Aleshire, Peter. *Fox and the Whirlwind: General George Crook and Geronimo, a Paired Biography.* Victoria, British Columbia, Canada: Castle Books, 2009.

Ball, Eve, Nora Henn, and Lynda A. Sánchez. *Indeh: An Apache Odyssey.* Reprint. Norman: University of Oklahoma Press, 1988.

Gatewood, Charles B. *Lt. Charles Gatewood & His Apache Wars Memoir.* Edited by Louis Kraft. Lincoln, NE: Bison Books, 2009.

Geronimo. *The Autobiography of Geronimo.* St. Petersburg, FL: Red and Black Publishers, 2011.

Goddard, Pliny Earle. *White Mountain Apache Texts.* Whitefish, MT: Kessinger Publishing, 2010.

Goddard, Pliny Earle. *Myths and Tales of the White Mountain Apache.* Whitefish, MT: Kessinger Publishing, 2011.

Goodwin, Grenville. *Myths and Tales of the White Mountain Apache.* Whitefish, MT: Kessinger Publishing, 2011.

Record, Ian W. *Big Sycamore Stands Alone: The Western Apaches, Aravaipa, and the Struggle for Place.* Norman: University of Oklahoma Press, 2008.

Shapard, Bud. *Chief Loco: Apache Peacemaker.* Tucson: University of Oklahoma Press, 2010.

Smith, Victoria. *Captive Arizona, 1851–1900.* Lincoln: University of Nebraska Press, 2009.

Watt, Eva Tulene, and Keith H. Basso. *Don't Let the Sun Step over You: A White Mountain Apache Family Life (1860–1976)*. Tucson: University of Arizona Press, 2004.

PERIODICALS

Adley-Santamaria, Bernadette. "Interrupting White Mountain Apache Language Shift: An Insider's View." *Practicing Anthropology* 21, no. 2 (1999): 16–19.

Welch, John R. "White Mountain Apache Heritage Program Operations and Challenges." *Society for American Archaeology* 16, no. 1 (January 1998). Available online from http://www.saa.org/Portals/0/SAA/publications/SAAbulletin/16-1/SAA9.html (accessed on July 20, 2011).

WEB SITES

Adley-SantaMaria, Bernadette. "White Mountain Apache Language Issues." *Northern Arizona University*. http://www2.nau.edu/jar/TIL_12.html (accessed on July 20, 2011).

Center for American Indian Economic Development. "The White Mountain Apache Tribe." *Northern Arizona University*. http://www.cba.nau.edu/caied/tribepages/WMAT.asp (accessed on July 20, 2011).

"The Children of Changing Woman." *Peabody Museum of Archaeology and Ethnology*. http://www.peabody.harvard.edu/maria/Cwoman.html (accessed on July 20, 2011).

Center for American Indian Economic Development. "The White Mountain Apache Tribe." *Northern Arizona University*. http://www.cba.nau.edu/caied/tribepages/WMAT.asp (accessed on July 20, 2011).

Cline Library. "Indigenous Voices of the Colorado Plateau: White Mountain Apache." *Northern Arizona University*. http://library.nau.edu/speccoll/exhibits/indigenous_voices/white_mountain_apache/overview.html (accessed on July 20, 2011).

Gerke, Sarah Bohl. "White Mountain Apache." *Arizona State University*. http://grandcanyonhistory.clas.asu.edu/history_nativecultures_whitemountainapache.html (accessed on July 20, 2011).

Jacks, Stewart. "Apache Trout Recovery: History in the Making." *U.S. Fish and Wildlife Service—Region 2*. http://www.fws.gov/southwest/fisheries/azfro/PDF/Briefings/AZFROApacheTroutBriefing.pdf (accessed on July 20, 2011).

"Nohwike Bagowa: House of Our Footprints" *White Mountain Apache Tribe Culture Center and Museum*. http://www.wmat.us/wmaculture.shtml (accessed on July 20, 2011).

Shii né: The Mind-Land Harmony: Conservation on White Mountain Apache. Boulder, CO: Rocky Mountain Natural Resource Center, 2006. Available online from http://www.nwf.org/~/media/PDFs/Regional/Rocky-Mountain/WhiteMtnFinal2.ashx (accessed on July 20, 2011).

Sreenivasan, Hari. "'Apache 8' Follows All-Women Firefighters On and Off the Reservation." *PBS NewsHour.* http://video.pbs.org/video/2006599346/ (accessed on July 20, 2011).

"White Mountain Apache Indian Reservation." *Arizona Handbook.* http://www.arizonahandbook.com/white_mtn_apache.htm (accessed on July 20, 2011).

"White Mountain Apache Tribe." *InterTribal Council of Arizona.* http://www.itcaonline.com/tribes_whitemtn.html (accessed on July 20, 2011).

"White Mountain Apache Tribe: Restoring Wolves, Owls, Trout and Ecosystems" *Cooperative Conservation America.* http://www.cooperativeconservation.org/viewproject.asp?pid=136 (accessed on July 20, 2011).

WMAT: White Mountain Apache Tribe. http://wmat.us/ (accessed on July 20, 2011).

Zeig, Sande. *Apache 8* (film). http://www.apache8.com/ (accessed on July 20, 2011).

Hopi

Name

Hopi is the shortened form of the tribe's original name, *Hopituh Shi-nu-mu.* Its most commonly given meaning is "peaceful people." The Hopi are sometimes referred to as the Moqui, a name given to them by the Spanish, who misunderstood and thought the Hopi word *móki,* meaning "death", was the tribe's name.

Location

The Hopi reservation is located in northeastern Arizona, just east of the Grand Canyon in the Four Corners area, where Arizona, Utah, Colorado, and New Mexico meet. Most of the twelve Hopi villages are situated atop three rocky mesas (called First Mesa, Second Mesa, and Third Mesa) that rise 600 feet (180 meters) from the desert floor. A mesa (the Spanish word for table) is a large hill with steep sides and a flat top. Some Hopi also live on the Colorado Indian Tribes Reservation in Parker, Arizona.

Population

In 1680, there were an estimated 2,800 Hopi. In the 1990 U.S. Census, 11,791 people identified themselves as Hopi. By the 2000 census, that figure had decreased to 10,336; of that number, 6,946 lived on the Hopi Reservation in Arizona. According to 2004 tribal records 12,053 Hopi were enrolled as tribal members. In 2011, tribal enrollment had reached 13,299.

Language family

Uto-Aztecan.

Origins and group affiliations

Scientists say the Hopi tribe has lived in its present location for at least one thousand years. Hopi tales tell how their ancestors developed from small creatures in another world. The Hopi are the westernmost of the Pueblo Indian tribes. The Hopi, however, are the only Pueblo people who speak a Shoshonean language of the Uto-Aztecan language family. Hopi

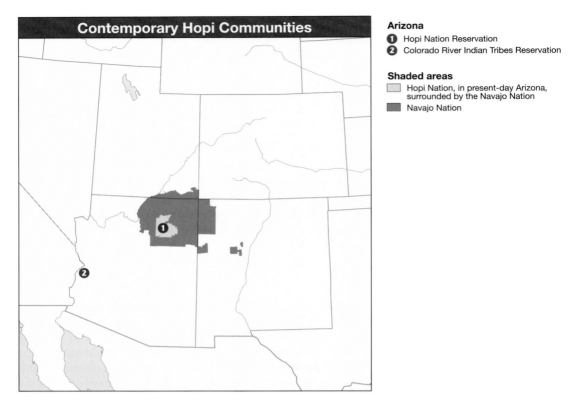

Contemporary Hopi Communities

Arizona
1. Hopi Nation Reservation
2. Colorado River Indian Tribes Reservation

Shaded areas
- Hopi Nation, in present-day Arizona, surrounded by the Navajo Nation
- Navajo Nation

A map of contemporary Hopi communities. MAP BY XNR PRODUCTIONS. CENGAGE LEARNING, GALE. REPRODUCED BY PERMISSION OF GALE, A PART OF CENGAGE LEARNING.

living on the Colorado Indian Tribes Reservation share the land with the Mohave, Navajo (see entries), and Chemehuevi. Over the years, the Hopi who live on the Hopi Reservation have struggled with the Navaho over land rights.

The Hopi people regard themselves as the first inhabitants of America. They excel at the challenge of farming and gardening in their extremely dry climate. According to this deeply religious tribe, their way of life focuses on humility, cooperation, respect, and caring for the earth. As Hopi traditional elder Thomas Banyacya said about his people: "Our goals are not to gain political control or monetary wealth, but to pray and to promote the welfare of all living beings and to preserve the world in a natural way." The Hopi's isolated location, customary secrecy, and the fact that their community remains largely closed to outsiders have helped preserve their culture.

HISTORY

Prior to Spanish contact

Most scholars believe that the region where the Hopi live has been occupied for at least ten thousand years. Evidence suggests that as far back as 1,500 years ago, ancestors of the Hopi made use of ceremonies, technology, and architecture very much like that seen on the Hopi reservation in modern times.

From 1350 to 1540, Hopi villages grew larger and required greater social organization. At that time, chieftains, or heads of the villages, expanded their power. The period also saw the first use of *kivas,* underground ceremonial chambers found in every village. In addition, coal was mined on tribal land, and the Hopi people were among the world's first to use coal for firing pottery to strengthen it.

Other Native nations call the Hopi, whose complex culture was firmly in place by the 1550s, "the oldest of the people." Their village of Oraibi dates back to at least 1550 and is the oldest continuously occupied settlement in the United States. Hopi traditions include an annual series of ceremonies and a social system based on clans (groups of related families that trace themselves back to a common ancestor).

An illustration made for a description of the ancient Hopi village of Oraibi by an observer in the 1870s show terraced houses and an entrance to a kiva in the foreground.

Important Dates

1540: The Hopi first meet Europeans when Spanish soldiers led by Coronado arrive.

1680: The Hopi and other Pueblo groups force the Spanish out of their area in the Pueblo Revolt.

1882: President Chester A. Arthur establishes the Hopi Indian Reservation.

1934: The Hopi Tribal Council starts to deal with Hopi-U.S. government relations.

1974: The Navajo-Hopi Settlement Act returns 900,000 acres to the Hopi that had been taken by the Navajo.

1996: The Navajo-Hopi Land Dispute Act allows more time for Navajos to relocate, but some stay and, with help of Hopi traditionalists, resist the desecration of Big Mountain.

Spanish impose Christianity

The Hopi had their first contact with Europeans in 1540 when a group of Spanish soldiers, led by explorer Francisco Vásquez de Coronado (c. 1510–1554), arrived in Hopi territory. They were looking for the legendary "Seven Cities of Gold"—places that were supposed to be full of riches. When the Spaniards searched and found no gold in Hopi villages, they destroyed part of a village and left. The Hopi did not face further interference from the Spanish until 1629, when the first Spanish missionaries arrived. These Roman Catholics built missions in Oraibi and at two other villages. Most tribal members pretended to adopt the new religion while practicing their own beliefs in secret.

Some Spaniards had come seeking gold, and they believed the tribe knew where it was located. Hopi oral tradition tells that the people were tortured to extract this nonexistent information. In addition, the priests banned Hopi rituals and ceremonies. The Hopi finally rebelled against Spanish rule and religious oppression when they joined the rest of the Pueblo people in a unified revolt known as the Pueblo Revolt of 1680. (For more information, see Pueblo entry.) During this uprising the Native allies took the lives of Catholic priests and Spanish soldiers and kept up a several-day attack on Santa Fe, New Mexico. After the battle, the Hopi returned to their villages and killed all the missionaries.

Spanish interference ends

To protect themselves from retaliation, the Hopi moved three of their villages to the mesa tops. The Spanish returned in 1692 and reconquered the nearby Rio Grande area. (The Rio Grande is the river that separates Mexico from Texas.) Many Natives from the region fled west to the Hopi lands, where they were welcomed. Over the next few years, a number of the people who lived at the Hopi village of Awatovi invited the Spanish priests back. This situation caused a serious break between those who wanted to preserve the old ways and those who embraced Christianity.

Finally, in 1700, Hopi supporters of the old ways killed all the Christian men in Awatovi and then destroyed the village.

The destruction of Awatovi marked the end of Spanish interference in Hopi life. For the most part, the Hopi had no further contact with outsiders until about 1850. At that time, the U.S. government appointed an Indian agent to oversee the Hopi and other Native inhabitants of the region. U.S. officials' visits to Hopi lands caused a terrible smallpox epidemic that killed hundreds of people in 1853 and 1854. A subsequent drought reduced the population of Oraibi from eight hundred people to two hundred. When the American Civil War (1861–65; a war between the Union [the North], which was opposed to slavery, and the Confederacy [the South], which was in favor of slavery) began, the military withdrew from the Southwest to fight the war. Without soldiers to stop them, the Navajo increased their attacks on Hopi villages.

Navajo intrusion

In 1882, aware that the Navajo were attacking the Hopi and taking over their land, U.S. president Chester A. Arthur (1829–1886; served 1881–85) ordered the establishment of the Hopi Reservation. He granted the tribe 2.6 million acres of land. Because of the wording of his order, however, Navajo takeover of Hopi land continued for nearly a century, until the passage of the Navajo-Hopi Indian Land Settlement Act of 1974. The act returned approximately half of the property in question to the Hopi. Some land disputes between the Hopi and Navajo, however, still remain unresolved (see "Current Tribal Issues").

In 1950, the U.S. Congress passed the Navajo-Hopi Act and spent $90 million to improve reservation facilities such as roads, schools, hospitals, water, electricity, and sewers. In 1961, the Hopi tribal council received permission to lease tribal lands to outsiders. As a result, the council allowed the Peabody Coal Company to lease 25,000 acres of land for mining, a process that began at Black Mesa in 1970 and has brought some money to the Hopi. Since the 1960s, farming has greatly decreased on Hopi lands, and by 1980, the major source of income had become wage labor (see "Economy").

In the first decades of the 2000s, most Hopi had jobs in area coal mines, in the service industry, or in the tourist trade. Many also worked as artists and craftspeople. One difficulty the Hopi find is that working for wages does not allow the necessary time for farming or participating in religious ceremonies. Nevertheless, most families try to maintain their culture in spite of the changes brought about by modern living.

RELIGION

Dependence on the gods

The Hopi religion is a highly developed belief system. It has many gods and spirits, including Earth Mother, Sky Father, the sun, the moon, and the many *kachinas,* or invisible spirits that inhabit living and nonliving things. The religion features a complex yearlong schedule of rituals, songs, recitations, and prayers.

The Hopi have long believed that the nonreligious elements of their lives must be based upon their religious patterns, the patterns of Creation. The Hopi are deeply connected to the earth. They have faith that if they perform their cycle of ceremonies successfully, the world will remain in harmony, the gods will be pleased, and sufficient rain will fall. In the 1990s, reports showed that more than 95 percent of the people remained faithful to their Hopi religious beliefs. Although some people have since converted to Christianity, the number of followers of the Hopi tradition was estimated to be close to 90 percent in 2011.

Kivas and prayer feathers

Central to the religious ceremonies of the Hopi are the kiva, the *paho,* and the Corn Mother. The kiva, an underground ceremonial chamber, is usually rectangular (although the ancient ones were circular) and is sunk into the village square. It symbolizes the place of emergence of the original Hopi people into this world. The kiva has a small hole in the floor that represents the entrance to the underworld and a ladder extending above the roof opening that represents the way to the upper world.

At the end of secret ceremonies held inside the kiva, ceremonial dances are performed in the square. The paho, a prayer feather, usually that of an eagle, is used to send prayers to the Creator. Pahos are used at all kiva ceremonies.

Corn Mother and kachinas

Corn, which has sustained the Hopi for centuries, plays a large role in Hopi ceremonies. For example, cornmeal is sprinkled to welcome the kachinas to the Corn Mother. The Corn Mother, who has been

Hopi Corn Dancers perform at an Intertribal Indian Ceremonial event in Gallup, New Mexico. © NORTH WIND PICTURE ARCHIVES.

described as "a perfect ear of corn whose tip ends in four full kernels," is saved for rituals.

Hopi kachinas are said to inhabit the sacred San Francisco Peaks. They come to live in Hopi villages for six months of the year to perform ceremonies and dances. They are mostly good spirits who have the power to pass on prayers for rain to the gods. Masked people dressed as these spirits perform the kachina dances, which are tied to the growing season, beginning in March and lasting into July.

LANGUAGE

The Hopi speak a single language, Hopi, a Shoshonean form of the Uto-Aztecan language family. Different Hopi groups have different dialects (varieties). For example, the Hopi people of the village of Hano speak *Tewa*, a Pueblo language derived from the *Azteco-Tanoan* language family.

The Powamu Ceremony and Bean Dance

The Hopi Powamu Ceremony is performed to request plentiful crops from the gods and to initiate children into a Kachina society. The sixteen-day rites begin during the new moon in February and prepare the Hopi and their dry lands for the upcoming planting season. Beans are blessed, planted in moist sand in boxes, and then grown in the hothouse environment of underground kivas. Ceremonies that center on planting are very important because they help seeds sprout and thrive when warm weather comes.

The Bean Dance celebrates the germination of the seeds. Kachinas dance into the village square along a path of cornmeal sprinkled before them by priests. The dancers call on the mysterious forces of nature and stay in the village for six months, dancing for rain, fertility, and other blessings.

The Crow Mother Kachina walks through the village on the last day of the Powamu Ceremony, carrying a basket of fresh bean sprouts that germinated in the kiva. These signify the abundance of crops to come. The Crow Mother is accompanied by her two sons, called the Whipper Twins. With eyes bulging and hair flying, they bare their teeth as they pretend to whip the children of the village with yucca fronds.

The Hopi language is difficult to translate, and only recently has it been written down. The strong Hopi oral tradition preserved it and passed it down from generation to generation, so that today, most Hopi, including the young people, still speak their language as well as English.

GOVERNMENT

Each independent Hopi village is governed by a *kikmongwi,* or village chief. Villages are only loosely connected politically as a confederation, although they have strong cultural connections in their shared history and religion and in the similarity of their ceremonies.

The Hopi tribe has always been organized according to a system of clans based on the mother's ancestry. In modern times, the people are part of some thirty clans. Clan membership helps to provide a singular Hopi identity. Although the Hopi Tribal Council has existed since 1934 to deal with matters between the Hopi and the federal government, it does not govern the tribe. The council is led by a chairperson and vice chairperson who serve four-year terms; council members serve two-year terms. Council members are either elected by their villages or appointed by the *kikmongwi*; only a few villages, though, send representatives to the council. Every village has its own government, but the Hopi Tribal Council sets general policies, oversees tribal business and laws, and represents the Hopi people in dealings with the external world.

In 2011, the majority of the Hopi rejected a new draft of their constitution. The original constitution drafted in 1936 contains the following provision: "Each village shall decide for itself how it shall be organized. ... and the Kikmongwi of such village shall be recognized as its leader." The new constitution called for a four-branched government, rather than the usual three-branched (executive, legislative, and judicial), with the villages as an additional branch. The traditional people did not want to give up village sovereignty, so they voted against the proposed changes.

ECONOMY

For many centuries, the Hopi stayed in one place and farmed. Men planted and harvested the crops, while women gathered other needed food. During a great drought from 1279 to 1299, the Hopi adopted inventive farming methods that took advantage of every possible source of moisture and are still in use today.

One Hopi irrigation method used wind to blow sand up against the sides of the mesas, forming dunes that trapped moisture. They planted crops in these dunes. Hopi farmers also planted in the dry washes (low ground that is flooded part of the time) as well as in the mouths of the streams. They sometimes irrigated crops by hand. The Hopi raised cotton in addition to edible crops, and men spun and wove cotton cloth into clothing and textiles for their own use and for trade.

In modern times, small farms and cattle and sheep ranches are a major part of the tribal economy. A number of people work on the reservation in the construction industry, either for private developers or for the tribal government. Tourism is also important as visitors come to see Hopi historical sites such as Oraibi Village or to discover more about Hopi farming techniques and life. Coal mining, arts and crafts, service businesses, and tribal government employ many people. Some have left the reservation to pursue careers.

DAILY LIFE

Families

Parents gave their children much love and attention to teach them the "Hopi Way" of peace and kindness. If a child or adult did not act according to these values, the tribe shunned them until they changed their behavior, but they quickly forgave those who repented. When children were bad, a scare-kachina with bulging eyes and long fangs often frightened them into better behavior.

Hopi Words

tiva	"dance"
tuwaki	"shrine in the kiva"
kahopi	"not Hopi"
kachada	"white man"
Hotomkam	"Three Stars in Line" or "Orion's Belt"
kachinki	"kachina house"
Hakomi?	"Who are you?"
Haliksa'i	"Listen, this is how it is"

Buildings

For centuries, Hopi villages were composed of houses built of local native stone and arranged around a center containing one or more kivas. Villages in the early twenty-first century are set up in much the same way.

From 1100 to 1300, the climate became drier, and people were forced to move into villages. It became difficult for farmers to grow enough food for everyone. To house the growing population, buildings in the villages grew larger, with some containing hundreds of rooms. Houses built from 1350 to 1540 were made of stone cemented with adobe (pronounced *uh-DOE-bee*; a sun-dried mud made of a mixture of clay, sand, and sometimes ashes, rocks, or straw) and then plastered inside. They were very similar to the older houses of present-day Hopi, except that they often had many stories. The houses of that time were heated with coal.

Currently, the Hopi live in both older-style houses and modern ones. The kiva remains largely the same as in ancient times: a rectangular room built of native stone, mostly below ground. Kivas are sometimes wider at one end to form the same "T" shape as the doorways found in all ancient Hopi ruins. Each kiva contains an altar and a central fire pit below the roof opening, with a ladder extending above the edge of the roof.

Clothing and adornment

In earlier times, Hopi men wore fur or buckskin loincloths (flaps of material that covered the front and back and were suspended from the waist). Some loincloths were painted and decorated with tassels, which symbolized falling rain. The men also wove robes and blankets out of the cotton they grew. Observers in 1861 reported that women wore loose black gowns with a gold stripe around the waist and at the hem, whereas men wore shirts, loose cotton pants, and a blanket around their shoulders.

Married women wore their long hair straight or in braids. Unmarried girls wore their hair in large twists on either side of their heads in a shape that resembled a squash blossom, a symbol of fertility. Unmarried women wear this time-consuming hairstyle today, but only for ceremonies. Some Hopi men still wear the traditional male hairstyle with straight bangs over the forehead and a knot of hair in the back with the sides hanging straight and covering the ears.

In modern times, some Hopi women and girls still wear the traditional Hopi dress, which is black and embroidered with bright red and green trim. For ceremonies and dances, Hopi men wear elaborate costumes that feature special headdresses, masks, and body paints. The costumes vary according to clan and ceremony.

Food

In earlier days, the staple crops of the Hopi were corn, squash, beans, and some wild and semi-cultivated plants such as Indian millet and wild potato. Salt was obtained during long, difficult excursions to the Grand Canyon area. Hopi women gathered piñon, prickly pear, yucca, berries, currants, nuts, and various seeds. In the sixteenth century, the Spanish introduced wheat, onions, chilies, mutton (sheep meat), peaches, and other fruits into the Hopi diet.

Many modern Hopi farmers still use the old methods of cultivation. They primarily raise corn, melons, gourds, and many varieties of beans. The six traditional Hopi varieties of corn include yellow, blue, red, white, purple, and sweet. Corn is ground for use in ceremonies, such as the annual corn roast, as well as to make *piki,* a traditional bread baked in layers on hot stones.

Hundreds of years ago, wild game was more plentiful than it is today, and Hopi men hunted deer, antelope, and elk. They also hunted rabbit using boomerangs (flat, curved sticks that can be thrown so that they will return near the thrower). By 1950, wild game had dwindled, leaving only rabbit and a few quail and deer.

Education

The Hopi made use of the interactive method of learning—speaking and listening. This was their main method for teaching their children about the Hopi ways. To teach their children about religion, parents gave them dolls called *tithu,* not as toys but as symbols of the *katsinum,* or kachinas. The first doll they received stood for *Hahai'i wuhti,* the mother of the *katsinum.*

The Hopi have always had a strong interest in education, and in 1886. a group of Hopi leaders requested that the Bureau of Indian Affairs build a school for their children. The following year, Keams Canyon Boarding School opened, and some Hopi families sent their children to the school, where they were taught English and Christianity. Traditionalists did not want their children to lose their own customs and language, so they did not cooperate, even when the government made school attendance mandatory. This issue was part of a larger conflict between the traditionalists, who wanted to maintain the old ways, and progressives, who wanted to adapt to mainstream society (see "Traditionalists vs Progressives" sidebar),

Traditionalists vs Progressives

During the 1800s, the Hopi experienced a major division in their tribe. Some people wanted to embrace the ways of the settlers and become more like them. They asked the Bureau of Indian Affairs for schools for their children, and they agreed with the U.S. government plans. Their cooperation earned them the nickname "friendlies," or progressives.

Other Hopi opposed the modernization of their land. They did not want mining or electrical lines on their lands, nor did they want to adopt American ways. They clung to their traditional beliefs and ways of doing things. When the government school opened, these Hopi refused to send their children. Because of their resistance to mainstream society, the traditionalists were sometimes called "hostiles."

The two groups often came into conflict with each other. When they did, the U.S. government sided with the progressives because those Hopi were acting in what the Indian agents called a "civilized manner," meaning the Hopi were following customary American behavior. Tensions reached a high point when, after disobeying orders to send their children to the reservation school, the traditionalists planted wheat on land that the progressives had been using. Although the land originally had belonged to the traditionalists, the U.S. government got involved in the dispute and sent troops to the area. They arrested nineteen men and shipped them to Alcatraz, a maximum security prison on an island off San Francisco, hoping to coerce the traditionalists into cooperating with the government.

and it led the government to arrest and imprison nineteen Hopi men who refused to comply with the order. After the children of the traditionalists had been sent to boarding school, most were not allowed to go home for summer vacation because administrators feared they might not return.

In modern times, Hopi children are educated at public schools on the reservation as well as at the boarding school in Kearns Canyon and a community college nearby. A partnership between Northland Pioneer College, Northern Arizona University, and the Hopi Nation allows students to take college classes while they are in high school. After they graduate, they may have as many as thirty college credit hours; this allows them to skip several college semesters. Not only does this program, called "Two Plus Two Plus Two," encourage students to go on to college, but it also lowers the costs of getting a college education.

Healing practices

Many Hopi healing methods rely on the power of suggestion—the fact that people often feel better if something is said or done to make them believe they will get better. The Hopi are also knowledgeable about the healing properties of certain plants and herbs.

Several healing societies perform curing rituals; some concentrate on only one type of illness. For example, snakebite is treated by the Snake Society on First Mesa, whereas rheumatism (muscle or joint discomfort) is treated by the Powamu Society.

Sometimes people become members of curing societies after suffering an accident or illness. For example, lightning-shocked people and those whose fields have been lightning-struck join the Flute Society, whose members can cure ear aches in babies. Other healers can suck out diseases from infants and children by holding cornmeal in their mouths and symbolically "spitting away" the disease. Certain kachina dances (including the Horned Water Serpent and the Buffalo Dance) are held specifically to help afflicted persons.

In addition to these age-old healing techniques, modern-day Hopi use medical science, including the services of doctors and hospitals. There are health clinics on the reservation and hospitals nearby. The U.S. Indian Health Service provides mental health services and substance-abuse programs.

ARTS

Hopi women make fine multicolored pottery. They also produce traditional textiles for trade or sale, Hopi kachina dolls, hand-woven baskets, and ornate jewelry. Each mesa is known for a particular art.

Oral literature

Hopi stories present tribal knowledge in such a way that both children and adults can learn something new at each hearing. Every clan has its own stories with information valuable to its members, and people learn only the stories of their clan. The tales contain more than enough truth to ponder for a lifetime. The Hopi consider their stories sacred and private.

CUSTOMS

Naming ceremonies

Newborn babies are kept out of the sun for their first nineteen days, then a naming ceremony is held. When sunlight touches the infant on the twentieth day, the child receives a name. A baby belongs to

Hopi Origin Tale

Hopi oral history teaches that their people originated in the first of Four Worlds, not as people but as insect-like creatures who fought among themselves. Displeased that the creatures did not grasp the true meaning of life, the Creator, the sun spirit *Tawa*, sent Spider Woman, another spirit, to guide them on a journey. By the time they reached the Third World, they were human beings. They reached the Fourth, or Upper World, by climbing up from the underworld through a hollow reed.

When the Hopi reached the Fourth World, they were given four stone tablets by *Masaw*, the spirit that protected the world and taught the people the proper way to live. Masaw described the travels they were to take—to the ends of the land in each of the four directions and how in time they would find the place where they were meant to settle.

As the migrations began, various clans started out in each direction. Their routes eventually formed a cross, the center of which was the Center of the Universe, their intended permanent home. According to this Hopi account of creation, their journeys finally led them to the plateau that lies between the Colorado River and the Rio Grande, in the Four Corners region (where Arizona, Utah, Colorado, and New Mexico meet). The people believe they were led there so that the scanty rainfall would encourage them to pray and remain close to the Creator to fulfill their needs.

Because the number four holds great significance in the Hopi religion, many ritual customs often call for repetitions of four.

its mother's clan, but it is named for the father's. Since one cannot be Hopi without a clan of birth, if the mother is not Hopi, neither are her children.

For the ceremony, a traditional stew is prepared at the home of a baby's maternal grandmother (mother's mother). During the naming ritual, the grandmother kneels and washes the mother's hair, then bathes the new baby, who is wrapped snugly in a blanket with only its head visible. Using a special ear of corn called the Corn Mother, the grandmother rubs a mixture of water and cornmeal into the baby's hair, applying it four times. Each of the baby's paternal aunts (from the father's side) also does the same, and each gives a gift and suggests a name. The grandmother chooses one of the names and then introduces the baby to the sun god just as the sun comes up. A feast follows the naming ceremony.

Adolescence

Both boys and girls are initiated into a kachina cult between the ages of eight and ten. The initiation ceremony includes fasting, praying, and a light whipping with yucca leaves. Each child is assigned a ceremonial mother (for the girls) or father (for the boys), who sees them through the ordeal. Boys usually join the society of their ceremonial fathers. There are four such societies—*Kwan, Ahl, Tao,* and *Wuwutcimi.* Joining one of these groups is part of the *Powamu* ceremony, a four-day tribal initiation rite for young men that traditionally takes place at planting time.

Ten-year-old girls once took part in a ceremony that involved grinding corn for an entire day at the girl's paternal grandmother's house. Some girls ground corn for four days to mark their first menstrual period. They then received a new name and adopted the squash blossom hairstyle (see "Clothing and adornment").

Festivals

The cycles of Hopi rituals are conducted in secrecy within the kivas. The dances that follow in the village square are rhythmic, mystical, and colorful. Outsiders are sometimes allowed to watch them.

One of the most important Hopi ceremonies is held at the winter solstice (the time when the sun is farthest south of the equator). This ceremony, called the *Soyal,* is the first ceremony of the year and the first kachina dance. The people believe this ceremony will make the sun return sooner. The Niman Ceremony or Home Dance, the last kachina dance of the year, is held in thanksgiving at the summer solstice (when the sun is closest to the equator). By this time, the last of the crops have been planted and the first corn has been harvested.

Hopi Snake Dancers perform with live and poisonous rattlesnakes, which are set free after the ceremony. © MARY EVANS PICTURE LIBRARY/THE IMAGE WORKS.

Other dances of less religious importance are the Buffalo Dance, held in January to commemorate the days when buffalo were plentiful; the Bean Dance, held in February to ask the kachinas to bless the next planting; and the Navajo Dance, which celebrates the neighboring Navajo tribe.

The relatively short (one hour) Snake Dance is preceded by eight days of secret preparations. During this rite, priests handle and even put snakes in their mouths. The secret of how they do this without being bitten has never been revealed to outsiders. At the end of the dance, the snakes are released back into the desert to ensure that the rains will come. Alternating every other year with the Snake Dance is the Flute Dance, which honors the spirits of people who have died during the preceding two years. Women's dances, such as the Basket Dance, are held near the end of the year.

Courtship and marriage

Some of the ancient Hopi marriage customs still survive, but many have fallen into disuse. For example, around 1950, courtship was still an elaborate procedure that involved a rabbit hunt and corn grinding, and marriages could only take place with family approval. A bride wore a traditional white tasseled robe, woven for the occasion by her uncles. She carried a similar, smaller white robe rolled up in a type of suitcase. This gown later served as her burial clothes. The young couple lived with the mother of the bride during their first year together.

In modern times, courtship is much less formal. Couples are often married in church or by a town official and then return to the reservation. Since many men no longer know how to weave, most uncles do not make the traditional robes.

There are several Hopi marriage customs still practiced in the early twenty-first century. A bride-to-be stays with her future in-laws for four days. During this period, she grinds corn all day and prepares the meals to show that she knows how to cook. Prior to the wedding, the aunts of the bride and groom participate in a good-natured free-for-all, throwing mud and trading insults, each suggesting that the other side is no good. Then the groom's parents use yucca for a ceremonial washing of the couple's hair. A huge feast follows at the house of the bride's mother.

Clan membership continues to play a role in partner selection. There are still rules that discourage marrying into one's own clan, but such marriages are no longer forbidden. The fact that marriage to nontribal members is extremely rare has helped to preserve Hopi culture.

Funerals

Among the Hopi it is desirable to grow old because the journey of life is almost complete, and the soul will go on to a better place. Because they believe the soul's journey to the land of the dead begins on the fourth day after death, bodies are customarily buried as quickly as possible. Any delay in burial could interfere with the soul's ability to reach the underworld.

A paternal aunt washes the hair of the deceased with yucca shampoo, and she decorates the hair with prayer feathers and covers the face with a mask of raw cotton that symbolizes clouds. The body is wrapped—a man's in a deerskin robe and a woman's in her wedding robe. The oldest son buries the corpse in a sitting position along with food, water, and cornmeal. Finally, a stick is inserted into the soil of the grave, creating a place for the soul to exit. If rain follows, it signifies that the soul has experienced a successful journey.

CURRENT TRIBAL ISSUES

Land claims

When the Hopi Reservation was originally established in 1882, nearly 2.5 million acres were set aside in northeastern Arizona for the Hopi and whatever other Native peoples the federal government settled there. The Hopi Reservation was centered within a larger area that the Hopi considered to be their ancestral land, but it was designated the Navajo Reservation.

As their population increased, the Navajo expanded their settlements beyond their own borders and onto the Hopi Reservation. The situation went on for many decades. Although the Hopi complained, the U.S. government failed to act. In time, the Navajo took over 1.8 million acres of the land originally designated for the Hopi, leaving the tribe with only about 600,000 acres. Recognizing the problem, Congress passed the Navajo-Hopi Settlement Act in 1974. The act returned 900,000 acres to the Hopi, but the dispute over resettlement and the remaining 900,000 original acres continued. In 1996, the Navajo-Hopi Land Dispute Act reaffirmed that the land belonged to the Hopis, but it allowed more time for Navajos to relocate. Some Navajos remained, however, and the question of land ownership remains ongoing. Being landlocked by the Navajo reservation also causes difficulties for the Hopi because it prevents access to businesses and industries on Hopi land.

Preserving the "Hopi Way"

Concerns about the preservation of the "Hopi Way" have divided the tribe into two factions: traditionalists and progressives. Traditionalists, who want to keep the old ways, fear that modern influences will break down Hopi culture. Conversely, progressives feel that adopting some aspects of current American life is necessary if the tribe is to survive and grow.

Hopi people are disturbed that the privacy surrounding their rites and practices has been violated for the benefit of non-Hopi people. For example, stories told to visitors and photographs of rites have been published in books without permission, observers have taped Hopi ceremonies and sold the tapes to the public, clothing and ceremonial dance steps have been copied and sold in nonsacred settings, and designs from Hopi potters and kachina doll makers have been reproduced.

In 2011, the Hopi asserted their views on village sovereignty (self-government) by voting down proposed changes to their 1936 constitution (see "Government"). The majority wanted to keep the original style of government rather than adopting a form of government similar to other Native nations.

Environmental concerns

Coal mines have changed the Black Mesa area. They pump a large amount of water daily from the ground. Large sinkholes have opened in the ground, some as deep as thirty feet. Experts say this could indicate that the water is drying up. If so, it could mean forced relocation for the tribe. As of 2005, the Navajo Nation Council voted to stop the water pumping done by Peabody Energy, which was expected reduce future problems, but recovery of the land is still a problem.

Reclaiming the land stripped by the mines is another ongoing project. Holes are filled with dirt and rocks. They are then reshaped so they look similar to the original landscape, and twenty pounds of seeds per acre are sown. It will take many years before the land is restored to its original condition. Meanwhile, new areas are being mined that will also require extensive cleanup and reclamation.

Another major concern in this arid area is water. In addition to ensuring safe drinking water by monitoring for contamination, the tribe is working to identify dependable, long-term water supplies that will meet future needs.

NOTABLE PEOPLE

Louis Tewanima (c. 1879–1969) was a world-class Hopi athlete. He won a record-setting silver medal in the 1912 Olympic Games in Stockholm, Sweden, in the 10,000-meter race. Tewanima returned to his home on the reservation to tend sheep and raise crops, but still kept active well into his nineties. In 1954, he was named to the All-Time United States

Olympic Track and Field Team. In 1957, he was the first person to be inducted into the new Arizona Sports Hall of Fame.

Hopi Charles Loloma (1921–1991) designed jewelry that is among the most distinctive in the world. His unique designs combined non-traditional materials such as gold and diamonds with typical Hopi materials like turquoise. Loloma also received great recognition as a potter, silversmith, designer, and painter of murals.

Other notable Hopi include the first Hopi to receive a doctorate in sciences, the geneticist Frank C. Dukepoo (1943–99; Pu-mat-uh-ye-Aye Tsi Dukpuh); the traditional artist Fred Kabotie (c. 1900–86); the "single most influential Indian woman creator in clay," Otellie Loloma (1922–92); the award-winning artist and teacher Linda Loma-haftewa (1947–); a ceramicist who helped revive Indian arts, Nampeyo, (c.1860–1942); an influential periodical publisher and editor who helped tribal communities locate funding, Rose Robinson (1932–95); the anthologized poet Wendy Rose (1948–); and the weaver Ramona Sakiestewa (1949–).

BOOKS

Anthony, Alexander E., Jr., David Neil Sr., and J. Brent Ricks. *Kachinas: Spirit Beings of the Hopi.* Albuquerque, NM: Avanyu Publishing, 2006.

Benally, Malcolm D., ed. and trans. *Bitter Water: Dinè Oral Histories of the Navajo-Hopi Land.* Tucson: University of Arizona Press, c. 2011.

Bjorklund, Ruth. *The Hopi.* Tarrytown, NY: Marshall Cavendish Benchmark, c. 2009.

Bonvillain, Nancy, and Ada Deer. *The Hopi.* Minneapolis, MN: Chelsea House Publications, 2005.

Fewkes, Jesse Walter. *Hopi Snake Ceremonies: An Eyewitness Account.* Albuquerque, NM: Avanyu Publishing, 2000.

Gilbert, Matthew Sakiestewa. *Education beyond the Mesas: Hopi Students at the Sherman Institute, 1902–1929.* Lincoln: University of Nebraska, 2010.

Kavasch, E. Barrie. *Enduring Harvests: Native American Foods and Festivals for Every Season.* Old Saybrook, CT: The Globe Pequot Press, 1995.

Koyiyumptewa, Stewart B., Carolyn O'Bagy Davis, and the Hopi Cultural Preservation Office. *The Hopi People.* Charleston, SC: Arcadia Publishing, 2009.

Lockett, Hattie Greene. *The Unwritten Literature of the Hopi.* Boston: Qontro Classic Books, 2010.

Parsons, Elsie Clews. *Hopi and Zuñi Ceremonialism.* New York: Harper and Bros., 1950. Reprint. Millwood, NY: Kraus Reprint, 1976.

Pritzker, Barry, and Paul C. Rosier. *The Hopi.* New York: Chelsea House, c. 2011.

Silas, Anna. *Journey to Hopi Land.* Tucson, AZ: Rio Nuevo Publishers, 2006.

Stirling, M.W. *Snake Bites and the Hopi Snake Dance.* Whitefish, MT: Kessinger Publishing, 2011.

Stout, Mary. *Hopi History and Culture.* New York: Gareth Stevens, 2011.

Thompson, Laura. *Culture in Crisis: A Study of the Hopi Indians.* Ann Arbor, MI: University Microfilms, 1969.

Waters, Frank. *Book of the Hopi.* New York: Viking Press, 1963.

Wright, Barton. *Clowns of the Hopi: Tradition Keepers and Delight Makers.* Walnut, CA: Kiva Publishing, 2004.

WEB SITES

"About the Hopi." Restoration. http://hopi.org/about-the-hopi/ (accessed on July 20, 2011).

Banyacya, Thomas. "Message to the World." *Hopi Traditional Elder.* http://banyacya.indigenousnative.org/ (accessed on July 20, 2011).

"Camp Grant Massacre—April 30, 1871." *Council of Indian Nations.* http://www.nrcprograms.org/site/PageServer?pagename=cin_hist_campgrantmassacre (accessed on July 20, 2011).

Center for American Indian Economic Development. "Hopi Tribe, Hopi Reservation." *Northern Arizona University.* http://www.cba.nau.edu/caied/tribepages/Hopi.asp (accessed on July 20, 2011).

Cline Library. "Indigenous Voices of the Colorado Plateau: Hopi." *Northern Arizona University.* http://library.nau.edu/speccoll/exhibits/indigenous_voices/hopi/overview.html (accessed on July 20, 2011).

Eck, Pam. "Hopi Indians." *Indiana University.* http://inkido.indiana.edu/w310work/romac/hopi.htm (accessed on July 20, 2011).

Gilbert, Matthew Sakiestewa, "Letter to Hopi and Tewa People Regarding Hopi Constitution." *Beyond the Mesas.* January 21, 2011. http://beyondthemesas.com/2011/01/22/letter-to-hopi-and-tewa-people-by-benjamin-h-nuvamsa/ (accessed on July 20, 2011).

Holzman, Allan. "Beyond the Mesas [video]." *University of Illinois.* http://www.vimeo.com/16872541 (accessed on July 20, 2011).

Holzman, Allan. "The Indian Boarding School Experience [video]." *University of Illinois.* http://www.vimeo.com/17410552 (accessed on July 20, 2011).

"Hopi." *Four Directions Institute.* http://www.fourdir.com/hopi.htm (accessed on July 20, 2011).

"Hopi." *Southwest Crossroads.* http://southwestcrossroads.org/search.php?query=hopi&tab=document&doc_view=10 (accessed on July 20, 2011).

"Hopi Indian Tribal History." *Access Genealogy.* www.accessgenealogy.com/native/tribes/hopi/hopeindianhist.htm (accessed on July 20, 2011).

"Hopi Pueblo Pottery Collection." *ClayHound Web.* http://www.clayhound.us/sites/hopi.htm (accessed on July 20, 2011).

"Hopi Tribe." *Inter Tribal Council of Arizona, Inc.* http://www.itcaonline.com/tribes_hopi.html (accessed on July 20, 2011).

National Park Service. "Alcatraz Island: Hopi Prisoners on the Rock." *U.S. Department of the Interior.* http://www.nps.gov/alca/historyculture/hopi-prisoners-on-the-rock.htm (accessed on July 20, 2011).

"The Official Hopi Cultural Preservation Office." *Northern Arizona University.* http://www.nau.edu/hcpo/index.html#table (accessed on July 20, 2011).

"People of the Colorado Plateau: The Hopi." *Northern Arizona University.* http://www.cpluhna.nau.edu/People/hopi.htm (accessed on July 20, 2011).

"Proposed Hopi Constitution." Hopi Tribal Operations Office. http://www.hopiwethepeople.org/ (accessed on July 20, 2011).

"The Pueblo Revolt against the Spanish: A First Mesa Account." *Southwest Crossroads.* http://southwestcrossroads.org/record.php?num=553&hl=hopi (accessed on July 20, 2011).

Redish, Laura, and Orrin Lewis. "Hopi Indian Fact Sheet." *Native Languages of the Americas.* http://www.bigorrin.org/hopi_kids.htm (accessed on July 20, 2011).

Smith, L. Michael. "Hopi." *Four Corners Post Card.* http://www.ausbcomp.com/redman/hopi.htm (accessed on July 20, 2011).

"Vocabulary Words in Native American Languages: Hopi." *Native American Language Net.* http://www.native-languages.org/hopi_words.htm (accessed on July 20, 2011).

Weiser, Kathy. "The Hopi—Peaceful Ones of the Southwest." *Legends of America.* http://www.legendsofamerica.com/na-hopi.html (accessed on July 20, 2011).

Mohave

Name

Several meanings for the name Mohave, or Mojave (both pronounced *moe-HAH-vee*), have been suggested. It may come from the Native word *hamakhava,* which means "mountain peaks," referring to the Needles, mountain peaks in California, or it may come from the word *ahamakav* or *ahamecav,* which means "people who live along the river." The people call themselves *'Aha Makhav* or *Pipa Aha Macav,* which means "people by the river."

Location

The Mohave lived in sprawling settlements on both sides of the Colorado River, which separates California and Arizona and extends into lower Nevada. Their homeland was once about 200 miles (320 kilometers) long and 25 miles (40 kilometers) wide. Modern-day members of the tribe live with descendants of three other tribes—Chemehuevi, Hopi, and Navajo—on or near the 270,000-acre Colorado River Indian Tribes Reservation (located mostly in Arizona, with about 43,000 acres on the California side). The people of that reservation are collectively known as Colorado River Indians. Other Mohave live on or near Fort Mohave Reservation, which has acreage in California, Arizona, and Nevada, and tribal offices in Needles, California. Some members of the tribe live on the Fort McDowell reservation in Arizona along with the Apache and Yavapai.

Population

In 1800, there were about 3,000 Mohave. In 1900, there were about 2,000, with 500 on the Colorado River Reservation, about 1,000 near Fort Mohave, Arizona, and about 200 in Needles, California. In the 1990 U.S. Census, 1,645 people identified themselves as Colorado River Indians; no one identified themselves as Mohave. The 2000 census showed 1,707 Colorado River Indians in the United States; of those, 1,412 lived in Arizona. Population for the Fort Mojave Indian Tribe of Arizona was 1,519. In 2011, the Colorado River Indian Tribes had 3,500 enrolled members.

Language family

Yuman.

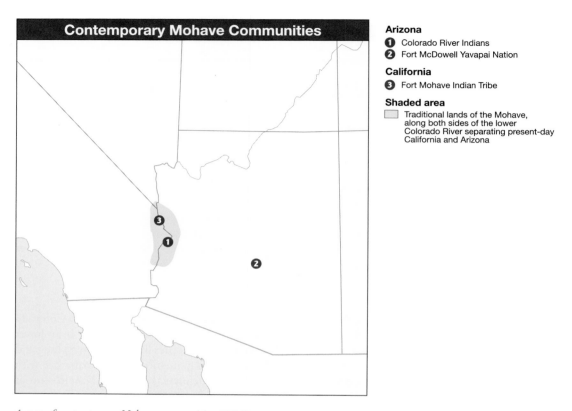

A map of contemporary Mohave communities. MAP BY XNR PRODUCTIONS. CENGAGE LEARNING, GALE. REPRODUCED BY PERMISSION OF GALE, A PART OF CENGAGE LEARNING.

Origins and group affiliations

The Mohave were the largest of the Yuman-speaking tribes living along both sides of the lower Colorado River. (The other Yuman-speaking tribes were the Yavapai, Maricopa, Quechan, Hualapai, Havasupai, Paipai, Kumeyaay, Cocopá, and Kiliwa) The Mohave were a desert people descended from the Patayan of late prehistoric times. Most Mohave migrated to the Mohave Valley (where Fort Mohave Reservation now stands) from the Mohave Desert to the east, settling along the Colorado River around 1150. The tribe later divided into two factions or groups: one preferred peace with whites and neighboring tribes; the other favored war.

Friends and allies of the Mohave included the Quechan, Yavapai, Cahuilla (see entry), Chemehuevi (a Southern Paiute tribe; see Paiute entry), and Tipai-Ipai. Their enemies included the Halchidhoma, Maricopa, Cocopa, Pima (see entry), Tohono O'odham (see entry), and, occasionally, the Walapai.

An illustration of two Mohave warriors and a Mohave woman shows them with elaborate tattoos covering most of their bodies. © MARY EVANS PICTURE LIBRARY/THE IMAGE WORKS.

The Mohave have lived, they say, longer than anyone—living or dead—could ever remember in a hot, dry area made fertile by the yearly flooding of the Colorado River. An active and adventurous people, they made a name for themselves as expert runners. The Mohave traveled far and wide to trade and created a trail to the Pacific Coast that U.S. settlers later found useful. The tribe was feared because of its fierce warriors. Although trappers and settlers characterized them as warlike, the majority of the Mohave preferred peace. Most attacks were carried out by *kawanamis,* or "brave men." These were professional warriors who had special dreams that encouraged fighting. Reports of their attacks

Important Dates

1827: A battle breaks out between the Mohave and Jedediah Smith's expedition.

1858: Fort Mohave is established to protect American settlers from Indian attacks.

1859: The Mohave are defeated, ending resistance against U.S. settlement.

1865: The Colorado River Reservation is established, with acreage in Arizona and California.

1870: Fort Mohave Reservation is established, with acreage in California, Arizona, and Nevada.

c. 1945: Members of the Hopi and Navajo tribes join the Mohave and Chemehuevi on the Colorado River Indian Tribes Reservation.

1963: The Colorado River Indian Tribes win an important water rights case, and reservation economy improves.

1983: The state of California passes legislation calling for the development of a radioactive waste depository. Ward Valley, 22 miles from Fort Mohave Indian Reservation, is chosen as the site. Native opposition to the proposal begins.

on California-bound wagon trains brought the Mohave to the attention of the U.S. military, and by 1865, they were being settled on reservations. There the people lived unhappily and impoverished for many years. By the late 1990s, though, with modern irrigation methods in place for more than thirty-five years, the Mohave enjoyed considerable prosperity.

HISTORY

Uneventful contacts with Spanish

Long before the Spanish first saw them, the Mohave were a large, unified tribe, even though families lived on sprawling, individually owned farms rather than in villages. Their lives were simple and marked by few ceremonies or festivals. The Mohave people came together to defend their territory or to attack other tribes. The first overwhelming threat to their way of life came hundreds of years after their first contact with Europeans.

The tribe first encountered the Spanish in 1604, when Juan de Oñate (1552–1626) of Mexico explored the region where the Colorado and Bill Williams Rivers come together. It was another 172 years before the Spanish actually reached the Mohave Valley. When a Spanish priest, Father Francisco Garcés (1738–1781), arrived in 1776, he estimated the Mohave population to be three thousand. As far as the Spanish were concerned, however, the Mohave Valley was too dry, barren, and remote to be of any interest. Contact between the two groups remained minimal, except for an occasional Mohave raid for horses at Spanish missions in California.

War with outsiders

During the 1820s, American fur trappers traveled through Mohave country, prompting considerable bloodshed. One of the best-known battles occurred in August 1827 when the Mohave nearly wiped out a trapping expedition led by American fur trader and explorer Jedediah Smith (1799–1831). In 1851, the tribe attacked a group led by Lorenzo Sitgreaves (1810–1888), who was looking for a route for a transcontinental (spanning the nation from coast to coast) railroad. At other times, the tribe cooperated with outsiders. They guided an expedition of U.S. travelers through the desert to the Pacific Coast from 1853 to 1854, but when faced with the destruction of their natural resources by outsiders, they defended their territory.

Throughout the early period of American trapping and westward expansion, the Mohave also warred with neighboring tribes. Between 1827 and 1829, they fought the Halchidhoma, who invaded their land. The Mohave expelled the tribe from their valley. The Mohave later permitted the poverty-stricken Chemehuevi to occupy their lands until war broke out between the tribes in 1865. The Chemehuevi were driven back into the desert, but they reached peace with the Mohave in 1867.

The Mohave suffered a disastrous military defeat at the hands of the Pima and Maricopa tribes in 1857, but they persisted with attacks on U.S. settlers. Their 1858 attack on a wagon train bound for California was a call to action for the U.S. military. It resulted in the establishment of a U.S. Army post in the Mohave Valley for the protection of American settlers. (This post was later named Fort Mohave.) The post's commander was ordered to bring the Mohave into "submission." Mohave resistance did not end until many Mohave warriors had been slain by American soldiers in an 1859 battle.

Reservation lands lost

The Colorado River Indian Reservation was established in 1865 for all the Native peoples living along the Colorado River and its tributaries. The Mohave and the Chemehuevi were confined to nearly 270,000 acres on both sides of the river. The government promised to build modern irrigation works on the reservation, and Mohave Chief Irretaba settled there with a fairly large group of people. Another Mohave chief named Hamoseh Quahote, along with a great majority of the tribe, refused to leave the Mohave Valley. Later, after a railroad was built through Mohave lands, some Native people changed their minds and moved south to the Colorado River Indian Reservation. Those who remained behind were settled at Fort Mohave Reservation, established in 1870, where they endured prejudice and humiliation by U.S. settlers.

Two Mohave men in western Arizona, circa 1870.
NATIONAL ARCHIVES AMERICAN INDIAN SELECT LIST PHOTO NUMBER 136.

The Mohave had been on their reservations for only a short time before their lands were reduced. By 1887, the Santa Fe Railroad company owned a large portion of Fort Mohave Reservation land.

In 1941, when the Japanese bombed Pearl Harbor, Hawaii, and the United States entered World War II (1939–45; a war in which Great Britain, France, the United States, and their allies defeated Germany, Italy, and Japan), the federal government interned Japanese Americans, confining them to camps because of their race. (The government feared that Americans of Japanese descent might help Japan invade the United States, although no evidence of this ever existed.) Many Japanese Americans were detained at the Colorado River Indian Tribes Reservation. In return for accommodating these prisoners, the U.S. War Department promised the Native nations it would not keep the land permanently and would make land and irrigation improvements on the reservation.

After World War II, the United States developed a new policy of moving "surplus" Indians from one reservation to another. The government offered farming land on the Colorado River Indian Reservation to some Hopi and Navajo (see entries), and some members of those tribes are now considered Colorado River Indians.

Government "civilizes" Mohave

As the Mohave mourned the loss of their ancient homeland, the government set about assimilating them by educating them in American culture and religion. Schools and churches were built, and the Native people were instructed in modern farming techniques. Between 1870 and 1890, the Mohave were plagued by disease and poverty. Improved irrigation methods brought some prosperity in the twentieth century, but much of the tribe's traditional culture has been lost over the years.

RELIGION

The Mohave believe they were sent forth from Avikomé Spirit Mountain (Mt. Newberry in Nevada) by their spiritual guides, Mutavilya and Mastamho, to be the earth's caretakers. Mutavilya built a Great Dark House, the place where the first Mohave dreamers received knowledge from their spirit guides.

The people have always relied upon dreams for spiritual guidance and knowledge. All the talents, skills, and successes they enjoy in life are received in dreams. Great dreams came only to a few chiefs, braves, healers, and singers who had to perform courageous deeds to show their dreams were real. According to Mohave beliefs, these great dreams first occurred in the womb, were forgotten, and then reoccurred in adolescence. The Mohave had few religious ceremonies; religious expression occurred mainly through songs. (See "Oral literature.")

The Mohave believed that four days after a body was cremated (burned), the spirit went to the land of the dead, where deceased relatives met the ghost. A pleasant, pain-free period followed, with plenty of good things to eat. The soul then died again and was cremated by other ghosts, repeating the cycle until, eventually, the soul turned to charcoal

Mojave Words	
a'avk	"hear"
aha	"water"
amam	"eat"
'anya	"sun"
haly'a	"moon"
hatchoq	"dog"
'iipa	"man"
isvark	"sing"
iyuuk	"see"
thinya'aak	"woman"

in the desert. The Mohave who had not been tattooed in life were thought to pass down a rat hole at death.

Religious leaders, whose names meant the "one who is good," gave feasts and hosted victory celebrations. The importance of these leaders declined after European contact, when public religious ceremonies began to vanish in Mohave life.

Christian missionaries came to the reservations to convert the Mohave at the beginning of the twentieth century. The first Presbyterian church was built in 1914, and many other groups have had an influence on the tribe since then. Religious denominations with followers on the reservations include Catholics, Pentecostals, Mormons, and Jehovah's Witnesses. Some Mohave still practice their Native religion.

LANGUAGE

The Mohave are regarded as the first speakers of the Yuman (see entry) language. In 1997, about 5 percent of Fort Mohave tribal members still spoke the language; the figure at the Colorado River Indian Reservation was 15 percent. In addition to English, many tribal members speak Spanish. Efforts to revive the Native language have been undertaken by Fort Mohave's Aha Makav Cultural Society. According to studies done by the Summer Language Institute (SIL) International in 2000, most adults on the reservation speak Mohave, but many children do not.

GOVERNMENT

The Mohave did not have a formal government but were a unified tribe and joined together in defense against enemies. Long ago, any man who had special power bestowed on him in a dream claimed the position of head chief, but at some point in the tribe's history, the position became hereditary, passed down from father to son. Although they had a chief, no single person or group held a great deal of power over any other. The tribal chief served mainly as an overseer, looking after tribal welfare and providing an example of proper behavior to his people. During battles, he took charge of the war chiefs, whom he chose.

The last Mohave chief died in 1947. Present-day Mohave reservations are governed by elected tribal councils in accordance with the Indian Reorganization Act of 1934. The Colorado River Indian Reservation has a nine-member tribal council, led by a chairperson. At Fort Mohave, a tribal chairperson and an elected seven-member council govern the reservation. The task of tribal councils is complicated by the fact that, when governing, the councils must take into account tribal laws and the laws of the states of California, Arizona, and Nevada.

ECONOMY

Farming was the main economic activity among the Mohave. The men cleared the land and planted and tended the fields, which were then harvested by women. Unlike many other Native groups, the Mohave recognized ownership of property. A piece of land not already in use could be taken over, cleared, and planted; it was then considered private property. In years when the Colorado River did not rise high enough to flood their fields, the Mohave depended on hunting, fishing, and gathering food.

On the reservations, the tribe endured poverty and hardship when the federal government was slow to deliver on promises of improved irrigation techniques. When a reliable system was introduced in the early twentieth century, the economy improved.

Farming remains the major source of income for the Mohave. Cotton, alfalfa, wheat, feed grains for livestock, lettuce, garbanzo beans, peanuts, tomatoes, and melons are their major crops. The Fort Mojave Reservation also supplies Bermuda grass seed to the turf-grass industry. The Mohave attained a higher standard of living beginning in the 1960s, when they started leasing reservation lands to development corporations and farming operations. Unemployment on the reservations remained extremely high for the next two decades; at one point, 41 percent of job seekers at Fort Mohave and 25 percent of job seekers at the Colorado River reservation unable to find work.

With the opening of casinos and tourist facilities in the 1990s, the unemployment situation improved. Many service businesses both on and off the reservation brought in additional income. Tribal employment is also a major source of jobs. Leasing property has provided extra income and led to land development and home building. By the early 2000s, the unemployment rate at Colorado River was less than 10 percent; Fort Mojave's unemployment had fallen to less than 5 percent.

A Mohave father (right) and son. COURTESY OF THE BRAUN RESEARCH LIBRARY, AUTRY NATIONAL CENTER.

DAILY LIFE

Families

Families usually consisted of seven or eight persons, including parents, children, and other relatives. Families related to each other through the male line might settle near one another for a time, but the people moved about frequently.

Buildings

During most of the year, the people lived in single-family, open-sided, flat-roofed structures that provided more shade than shelter. Winter homes were low, sloping, rectangular structures made of arrowweed (a large brushy shrub that grows in clumps resembling corn shocks)

U•X•L Encyclopedia of Native American Tribes, 3rd Edition

attached to poles and covered with mud. The Mohave built their dwellings over a circular hole in the ground. From floor to ceiling, the homes measured about 5 feet (1.5 meters) high, but almost half of that was underground. A low door on the eastern side of the dwelling served as both an entrance and an escape hole for smoke from indoor fires. Although they lived along the Colorado River, the Mohave did not build boats or canoes.

Clothing and adornment

The Mohave were big-boned, exceptionally tall, and physically stronger than any other tribe in the United States. The desert region where they lived was subject to extremes of heat and cold, and when it was hot, the Mohave wore little or no clothing. Men sometimes wore narrow breech-cloths, garments with front and back flaps that hung from the waist. Women sometimes wore front and back aprons or short skirts woven from the fibrous inner layer of willow bark.

Blankets made from strips of rabbit, badger, or rat skin provided warmth in the evenings and during cold weather, and badger skin sandals protected people's feet during travel. Both men and women wore their hair in bangs over the forehead. Women let their hair hang long in back, while the men twisted theirs into many thin strands and held them in place with mesquite gum. Both sexes took pride in their long, glossy black hair, frequently cleaning it by plastering it with a mixture of mud and boiled mesquite bark. Both sexes painted their faces, and face and body tattooing was common.

During the early to mid-twentieth century, Mohave men often wore overalls, tight undershirts, usually painted black or striped, and bright handkerchiefs around their necks. Many Mohave women adorned themselves with creative glass bead decorations.

Food

Plant life The Mohave lived in small farming communities scattered in clusters along the bottomlands of the lower Colorado River. The region's vegetation consisted of piñon (pine nut) trees, desert shrubs, cactus, mesquite shrubs, and screwbeans (the spiral-shaped pod of the screwbean tree). Arrowweed, cottonwoods, cane, and willows grew at the river bottoms. The sandy earth sloping upward from the river supported cacti and creosote bushes (pronounced *KREE-uh-sote*; evergreen desert shrubs).

The people grew more than half of the food they ate. Their crops included corn, melons, pumpkins, squash, gourds, beans, sunflowers, grasses, and herbs. They also grew tobacco and cotton. Men punched holes in the moist river soil using a planting stick with a wedge-shaped point. Women followed, dropping seeds in each hole and covering them with soil by hand. No fertilization was necessary because flooding enriched the soil.

Animal life Scarce food and water forced wildlife to roam widely, and the Mohave rarely saw big game. They hunted an occasional deer, a project that required a profound understanding of life in the desert and a keen eye. When a hunter caught a deer, he traded it to other Mohave for fish and farm products because it was bad luck for him to eat his own kill. Mostly, though, meat came from quail, rabbits, rodents, and fish. Men set up weirs (small fences of sticks built across a river or stream) or heated and bent cactus thorns into hooks to catch fish. They broiled mullet or lumpfish on hot coals or prepared them with corn as a stew. Sometimes communal rabbit drives were held. The Mohave occasionally relied on insects, snakes, and lizards for food when game was scarce, or they dug up nourishing roots.

Education

The Mohave placed little pressure on children to learn because they believed skills and talents came through dreaming. Children spent much time in play activities, often imitating adult behavior.

Once the Mohave were on reservations, the U.S. government took over the schooling of the children. They built boarding schools for Native youth to limit or remove their connections to their culture. Children were forbidden to speak their Native language and were even given new "American" names. By the end of the twentieth century, a few Mohave reservation children still attended government-run boarding schools, but most children had enrolled in area public schools. By the start of the twenty-first century, the Mohave had established schools or cultural centers where children could learn their Native language and traditions.

Healing practices

A medicine man's power came from dreams, which were sent before birth or in early childhood by Tinyam, "The Night." Tinyam stood beside the young child and provide instruction on how to perform certain cures. Mohave medicine men were specialists; each could only cure one type of illness. Evil medicine men could cause illness.

The curing specialist might blow breath or spit on a patient with a fever or suck a swollen part of the ill person's body to release evil. The identity of an evil medicine man who had caused an illness usually came to the patient in a dream. In ancient times, relatives of sick people sometimes killed a medicine man they thought caused an illness. Some medicine men welcomed such a death because they believed a special fate would be theirs if they died violently.

Mohave medicine men mistrusted white remedies. During the 1900s, the medicine man's influence all but disappeared, in part because the U.S. government discouraged these practices. Modern-day Mohave on the reservations have access to community hospitals as well as to hospitals operated by the Indian Health Service. The Colorado River Indian Tribes employ health experts and operate facilities on the reservation to deal with psychological problems and alcohol abuse.

Games

The Mohave enjoyed gambling and games involving skill, strength, and endurance. Among these was a hoop and pole game that required a person to have both a sure aim and good judgment under pressure, since participants bet heavily on the outcome. First, a hoop was set rolling; then one player slid a pole along the ground, trying to calculate when the hoop would roll onto the pole and stop. Dice-like counting games were played by women using counters made from shells.

ARTS

Petroglyphs

Petroglyphs (carvings or drawings on rock) left behind by ancient Mohave peoples can still be seen on the walls of Grapevine Canyon, the entrance to Spirit Mountain (Mt. Newberry in Nevada), where the Mohave people believe they originated. The petroglyphs tell how the Mohave came to be and record important information such as who passed through their territory and where water sources were located.

A Mohave woman sits with pottery and a cup. COURTESY OF THE BRAUN RESEARCH LIBRARY, AUTRY NATIONAL CENTER.

Crafts

Women wove burden baskets, made pottery, and fashioned glass beads until European trade beads became more common. The beads they made came from ingredients they took from the necks of insects; some early observers thought these bugs might have been black beetles. Along with several other Yuman tribes, the Mojave used either large watertight baskets or huge pottery bowls up to 3 feet (1 meter) in diameter to float supplies and children across streams when moving from place to place.

Oral literature

Mohave song cycles passed along tribal history, morals, and myths. These groups of songs were extremely long and complicated and full of details about time and place. For example, Mohave Bird Songs describe a travel route through the desert to the Pacific Coast and list every type of bird encountered on the way. One song cycle could consist of fifty to two hundred songs, and thirty cycles were sung at one time. The words to the songs came to the singer in dreams. Some song cycles required several days and nights to perform; they were often accompanied by the music of a gourd rattle or by drumming on a basket. By the 1970s, there were few Mohave people left who knew how to perform the song cycles, and only fragments of the tribe's oral literature were remembered.

CUSTOMS

Festivals and ceremonies

The Mohave did not wear masks or ceremonial costumes, nor did they have rituals for rainmaking or crop growth, except when members of the tribe sometimes drank cactus wine to bring forth rain in the very early times. The main celebrations included the Scalp Dance (see "War rituals") and girls' puberty ceremonies, both of which died out by the early 1900s. Songs for cremation and the Mourning Chant were the only rituals still practiced in recent times.

War rituals

The Mohave were warlike because their spirit guide, Mastamho, predicted that each generation would have men with war powers. Therefore, when not hunting or gathering, Mohave warriors fulfilled that prophesy by going to war. Warfare was carried on by men who had experienced "great dreams" that gave them power in battle. However, if they were needed, most Mohave men were willing to fight, whether they had had a great dream or not.

To carry out small raids, ten to twelve men performed the task without ceremony or ritual. For major battles, scouts were sent ahead to stake out a route, noting the location of water holes and enemy camps. Warriors then made surprise attacks on the enemy at dawn.

Mohave warriors divided into two groups: the first group were archers, who used 5-foot-long (1.5-meter-long) bows and arrows for long-distance fighting; the second group were clubmen, who rushed in for close fighting using heavy clubs and sticks. Each warrior carried a round shield made of horsehide or deerskin and a feathered stave (wooden pole). A fighter would plant his stave firmly in the ground and defend it to his death.

A special scalper always accompanied war expeditions, and the return of warriors was celebrated with a victory dance around enemy scalps mounted on poles. Young female prisoners were given to old men of the tribe to insult the enemy.

Running

Much of Mohave traveling took place on foot, and men were especially adept, often covering up to 100 miles (160 kilometers) a day across the desert. Running was an opportunity to meditate and to escape from evil spirits; it served a practical purpose as well. Teams of relay runners could communicate the location of enemies or water holes.

Puberty and pregnancy

Unlike many other tribes, the Mohave did not regard puberty and pregnancy as occasions for complicated rituals. Menstruating girls sat in a secluded corner of their homes, resting quietly and avoiding meat and salt. At night, they were laid in a warm pit. A pregnant woman was cared for tenderly, since the unborn child would be having its first—and possibly "great"—dream, and the dream might be adversely affected if the mother were unhappy or upset.

Courtship and marriage

A Mohave man courting his future bride brought her many gifts. If the young woman accepted the man's advances, the couple began to live together. No ceremony was necessary to validate the marriage. The couple could live wherever they chose. They might, for example, take up residence at the bride's home with her parents until they built a home of their own. If the partners' union failed, they separated. Divorces were fairly common. Most men had only one wife, although it was permissible to have more than one. Divorces and remarriages remain common in modern Mohave society.

Funerals

The funeral involved more ritual than any other Mohave ceremony. Mourners typically gathered around the dying person to sing and wail.

After death, they wrapped the corpse in a blanket and burned the body, and the mourners continued to wail and watch as the body departed to the afterworld. The person's home and personal possessions were also burned. The Mohave never again spoke the name of the dead person. A child who was born after a parent died never knew his or her parents' name.

A special mourning ceremony was held for certain warriors and chiefs after their cremation. This ceremony involved a ten-hour ritual in which men in war costumes ran back and forth carrying replicas of real weapons. The special house that was built to hold the spectators at this ritual was later burned together with the replica weapons. Runners then fled to the river and jumped in for purification.

The cremation and wailing ceremony continue to be the manner in which most Mohave mourn their dead. Some personal property is also burned when a person dies.

CURRENT TRIBAL ISSUES

In the nineteenth century, the Mohave gave up a large part of their homeland to the American government. By the end of the twentieth century, they were being pressured by the state of California to permit the building of a radioactive waste dump in Ward Valley, a site 22 miles (35 kilometers) west of Needles in traditional Mohave territory. The Mohave and the Chemehuevi, who were also affected by the proposal, claimed such a dump would contaminate the sacred Colorado River, threaten the tribes' health and livelihood, and destroy the habitat of the desert tortoise, an important tribal symbol. Furthermore, the tribes asserted that the project was a violation of their rights and considered it as yet another attack on Native American culture, lands, and futures. In 2002, the state cancelled the project. Every year, the Mohave and other groups involved in the court cases to protect the land gather for a celebration and to continue advocating for the protection of their sacred areas.

Little of traditional Mohave culture remains, as a result of longstanding efforts on the part of the federal government and other agencies to force the people to assimilate (become part of the larger American culture). Recent efforts, however, have been made to revitalize aspects of the culture. The tradition of running, for example, is gaining renewed meaning and popularity at Fort Mohave. Runner clans—groups of men and women who receive in dreams the desire and the power to run— have formed at the reservation. Ward Valley, the site of a proposed waste dump, became the site of "Spirit Runs," communal relay runs with both a political and a spiritual purpose.

In addition to protecting their water rights, the Fort Mojave people have been working with state and federal agencies to restore habitats for many endangered species, such as the desert willow flycatcher, the Yuma clapper rail, and the yellow-billed cuckoo. They are also active in presenting environmental education programs to schools and the surrounding communities.

BOOKS

Boule, Mary Null. *Mohave Tribe.* Vashon, WV: Merryant Publishers Inc., 2000.

Curtis, Edward S. *The North American Indian.* New York: Johnson Reprint Corporation, 1908.

Furst, Jill Leslie McKeever. *Mojave Pottery, Mojave People.* Santa Fe, NM: School of American Research Press, 2001.

Kroeber, Alfred Louis. *Seven Mohave Myths.* Whitefish, MT: Kessinger Publishing, 2007.

Mifflin, Margot. *The Blue Tattoo: The Life of Olive Oatman.* Lincoln: University of Nebraska Press, 2011.

Ortiz, Alfonso, ed. *Handbook of North American Indians,* Vol. 10: *Southwest.* Washington, DC: Smithsonian Institution, 1978.

Swanton, John R. *The Indian Tribes of North America.* Washington, DC: Smithsonian, 1979.

Williams, Jack S. *The Mojave of California and Arizona.* New York: PowerKids Press, 2004.

PERIODICALS

Fikes, Bradley J. "Ward Valley Sides Spar over Review Panel." *San Diego Business Journal,* April 10, 1995.

Stewart, Kenneth M. "Mohave Warfare." *Southwestern Journal of Anthropology* 3, no. 3 (Autumn 1947): 257–78.

WEB SITES

"Desert Native Americans: Mohave Indians." *Mojave Desert.* http://mojavedesert.net/mojave-indians/ (accessed on July 20, 2011).

"Fort Mojave Indian Tribe." *Inter Tribal Council of Arizona, Inc.* http://www.itcaonline.com/tribes_mojave.html (accessed on July 20, 2011).

"Mohave Indian Tribe History." *Access Genealogy.* http://www.accessgenealogy.com/native/tribes/mohave/mohaveindianhist.htm (accessed on July 20, 2011).

"Mohave National Preserve: Mohave Tribe: Culture." *National Park Service.* http://www.nps.gov/moja/historyculture/mojave-culture.htm (accessed on July 20, 2011).

Navajo

Name

Navajo (pronounced *NAH-vah-ho.*). The name comes from a Tewa (Pueblo) Indian word, *Navahu,* meaning "large area of cultivated fields." The Navajo call themselves *Diné* ("the People").

Location

The Navajo make their home on a federal reservation called the Navajo Nation. The largest reservation in the United States, it covers more than 27,000 square miles (43,450 square kilometers) of their former homelands in the canyons, mountains, deserts, and forests of northeastern Arizona, northwestern New Mexico, and southeastern Utah. Three other bands live on small reservations in western New Mexico. Some Navajo also share the Colorado River Indian Tribes Reservation in Arizona with the Hopi, Mohave, and Chemehuevi.

Population

In 1868, there were about 10,000 Navajo. In the 1990 U.S. Census, 225,298 people identified themselves as Navajo. In 2000, that number increased to 276,775. The 2010 census counted 286,731 Navajo, with 332,129 people claiming some Navajo heritage. According to the Navajo Nation, the population had reached 300,024 in 2011.

Language family

Athabaskan.

Origins and group affiliations

Navajo accounts of their own history correspond with what scientists and historians say about Navajo ancestors moving from the far North to the Southwest over long periods of time. The Navajo traditions tell of the First World, or Black World, which is similar to that of a frigid flatland area, possibly the far north in Alaska. The Navajo Second World (Blue-Green World) features landmarks and animal life similar to those found

Contemporary Navajo Communities

Navajo Nation Today

Federal reservation: 26,000 square miles of former homelands in northeastern Arizona, northwestern New Mexico, and southeastern Utah.

Shaded areas

Navajo Nation, in present-day Arizona at the Four Corners area, where Arizona, Utah, Colorado, and New Mexico meet.

Hopi Nation

A map of contemporary Navajo communities. MAP BY XNR PRODUCTIONS. CENGAGE LEARNING, GALE. REPRODUCED BY PERMISSION OF GALE, A PART OF CENGAGE LEARNING.

in western and central Canada. The Navajo Third World (Yellow World) contains mountains and plains that resemble those on the eastern slope of the Rocky Mountains and the Southwest. The Navajo Fourth World (Glittering World) reflects the surroundings at the Navajo Nation today in northwestern New Mexico. The Navajo have probably inhabited the Southwest for nearly one thousand years. Their closest allies were the Apache and the Pueblo.

Once a group whose fierce warriors struck fear in the hearts of their enemies, the Navajo are a mysterious, complex people who have maintained more of their culture than most other tribes. In the early twenty-first century, the majority of Navajo were under the age of thirty, and nine out of ten tribal members inhabited reservation lands. Although the people live a variety of lifestyles and work at many different jobs, they value their traditions and strive to keep alive the ancient Navajo ways.

HISTORY

Outside influences

The Navajo may have arrived in the American Southwest as early as the eleventh century. Until about 1650, the people were mainly hunters and gatherers who noted the practices of other societies and adopted those that they thought would be useful to them.

The Spanish came to Diné Bikéyah, or Navajoland, in the seventeenth century and tried to convert the Native peoples to the Spanish way of life. From around 1650 to 1775, the Navajo learned from both the Spanish and the Pueblo (see entry) how to farm corn, herd sheep, weave wool, and work silver. The Spanish also taught them how to grow new fruits and vegetables, such as peaches, wheat, and potatoes, and they introduced them to the cattle, sheep, and horses that over time would become important to the Navajo way of life. By the late 1600s, the use of horses allowed the Navajo to travel far distances on horse raids and increase the scope of their trading. Very few Navajo converted to the Catholic religion of the Spanish, perhaps because the Spanish showed disrespect for the Native culture.

Important Dates

1626: The Spanish first encounter the Navajo people.

1864: The devastating Long Walk, a forced removal from their homelands, leads the Navajo to a harsh exile at Bosque Redondo.

1868: The Navajo reservation is established by treaty with the United States, and the people return from Bosque Redondo.

1923: The Navajo unify under a tribal council.

1941–45: Navajo Code Talkers send and receive secret messages in their Native language, making a major contribution to the U.S. war effort during World War II.

1974: The U.S. Congress passes the Navajo-Hopi Land Settlement Act, which established a Joint-Use Area and requires the relocation of individual tribe members to their own tribal lands.

1996: The Navajo-Hopi Land Dispute Act allows the Diné more time to relocate, but some stay.

Beginning in the late 1600s, the Navajo moved westward into the lands of present-day New Mexico and Arizona because of hostilities with Comanche and Ute tribes (see entries) and Spaniards who lived on three sides of their territory. The Navajo did not like the customs of the Spanish, who fought with the Native peoples and sometimes took them as slaves. The Navajo joined the Pueblo and Apache (see entry) to fight off the Spanish. Around 1750, the tribe established a fortified town in Canyon de Chelly (pronounced *shay*). The next several decades were marked by the development of the arts and intricate ceremonies.

U.S. government dealings with Navajo

Even though they were mainly farmers and herders, the Navajo sometimes raided neighboring societies. They did this to feed themselves after a crop failure, to get more horses and other livestock, or to rescue their children who had been captured for the slave trade.

In the early 1800s, the original Spanish colonists in the Southwest rebelled against Spain and founded the nation of Mexico. Although they claimed the northern territory where the Navajo lived as their own, most Mexicans lived farther south. The United States took possession of most of the Southwest in 1848 as a result of the Treaty of Guadalupe-Hidalgo, which ended the Mexican-American War (1846–48; a war during which Mexico lost about one-half of its national territory to the United States). At first, the United States made an effort to establish a treaty-based relationship with the Navajo. The Americans, however, mistakenly assumed that the leaders of the Navajo bands who signed various treaties represented all Navajo people. In fact, each headman represented only his own band.

When bands who had not signed treaties continued to raid, the Americans thought their agreements had been violated. As further land disputes arose, people on both sides were killed. In 1864, the U.S. government decided to settle the problem by adopting an all-out policy of subduing the entire Navajo population. Kit Carson (1809–1868), an early frontiersman, led the American troops. Rather than engaging in military battles, Carson and his army proceeded through Navajo lands taking livestock and burning homes and crops. In the process, some women and children were molested, and some of the captured women were sold into slavery. Finally, Carson's troops attacked Canyon de Chelly, crushing most of the remaining Navajo resistance. Thousands of nearly starving Navajo surrendered.

The Long Walk

In 1864, eight thousand Navajo were resettled at a place called Bosque (pronounced *bosk*) Redondo near Fort Sumner in east central New Mexico. They made the 300-mile (480-kilometer) journey on foot, a terrible event that has become known as the Long Walk. Those who could not keep up were either taken into slavery or were shot by military guards. People who complained of illness, including women soon to give birth, were also shot. More than two thousand died during the forced march.

IN COMMEMORATION OF THE NAVAJOS
WHO LIVED HERE IN EXILE, 1863-1868.
THE CENTENNIAL RE-ENACTMENT OF THE
SIGNING OF THE TREATY OF PEACE (1 JUNE 1868)
TOOK PLACE ON THIS SPOT.
ERECTED BY THE NAVAJO TRIBE AND THE
PLATEAU SCIENCES SOCIETY, WINDOW ROCK,
ARIZONA, FEBRUARY 1971.

Navajo memorial to the Bosque Redondo, or "Long Walk," stands beside the Pecos River in Fort Sumner, New Mexico. © NORTH WIND PICTURE ARCHIVES.

Once they arrived at the forty-square-acre reservation at Fort Sumner, the Navajo found the land unsuitable for growing adequate food. On this land where agriculture was impossible, the people were expected to become farmers. The water was bad, firewood was in short supply, and insects plagued them. They also fell victim to raids by enemy tribes. More than two thousand additional Navajo died at Bosque Redondo from starvation and diseases.

During their period of exile at Bosque Redondo, only about half of the Navajo survived. Hundreds of people escaped and returned to their homelands to join the thousands of other Navajo who had remained free. Those who avoided the relocation by hiding on their lands grew crops, gathered wild foods, and raised livestock, confident that in time the others would come home from the Long Walk. They built homes and planted gardens, trying to reestablish their former way of life before their kinspeople returned.

The U.S. government did little to help the sick and dying Navajo until a Santa Fe newspaper wrote about the terrible conditions on the reservation, and the American public protested. In time, the U.S. government admitted that the resettlement had been a terrible mistake. In 1868, Congress created a reservation within the original Navajo homelands, and the Navajo people were invited to return from Bosque Redondo. However, they were only permitted to return to an area called "Treaty Reservation," a section of land that was only 10 percent of their former lands. This land was surrounded by non-Natives who had moved in while the Navajo were gone and had established towns and trading posts. Before long, the Santa Fe Railroad brought even more U.S. settlers to the area.

Four Navajo reservations

The 3.5-million-acre Navajo Nation reservation established by the U.S. government was expanded over time by additional grants of land. The reservation is now the largest Native American reservation in the United States; it includes more than 17 million acres and is about equal to the size of West Virginia.

After their departure from Bosque Redondo, three bands of Navajo chose to settle apart from the main tribe. These bands established three small, isolated offshoot reservations in western New Mexico. Today, more than 5,800 Navajo live on the Ramah, Cañoncito (now called To'Hajiilee), and Alamo Reservations. The vast Navajo Nation boasts spectacular scenery, but not much of the land is useful for farming or grazing.

Modern life

Many Navajo volunteered for military service in World War I (1914–18; a war in which Great Britain, France, the United States, and their allies defeated Germany, Austria-Hungary, and their allies). In 1924, all Native Americans were granted U.S. citizenship largely because of that. The Navajo made a very important contribution during World War II (1939–45; a war in which Great Britain, France, the United States, and their allies defeated Germany, Italy, and Japan). Men called Navajo Code Talkers used the Navajo language to send secret messages to branches of the American military. Their messages baffled enemy Japanese code-breakers. Survivors of the 420 Code Talkers who served with the U.S. Marines remained among the most respected elders of the Navajo Nation.

Coal and oil were first found in the Navajo Nation around 1920, and the people have made some money from these resources. In 1997,

The Navajo Code Talkers

After Japan bombed Pearl Harbor, Hawaii, on December 7, 1941, the U.S. government declared war on Japan and entered World War II (1939–45). Americans discovered that the Japanese were eavesdropping on the U.S. Marines and decoding their secret messages. In early 1942, a non-Native man who had been brought up at the Navajo Nation suggested that the military could use Navajo men to devise unbreakable codes. Other than fifty thousand Navajo, fewer than thirty people in the world knew the Navajo language; none were Japanese.

Young Navajo men were recruited as Code Talkers. Because the Navajo language lacked words for modern military terms, Navajo Code Talker Carl Gorman (1907–1998) and others worked out a two-tier code in which English military words were represented by different Navajo words. For example, Navajo words for different birds were used for names of planes. When the Japanese figured out Marine radio operators were speaking Navajo, they forced a captured soldier who spoke the language to translate. Although he knew a term such as *chay-da-gahi* meant turtle, he did not know that "turtle" meant "tank" to the code talkers.

In addition to their language skills, young Navajo soldiers also proved to be adept at night scouting and were excellent undercover fighters. They lived off the land in Japan and made stew from chickens, goats, and horses they killed with slingshots. Ultimately, the Navajo, who at one time were forbidden to speak their own language by the Bureau of Indian Affairs, used that language to help the United States win the war. In 1982, President Ronald Reagan (1911–2004; served 1981–89) proclaimed August 14 as National Navajo Code Talkers Day. Most Code Talkers who were still alive did not partake in the celebrations, however, because they did not believe in glorifying war. By 2011, only one of the original code talkers was still living.

concerned over resources being mined for others' use while many tribal members had no electricity or gas in their homes, the nation created the Navajo Oil and Gas Company. By the early 2000s, mining had become one of the largest sources of income for the tribe. Along with coal and oil, natural gas brought in more than $75 million in royalties for the tribe in 2007. However, concerns about people's health and the impact on the environment led the Nation to set mining restrictions.

The Navajo-Hopi land dispute

Since the founding of their reservations, the Navajo and Hopi have been engaged in a land dispute. The original Navajo Nation authorized by Congress included only ten percent of the tribe's original land. The Hopi reservation was created adjoining the Navajo Nation in 1882, and in 1934, Congress expanded the Navajo reservation so that it completely surrounded the Hopi reservation. Each tribe thought that land given to the other was rightfully its own.

In 1962, a federal court ruling established an area surrounding the Hopi land as a Joint Use Area (JUA) for both tribes. The discovery of oil and coal in the JUA made the tribes more interested in clearly defining ownership. When the U.S. Congress passed the Navajo-Hopi Settlement Act in 1974, it authorized the division of the JUA between the two tribes and required people living on the other tribe's land to relocate. (This applied to nearly ten thousand Navajo.) Thousands of people voluntarily moved, but many became separated from their extended families and relocated to suburban-area homes where they could not find work. In time, one-third of them lost their new homes.

After a long delay, the matter neared a resolution in 1997. The Navajo still living on Hopi land were permitted to stay in their homes if they signed a nonrenewable, seventy-five-year lease and agreed to live under Hopi regulations. The choice was a difficult one for the Navajo because of spiritual ties; they would be obliged to ask for Hopi permission to conduct many of their ceremonies, and they would not be allowed to bury their dead on the leased land. Still, most Navajo signed the lease in March 1997. Nevertheless, the long dispute disrupted many lives and further strained relations between the two tribes.

The Navajo today

At the start of the twenty-first century, the Navajo educational system, economy, and government had grown strong despite the misuse of money by some of its tribal leaders. Young Navajo continued to learn their language and participate in tribal ceremonies, and the tribe has been working to preserve its ancient culture.

RELIGION

The Navajo religion helps the people strive for harmony with nature and with others. The tribe sees the universe as orderly. Everything in the world, no matter how tiny, has an important place.

Among the Navajo gods are many Holy People, including Changing Woman (who created the people from cornmeal and flakes of skin that had fallen from her own body), Spider Woman (who taught the people to weave), Talking God (who showed the people how to build their houses), and Coyote (an occasionally helpful, clever prankster whose tricks provide many lessons). Ceremonies called "Blessingways" are given in thankfulness for a long and happy life or to celebrate the occasion of a new house or a new marriage.

Mountain Earth bundles are the most important ceremonial objects. They are made of tanned, undamaged buckskin taken from a deer suffocated during a special ritual. The bundle contains small pouches of soil and other items from the top of each of the four sacred mountains that surround the Navajo homeland.

Navajo Christians

Roman Catholic missionaries in the 1600s were only the first of various Christian groups that tried to convert the Navajo to their faith. In the late 1860s and 1870s, Presbyterian and Mormon missionaries were a presence on the reservation. In the 1890s, Catholic priests began a mission, St. Michael's, and later opened a school that became a center for studying the Navajo religion, language, and way of life. In time, other Protestant denominations also began churches and schools, and many Navajo became Christians.

Present-day Navajo often combine Christianity with their traditional religious beliefs and practices. About 25,000 Navajo are members of the Native American Church, which was formed in 1918 by followers of the Peyote (pronounced *pay-O-tee*) religion, who had developed an intricate belief system embracing traditional Native values and visions of the spiritual world attained through the use of dreams, prayers, rituals, and the peyote plant. Thousands more participate in peyote ceremonies without claiming membership in the church. Peyote is a substance that comes from cactus; when takers consume it, they go into a trance-like state and see visions. The use of peyote was prohibited on the Navajo Nation for twenty-seven years, until the tribal council legalized its religious use in 1967.

LANGUAGE

Navajo and six Apache dialects (varieties) make up the southwestern branch of the Athabaskan language family. The language includes sounds from the natural world, and pronunciation requirements are very strict.

Navajo Words

ahe'ee	"thank you"
at'ééd	"girl"
aoo'	"yes"
ashkii	"boy"
gah	"rabbit"
hooghan	"home"
łíí'	"horse"
nahosdzáán	"earth"
ólta'	"school"
deesháál	"I will come/go."
jiní	"it is said"

Spoken Navajo has a mechanical flavor about it that almost sounds like the talk of a robot. Language experts say that the only people who can pronounce Navajo perfectly are the native-born.

The Navajo believe that some words have the power to ward off evil, whereas others are so dangerous that only special persons under specific conditions can speak them. Unlike many other nations, the Navajo rarely add words from other languages into their vocabulary. Instead, they combine traditional terms to describe new objects or events. For example, the Navajo word for "elephant" means "one that lassoes with his nose." An automobile is a "chuggi," which sounds like a car's engine, and gasoline is described as "car's water."

GOVERNMENT

Until modern times, the tribe consisted of small, independent bands headed by chiefs or headmen. The discovery of coal and oil on the Navajo Nation in 1920 made it necessary for the tribe to organize in a different way. The U.S. government founded the Navajo Business Council in 1922 to grant oil and mineral leases in the name of the Navajo Nation, but many leases were not favorable to the Navajo.

In 1938, the Navajo rejected the Indian Reorganization Act (IRA), which would have given them a federally structured tribal government and constitution. Instead, with the federal government's permission, they held their own constitutional convention. The tribe wrote a constitution that would give them independence from the federal Bureau of Indian Affairs (BIA). The U.S. government rejected this plan and formed a new Navajo Business Council. This council was composed of seventy-four elected Navajo members and became known as the "Rule of 1938." This was the basis for the present Navajo Tribal Council.

Since 1922, the local government has been organized into chapters, each with its own chapter house. (Chapter houses are local meeting places where residents from that area gather to discuss and decide on legislation that affects them.) The nation is headed by an eighty-eight member council representing the 110 chapters, and it has a three-branch government—executive, legislative, and judicial—headed by a president who is elected every four years. A speaker is elected every two years to head the legislative branch. A chief justice is appointed to oversee the court system.

ECONOMY

Farming and ranching

Traditionally, Navajo farmers did not irrigate their fields; their seeds could be sustained by underground water. In time, however, farming methods have changed. In the 1960s, Congress approved the Navajo Irrigation Implementation Project (NIIP). The system used canals, pipelines, pumping stations, and sprinklers to irrigate crops. Water was stored thirty miles away behind a new dam on the San Juan River. In the mid-1990s, a 70,000-acre tribal farm called Navajo Agricultural Products Incorporated (NAPI) began producing profitable harvests of alfalfa, pinto beans, potatoes, onions, and mushrooms. In addition to growing crops, NAPI processed and packaged them.

The entrance to the Navajo Nation Tribal Government Center, which is in Window Rock, Arizona. © NORTH WIND PICTURE ARCHIVES.

Traditional ranching, too, underwent changes. Since the seventeenth century, sheep herding has been a vital part of Navajo life. Sheep provided meat, their tendons made bowstrings, and their wool was woven into clothing and blankets. During the late 1930s, an extreme drought made the central and southern United States so dry that the area was called the "dust bowl." At this time, the U.S. government decided that the Navajo were raising too many sheep and that their grazing resulted in soil erosion by stripping plant cover from the topsoil, causing it to dry out and blow away. Agricultural Department agents killed tens of thousands of Navajo sheep. For several decades after this, relations between the Navajo and the U.S. government were hostile. During the twentieth century, cattle raising largely replaced sheep herding on the reservation.

Other sources of income

In the mid-1990s, the Navajo Oil and Gas Company built its own oil refinery. In the early twenty-first century, in addition to tax revenue, the Navajo Nation gained income by leasing its land for gas and oil drilling as well as through coal mining, forestry, and the operation of eight industrial parks. Manufacturing businesses on reservation lands produce missiles, wood products, circuit boards, locomotive computers, modems, computer parts, and many other products. More than 250 trade operations, including shopping centers and banks, also operate on the reservation, and construction workers are building new homes and buildings there.

Navajo weavers command good prices for their handmade woolen rugs, belts, and blankets. Navajo trading posts sell craft objects such as silver work, an art form the people learned from the Mexicans. Navajo artisans make silver bracelets, rings, earrings, necklaces, and belts decorated with the opaque blue stone called turquoise.

Service businesses make substantial profits from the more than 2.5 million annual visitors who come to the reservation. Several resort facilities operate there, and in 1997, the tribe entered into a partnership with the U.S. National Park Service. Together, they developed a new resort and marina complex at Antelope Point on Lake Powell.

DAILY LIFE

Families

Navajo family units were made up of two or more families centered on a mother and her daughters. The unit was bound together by ties of marriage and close relationships. Women held an important social position.

Navajo society is based on clans (groups of people who claim descent from a common ancestor). Some clans trace their origins to creation by the Holy People. The original clans were Towering House, Bitterwater, Big Water, and One-who-walks-around. Other clans arose when new groups became Navajos. Each Navajo person is associated with four different unrelated clans.

Among the Navajo, a person's ancestry is traced through the mother's side of the family and determines the clan to which a person belongs. A child must marry outside his or her clan. Navajo relationships are often hard for outsiders to understand, as the people have different terms for aunts, uncles, cousins, and other relatives.

A Navajo log hogan of the style adopted in the 1800s sits in Canyon de Chelly, Arizona. © NORTH WIND PICTURE ARCHIVES.

Buildings

Traditional Navajo houses are called hogans. Older versions, built around a wooden post frame, were cone-shaped. Beginning in the mid-1800s, log cabins with beehive-shaped log roofs became more popular. Usually the roofs, and sometimes the walls, were covered with packed earth. A smoke hole was left at the center of the roof. When wood was scarce, hogans were built of stones held together with mud mortar.

In recent years, cinderblock houses have become more popular, and family homes usually include several additional structures. There are corrals made of brush, open-walled workspaces with flat roofs, and storage structures or dugouts. Typically, a sweat lodge, built like a small version of the old, conical hogans, sits nearby in a secluded spot, since curing ceremonies can only be conducted in the traditional structure.

Newly built hogans are sprinkled with corn pollen or cornmeal, and prayers are offered to ensure they will be places of happiness. According to legend the Holy People built the first hogans from such precious materials as turquoise, jet, or shell. Now, as then, hogan doors face east, toward the rising sun. Navajo families often have two homes: one to live in during the cold winter months, and one to stay in while farming in the summer.

Clothing and adornment

Early Navajo clothed themselves in breechcloths (flaps of material that cover the front and back and are suspended from the waist), leggings, skirts, and blankets that were either woven from cedar bark or yucca plant material or made of fur. Animal skins were used to make moccasins with braided yucca soles.

By the early seventeenth century, men wore tanned buckskin clothing, and women wore dresses of fabric, often wool. By the time of the Long Walk, clothing had become quite colorful. Some men wore knee-length buckskin pants decorated with brass and silver buttons along the outer seams and woolen leggings dyed blue and held up by bright red garters. Women's ankle-length dresses, fashioned from two woven panels and sewn together along the sides and over both shoulders, were belted at the waist with a red woven sash. Women also wore leggings made by wrapping strips of dyed buckskin around their legs from ankle to knee; these were adorned with silver buttons.

During the late nineteenth century and early twentieth century, women usually wore long, full skirts of cotton with bright blouses, often made of velveteen fabric. Men usually wore blue jeans, colorful shirts (sometimes of velveteen), boots, belts decorated with decorative silver disks, and headbands made of rolled kerchiefs. Both men and women have traditionally worn their hair long, wound into an hourglass shape at the base of the neck and bound with wool string. Silver and turquoise necklaces, earrings, and bracelets have long been popular with both men and women.

Food

When they first moved to the Southwest between the ninth and twelfth centuries, the Navajo hunted and gathered wild vegetation. They learned from the Pueblo Indians how to grow corn, beans, and squash. The Spaniards, who came in the 1600s, taught the Native Americans to grow wheat and oats and to herd sheep and goats.

At the time of their exile to Bosque Redondo, the Navajo commonly ate mutton (sheep meat), corn, frybread (plate-sized disks of bread fried in hot fat), and coffee laced with sugar and goat's milk. They picked corn early to avoid frost damage, then they husked, sun dried, and removed it from the cob before storing it in bags for later use. Fresh corn was served as a special treat. The people often ate a cooked mush made from cornmeal or wild seed meal mixed with water or goat's milk. This substance was used to prepare many foods. The addition of garden vegetables and meat—prairie dog continues to be a favorite—made the mush a well-balanced meal.

Education

For centuries, Navajo children learned skills by observing their parents and members of their extended families. During the nineteenth century, the Navajo opposed efforts to start American-style schools for their children. Missionaries ran most of the schools and tried to change the student's religion. Navajo parents saw these schools as a threat to their way of life and to their families. In addition, about two-thirds of Navajo families had suffered when their children were sold into slavery during the early and mid-1800s. Rival tribes, Mexicans, and even the U.S. Army kidnapped children and sold them in Mexico, where many were forced to work in the mines. As a result, most Navajo parents were reluctant to let their other children leave home to attend boarding school for anywhere from two to eight years.

In spite of the tribe's objections, children were taken from their parents and sent to boarding schools, where they were taught to speak, act, and dress like others in U.S. society. In 1907, a Navajo who protested against children attending Shiprock Boarding School was jailed and remained in prison with no trial for more than a year.

During World War II, many families lived off the reservation to take advantage of work opportunities, and their children attended public schools. In the early 2000s, the Navajo Nation's educational facilities included state schools that served students in kindergarten through twelfth grade, as well as several Bureau of Indian Affairs boarding schools and some private mission schools. Northland Pioneer College, Crownpoint Institute of Technology, and Diné Community College (formerly Navajo Community College) in Tsaile, Arizona, along with its five branch campuses, offer students a variety of courses of study.

Navajo medicine man attends a dedication ceremony for a new hospital at Fort Defiance, Arizona, in 1938. © AP PHOTO.

Healing practices

For the Navajo, sickness is an indication of disharmony. Curing ceremonies treat the cause of the ailment rather than the symptoms. When a person gets sick, he or she normally goes to a person called a stargazer or hand trembler, who tells the patient the cause of the illness. The stargazer then recommends that the person see a special medicine person and take part in a particular ceremony. Illnesses can be caused by the accidental or intentional breaking of one of the society's many taboos, by contact with a ghost, or by the spell of a witch.

The medicine person recommended by the stargazer is known as a *hataali* ("singer"). The *hataali* conducts a ceremony in which both the patient and his or her relatives participate. The ceremony may last nine nights and include the performance of more than five hundred songs. The singer is sometimes assisted by dancers who wear masks representing appropriate spirits, called *Yeis*. A sand painting, created during the ritual, is destroyed at the completion of the ceremony. (Sand painting is a Navajo and Pueblo tradition in which sands of different colors are used to create a ceremonial design.) During a ceremony, the healer may employ objects with special powers, medicines made from plants, and lengthy prayers. Ideally, curing rituals are followed by the singing of the Blessingway, a prayer to restore harmony that has been called the backbone of the Navajo healing system.

In modern times, with the breakdown of the traditional, family- and clan-based educational systems, Diné Community College and other institutions have begun teaching Native healing arts. At the Medicine Man School in Rough Rock, Arizona, aspiring singer-healers are taught their trade from experienced healers. The students learn during actual ceremonies, because it is considered to be wrong to address the spirits without a genuine need for healing or blessings. Because the training period cannot be scheduled and the ceremonies are complex, it can take four to six years to learn one of the longer rituals. Each singer is trained in a specialty that includes the ability to perform between one and six different ceremonies. Although women are permitted to become singers, they rarely do, perhaps because they fear that some event or spirit they could encounter might affect their unborn children.

In the early twenty-first century, Indian Health Service hospitals on the reservation have special rooms where traditional healers can conduct traditional curing ceremonies. This new spirit of cooperation between modern and traditional medical people is bringing more Navajo people in for treatment. Navajo healers have a knowledge of herbs that can be used for birth control, mild diabetes, and seizures.

ARTS

Navajo women in traditional times were known for their excellent pottery, including ladles, jars with pointed bottoms, and decorated bowls. They also made coiled baskets, food containers, and water bottles. The women learned to weave from the Pueblo people and produced rugs and blankets with intricate, unique designs that they colored with natural dyes. Navajo craftspeople are also renowned for their unique silver and turquoise creations.

A Navajo family sits in front of their blanket loom, circa 1900. © NORTH WIND PICTURE ARCHIVES.

CUSTOMS

Taboos

The Navajo believe that the sacred order of the world must be maintained to avoid illness or other misfortunes. They accomplish this, in part, by observing many taboos. A few of the thousands of actions that are forbidden include touching lightning-struck trees; killing coyotes, bears, snakes, and certain birds; combing their hair at night; and stepping over the body of another person sleeping in a hogan, no matter how crowded it may be. Pregnant women and their husbands or a person who has recently undergone a curing ritual observe even more taboos.

Puberty

Young girls undergo one of the oldest ceremonies of the Navajo culture, the *kinaaldá*. The two-day ritual takes place after a girl's first menstrual period and is designed to teach her lessons she will need in adult life. The girl must perform several exhausting runs to ensure her physical conditioning and endurance. In addition, she must grind by hand some of the cornmeal and wheat she will use to prepare a traditional cake; the chanted prayers of a medicine man accompany the process. Near the end of the ceremony, a female relative massages the girl's body to make it more beautiful. The girl then prays over a group of young children. Following the ritual, she is accepted into the community as an adult and is considered to be ready for marriage.

For boys, puberty is often marked by the deepening of the voice. Their puberty ceremony is similar to that recorded in oral history for Monster Slayer and Born for Water, Changing Woman's twin sons (see "Religion"). During the ritual, boys sing and yell as they run to the east. Their skin is covered with cornmeal. Participating in giveaways and learning proper behavior for men are also important activities. Other parts of the ceremony include fasting, sweating, and learning songs. Following this celebration, boys take their place as adults in the tribe and assume male responsibilities.

Courtship and marriage

Traditionally, relatives arranged Navajo marriages after the boy reached the proper age. An expensive gift (sheep or horses) was often given to the girl's family by the boy's family. When a couple married, the grandmother of the bride presented the new couple with a basket of cornmeal at the wedding site. The bride and groom then exchanged a pinch of cornmeal, from which they received the strength and blessing of the spirit world. Some couples still observe this custom during the wedding ceremony.

Newly married couples usually built their houses near the home of the wife's mother. This allowed the wife and her children to have close contact with the maternal grandmother. A large space was left between the homes, however, because a man was forbidden to look at or speak to his mother-in-law.

Funerals

In the past, the Navajo feared dead people and ghosts. Immediately after the death of a family member, close relatives showed their sadness by weeping and wailing, cutting their hair, and putting on old clothing. Elderly relatives washed the deceased's hair and body and dressed the body in fine clothes. Burial took place in the daytime, and as soon as possible. The people placed the corpse on a horse along with many personal possessions and took it far away, possibly to the hill country. A crevice in the rocks that could be covered with brush served as a grave. The horse was killed at the grave site, so that it could be used by the dead person in the afterworld.

Those who accompanied the body returned home and burned their own clothing. The mourners then burned sage, or some other strong-smelling plant, and bathed in the smoke. Ashes were scattered around the camp to discourage the return of the dead one. The remaining possessions were broken or burned; nothing was kept that would remind the living of the dead person. No one mentioned the name of the deceased again. The building in which the death occurred was moved to different site. For a time, mourning relatives did not participate in social events.

Ceremonies and festivals

Traditional rituals Rituals were developed in ancient times to cope with the dangers and uncertainties of the universe. The Navajo have been able to preserve their traditional beliefs and practices in the face of long-time pressure from mainstream American culture. Many Navajo ceremonies are healing rituals used for physical and emotional imbalances and problems of social maladjustment.

The most common ceremony may be the War Dance, which has the official name of "The Enemyway." This three-day ceremony held in summer comes from the legend of Changing Woman's twin sons, who went to see their father, the sun, to seek his help in slaying the monsters who inhabit the earth to make it safe for the Navajo people.

The Enemyway sounds like a ritual to get ready for war, but it is actually a way for a patient to be rid of the effects of an "enemy." For example, it is held for people who feel weak or faint at the sight of blood or who have scary dreams. The ceremony involves the use of a rattle stick, a piece of juniper about 18 inches (46 centimeters) long, carved with meaningful designs. Burnt herbs and melted wax are placed on the stick and on the face of the afflicted, and a complicated ceremony follows, ending with "killing" the enemy ghost and scattering his ashes, followed by a feast and final dance.

Modern festivals Throughout the year a number of fairs, festivals, and rodeos are held at various sites around the reservation. As part of these activities, people use sand painting, singing, and dancing by masked impersonators of Holy People as well as cornmeal, corn pollen, feathered prayer sticks, and bundles containing sacred items.

Each year, more than one hundred thousand people attend the Navajo Nation Fair, a five-day festival in Window Rock, Arizona, the capital of the Navajo Nation. The fair features Navajo traditions centering on the sacredness of food. It also offers art, crafts, chants, dances, and stories.

CURRENT TRIBAL ISSUES

A current Navajo land ownership issue revolves around a 7,000-square-mile (18,130-square-kilometer) area known as the Checkerboard. When railroads were built in the late 1800s, alternating sections in this region were granted to the railroad companies. Federal programs in the early twentieth century further fragmented lands in the area. At present, nearly thirty thousand Navajo live in the Checkerboard. The nation is making efforts to trade or buy land to create larger, more useful parcels.

One major concern of the tribe today is the high rate of cancer, especially in young females. Many believe it is a result of environmental pollution from uranium mining, which the Navajo are fighting against. With the reservation sitting on more than one hundred million pounds of uranium, the battle for control of these resources has been of major concern to the Navajo nation. In 2010, the court ruled that Churchrock, a uranium-mining site, was not on Navajo land, so the tribe had no right to sue to block the mining. The Navajo Nation says that their people will still be affected. They point to a disaster from more than thirty years ago that is still causing problems for the tribe. On July 16, 1979, a dam burst and contaminated more than 80 miles (130 kilometers) of the Puerco River with radioactive tailings and toxic wastewater. In 2011, the nation held a ceremony to remind people of the devastation that occurred on that date.

Mining has also caused other difficulties in the region, including the development of sinkholes at the Hopi reservation. A study published in

2011 showed that a major coal mine in Black Mesa was draining the area's water supply. For a nation in an arid climate, the consideration of the impact on future drinking water and irrigation is critical. Several action groups are using the information from this environmental assessment as ammunition in their fight to stop mining permit renewals.

A related environmental problem—construction of the coal-fired Desert Rock power plant, the third power plant in the Four Corners area—led to clashes between Navajo politicians and Diné Citizens Against Ruining the Environment (Diné CARE). Whereas politicians point out the benefits of additional power as well as more employment for the Navajo Nation, Diné CARE members' concerns are expressed by Bradley Angel of Greenaction, who opposes "a coal-fired power plant that would contribute to global warming, contaminate the air with asthma-inducing pollutants and cause the eviction of Navajo elders from their homes ... and of course, disturb the burials and cultural sites in the immediate vicinity of Desert Rock."

NOTABLE PEOPLE

Navajo Peterson Zah (1937–), who at one time was a teacher on his reservation, served as chief executive officer of the Navajo Nation government and chief fundraiser for the Navajo Education and Scholarship Foundation. In 1988, he founded a private firm that provided educational services to school districts on and off the reservation and worked to secure funds for new school construction on the Navajo and San Carlos Apache (see entry) reservations.

Annie Dodge Wauneka (1910–1997), the first woman to be elected to the Navajo Tribal Council, was a strong advocate for the Navajo people in politics, economics, and health. In 1964, she became the first Native American to receive the Presidential Medal of Freedom.

Manuelito (1818–1994) was a powerful warrior in raids against the Mexicans, Hopi, and Zuñi(see entry) and rose to prominence within his band. Of all the resistant Navajo bands, Manuelito's held out the longest against Kit Carson's troops, who tried to kill hostile Navajo and relocate the rest to Bosque Redondo. Pursued by the U.S. Army and facing starvation, Manuelito surrendered with his remaining warriors. He later traveled to Washington, D.C., to petition for the return of the Navajo homelands, and he successfully served as principal Navajo chief and chief of tribal police.

Over a period of seventy years, Henry Chee Dodge (c. 1857–1947) played a major role in forming a modern identity for the Navajo nation. Following the death of Manuelito, Dodge was chosen as Navajo head chief. Under his leadership, the tribe participated with the federal government in making and carrying out policies for mineral development, land rights issues, and federal programs such as school development. In 1923, he was elected chairperson of the first Navajo tribal council.

BOOKS

Bahti, Mark, and Eugene Baatsoslanii Joe. *Navajo Sandpaintings.* 3rd ed. Tucson, AZ: Rio Nuevo Publishers, 2009.

Becenti, Karyth. *One Nation, One Year: A Navajo Photographer's 365-Day Journey into a World of Discovery, Life and Hope.* Los Ranchos, NM: Rio Grande Books, 2010.

Benally, Malcolm D., ed. and trans. *Bitter Water: Dineì Oral Histories of the Navajo-Hopi Land.* Tucson: University of Arizona Press, 2011.

Brugge, Doug, Timothy Benally, and Esther Yazzie-Lewis. *The Navajo People and Uranium Mining.* Albuquerque: University of New Mexico Press, 2006.

Denetdale, Jennifer. *The Long Walk: The Forced Navajo Exile.* New York: Chelsea House, 2008.

Denetdale, Jennifer. *The Navajo.* New York: Chelsea House, 2011.

Dutton, Bertha P. *Indians of the American Southwest.* Englewood Cliffs, NJ: Prentice-Hall, 1975.

George, David Lane. *Spirit Warrior: Suspended between Ancient Terrors and Modern Insanities, a Young Navajo Searches for Truth.* Hagerstown, MD: Review and Herald, 2007.

Girdner, Alwin J. *Diné Tah: My Reservation Days 1923–1938.* Tucson: Rio Nuevo Publishers, c2011.

Kristofic, Jim. *Navajos Wear Nikes: A Reservation Life.* Albuquerque: University of New Mexico Press, 2011.

Lamphere, Louise, Eva Price, Carole Cadman, and Valerie Darwin. *Weaving Women's Lives: Three Generations in a Navajo Family.* Albuquerque: University of New Mexico Press, 2007.

Navajo Woven Prayers. San Diego, CA: Mingei International Museum, 2011.

Nez, Chester, and Judith Schiess Avila. *Code Talker.* New York: Berkley Caliber, 2011.

Page, Susanne and Jake. *Navajo.* Tucson, AZ: Rio Nuevo Publishers, 2010.

Pasternak, Judy. *Yellow Dirt: An American Story of a Poisoned Land and a People Betrayed.* New York, NY: Free Press, 2010.

Reid, Betty. *Navajo Women: Sáanii.* Tucson, AZ: Rio Nuevo Publishers, 2007.

Schwarz, Maureen Trudelle. *"I Choose Life": Contemporary Medical And Religious Practices in the Navajo World.* Norman: University of Oklahoma Press, 2008.

Sonneborn, Liz. *The Navajos.* Minneapolis, MN: Lerner Publications, 2007.

Spragg-Braude, Stacia. *To Walk in Beauty: A Navajo Family's Journey Home.* Santa Fe: Museum of New Mexico Press, 2009.

Wolfkiller: Wisdom from a Nineteenth-Century Navajo Shepherd. Recorded by Louisa Wade Wetherill; compiled by Harvey Leake. Salt Lake City: Gibbs Smith, 2007.

PERIODICALS

Bergman, Robert. "A School for Medicine Men." *American Journal of Psychiatry* 130, no. 6 (1973): 663–66.

WEB SITES

Alamo Chapter. http://alamo.nndes.org/ (accessed on July 20, 2011).

Cline Library. "Indigenous Voices of the Colorado Plateau: Navajo." *Northern Arizona University.* http://library.nau.edu/speccoll/exhibits/indigenous_voices/navajo/overview.html (accessed on July 20, 2011).

Faunce, Hilda. "Desert Wife." *Southwest Crossroads.* http://southwestcrossroads.org/record.php?num=814 (accessed on July 20, 2011).

"Impacts of Resource Development on Native American Lands: The Navajo Nation and Uranium Mining." *Carelton College.* http://serc.carleton.edu/research_education/nativelands/navajo/index.html (accessed on July 20, 2011).

Kawno, Kenji. "Warriors: Navajo Code Talkers." *Southwest Crossroads.* http://southwestcrossroads.org/record.php?num=387 (accessed on July 20, 2011).

"The Long Walk." *Council of Indian Nations.* http://www.nrcprograms.org/site/PageServer?pagename=cin_hist_thelongwalk (accessed on July 20, 2011).

Myers, Tom. "Navajo Reservation" (video). *University of Illinois.* http://www.vimeo.com/8828354 (accessed on July 20, 2011).

"Navajo (Diné)." *Northern Arizona University.* http://www.cpluhna.nau.edu/People/navajo.htm (accessed on July 20, 2011).

Navajo Indian Tribes History. *Access Genealogy.* http://www.accessgenealogy.com/native/tribes/navajo/navahoindianhist.htm (accessed on July 20, 2011).

Maryboy, Nancy C. and David Begay. "The Navajo of Utah." *Utah's History to Go: State of Utah.* http://historytogo.utah.gov/people/ethnic_cultures/the_history_of_utahs_american_indians/chapter7.html (accessed on July 20, 2011).

The Navajo Nation. http://www.navajo-nsn.gov/history.htm (accessed on July 31, 2007).

"Navajo Pottery." *ClayHound Web.* http://www.clayhound.us/sites/navajo.htm (accessed on July 31, 2007).

"Navajo Tourism Video Series." *Navajo Tourism Department.* http://discovernavajo.com/ (accessed on July 20, 2011).

"Navajo War." *Council of Indian Nations.* http://www.nrcprograms.org/site/PageServer?pagename=cin_hist_navajowar (accessed on July 20, 2011).

"Navajo Wedding Legend." *Twin Rocks Trading Post.* http://www.twinrocks.com/legends/128-navajo-weddings.html (accessed on July 20, 2011).

Peterson, Leighton C. "Tuning in to Navajo: The Role of Radio in Native Language Maintenance." *Northern Arizona University.* http://jan.ucc.nau.edu/~jar/TIL_17.html (accessed on July 20, 2011).

Ramah Navajo Chapter. http://ramah.nndes.org/ (accessed on July 20, 2011).

To'hajiilee Navajo Chapter. http://tohajiilee.nndes.org/ (accessed on July 20, 2011).

Weiser, Kathy. "The Navajo—Largest in U.S." *Legends of America.* http://www.legendsofamerica.com/na-navajo.html (accessed on July 20, 2011).

Pima

Name

The Pima (pronounced *PEE-mah*) referred to themselves as *Akimel O'odham* (pronounced *AH-kee-mul oh-OH-tum*) or *Akimel O'othom* (pronounced *AH-kee-mul AU-authm,* meaning "River People." Legend has it that Spanish explorers asked several questions of the first Pima Indians they encountered. When the Natives answered their questions with the phrase *pi-nyi-match* ("I do not know"), the Spanish misunderstood and thought they were saying *Pima.* Thereafter, the Spanish explorers referred to the people as Pima.

Location

The Pima were desert dwellers from various portions of the 100,000-square-mile (259,000-square-kilometer) Sonoran Desert. The people that the Spanish called Upper Pimans came from southern Arizona and southeastern California; Lower Pimans inhabited western Sonora (a section of the desert that extends into Mexico). Modern-day descendants of the Upper Piman Indians live with members of the Maricopa tribe on the Gila River Reservation and the Salt River Reservation in southern Arizona. Some Pima also live on the Ak-Chin (Maricopa) Reservation in Maricopa, Arizona. (Lower Pimans are now called Tohono O'odham.)

Population

In 1694, there were an estimated 2,000 to 3,000 Pima. In the 1990 U.S. Census, 15,074 people identified themselves as Pima, making the tribe the sixteenth-largest in the United States at that time. The 2010 census counted 22,040 Pima. In 2011, the Ak-Chin Indian Community had a tribal enrollment of 770, Salt River had 8,700 members, and Gila River had 14,000 people enrolled.

Language family

Uto-Aztecan.

Origins and group affiliations

The Pima believe they originated in the Salt River Valley and later spread to the Gila River area. They most likely descended from the prehistoric Hohokam people, whose culture faded about 1450. The Pima Nation

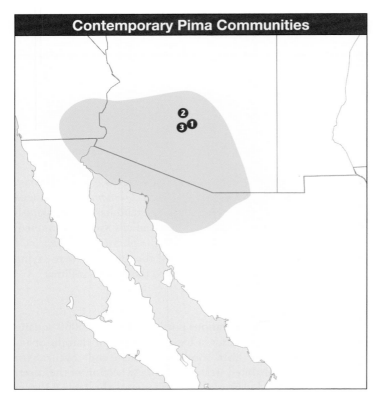

Contemporary Pima Communities

Arizona

❶ Gila River Pima–Maricopa Indian Community
❷ Salt River Pima–Maricopa Indian Community
❸ Ak-Chin Indian Community

Shaded area

Traditional lands of the Pima in the Sonoran Desert in present-day southern Arizona, southeastern California, and northern Mexico

A map of contemporary Pima communities. MAP BY XNR PRODUCTIONS. CENGAGE LEARNING, GALE. REPRODUCED BY PERMISSION OF GALE, A PART OF CENGAGE LEARNING.

shares a similar language and certain traits with tribes in Sonora, Mexico—especially with the neighboring Tohono O'odham (often called the Papago). The Pima were friends and allies of the Maricopa and enemies of the Apache and Quechan tribes, who often raided and stole from them.

Once a farming people, the Pima were known for their courtesy and generosity. As they employed Spanish agricultural knowledge and technology, they became prosperous large-scale farmers in their own right. Their newfound wealth was said to have changed them from a gentle people into warriors forced to protect their surplus crops from enemy raiders. The Pima frequently supplied produce to American settlers passing through their seemingly barren desert territory. Carrying on a tradition now hundreds of years old, the people continue to farm the arid (dry) lands of Arizona, but their difficult job has been eased somewhat by modern irrigation techniques.

HISTORY

Early encounters with the Spanish

No one knows for sure how long the Pima Indians have lived in Arizona and Mexico. By the time the Spanish encountered them in 1694, the tribe had adapted to the widely varying environments in their homeland, which ranged from extremely dry sections where food and water were in short supply to regions that supported crops quite well.

Historians believe that when the Spanish first encountered them, the Pima were in decline, having suffered from plagues of diseases for the previous 170 years. The Pima lived in several farming communities, where people worked together to plant and harvest crops. For some time after their arrival in the New World, the Spanish were busy in other regions, trying to convert Native peoples to the Catholic faith and make them a useful part of the Spanish empire. Tribes such as the Pueblo (see Pueblo entries) rebelled against the Spanish, but Pima participation in the revolts was minimal for three main reasons: (1) their location was remote, (2) they were busy with their farms, and (3) they had less contact with outsiders.

The Spanish government knew little about the Pima, but they approved of the tribe's industrious nature and its policy of noninvolvement in the numerous Native uprisings that occurred in the eighteenth century. Hoping to win the tribe's confidence and support, the Spanish introduced new farming techniques to them.

Spanish innovations assist farming

The Pima reaped immediate benefits from Spanish farming methods. They gained a new food crop—winterwheat—and thus were able to farm year-round. After learning to grow more food with advanced irrigation techniques, the tribe became an important economic force in the region, and years of prosperity followed.

Important Dates

1694: First contact with Spanish explorers.

1848: Pima lands become U.S. territory following the Mexican-American War.

1859: American surveyors map out a reservation on the Gila River for the Pima and Maricopa Indians. It includes fields, but no water.

1871: New non-Native settlements reduce the water supply to Pima lands, thus destroying the tribe's farms.

1879: The Salt River Indian Reservation is established.

1895: Congress formally establishes the Gila River Indian Community, setting aside 375,000 acres of land for the Native nations.

1993: Gaming is approved; tribe opens casinos.

A surplus of grain and cotton allowed the Pima to engage in trade. Their visibility in the trading community brought them to the attention of the Apache (see entry), who took note of Pima surpluses and began to raid their communities. This forced the Pima to cut down on their travel, to move into fewer, larger settlements for protection, and to sharpen their fighting skills.

In 1848, following the American victory in the Mexican-American War (1846–48; a war fought between the United States and Mexico that led to loss of about half of Mexico's national territory to the United States), the United States acquired Pima lands. The Pima hoped to learn more about farming from the Americans but were disappointed when no such help was given. For their part, the Pima proved to be good friends to the United States. They supplied food and livestock to pioneers who traveled through Pima lands during the California gold rush, which began in 1848. When American frontiersman Kit Carson (1809–1868) asked to buy food in 1846, the Pima chief replied, "Bread is to eat, not to sell. Take what you want."

The Pima also helped the U.S. Army protect settlers against Apache raiders and supplied farm goods to U.S. troops. The Pima hoped to receive guns and shovels in return, but U.S. officials failed to deliver on their promises. The tribe's anger and confusion grew when the federal government— without explanation—supplied farming implements to the Pima people's traditional enemy, the Apache. (Apache Indians were not farmers and therefore were not likely to use the implements.) The U.S. failure to repay the Pima's generosity must have been especially bewildering to the tribe because of their gift-based bartering system (see "Economy").

Around the same time, the Apache were also raiding Maricopa Indian villages to the west, forcing the Maricopa toward Pima territory. In 1859, American surveyors plotted out the Salt River Pima–Maricopa Indian Community Reservation for both the Pima and Maricopa Indians. The reservation included fields but no water, and the era of Pima farming wealth quickly faded.

"Years of famine"

The Pima economy collapsed in 1871, after the construction of a dam that diverted water from the Gila River to lands settled by whites. Some Pima moved south to a location on the Salt River; in 1879, their new settlement became the Salt River Indian Reservation.

A Pima Indian woman carries a pot on her head at the Gila River Reservation in Arizona. NATIONAL ARCHIVES AND RECORDS ADMINISTRATION.

The Pima way of life disappeared completely between 1871 and 1918, a period the tribe remembers as the "years of famine." Those who wanted to work became dependent on wages earned performing labor for the settlers. Presbyterian missionaries arrived, discouraged the Pima from practicing their traditional religion, and assumed control of the education of their children. Many members of the tribe turned to alcohol. Tensions within the group escalated. Isolated from the world and unwilling to learn English or adopt the American ways, the people fell into poverty and despair.

Adapting to the outside world

Pima contact with the outside world was almost nonexistent at the beginning of the twentieth century. Their isolation lessened somewhat after they acquired battery-powered radios and began to learn English. Some Pima men served in the U.S. military during World War II (1939–45) and returned to the reservations with a wider worldview and a determination to bring their fellow Pima into modern life. This process was further hastened by a tremendous postwar population explosion in the nearby city of Phoenix, which grew from about 107,000 people in 1945 to 790,000 people thirty years later.

Major technological advances took place in Arizona in the first half of the twentieth century. Among them were the expansion of the Southern Pacific Railroad, the building of the Roosevelt Dam on the Salt River, and other significant water projects that returned some water to the Pima. Since then, the Pima have become involved in the expanding economy of the surrounding urban areas. Forward-thinking Pima leaders have been working hard to take on the challenges of the twenty-first century. They predict that the tribe will embrace and adopt worthwhile aspects of the larger American culture, modify its farming lifestyle to keep up with the competition, and expand its economic base by developing nonagricultural means of support.

RELIGION

Not much is known about early Pima religious practices. According to the Pima origin story, the Earthmaker created a world populated by supernatural beings such as Coyote the trickster and a man-eating beast. A great flood later caused the supernatural beings to flee, but Elder Brother returned, created the Pima and their neighbors, and taught them the arts and ceremonies they practiced. Like other Southwestern Native nations, the Pima celebrated the corn harvest, fertility (the ability to conceive and bear children), and rainmaking.

Early Spanish Catholic missionaries had little influence on the Pima. The people accepted some Catholic rituals such as baptism, but they blended them with their own traditional ceremonies. Presbyterian missionaries were much more successful. They arrived during the 1870s and had a profound effect on the Pima. By the 1890s, they claimed about 1,800 Pima as members. Officials of the Catholic Church returned and started the first missions among the Pima around 1900, but the tribe did not accept this attempt to convert them to a different kind of Christianity.

LANGUAGE

The Pima speak a single dialect (variety) of the Piman language. By way of comparison, their relatives, the Tohono O'odham (see entry), speak the same language but have maintained several distinct dialects. As longtime allies and neighbors, the Pima and Maricopa traditionally have known each other's languages.

In the twentieth century, the Pima people began learning English. Statistics from the U.S. Bureau of the Census in 2000 showed that of almost 10,000 O'odham speakers, about 8 percent spoke little or no English. Conversely, only 4 percent of the younger generation (under age fifteen) did not speak English well. In 2010, statistics indicated that close to 11,000 people spoke Pima, and children were learning their native language, beginning in elementary school.

GOVERNMENT

Long ago, the Pima were a loosely organized society. Each independent farming community had a designated leader and one or more influential persons called shamans (pronounced *SHAH-munz* or *SHAY-munz*), who specialized in healing, controlling the weather, or ensuring success in battle. As the Pima began farming on a greater scale and interacting more with outsiders during trade and warfare, the position of leader (or governor) became increasingly important and was passed down from father to son.

The Pima people earned considerable distinction as farmers and then as soldiers. Their uncompromising work ethic and impressive organizational skills secured their title as a "nation" in the eyes of the Spanish, Mexican, and U.S. governments. The Pima Nation elected its own governor and tribal council.

The Pima of the early twenty-first century lived on reservations held jointly with the Maricopa tribe, a traditional neighbor and ally. The Gila

---

Pima Bajo Words

Most of these words are used by the Mexican Pima. Many Pima words used in the United States are similar to those in the Tohono O'odham (see entry) dialect (variety of language).

goka	"two"
himak	"one"
kai	"seed"
kili	"man"
maakov	"four"
masadi	"moon"
maviis	"five"
okosi	"woman"
sudagi	"water"
tasa	"sun"
vaika	"three"

River Indian Community is governed by an elected tribal council representing seven districts, as well as a governor and a lieutenant governor. The tribal council encourages and facilitates youth participation in government.

The official governing body of the Salt River tribe is the Salt River Pima–Maricopa Indian Community Council, whose seven elected members include a president and a vicepresident. Council members are elected from one of two electoral districts for four-year terms. Ak-Chin Reservation has a Community Council of five members.

ECONOMY

Early farming

The Pima Indians have always been farmers. Tribal members became traders only after the Spanish arrived in the New World. Before the Pima developed their own "buying and selling" economy like that of the settlers, they had an interesting way of exchanging goods: they distributed most items as gifts. In this system of give and take, a person offered a possession to another person, who had to accept it. The giver gained power or importance, and the recipient was obliged to return the gift in some way. The presenter sometimes used lines to mark the value of a gift. For example, when offering grains or beans in a basket, the donor marked lines on the basket to show how high up the sides the grain or beans came. This ensured that when the receiver returned in the basket, the amount matched or exceeded the original in worth. Merchandise also changed hands based on the outcome of games and foot races.

After contact with the Spanish, the Pima began growing winter wheat and used more elaborate irrigation methods to increase the productivity of their crops. Agricultural development supported more people and allowed the Pima to trade surplus grain with other tribes and with non-Natives. Eventually, the Pima sold crops for gold and silver.

During the period of greatest prosperity, the tribe's surplus goods made them an attractive target for Apache raiders. To get back at the Apache thieves, the Pima sometimes kidnapped and sold Apache children to the Spanish for use as slaves. They later traded wheat, baskets, and blankets to the Mexicans and to other tribes for items such as hides and wild peppers—items not available in Pima homelands.

Where they had once grown only as much food as their own needs demanded, the Pima responded to increased outside demands for their grains and produce by growing more. The resulting prosperity introduced the concepts of personal possessions and wealth to Pima culture. By the time they lost the water they needed to grow their many crops, the Pima had also lost the old ways of farming their land as a cooperative group and sharing the proceeds with others. Farming was not reestablished as a productive way of life for nearly a century.

Modern economy

The water crisis of the late 1800s and the period of famine that followed forced some Pima to turn to low-paying wage jobs and government welfare until farming became practical once again. The reservations looked for other ways to use their land, such as leasing it to such outside industries as research and development companies, a brass foundry, telecommunications businesses, and manufacturing plants. These industries brought jobs to the reservations.

With modern irrigation techniques in place, agriculture is once again an important source of income for the Pima. In addition to their very fine Pima cotton, the nation grows wheat, millet (small-seeded cereal grasses), alfalfa, barley, melons, pistachios, olives, citrus fruits, and vegetables. The prime location of the reservations territory attracts many tourists, who are drawn by artifacts offered at the Hoo-hoogam Ki Museum and the Gila Indian Center. Golf courses, a marina complex, an international racepark, and many tribal annual events are also open to the public.

After gaming was authorized in 1993, the Pima constructed casinos. They also developed tourism, built industrial parks, and opened businesses on the reservation. Although all of these have proved profitable, unemployment remains high on the reservations. In 2000 at Gila River, almost 25 percent of the people who wanted to work could not find jobs; unemployment at the other reservations was about 10 percent. By 2011, that figure had dropped to 8 percent for both the Pima and Maricopa peoples.

Pima Cotton: Among the World's Finest

Extra-long staple (ELS) cotton has been grown in the Southwest since the early 1900s. It was previously called American-Egyptian cotton. In 1951, a seed was developed that produced a superior ELS cotton known for its outstanding silkiness. It was called Pima cotton in honor of the Pima tribe, who were raising the cotton on a U.S. Department of Agriculture experimental farm in Sacaton, Arizona, which was headquarters of the Gila River Pima–Maricopa Indian Community. Pima cotton is used by the world's finest textile (clothmaking) mills.

DAILY LIFE

Families

Pima families included a husband and wife, their young children, their unmarried adult daughters, and the families of their married sons.

Buildings

The early Pima built small, round, flat-roofed houses called *ki* (pronounced *kee*). The typical ki measured 10 to 25 feet (3 to 8 meters) in diameter. Four posts and two main support beams propped up the roof. The Pima bent light willow poles in a circle around this square frame and tied them to it. Support beams, in turn, braced several lighter cross poles. The people used arrowwood, cattail reeds, wheat straw, or corn stalks

A woman sits outside a ki, a traditional Pima home made of straw, reeds, or corn stalks, in 1907. LIBRARY OF CONGRESS, EDWARD S. CURTIS COLLECTION, LC-USZ62-101255.

over the cottonwood frame. Dirt on top of this brush or straw covered the domelike structures. Although they often leaked, these homes could survive strong winds.

Other buildings in the traditional Pima village included a rectangular council house, storehouses, a lodge for women who were menstruating, and cottonwood arbors that protected people from the heat of the sun.

The people worked together as a community. If someone in the village lost a house through fire or another disaster, everyone gathered, and both men and women rebuilt the home. Families all donated food, which the women cooked to feed the workers.

Even after centuries of contact with people who lived in adobe (pronounced *uh-DOE-bee*) homes, the tribe persisted in building the ki single-family home until the late 1800s. (Adobe is a sun-dried mud made of a mixture of clay, sand, and sometimes ashes, rocks, or straw.) The Pima began building pueblo-style adobe houses around the turn of the twentieth century, but cement-block construction later became a more popular method of construction.

Clothing and adornment

Before the Spanish arrived in Pima territory, the people wore little clothing. Men dressed in breechcloths, apronlike garments that hung from the waist. Women wore skirts made of cotton or of the inner part of cottonwood bark; padding under the skirts made them stand away from the body. Sandals and cotton blankets added protection and warmth when needed. Later on Pima men wore Spanish-style clothing.

The Pima paid particular attention to hairstyles, body painting, and tattooing. Men and women wore their hair long. Whereas women wore theirs loose with bangs, men braided or twisted theirs into locks and added human or horse hair or even woven headbands to make it look bulkier and fuller. Frequent brushings and a dressing of river mud and mesquite gum kept their hair dark and shiny. The Pima sometimes painted their hair, faces, and bodies. Both sexes had their lower eyelids lined with tattoos, usually at the time of puberty or marriage. Men also tattooed lines across the forehead; women added lines along each side of the chin. Grease applied to the face protected against chapping.

Food

For many centuries, Pima farmers used just two implements: a digging stick and a sharpened board that served as both hoe and harvester. They concentrated on farming the islands in the Gila River and the land on the surrounding floodplain. The tribe's most important crops were corn and tepary beans (pronounced *TEH-puh-ree*), supplemented with wild foods such as mesquite beans and saguaro (*suh-WAHR-uh*) cactus fruit.

Although their early farming methods were primitive, the Pima usually met their primary food needs without having to hunt or gather. When drought or other catastrophes damaged their crops, they fished or hunted deer, rabbit, quail, and doves. They also searched for food to make up for the lost grains and vegetation. The area where they live abounds with cactus. Most cacti had fruit that the tribe stewed into preserves or made into syrup or wine. After cooking the fruit from the cholla cactus for half a day in a pit lined with hot stones, the women ground it into meal and mixed it with wheat flour to make mush.

Education

In early times, Pima chiefs and parents were a child's primary source of knowledge. Their role was taken over by missionaries and government agents during the early reservation period, but the Pima were so impoverished at the time that they had little interest in education of any kind.

Present-day Pima recognize the importance of education and training to ensure that young people attain good high-paying jobs. Education begins early with a Head Start program for preschoolers. There are elementary schools on the reservations, and children attend high school at public schools in nearby cities. Pima children are encouraged to attend college and return home to use the skills they acquire for the betterment of the tribe. The tribe contributes millions of dollars every year to pay for higher education for Pima students.

Healing practices

The early Pima believed that people could be made ill by behaving badly toward animals or by offending clouds or lightning. They called on healers called shamans for help. Shamans gained their powers through dream visions in which they met powerful supernatural beings. Later, these healers called upon these supernatural beings to heal the sick.

A Pima medicine man performs a morning prayer during the winter solstice. © ARNE HODALIC/CORBIS.

To find out what ailed a person, the shaman breathed tobacco smoke over the patient's body and sometimes used an eagle feather or crystal to connect with the spirit world. This ritual allowed the shaman to see what spirits had visited the body and harmed its health. If these steps did not work, the shaman sang to the spirits, asking them to communicate the nature of the illness. Then a curing ritual was performed.

The Pima thought of shamans as heroes, but white missionaries encouraged the people to look upon shamans with suspicion. Because of this, in 1860 and 1861, the tribe blamed three shamans for causing a plague; they then killed the shamans. Other shamans were also murdered over the years following epidemics (uncontrolled outbreaks of deadly diseases). By the late twentieth century, though, shamans had regained the respect once given them, but the number of these healers had decreased dramatically.

Modern-day Pima have become a subject of great interest to U.S. health officials. Native Americans are more likely than other Americans to contract diabetes. In diabetic patients, blood sugar levels rise well above normal limits. The frequency of a certain type of diabetes at the Gila River Indian Reservation is the highest known in the world. For more than three decades, the Pima people have been cooperating with medical researchers who are studying the causes of the disease. Because the Pima people usually intermarry and remain in the same community,

A Pima woman poses with pottery on her head in 1907.
© EDWARD S. CURTIS/CORBIS.

researchers can eliminate outside factors in their research. Pima diabetics are studied and treated for the disease at a sophisticated health center located on the reservation. The results of these studies will benefit diabetics around the world.

ARTS

The Pima made beautiful and functional baskets and woven cotton blankets. Many baskets were shaped like large, round trays that could be carried on people's heads. The Pima wove them of willow or cottonwood and dyed some fibers black with the pods of devil's claw, an acacia bush. They made larger burden baskets from four giant cactus ribs that they tied together with rope braided from human hair. Women carried these baskets on their backs, but they also supported full baskets with a strap across their foreheads.

Pima pottery was more practical than decorative. Early pottery was cream-colored. Redware was developed later; it was decorated with black designs made using mesquite gum.

CUSTOMS

Marriage and divorce

Parents usually arranged marriages for their children, but children could freely express their wishes about their future mates. Marriages in Pima society were quite informal. The couple lived together and declared themselves married with no ceremony to mark the occasion. Divorce and remarriage were also relatively simple.

War rituals

The Pima began as a society of gentle people who valued peace. The wealth they gained from growing surplus crops changed their lives. They were forced to station guards around their settlements and defend themselves from raids by tribes who wanted what they had. Warring became far more frequent as the tribe carried out counter-raids to punish thieves. The Pima trained their men to be outstanding warriors; they fought with heavy clubs and shot arrows treated with rattlesnake poison. However, the people still considered the concept of war as evil. When a Pima warrior killed someone, he tried to make up for the person's death by secluding himself for a

A dancer in traditional dress and face paint performs at a Salt River Pima–Maricopa Indian Community powwow in Scottsdale, Arizona.
© DOUG JAMES/ SHUTTERSTOCK.COM.

sixteen-day purification period, which involved fasting and special rites performed by a shaman to cleanse the warrior's weapons.

Festivals and ceremonies

In ancient times, the Pima had few ceremonies, although there may have been a simple puberty ritual for girls. Modern Pima celebrate many occasions. Annual happenings include a New Year's Chicken Scratch Dance; the "Mul-Chu-Tha," a tribal fair that raises money for youth activities and features a parade, Native American rodeo, arts and crafts, and dances; and the Red Mountain Eagle Powwow. A powwow is a traditional celebration that includes singers and dancers from many different tribes. Several sports tournaments, a beauty/talent pageant, a fall carnival, and Rodeo Days are more recent additions to their lineup of public events.

CURRENT TRIBAL ISSUES

Because water was diverted by non-Native farmers farther upstream, the Gila River ran dry. This loss of water, combined with periods of drought, caused crop failure and famine. For almost one hundred years, the Pima engaged in legal battles to reclaim their water rights. The issue was settled in 2005 by a federal law that allotted a percentage of the upstream water to flow into the Gila River territory, but water is still a concern for other reservations in this arid area. In 2011, the Ak-Chin Indian Community began a water reclamation project that included plans for a surface water treatment plant,which will help bring clean drinking water to the community. That same year, the Gila River Reservation developed plans for an extensive irrigation project that would channel water to areas where it was scarce.

The Gila River Reservation also struggled with the cleanup of a hazardous waste dump on land it had leased to a tire recycling company. More than eleven thousand tons of tires had been piled up on the property. When an arsonist set them on fire, they smoldered for months, causing air pollution and forcing many tribal members to be evacuated. Redevelopment grants in 2010 and 2011 allowed the community to move forward with major cleanup projects. Soil contamination is another concern connected with the dumping area.

Like other Southwestern nations, the Pima are working to improve the quality of education and health care on their reservations. Although many Southwest tribes have at least partially closed their communities to outsiders and protect aspects of their culture through secrecy, the Pima have allowed outsiders to observe their culture. Modern Pima regard themselves as a people with their own history and traditions, which they have retained despite all outside attempts to change them.

NOTABLE PEOPLE

Ira Hamilton Hayes (1923–1955) was probably the most famous Native soldier of World War II. In February 1945, his unit landed on Iwo Jima, a barren island in the Pacific Ocean. Iwo Jima served as a base for launching U.S. air strikes against Japan, the United States' greatest rival in the war. Hayes became one of six marines who raised the U.S. flag on the summit of the island's now-famous Mount Suribachi in the midst of heavy enemy fire. The Associated Press photograph that captured the moment on film became the basis for the bronze monument in Washington, D.C., that commemorates the battle of Iwo Jima. After he finished his military service, Hayes returned to the Pima Reservation, but the taste of fame that came with his war exploits had a destructive effect on him in the postwar years. He became a drifter, an alcoholic, and a lawbreaker. Hayes died of exposure in the Arizona desert on January 24, 1955. He was buried alongside many of his fallen comrades in Arlington National Cemetery, not far from the bronze statue that captures the pivotal moment in his life.

The Man in the Maze

Many Arizona tribes use the symbol of the maze, which represents the house of Elder Brother. The maze can be seen on the Great Seal of the Salt River Pima–Maricopa Indian Community. This pattern carries the meaning of life, and children are told that it shows the journey of life.

Daily life has many twists and turns just as the maze does. Sometimes bad events happen that require a turn in the path. Over time, a person reaches the center of the maze. There, he or she meets the Sun God and moves into the next world. Alfretta Antone explains the meaning passed down from generation to generation.

> "The maze is a symbol of life … happiness, sadness … and you reach your goal … there's a dream there, and you reach that dream when you get to the middle of the maze … that's how I was told, my grandparents told me that's how the maze is."

SOURCE: Myers, John, and Robert Gryder. "The Man in the Maze." *The Salt River Pima-Maricopa Indians.* Phoenix: Life's Reflections, 1988.

The 1961 film *The Outsider*, starring Tony Curtis, is loosely based on the life of Ira Hayes. Folksinger and songwriter Bob Dylan's single "The Ballad of Ira Hayes," released in 1965, provides a far more realistic account of this tragic hero's experiences. For a generation of young Native Americans who came of age during the late 1960s and early 1970s, Hayes took on new prominence, becoming a modern symbol of the wronged Native American warrior: he fought for the United States and gained celebrity, but he died in near obscurity.

BOOKS

Bahr, Donald. *How Mockingbirds Are: O'odham Ritual Orations*. Albany: State University of New York Press, 2011.

Cook, Charles H., and Isaac T. Whittemore. *Among the Pimas; or, the Mission to the Pima and Maricopa Indians (1893)*. Whitefish, MT: Kessinger Publishing, 2010.

DeJong, David H. *Forced to Abandon Our Fields: The 1914 Clay Southworth Gila River Pima Interviews*. Salt Lake City: University of Utah Press, 2011.

DeJong, David H. *Stealing the Gila: The Pima Agricultural Economy and Water Deprivation, 1848–1921*. Tucson: University of Arizona Press, 2009.

Ezell, Paul H. "History of the Pima." In *Handbook of North American Indians,* Volume 10: *Southwest,* edited by Alfonso Ortiz. Washington, DC: Smithsonian Institution Press, 1983.

Lloyd, J. William. *Aw-aw-tam Indian Nights: The Myths and Legends of the Pimas*. Westfield, NJ: The Lloyd Group, 1911. Available online from http://www.sacred-texts.com/nam/sw/ain/index.htm (accessed on July 20, 2011).

Rea, Amadeo M. *Wings in the Desert: A Folk Orinthology of the Northern Pimans*. Tucson: University of Arizona Press, 2007.

Russell, Frank. *The Pima Indians*. Whitefish, MT: Kessinger Publishing, 2010.

Underhill, Ruth. *The Papago Indians of Arizona and their Relatives the Pima*. Whitefish, MT: Kessinger Publishing, 2010.

Webb, George. *A Pima Remembers*. Tucson: University of Arizona Press, 1959.

WEB SITES

Ak-Chin Indian Community. http://www.ak-chin.nsn.us/ (accessed on July 20, 2011).

"Ak-Chin Indian Reservation." *Northern Arizona University.* www.cba.nau.edu/caied/tribepages/AkChin.asp (accessed on July 20, 2011).

"Edward S. Curtis's The North American Indian." *Northwestern University Digital Collections.* http://curtis.library.northwestern.edu/curtis/toc.cgi (accessed on July 20, 2011).

Field Division of Education. "Material Culture of the Pima, Papago, and Western Apache." *National Park Service*. http://www.cr.nps.gov/history/online_books/berkeley/beals1/beals1i.htm (accessed on July 20, 2011).

Gila River Indian Community. http://www.gilariver.org/ (accessed on July 20, 2011).

Meeks, Heather, Michael Mensah, and Ashley Cobb. "Waila Music." *University of Arizona*. http://parentseyes.arizona.edu/msw/waila/index.html (accessed on July 20, 2011).

"O'odham (O'odhamñiok)." *Omniglot*. http://www.omniglot.com/writing/oodham.htm (accessed on July 20, 2011).

"Pima (AkimelO'odham)." *Four Directions Institute*. http://www.fourdir.com/pima.htm (accessed on July 20, 2011).

"Pima Indian Tribe History." *Access Genealogy*. www.accessgenealogy.com/native/tribes/pima/pimaindianhist.htm (accessed on July 20, 2011).

"The Pima Indians: Pathfinders for Health." *National Diabetes Information Clearinghouse*. http://diabetes.niddk.nih.gov/dm/pubs/pima/index.htm (accessed on July 20, 2011).

"Pima Language." *Global Recordings Network*. http://globalrecordings.net/en/language/237 (accessed on July 20, 2011).

"Pima-Papago—Religion and Expressive Culture." *Countries and Their Cultures*. http://www.everyculture.com/North-America/Pima-Papago-Religion-and-Expressive-Culture.html (accessed on July 20, 2011).

Redish, Laura, and Orrin Lewis. "TohonoO'odham (Papago) and AkimelO'odham (Pima)." *Native Languages of the Americas*. http://www.native-languages.org/papago.htm (accessed on July 20, 2011).

Salt River Pima–Maricopa Indian Community. http://www.srpmic-nsn.gov/ (accessed on July 20, 2011).

Pueblo

For more information on the Pueblo people, see Acoma Pueblo, Jemez Pueblo, San Juan Pueblo, Taos Pueblo, and Zuñi Pueblo entries.

Name

Pueblo (pronounced *PWEB-loh*). Early Spanish explorers gave this name to various Native groups living in territory that is now part of the American Southwest. A *pueblo* is a stone and adobe village inhabited by various tribes in the southwestern United States. The broad Spanish name now refers to both the Pueblo people and the pueblos (cities) where they live.

Location

The Pueblo people have always lived in New Mexico and northeastern Arizona. The surviving New Mexico pueblos are located at Acoma, Cochiti, Isleta, Jemez, Laguna, Nambé, Picuris, Pojoaque, Sandia, San Felipe, San Ildefonso, San Juan, Santa Ana, Santa Clara, Santo Domingo, Taos, Tesuque, Zia, and Zuni. Most are located on the Rio Grande River and its branches. The Hopi people live in Arizona, and Ysleta del Sur Pueblo, near El Paso, Texas, was begun by refugees from the New Mexican Isleta Pueblo.

Population

There were an estimated 250,000 Pueblo in the early 1600s. They lived in 134 or more villages in the early sixteenth century. Between 1540 and 1700, the number of villages dwindled to 19, where it remains today. In the 1990 U.S. Census, 55,330 people identified themselves as Pueblo. By 2000, that number had risen to 59,621. The 2010 census counted 49,695 Pueblo, with a total of 62,540 people claiming some Pueblo heritage.

Language family

Pueblo languages belong to four different families: Keresan, Tanoan, Zunian, and Uto-Aztecan.

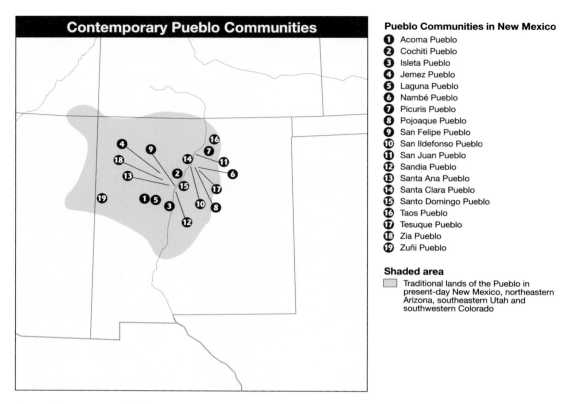

Contemporary Pueblo Communities

Pueblo Communities in New Mexico

1. Acoma Pueblo
2. Cochiti Pueblo
3. Isleta Pueblo
4. Jemez Pueblo
5. Laguna Pueblo
6. Nambé Pueblo
7. Picuris Pueblo
8. Pojoaque Pueblo
9. San Felipe Pueblo
10. San Ildefonso Pueblo
11. San Juan Pueblo
12. Sandia Pueblo
13. Santa Ana Pueblo
14. Santa Clara Pueblo
15. Santo Domingo Pueblo
16. Taos Pueblo
17. Tesuque Pueblo
18. Zia Pueblo
19. Zuñi Pueblo

Shaded area

Traditional lands of the Pueblo in present-day New Mexico, northeastern Arizona, southeastern Utah and southwestern Colorado

A map of contemporary Pueblo communities. MAP BY XNR PRODUCTIONS. CENGAGE LEARNING, GALE. REPRODUCED BY PERMISSION OF GALE, A PART OF CENGAGE LEARNING.

Origins and group affiliations

Ancestors of the Pueblo people were the Hisatsinom, or Ancestral Puebloans (see Anasazi entry), a group of wandering hunters who settled down between 400 and 700. They grew corn and other crops and built houses in caves and cliffs. At the end of the twentieth century, the people called Pueblo were actually nineteen independent tribes in New Mexico, one in Arizona, and one in Texas.

The Pueblo believe that the first humans came out of the earth through an opening called *sipapu*. Unlike other Native nations who were moved onto reservations by the U.S. government, the Pueblo still inhabit their ancestral lands, and their culture has not undergone a great deal of change. Historically, the many Pueblo groups were alike in key ways: they built permanent homes, had similar religious customs, made pottery, and grew corn, beans, and squash.

HISTORY

The "ancient ones"

Although the ancestors of the Pueblo lived in the American Southwest for more than twelve thousand years, not much is known about them, partly because the Pueblo will not allow archaeologists to dig extensively on Pueblo land. (Archaeologists are scientists who recover and study the evidence of past cultures.) Thousands of years ago, the ancestors of the Pueblo, the Anasazi (see entry), lived in the Four Corners area, where the present-day states of Arizona, Colorado, New Mexico, and Utah meet.

Until the 700s, the Anasazi lived by hunting and growing small crops of corn and beans. Over the next few centuries, they cultivated cotton, created pottery, and built *kivas* (rooms where ceremonies and sacred meetings took place). They also constructed cities, later called "pueblos" by the Spanish, who arrived in the New World in the 1500s. In time, Spanish colonists gave each pueblo a Spanish name based on a geographic trait, a Catholic saint's name, or a Spanish pronunciation of the Indian name for the pueblo.

Important Dates

1539: The Pueblo encounter Spanish explorers.

1680: The Pueblo Revolt drives out the Spanish.

1692: The Spanish begin their reconquest of Pueblo land.

1850: New Mexico, land of the Pueblo people, is declared a U.S. territory.

1922: The All Indian Pueblo Council meets to fight for land and water rights.

1924: The Pueblo Lands Act of 1924 passes. The U.S. government pays for or returns land to the tribe.

1970: Congress returned the sacred area of Blue Lake and 48,000 surrounding acres of land to the Pueblo.

Pueblos thrive, then decline

By the 1300s, the pueblos were flourishing. Pueblo architecture grew more complex, pottery and weaving methods had improved, and farming practices were refined. The ancient Anasazi people built spectacular cities, including the famed Pueblo Bonito, which was constructed between 920 and 1130 CE. The city centered on a huge, D-shaped apartment building of eight hundred rooms that rose five stories high.

A severe drought struck the Southwest around 1276 and lasted into the early 1300s, forcing many of the Pueblo peoples to abandon their villages in search of water. At that time, they joined other Puebloans farther north in central New Mexico and northeastern Arizona. A second series of migrations took place during the fifteenth century. When the Spanish arrived in the 1500s, they discovered many abandoned Pueblo towns.

Spanish drawn to Pueblo lands

In 1529, four Spanish shipwreck survivors spent eight years wandering the Southwest before finding their way back to their countrymen. With great excitement, they returned to Spain telling tales of magnificent cities of gold. It was not long before treasure-seeking Spanish explorers made their way to the new land. The Spanish began exploring Pueblo country in 1539, eighty years before the Pilgrims landed at Plymouth Rock. Some of the cities the Spaniards visited were already 250 years old.

The Spanish introduced horses and firearms to the Pueblo. Later, European settlers brought new crops and inventions, but they also spread diseases to which the Native peoples had no immunity. Some anthropologists (scientists who study ancient cultures) believe that during the period between 1540 and 1700, when the Spanish controlled what is now New Mexico, the Pueblo population decreased by half.

Spanish settlers had little regard for the Native people's land, their culture, or their traditions. In 1540, a Spanish expedition led by Francisco Vásquez de Coronado (c. 1510–1554) landed in the region. They camped in the Tiwa province of Tiguex, putting twelve villages of people out of their homes. Using the area as a base camp, the party searched in vain across the plains of Kansas for an incredibly wealthy mythical city, but they returned to Mexico empty-handed.

Around 1580, new groups of Spaniards arrived in Pueblo territory. They established settlements and brought Christianity to the Native peoples. Juan de Oñate (1552–1626) established a government at Santa Fe, New Mexico, and quickly stripped the Natives of their freedoms. The Pueblo people were required to give corn and woven cloth to the Spanish settlers and perform backbreaking labor for them. Traditional Puebloan religious practices were banned as superstitious. Anyone who refused to obey Spanish rule paid with the amputation of a hand or foot, forced slavery, or even execution.

The "First American Revolution"

The Pueblo Revolt of 1680 was the first and only successful move by Native North Americans to throw colonists off their lands. The Puebloans organized what some call the "First American Revolution." The Jemez (pronounced *HAY-mes*; see entry), one of the Pueblo groups of New Mexico, helped ensure the success of the revolt that was organized by Popé (died 1692), a religious leader from the San Juan Pueblo (see entry).

For the first time in their history, the many different Pueblo groups acted as a single force, and in August 1680, they killed four hundred Spaniards in one day, including twenty-one Catholic priests. The tribes drove the Spanish out of New Mexico, but only for a short time.

Twenty percent of the Spaniards in the region died in the rebellion, and those who survived fled to Mexico. Not all the Pueblo people agreed that the Spanish should be expelled, however. Some wanted the foreigners nearby for protection from the Apache and the Navajo (see entries), because those tribes had acquired horses and firearms. Some Pueblo even followed the Spanish to the South. Within a few years, other groups invited the Spanish to return.

Return of the Spanish

For twelve years, the Jemez tried to reestablish their pueblos and their way of life, but in 1692, Don Diego de Vargas (1643–1704) returned to the area to reclaim New Mexico for Spain. De Vargas forcibly took over San Diego Canyon in 1694, killing 84 warriors and taking 361 Jemez as prisoners. The Spanish again established colonies in the Pueblo region, and the Pueblo who remained in the area were forced to convert to Catholicism and to work on Spanish ranches. Over time, Spanish rule became less strict, and officials permitted the Pueblo peoples to resume some traditional religious practices.

After the Mexican Revolution of 1821, Mexico became independent of Spain, and the new Mexican government took charge of the pueblos. Twenty-five years later, Mexico fought with the United States over land in the present-day American Southwest. America's victory in this conflict (known as the Mexican-American War; 1846–48) made New Mexico— the land of the Pueblo peoples—part of U.S. territory. The Pueblo, as Mexican citizens, were automatically granted U.S. citizenship. (Most other Native groups were not given U.S. citizenship until 1924.) As U.S. citizens, the Pueblo did not receive the rights and protections granted through treaties that these other tribes gained as independent nations.

Pueblo lose, then regain land

Spanish laws passed in 1689 had given the Pueblo ownership of their ancestral lands. After New Mexico became part of the United States, the federal government pledged that it would recognize this agreement. Under the terms of ownership, Pueblo land was made off limits to settlement. Near the end of the nineteenth century, though, illegal settlement on the lands increased greatly. The Pueblo asked for, and then sued for, Indian status, which they gained in 1916.

The All Indian Pueblo Council (see "Government") came together in the early 1920s to oppose U.S. government interference in Pueblo land ownership and water rights. Using tactics such as an around-the-country lecture tour and appearances before Congress, the council secured passage of the Pueblo Lands Act of 1924. This act returned Pueblo lands that non-Native Americans had owned for less than twenty years. It also paid the Pueblo people for lost lands. The Puebloans used the money to purchase land for irrigation projects.

In the early 1970s, the All Indian Pueblo Council again acted on behalf of the tribes to oppose federal action that would interfere with their tribal water rights. In 1996, representatives from all the New Mexico pueblos, as well as two Apache tribes and the Navajo Nation, began holding quarterly meetings with New Mexico state officials to improve communication and cooperation among the various groups.

RELIGION

Ancient beliefs and practices preserved

The Pueblo considered a person's spiritual beliefs central to his or her daily life. The people saw themselves as the earth's caretakers and called upon supernatural beings to ensure health, happiness, and abundant crops.

Many Pueblo converted to Christianity, but Catholic and Protestant missionaries were not successful in eliminating traditional beliefs and practices. Even in the early twenty-first century, many Pueblo Catholics followed the beliefs of their ancestors and practiced their ceremonies. Tribal members belong to religious societies devoted to weather, fertility, healing, hunting, and entertainment. Centuries ago, during times of religious intolerance, the Pueblo people learned to keep their ceremonies secret. Many of their religious ceremonies remain hidden from outsiders.

Kachinas

The Pueblo believe in a Creator ("Great Spirit") who is always present. They honor the earth as their Mother and respect everything in it, whether living or not. According to Pueblo belief, every visible object has a spirit (the *kachina*) that is as real as the thing itself. The Pueblo honor three hundred major kachinas that represent the most important objects in their lives.

The Kachina religion practiced by the modern-day Pueblo people may have begun with the ancient Anasazi. Kachinas were said to be reincarnated (reborn after death) ancestors who served as messengers between the people and their gods. The term *kachina* also refers to the dolls that represent Pueblo Indians' ancestral spirits and the masked dancers who perform at agricultural and religious ceremonies.

Pueblo Indians of the early twenty-first century still stay in touch with the spirit world. For example, hunters ask permission of the spirit of an animal before killing it for food, and persons seeking strength often pray to receive the spirit of an especially powerful or beloved kachina.

Many Pueblo tales feature Salt Woman or Salt Mother, an elderly woman who freely helps anyone who asks her. The Pueblo used salt for healing rituals, burial ceremonies, food preparation and preservation, and even love potions. They also traded it. People used to make pilgrimages to the place where Salt Woman lived to obtain the precious seasoning.

Masked Dancers

During religious dance ceremonies, men dressed as kachinas act out the story of the first appearance of the Pueblo people. The men appear as animals (owl, crow, butterfly, or dog, for example) or as major crops (usually corn or squash).

Kachina clowns serve as comic relief, helping the Native people forget their troubles for a while. They entertain people and discourage undesirable behavior by ridiculing those who misbehave. Clowns sometimes poke fun at religious ceremonies or pretend to make fun of important people in song.

Religious freedom

During the 1920s, outside groups tried to stop the Pueblo from practicing traditional religious ceremonies. Laws were passed in the 1930s to protect the tribe's freedom of religion, but they were not always successful in doing so. Even as late as the 1960s, U.S. government officials attempted to "civilize" the people by forcing them to give up their traditional ways. The Pueblo received an important religious concession in 1970 when Congress returned the sacred area of Blue Lake and 48,000 surrounding acres of land to the Taos people. The tribe had been asking for thirty years for the return of this land, which they believe is the place where the Great Spirit first created people. (For more information, see Taos Pueblo entry.)

LANGUAGE

Most of the Pueblo speak dialects (language varieties) that derive from four separate language families: Tewa, Tiwa, Towa, and Keresan. Although the Pueblo share similar cultures, they are not typically fluent in each other's languages. Throughout their history, though, some Pueblo people have been able to speak several Pueblo languages. During the time of Spanish rule, many also spoke Spanish.

Many elders believe the Pueblo language should not be written but instead passed down orally, in keeping with ancient traditions. Others disagree, saying that writing will preserve the language for future generations. Even though the Pueblo languages are still unwritten, they continue to survive in most of the villages. Most modern Pueblo speak both English and their Native tongue.

GOVERNMENT

In early times, the Western Pueblo were ruled by religious leaders. Public opinion, expressed through gossip, kept people in line. The Eastern Pueblo separated religious and political authorities and developed a stronger central government. A tribal council decided how land was to be divided and could take back a person's right to live in a given pueblo.

Beginning in 1620, a Spanish-style system of government featuring a tribal governor and his assistants became widespread among the tribes. By the twentieth century, each pueblo maintained its own separate elected government.

All of the pueblos are self-governed and fiercely independent, but they each participate in the All Indian Pueblo Council, a loose federation or grouping. The All Indian Pueblo Council began with the Pueblo Revolt against the Spanish in 1680. It became an important force in the 1920s in organizing delegates from each pueblo to regain the land illegally seized from them by American settlers. Through their participation in the All Indian Pueblo Council, the governors of the New Mexico pueblos continue to meet and discuss issues such as water rights, education, health, and economic development.

ECONOMY

Prior to the arrival of the Europeans, the most important task at each pueblo was the construction of homes. Workers were paid with food, but because food was costly, only a minimal number of builders was hired for each project. Men usually made the adobe (pronounced *uh-DOE-bee*) bricks, while women did the plastering and constructed the roofs of the houses. (Adobe is a sun-dried mud made of a mixture of clay, sand, and sometimes ashes, rocks, or straw.) Members of the tribe also made their

A Pueblo village in New Mexico, circa 1800s. © NORTH WIND PICTURE ARCHIVES.

own personal tools—grinding stones, knives, hammers, arrowheads, and even fireplaces and ovens—from stone or bone.

Many Pueblo fought during World War II (1939–45; a war in which Great Britain, France, the United States, and their allies defeated Germany, Italy, and Japan), and when they returned home, they used their war benefits to obtain higher education or to open businesses. During the 1960s, federal programs were set up to provide financial assistance to Native peoples, and tourism on Pueblo lands began to thrive. Tourists are drawn to New Mexico by their fascination with the ancient pueblos and the Pueblo lifestyle.

The Spanish introduced new crops along with sheep and cattle ranching in the 1600s, and these economic activities are still important among the Pueblo in the twenty-first century. Some modern-day Pueblo people continue to work their own farms but make use of modern equipment. Others have taken nonagricultural jobs off the reservation and have moved to cities.

DAILY LIFE

Families

In Pueblo families, children belonged to their mother's clan (a group of related families). A household consisted of a husband and wife, their children, and the wife's brothers, along with their wives and children.

Pueblo women and girls built houses and ovens, made baskets and pottery, and tended small vegetable gardens. Men and boys took care of cornfields, hunted, and did weaving, knitting, and embroidering.

Buildings

Architecture The unusual Pueblo style of construction dates back to the Anasazi culture of about 700 and remains popular with some modern Pueblo people. Structures were made either of sandstone slabs cemented into place with mud or, more commonly, of adobe. Because adobe was also used in European countries on the Mediterranean Sea, the Spanish were already familiar with it when they discovered the Puebloans. In fact, the Spanish taught the people to make adobe bricks. Thereafter, bricklaying replaced the earlier practice of forming mud walls between wooden poles.

The Pueblo carried on the architectural traditions of their Anasazi ancestors. They built multistoried apartment-style buildings, usually three to six stories tall. First-floor rooms served mostly for food storage, whereas the living quarters were located on upper levels. To provide safety from invaders, the first floor had no doors. Lower rooms were entered through hatches (holes in the ceiling); during rainstorms the hatches could be covered with large slabs of stone. Modern homes have doors on the first floor.

Upper stories were terraced (staggered) toward the rear of the building. As a result, each upper-story room had a patio area provided by the roof of the room below. People used ladders or, less often, adobe stairs to go from one level to the next. The ladders could be pulled up in case of an enemy attack. Some ladders were wide enough for two people to pass at the same time.

House interiors Because wind and rain wore away at the earthen walls of the pueblos, a coating of mud plaster had to be reapplied to the exterior every year. To make the dwelling clean and attractive, interior surfaces were whitewashed. This time-consuming process involved combining a mineral substance called gypsum with cattle dung and baking the mixture like pottery. Then the Pueblo pounded this material into a powder, mixed it with water, and applied it to the walls. The thick adobe walls kept the rooms cool in the summer and warm in the winter.

Families slept on rugs or animal skins that they rolled up in the morning and used for seating. Pegs and poles, somewhat like modern towel racks, served as clothes hangers. The fireplace occupied one corner of the room, with cooking pots and gourds (dried, hollowed-out vegetables) for carrying water nearby. Before the nineteenth century, the smoke was vented through the pueblo's entrance. Later, a hood and flue (pipe) sent smoke outside the house. The Puebloans built special storage containers for grain into the floor.

During planting season, whole families sometimes camped in the fields, living in the remains of ancient settlements or building temporary villages. They constructed light shelters of brush and stone for protection from the blazing sun.

In the early twenty-first century, the majority of Pueblo residents lived in modern, single-family homes, most made of cinder block. At Acoma and Taos (see entries), some people still inhabited their centuries-old, apartment-style adobe buildings. Those who did chopped wood for fuel and lived for the most part without modern conveniences.

Kivas Central to the spiritual life of each pueblo was a circular room called the kiva, often built below ground level. Some pueblos had one or two kivas, while others had many. Most kivas contained a fire pit, an adobe bench attached to the wall, an altar, and a *sipapu*, a hole through which kachinas could emerge from the underworld for ceremonies. The men of a religious society used kivas to prepare for tribal ceremonies and as a place for social gatherings. Traditionally women could enter a kiva only to plaster the walls and attend occasional ceremonies.

Churches During the period of Spanish rule, a Catholic church was constructed in each pueblo. These huge adobe structures had walls as thick as 9 feet (3 meters) and were up to 40 feet (12 meters) tall. Their bell towers stretched even higher. The churches' roofs were made with strong wooden poles long enough to span the entire width of the structure. The poles were laid at intervals to make a base, with several layers of smaller wooden branches and brush in alternating directions arranged over them, they were then covered with packed earth. In the larger mission churches, tree trunks 40 feet (12 meters) long and weighing hundreds of pounds were harvested from the nearest forest. They were then hand-carried 30 miles (50 kilometers) or more to the construction site.

Clothing and adornment

The Pueblo wore cotton clothing as early as 800. In climates where it was too cold to grow cotton, they wore animal skins. They made winter coats by forming fluffy ropes from small animal pelts and turkey feathers. Rows of these ropes were sewn together with yucca twine, much like weaving a basket. After the Spanish taught the Puebloans to spin and weave wool, woolen clothing became popular. In the early days, weaving was a male occupation.

Men usually wore knee-length skirts or loincloths (flaps of material that covered the front and back and were suspended from the waist). They slipped a piece of cloth with a hole in the center over their heads to serve as a shirt. The Pueblo either went barefoot or wore sandals made of yucca fiber. Around 1300, they learned from other Native cultures to make animal skin moccasins and leggings. The people did not begin wearing long pants until around 1880. Even then, they sometimes slit the legs to accommodate tall moccasins or boots.

Women often wore simple knee-length dresses called *mantas* (pronounced *MAHN-tuhs*). These were made from a straight piece of cloth wrapped around the body and tied with a sash at the waist. The fabric passed under the left arm and fastened above the right shoulder. Mantas have been made of black wool since the time of Spanish rule. In the nineteenth century, women began wearing brightly colored silk blouses under their mantas. They later added colorful fringed shawls.

The Pueblo usually left their clothing undyed, but sometimes they colored fabrics with a bright blue-green dye made from copper sulfate. Later, when European fabrics became available, red cloth was especially popular. The fibers from such fabrics were carefully unraveled so the threads could be rewoven as decorative elements in Pueblo cloth.

Most Pueblo people wore their shoulder-length hair either loose or tied back, with bangs cut straight across the forehead. Men often tied their hair back at the nape of the neck, folded it up in half, and wrapped it with a leather strip into a long bundle called a *chongo*. Influenced by Plains Indians, some men in the Northern Pueblos braided their hair. Men painted their bodies for ceremonies, and women often decorated their cheeks with red powder made from crushed flowers.

Food

Because they farmed, the Pueblo settled in permanent cities. Corn made up about 80 percent of their diet. It was so important to Pueblo life that it was used in some form—as corn, cornmeal, or corn pollen—in nearly every ceremony. Fresh corn was boiled or roasted, or it was dried, ground, and stored as cornmeal. The Pueblo groups cultivated many varieties of corn, including a type called "flint corn" that could be stored for years because it was resistant to mold and rodents. In addition to the familiar white and yellow varieties, the tribes raised red, blue, dark purple, and speckled corn. The people often stored seed corn with an evergreen sprig or prayer feather in hopes of keeping the seeds fresh.

In addition to corn, the Pueblo raised squash, sunflower seeds, and several types of beans. The Spanish colonists introduced new crops, including apples, apricots, pears, grapes, wheat, and a variety of vegetables. Individual Pueblo families grew their own onions, peppers, chilies, and tobacco. They also made use of various wild plants, such as prickly pear cactus, berries, pine nuts, and yucca fruit. Other parts of the yucca plant were made into soap, fiber for sandals, and material for brooms and hairbrushes.

The Pueblo lived in a desert climate, so drought often harmed their crops. They planted in fields most likely to catch the summer rain and built dams to keep thunderstorm runoffs from washing away their crops. Women planted corn in holes up to 18 inches (46 centimeters) deep to allow the plant roots to use moisture well below the surface. They built a ridge of soil around each plant to retain water. As a result, cornfields took on a wafflelike appearance.

The tribe ate meat on rare occasions. Sometimes they hunted large animals such as deer, antelope, and buffalo using the "drive" method. A group of men and boys surrounded their prey and drove it into a canyon or corral where others could easily kill it. More commonly, they caught rabbits, gophers, squirrels, and other small animals in traps or killed them with clubs.

The Uses of Cornmeal

Pueblo girls and women spent three to four hours a day grinding several quarts of cornmeal by hand. They placed kernels on a grinding stone and crushed them with a cylinder-shaped stone. The texture of the stone determined how fine the cornmeal would be. Three or four workers often formed a team, each passing the meal she had ground to another worker with a finer stone.

Cornmeal added to boiling water produced a favorite morning drink. For travelers, cornmeal that had been thoroughly toasted between successive grindings and crushed extra fine could be carried easily and mixed with cold water for a nourishing beverage. Lumps of cornmeal dough dropped into boiling water made dumplings. A favorite food now known by its Mexican Indian name, *tamale* (pronounced *tah-MAH-lay*), consisted of meat or other filling encased in cornmeal, wrapped with a corn husk, and then boiled.

Cornmeal was also used for various types of bread, including tortillas (pronounced *tor-TEE-yahz*). *Piki* (*PEE-kee*) bread was prepared by quickly spreading thin batter made from blue cornmeal on a hot stone and almost immediately peeling off the paper-thin, cooked layer. Piki could be folded and stored for as long as a week.

Education

Tribal elders were respected for their wisdom. When they became too old for strenuous work, the elderly often joined the town council or became the head of a society. They also assisted in raising the children. They taught the youths about the Pueblo way of life and passed down the tradition of making kachina dolls. (Kachina dolls were carved from wood and then covered with white clay and painted in bright colors.)

During the late nineteenth century, the U.S. government wanted the Pueblo people to assimilate, or blend in with mainstream American society. Many of the children were sent far away from their parents to U.S.-run boarding schools to learn American ways. During the twentieth century, though, the Bureau of Indian Affairs built schools on Pueblo reservations, thereby enabling Pueblo youth to maintain a connection to their families and their heritage.

Healing practices

The Pueblo thought most illnesses had spiritual causes. A common treatment focused on restoring spiritual harmony between the ailing person and his or her environment. For example, the people believed that a baby who cried most of the time might be suffering back pain because his father mistreated horses before his birth. To cure his child, the father drove a team of horses hard, then took the horses' sweat and rubbed it onto the baby's back.

Healers were sometimes called on to perform special rituals. Some healers were ordinary people who had gained special healing powers in a dramatic way—through the bite of a snake, perhaps, or by being struck by lightning.

Plants were also used to treat and prevent illness. Crushed mustard leaves were applied to the body as a sunscreen. Other remedies such as rattlesnake oil, collected from snakes along the Mexican border, eased pains from rheumatism and cured poisonous snakebites by absorbing the venom.

In recent times, the Indian Health Service began cooperating closely with Native healers to improve the health status of the tribe.

ARTS

Pottery and stonework

Pueblo women have been known throughout history for a special kind of pottery featuring black designs painted on a white background. Their polished red and black pottery also remains popular today. The Pueblo groups are unique for their high level of craftsmanship in stonework, which allowed them to build houses with as many as thirty floors.

Pueblo Cultural Center

Exhibits on Pueblo history are on display at the Pueblo Cultural Center in Albuquerque, New Mexico. The exhibits trace the origins, traditions, arts, and craftsmanship of the people. The theater at the center depicts Pueblo culture through film, drama, and dance. Stage presentations and celebrations are also held on the grounds.

CUSTOMS

Childbirth

Various ceremonies surrounded childbirth. To ensure a healthy baby, expectant mothers and fathers avoided looking at snakes or harming animals. After a midwife or male healer assisted with a baby's birth, the newborn was washed, sprinkled with juniper ashes, and given an ear of white corn to keep as a reminder of its heritage. For twenty days following childbirth, a new mother drank juniper tea and took sweat baths in steam created by pouring water over a hot stone covered with juniper leaves.

Sometime between four and twenty days after birth, the baby was taken outside at dawn to be greeted by the sun. The father, or a healer called a shaman (pronounced *SHAH-mun* or *SHAY-mun*), then gave the child its name. After that, the baby was strapped to a wooden board, where it would spend its first few months learning the value of stillness.

Courtship and marriage

Prior to marriage, a woman usually spent three days grinding corn at the groom's home to prove her ability to perform this duty; sometimes she brought samples to prove her bread making talents. The groom-to-be and his relatives wove a special wedding garment for the bride. Before the wedding ceremony, the groom's mother washed the bride's and groom's hair. The groom's father then sprinkled a trail of cornmeal from his house to the bride's, where a feast was celebrated. In a final ceremony, the couple took a small bit of cornmeal, walked silently to the eastern part of the mesa (a large hill with steep sides and a flat top), breathed upon the cornmeal, threw it toward the rising sun, prayed, and returned to the village a married couple.

When a Pueblo man married, he went to live in the home of his wife's family, bringing along some of his family's carefully preserved seeds for planting.

Funerals

Although death was a sad occasion, the Pueblo believed the dead went on living in another, very different world—a world in which night was day, day was night, and the seasons were switched. Excessive mourning for the dead was discouraged as a waste of time.

Prior to burial, the Pueblo cleaned the body and dressed it in fine clothes. They placed feathers in the corpse's hands. For four days, attendants sat by the body; then they took it outside to be buried, along with food and tools. Dead children, believed to be too little to make the journey to the afterlife, were often buried underneath the family home. It was hoped that their souls would enter new babies born in the home.

Festivals and ceremonies

The Pueblo are sometimes referred to as "Rain Dance" people. Because water was so important in their desert environment, they held many of their traditional ceremonies to encourage adequate rainfall. Other dances expressed their sadness, told stories of the gods, and celebrated the growth of their crops. Dancers wore fancy costumes and sometimes used masks. They decorated themselves with paint, horns, branches, and feathers. They performed both carefully planned and free-style dances in ceremonies that went on for hours. During the Snake Dance, men fearlessly handled rattlesnakes. The rooftop terraces of pueblo homes provided a convenient place for people to sit and watch the ceremonial dances held throughout the year.

People attached prayer feathers to a house under construction to protect it. A "feeding the house" ceremony took place after the walls, roof, and floor were completed. People sprinkled crumbs along the rafters to insure the good health of those who would live inside. Because water, building materials, and firewood had to be transported up and down ladders to the pueblo homes, ceremonies were performed at the foot of the ladders to protect children and adults from accidents.

Modern Pueblo life is steeped in ritual. Festivals often combine traditional Native rituals with Christian celebrations. Each pueblo has its own celebrations throughout the year, including one on the feast day of the Catholic saint who serves as patron of the pueblo.

CURRENT TRIBAL ISSUES

An especially difficult challenge facing the Pueblo groups is the redevelopment of their economy. New methods of farming are being explored and refined. Some pueblos are encouraging tourism and related businesses. Many artists find success selling silver and turquoise jewelry, pottery, sculptures, and carved kachinas. And several New Mexico pueblos built casinos, generating considerable controversy in the process.

In an ongoing effort to hold on to their ancestral lands, the Pueblo people have appealed repeatedly to U.S. Congress and the court system. One of the most famous land rights battles was waged by the Taos Pueblo (see entry). The Pueblo are also trying to maintain their tribal culture and customs.

The All Indian Pueblo Council issued a statement in 2010 that identified the needs of the Pueblos. As proof of their sovereignty (self-government), the council wanted to establish nation-to-nation relationships with the U.S. government. It also called for a reform of the Bureau of Indian Affairs. At the same time, the council determined to address longstanding issues on the pueblos, such as health care, education, housing, and unemployment. Many Pueblo communities struggle with issues relating to water and land rights, lack of employment opportunities, and adequate health care. Roads and bridges need to be modernized, and the environment and natural resources must be protected. Preservation of the Pueblo culture is also a major priority.

NOTABLE PEOPLE

Joe Simon Sando (1923–2011; *Paa Peh* in Pueblo) was a Jemez Pueblo scholar and lecturer who wrote four books on the lives, culture, and history of the Pueblo Indians: *The Pueblo Indians, Pueblo Indian Biographies, Nee Hemish: The History of the Jemez Pueblo,* and *Pueblo Nations: Eight Centuries of Pueblo Indian History.*

Other notable Pueblo include the anthropologist, linguist, author, and educator Edward P. Dozier (1916–1971), who specialized in the study of his own people; Frank C. Dukepoo (1943–1999), a Hopi-Laguna Pueblo geneticist and founder of the National Native American Honor Society; the world-famous Santa Clara Pueblo artist Pablita Velarde (1918–2006); and her daughter, also an artist, Helen Hardin (1946–1984).

BOOKS

Bahti, Mark. *Pueblo Stories and Storytellers.* 3rd ed. Tucson, AZ: Rio Nuevo Publishers, 2010.

Carrillo, Charles M. *Saints of the Pueblos.* Albuquerque: LPD Press, 2008.

Croy, Anita. *Ancient Pueblo: Archaeology Unlocks the Secrets of America's Past.* Washington, DC: National Geographic, 2007.

Downum, Christian E. Hisatsinom: *Ancient Peoples in a Land without Water.* Santa Fe: School for Advanced Research Press, 2011.

Eaton, William M. *Odyssey of the Pueblo Indians: An Introduction to Pueblo Indian Petroglyphs, Pictographs and Kiva Art Murals in the Southwest.* Paducah, KY: Turner Publishing Company, 2002.

Kiowa and Pueblo Art: Watercolor Paintings by Native American Artists. Mineola, NY: Dover Publications, 2009.

Lekson, Stephen H. *Great Pueblo Architecture of Chaco Canyon, New Mexico.* Clinton Corners, NY: Percheron Press, 2007.

Márquez, Rubén Sálaz. *The Pueblo Revolt Massacre.* Albuquerque: Cosmic House, 2008.

Nickens, Paul and Kathleen. *Pueblo Indians of New Mexico.* Charleston, SC: Arcadia, 2008.

Pijoan, Teresa. *Pueblo Indian Wisdom: Native American Legends and Mythology.* Santa Fe: Sunstone Press, 2000.

Sando, Joe S. *Pueblo Recollections: The Life of Paa Peh.* Santa Fe: Clear Light Pub., 2008.

St. Lawrence, Genevieve. *The Pueblo And Their History.* Minneapolis, MN: Compass Point Books, 2006.

Sweet, Jill Drayson, and Nancy Hunter Warren. *Pueblo Dancing.* Atglen, PA: Schiffer Publishing, 2011.

Trimble, Stephen. *Talking with the Clay: The Art of Pueblo Pottery in the 21st Century.* Santa Fe: School for Advanced Research Press, 2007.

Wood, Nancy. *We Became as Mountains: Poems of the Pueblo Conquest.* Santa Fe: Western Edge Press, 2008.

PERIODICALS

Griswold, Eliza. "A Teen's Third-World America." *Newsweek.* December 26, 2010. Available online from http://www.thedailybeast.com/articles/2010/12/26/a-boys-third-world-america.html (accessed on July 20, 2011).

WEB SITES

All Indian Pueblo Council. http://www.20pueblos.org/ (accessed on July 20, 2011).

Indian Pueblo Cultural Center. http://www.indianpueblo.org/ (accessed on July 20, 2011).

National Museum of American History—Smithsonian Institution. "Pueblo Resistance: We Are Here." *Mexico State Record Center and Archives.* http://www.newmexicohistory.org/filedetails.php?fileID=23042 (accessed on July 20, 2011).

New Mexico Office of the State Historian. "1970—Restoration of Blue Lake to Taos Pueblo." New Mexico State Record Center and Archives. (accessed on July 20, 2011).

"Pueblo Indian History and Resources." *Pueblo Indian.* http://www.puebloindian.com/ (accessed on July 20, 2011).

"Pueblo Pottery." *University of Michigan and Drexel University.* http://www.ipl.org/div/pottery/classroom.htm (accessed on July 20, 2011).

"Pueblo Revolt." *Council of Indian Nations.* http://www.nrcprograms.org/site/PageServer?pagename=cin_hist_pueblorevolt (accessed on July 20, 2011).

"Research Starters: Anasazi and Pueblo Indians." *Scholastic.com.* http://teacher.scholastic.com/researchtools/researchstarters/native_am/ (accessed on July 20, 2011).

Weiser, Kathy. "Pueblo Indians—Oldest Culture in the U.S." *Legends of America.* http://www.legendsofamerica.com/na-puebloindians.html (accessed on July 20, 2011).

Acoma Pueblo

Name

Acoma Pueblo (pronounced *AH-koh-mah PWEB-loh*). Acoma is some-times spelled Akome, Acuo, Acuco, Ako and A'ku-me. Some tribal elders say the name *Acoma* means "a place that always was." Outsiders say it means "people of the white rock." A *pueblo* is a stone and adobe village inhabited by various tribes in the southwestern United States. The Spanish used the word *pueblo* to refer to both the people and their villages. The name of the main Acoma village, *Acu,* may mean "home for many ages" or "place of preparedness."

Location

Traditional Acoma lands may have consisted of some five million acres and many villages in present-day New Mexico. The modern-day Acoma Pueblo, a federal reservation, is located 60 miles (97 kilometers) west of Albuquerque, New Mexico. Most Acoma now live in one of the two more modern towns on the reservation, but fewer than fifty families maintain individual or group homes in the old city.

Population

The Spanish estimated that 5,000 to 10,000 people lived in the Acoma vil-lage in 1540. In 1582, there were about 6,000 Acoma people. By 1776, there were fewer than 600. In the 1990 U.S. Census, 3,938 people identified themselves as Acoma Pueblo. When the 2000 census was taken, that number had risen to 4,298. In 2004, the tribe recorded an enrollment of 4,754.

Language family

Keresan.

Origins and group affiliations

Modern-day Acoma people have four different groups of ancestors, one of which inhabited the Acoma homeland from prehistoric times. Some Anasazi people came and intermingled with them around the year 1200. The other

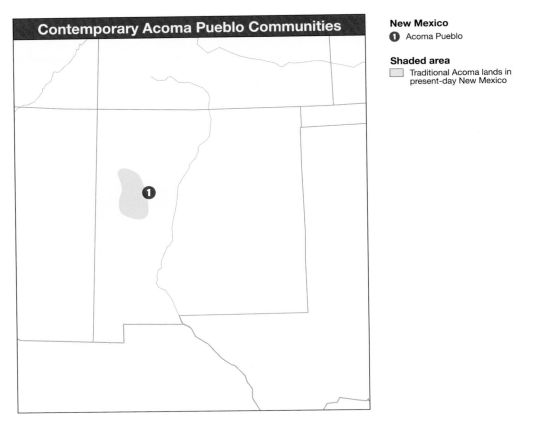

Contemporary Acoma Pueblo Communities

New Mexico
① Acoma Pueblo

Shaded area
☐ Traditional Acoma lands in present-day New Mexico

A map of contemporary Acoma Pueblo communities. MAP BY XNR PRODUCTIONS. CENGAGE LEARNING, GALE. REPRODUCED BY PERMISSION OF GALE, A PART OF CENGAGE LEARNING.

ancestral groups probably migrated to the area from the Cebollita Mesa region of New Mexico. The Acoma have close cultural ties with the Laguna Pueblo people.

Ancient tales tell that the Acoma once lived across the valley from their present-day settlement on an enchanted mesa (high, flat land shaped like a table) called Katsimo. One day, heavy rains separated the ground below from the land above. After that, the people built a village on top of a mesa for safety. The Acoma Pueblo, sometimes referred to as Sky City, sits like a mighty fortress high above the New Mexico countryside. Some say the Acoma Pueblo is the oldest continuously occupied settlement in the United States. This claim is challenged only by the Hopi Pueblo of Oraibi.

HISTORY

Contact with the Spanish

The Acoma say that their people have been living in the village of Acu for at least two thousand years. They were hunter-gatherers and farmers who apparently lived a contented life hunting for game and working their fields. The Acoma people first encountered Europeans in 1540, when the Spanish explorer Hernando de Alvarado (c. 1518–1550) and his party of twenty soldiers arrived on their land.

Alvarado was impressed by the pueblo, perched atop a large hill with steep sides and a flat top, the kind of terrain the Spanish call a *mesa*. It could only be entered by way of a hand-built stairway of two hundred steps, followed by a stretch of about one hundred narrower steps. Beyond the steps lay 20-foot (7-meter) high rocks with hand and toeholds for climbing to the entrance. The Spanish gave the name "Kingdom of Acu" to this astonishing place and recorded that five thousand to ten thousand warlike people lived there.

The next major contact with the Spanish came in 1598 when Juan de Oñate (1552–1626), the new governor of the region, toured the pueblo. A year later, the governor's nephew visited the Acoma Pueblo, but his trip ended in violence when the Acoma attacked the Spanish. According to the Acoma, Spanish soldiers assaulted some women in the village; the Spanish, however, maintained that they did nothing to provoke the assault.

Attack on Acoma

Only four Spanish men survived the attack and escaped. Six weeks later, the Spanish stormed the Acoma. With a cannon in tow, a dozen men scaled the tribe's mesa wall unseen and launched the bloody, two-day Battle of Acoma (1599). When it ended, the city lay in ruins, and eight hundred of the six thousand residents had been killed.

More than five hundred prisoners were taken to stand trial at the Spanish governor's headquarters. Warriors over the age of twelve were sentenced to twenty years of forced labor; men over the age of twenty-five had one foot cut off. This was the beginning of a long and unhappy relationship between the Spanish and the Acoma people.

Important Dates

1150: Acoma Pueblo is a well-established city.

1540: Spanish explorers visit Acoma Pueblo.

1599: Spanish soldiers destroy the pueblo in the Battle of Acoma. The tribe submits to Spanish rule.

1680: The Acoma people revolt against Spanish rule.

1699: The Acoma resubmit to Spanish rule.

1848: Acoma Pueblo land comes under the control of the United States.

1970: A financial settlement with the U.S. government allows the Acoma people to begin purchasing back parts of their traditional lands.

Acoma rebellion brews

Between 1629 and 1640, Spanish missionary priests forced the Acoma people to build a monumental Catholic church. The building was made of stone and adobe (a sun-dried mud made of a mixture of clay, sand, and sometimes ashes, rocks, or straw). The materials had to be hauled up to the top of the mesa in buffalo-hide bags and water jars. Native American workers carried massive timbers—some up to 40 feet long (12 meters)—more than 30 miles (48 kilometers) from Mt. Taylor. The logs apparently could not touch the ground during the backbreaking trip to the building site. Even the soil for a 2,000-square-foot (610-square-meter) cemetery had to be carried up the steep trail.

The Spanish tried to force all the Pueblo Indians to convert to the Catholic religion. They imposed severe penalties on any Natives who practiced their traditional religion. The Native Americans grew increasingly hostile. The forced labor, the imposition of a foreign religion, and the burden of keeping the Spanish supplied with food caused them to revolt in 1680.

Spanish return to Acoma

Although Acoma was some distance from the other pueblos, its people took part in the Pueblo Revolt of 1680 by killing the local priest and burning the Catholic church in their hometown. (For more information on the Pueblo Revolt of 1680, see Pueblo entry.) They were no match for the Spanish weapons, and in 1699, the Spanish again asserted their rule. They forced the Acoma to rebuild the church, a huge structure 150 feet (46 meters) long, 40 feet (12 meters) wide, and 35 feet (11 meters) tall, with walls 9 feet (3 meters) thick at their base. The church is still in use in the early twenty-first century.

The Acoma faced more hard times during the eighteenth century: the Apache (see entry) raided their land, and the Acoma suffered from diseases such as smallpox that had been brought by Europeans. By 1776, only 530 Acoma remained alive at the pueblo.

U.S. Congress affirms Acoma rights

Much of Pueblo territory, including Acoma land, was acquired by the United States in 1848 after its victory in the Mexican-American War (1846–48; a war in which Mexico lost about half of its national territory to the United States). Ten years later, Congress confirmed that the Acoma, along with other Pueblo tribes, could live on and farm their lands. An illegally built railroad, however, soon caused the loss of some reservation land. This left many Acoma unable to support themselves by farming; some left the reservation to find work as laborers, mechanics, electricians, and painters.

During the twentieth century, new laws were enacted that allowed the Acoma to regain ownership of portions of their homeland, including some major religious sites. In 1970, they received a cash settlement of $6.1 million from the U.S. government for the illegal loss of their lands (but none of the land was returned). The money enabled the Acoma to make several purchases during the 1970s and 1980s that added more than 15,000 acres to their tribal land holdings.

For a time in the late twentieth century, nearby uranium mines provided employment opportunities for the Acoma people; however, the uranium market was eventually depleted. The closing of the Ambrosia Lake Mine meant the loss of jobs for three hundred people on the reservation. Well into the mid-1990s, the number of Acoma Pueblo who could not find work remained extremely high. Since that time, the Acoma have sought to expand work opportunities for the residents of their ancient city by increasing tourism, offering gaming, developing service and retail businesses, and mining natural resources.

RELIGION

Historically, the Acoma have endured persecution because of their religious beliefs, so they maintain a great deal of secrecy about their spiritual traditions. Their chief gods are Ocatc (the sun, who is called "Father") and Iatiku (the mother of all Indians).

The Spanish Catholic missionaries were only partly successful in converting the Acoma to their faith. Christianity has never fully replaced the Native religion, but over the centuries, the tribe has blended elements of Catholicism with its traditional beliefs.

LANGUAGE

Acoma Keresan is still the primary language (the one they speak most of the time) of nearly 95 percent of the population on the Acoma reservation. Even in the early twenty-first century, many elders do not want the Keresan language to be written down but only passed along orally, because that has always been the tribal tradition. Other Acoma disagree, believing that writing could help to preserve the language for future generations. Even though the Keresan language was unwritten, it survived for centuries under Spanish rule.

Initiation of a War Chief

Elsie Clews Parsons (1875–1941), an anthropologist (a person who studies human behavior and culture), described the Acoma war chief ritual in her 1939 book, *Pueblo Indian Religion*:

> The outgoing war chief presented the new war chief with a prayer stick. The following day the war chief's two lieutenants, each carrying the cane of office and a quiver of mountain lion skin containing a smaller stick, gathered wood for additional prayer sticks. When they returned the war chief met them, singing, and made two lines of cornmeal for them to walk on.
>
> After making the prayer sticks the next day, the three men left them at the springs and returned with filled water jars. At three o'clock in the morning they asked to be admitted to the kiva. The Antelope clan bid them enter. The War Captain left four prayer feathers there as he prayed, then went to the east side of the mesa to pray. Just before sunrise, he called to the villagers who came out, greeted the sun, and sprinkled cornmeal on him.

The Acoma also struggled to hold on to their oral traditions and language during the 1900s when the U.S. government forced Native peoples to adopt white culture. Students attending federal or mission schools were forbidden to speak anything but English. Poet Simon J. Ortiz (1941–) recalled in *Woven Stone*, "Though it was forbidden and punishable with a hard crack by the teacher's ruler across the back or knuckles, we continued to speak in our Aacqumehdzehni [Acoma language], surreptitiously in the classroom and openly on the playground unless teachers were around."

In modern times, most Acoma residents speak English as well as Keresan, and many of the older Acoma people communicate in other Native languages of the region as well as in Spanish.

GOVERNMENT

Since the time of Spanish rule in the sixteenth and seventeenth centuries, the tribe has maintained a two-part governmental structure. The nonreligious government is led by a governor, his or her assistants, and a tribal council. They are responsible for interactions with the non-Native world. The religious tribal government is an ancient, god-centered system headed by members of the Antelope clan (a group of families who claim a common ancestor).

In 1863, President Abraham Lincoln (1809–1865; served 1861–65) presented the Acoma and other Pueblo tribes with silver-headed canes to commemorate their political and legal right to their land and self-government. The governors of each pueblo keep the canes during their official terms.

The tribe's first formal court system and written code of law was adopted in 1974. Today, the Acoma Pueblo are governed by five tribal officers and a twelve-member council. These leaders are appointed in the traditional manner. The Acoma also have a tribal court system. They have established business taxes and gaming ordinances.

ECONOMY

For centuries, the Acoma economy was based on agriculture. Men planted, harvested, built irrigation systems, and hunted. Women took care of housekeeping, childcare, and food preparation, including grinding cornmeal. After the people harvested fruits and vegetables, the chief distributed them equally among the tribal members.

During the past few decades, the Acoma have moved from a primarily agricultural economy to a business-based one. In modern times, the increasing pollution of the nearby San Jose River has cut down on Acoma farming. Cattle farming is now a major industry. Nearly 125 families work in ranching or farming. The tribal government employs more than half of the Acoma workforce to perform community projects or operate local facilities.

Tourism is important to the Acoma economy. Every year, at least eighty thousand tourists visit and provide income for the tribe. One popular attraction at Sky City is the San Esteban del Rey Mission, completed in 1640. The Sky City Cultural Center and Haak'u Museum opened in 2006 and offers additional tourist activities.

Pottery making provides the single largest private employment sector for the Acoma people. More than 120 self-employed potters sell their wares to visitors. The reservation also owns and operates a variety of service businesses along with farming and raising livestock. In addition, a small number of trees on the reservation are sold for lumber, and the tribe offers big game trophy hunting ventures. Sky City Casino provides employment and brings in revenue for tribal programs.

DAILY LIFE

Families

Acoma Pueblo society is matrilineal, meaning descent and inheritances are traced through the mother's side of the family. Aside from his or her inherited clan membership, each person is a member of a *kiva* (a ceremonial society named for the chamber in which the group's meetings are held) and participates in the tribal celebrations.

Buildings

Acoma buildings are aligned side by side in sets of three, forming east-west rows. Most contain kivas (meeting chambers for ceremonial societies).

The Acoma "Sky City" Pueblo in New Mexico has been occupied since the 1300s, despite having no utilities. © BOB DAEMMRICH/
THE IMAGE WORKS.

Acoma kivas are rectangular in shape rather than circular, as they are in many pueblos.

In the early twenty-first century, most Acoma live in modern-style villages. A few families still occupy the old villages, however, where buildings are maintained for the purposes of tradition, ceremonial gatherings, and tourism. The 250 dwellings in the original pueblo have neither running water nor sewer service. The families who choose to live there carry drinking water from natural stone catch-basins where water has been stored for a thousand years. The few radios and televisions in the old pueblo operate only on batteries, and all cooking and heating is done with wood.

Clothing and adornment

Like the other Pueblo people, Acoma men adopted Spanish dress of cotton pants and shirts. Women usually wore dresses that went over one shoulder. Acoma clothing, though, was more colorful than that of other pueblo dwellers. Garments are usually made from rectangular cloth strips with bright, embroidered designs along the borders.

Food

The Acoma enjoy many traditional foods, some of their favorites being blue corn drink (see "Food" in Pueblo entry for recipe), corn mush, pudding, wheat cake, corn balls, piki or paper bread, peach bark drink, flour bread, wild berries, wild banana, prickly pear fruit, and a chili-spiced stew.

Education

The Acoma Pueblo schools are overseen by a tribal school board that was created in 1978. Students also have the option of attending local public schools or private schools. Loan programs help students who wish to attend colleges and universities.

Acoma rainbow dancers perform at the Intertribal Indian Ceremonial event in Gallup, New Mexico. © NORTH WIND PICTURE ARCHIVES.

A traditional wedding vase is an example of the fine pottery skills of Acoma Pueblo artists. © AP IMAGES/MIKE YODER.

Public school education is supplemented by special classes taught by Acoma men who head various ceremonial societies. They conduct classes on such topics as proper behavior, care of the human spirit and the human body, astrology, child psychology, public speaking, history, music, and dancing. Spiritual teachings are learned mainly through participation in religious activities.

Healing practices

Traditionally, the Acoma had medicine societies that included male healers and female assistants. Healers called shamans (pronounced *SHAH-munz* or *SHAY-munz*) treated anyone who asked for help, and people gave them food or other useful items in payment. Shamans were said to receive their abilities from animals (for example, bears, eagles, snakes, or wolves), and they called on their powers with traditional songs and dances. To show off their skills, shamans might perform public feats such as swallowing swords, dancing on hot coals without injury, or producing green corn or fresh berries during winter. Three of the Acoma medicine societies remained in operation as of in the early 2000s.

Modern-day Acoma combine traditional practices with the latest medical techniques. For example, the Acoma hospital, which also serves the Navajo (see entry) and Laguna peoples, is equipped with a ritual curing room that resembles a hogan, a traditional home made of logs and mud. It contains a fireplace, an open pit area built into the earth, and a main door that faces east.

ARTS

A large percentage of Acoma people are keeping alive traditional crafts such as potterymaking, carving, and the weaving of blankets, belts, dresses, capes, socks, skirts, moccasins, and baskets. Acoma pottery is particularly prized for its thin walls and delicate decorations. The Acoma Pueblo has a visitor's center with a museum where tourists can see the thousand-year history of this ancient craft. The center also sells pieces by modern-day artists.

The Stolen Squashes

The Acoma composed many songs and poems, and some are used for teaching moral lessons. Coyote, an indestructible supernatural spirit with a humanlike mixture of good and evil qualities, is a popular character in Acoma oral literature. He appears in stories like this one about the terrible consequences of stealing:

There is a telling that one day Insect Man went out to weed his squash patch and found that one of his squashes had been eaten.

"Who can the thief be?" he chirped. "I'll think of a way to catch him." So he sat down and thought for a while.

Then he took a sharp stick and went from one squash to another, tasting them all until he found the sweetest one in the whole patch. He chewed a small hole in it and crawled inside. "Now I shall find out who is stealing my squashes," he said.

Soon Coyote came trotting along. He stopped beside the patch and began tasting each squash. When he came to the sweet one, he ate it up, Insect Man and all.

Down inside Coyote, Insect Man hunted about, singing as usual. Coyote looked first on one side and then on the other. He could not see anyone and was puzzled about that singing.

At last, Insect Man found what he was looking for. He pushed his sharp stick as deep as he could into Coyote's heart, and Coyote fell over dead.

Insect Man crawled out and went back to this weeding and singing.

When Coyote came to life again, he never stole another squash. But that is how it happened that Coyotes have false hearts.

SOURCE: Dahl Reed, Evelyn. From "The Stolen Squashes," in *Coyote Tales from the Indian Pueblos,* Santa Fe: Sunstone Press, 1988. Reproduced by permission.

CUSTOMS

Festivals and ceremonies

The major modern celebrations of the Acoma are the Governor's Feast, Easter, the Santa Maria Feast, Fiesta Day, and the Harvest Dance. The tribe gathers every year in the old village atop the mesa to celebrate the Feast of San Estevan, patron saint of Acoma. Both a Catholic mass and a traditional Harvest Dance are held, and fruits of the harvest are

Acoma Pueblo people walk in a procession to celebrate the feast day of their patron saint at San Estevan del Rey Mission, circa 1890. LIBRARY OF CONGRESS, MISCELLANEOUS ITEMS IN HIGH DEMAND, LC-USZ62-29347.

randomly distributed to attendees. Animals have always been highly respected by the Acoma, and the pueblo hosts Buffalo, Deer, and Turtle dances, as well as Basket and Turtle dances at Christmastime.

Children

On the fourth day after a baby was born, the Pueblo people named the child and took him or her outside at dawn to see the sun rise. By the early twenty-first century, babies were made full members of the tribe with both a Catholic baptism and the traditional presentation to Ocatc, the Pueblo sun god.

Funerals

Upon the death of a Catholic Acoma, a Roman Catholic mass for the dead is celebrated. Traditional Native prayers are also said to pave the way for the departed to be received by the Creator.

CURRENT TRIBAL ISSUES

Alcoholism among Acoma youth has become a matter of great concern to the tribe, not only because of its devastating physical and psychological effects but also because of its link to increased crime. The tribal court and police department seek to function as law enforcement agents, counselors, and educators to this troubled segment of Acoma society.

Beginning in the last half of the twentieth century, the Acoma started buying back their original lands. Since then, they have made land purchases that have added thousands of acres to their holdings.

One concern for the Acoma is maintaining the ancient buildings on the mesa, which are exposed to the elements. The tribe received a grant from the Getty Institute to preserve the San Esteban del Rey Mission, but because of the age of most of the building, maintenance of for the site will be an ongoing process.

NOTABLE PEOPLE

Simon J. Ortiz (1941–), who grew up in the village of McCartys, over-came alcohol addiction to become a sober and successful professional writer. In 1968, he received a fellowship from the International Writers Program to study at the University of Iowa. Despite having never earned a college degree, he has taught at several universities, held the post of consulting editor with the Pueblo of Acoma Press, and served as an interpreter and first lieutenant governor for his pueblo. Ortiz has written about Native life in essays, award-winning poetry collected in such books as *Going for the Rain* and *A Good Journey,* and story collections such as *Fightin'* and *Howbah Indians.*

Other notable Acoma Pueblo people include the painter and jewelry designer Wolf Robe Hunt (1905–1977); the potter Lucy Lewis (1898–1992), whose painted designs are based on ancient Native patterns; and the potter Lilly Salvador (1944–).

BOOKS

Bahti, Mark. *Pueblo Stories and Storytellers.* 3rd ed. Tucson, AZ: Rio Nuevo Publishers, 2010.

Carrillo, Charles M. *Saints of the Pueblos.* Albuquerque: LPD Press, 2008.

Cassidy, James J., Jr., ed. *Through Indian Eyes: The Untold Story of Native American Peoples.* Pleasantville, NY: Reader's Digest Association, 1995.

Keegan, Marcia. *Pueblo People: Ancient Tradition, Modern Lives.* Santa Fe, NM: Clear Light Publishers, 1999.

Little, Kimberley Griffiths. *The Last Snake Runner.* New York: Alfred A. Knopf, 2002.

Mails, Thomas E. *Dancing in the Paths of the Ancestors: The Culture, Crafts, and Ceremonies of the Hopi, Zuni, Acoma, Laguna, and Rio Grande Pueblo Indians of Yesterday.* Berlin, Germany: Marlowe and Company, 1999.

Ortiz, Simon J. *Woven Stone.* Tucson: University of Arizona Press, 2002.

Peaster, Lillian. *Pueblo Pottery Families: Acoma, Cochiti, Hopi, Isleta, Jemez, Laguna, Nambe, Picuris, Pojoaque, San Ildefonso, San Juan, Santa Clara, Santo Domingo, Taos, Tesuque, Zia, Zuni.* 3rd ed. Atglen, PA: Schiffer Publishing, 2008.

Sando, Joe S. *Pueblo Nations: Eight Centuries of Pueblo Indian History.* Santa Fe, NM: Clear Light Publishers, 1992.

Sweet, Jill Drayson, and Nancy Hunter Warren. *Pueblo Dancing.* Atglen, PA: Schiffer Publishing, 2011.

Trimble, Stephen. *Talking with the Clay: The Art of Pueblo Pottery in the 21st Century.* Santa Fe, NM: School for Advanced Research Press, 2007.

WEB SITES

"Acoma." *Southwest Crossroads.* http://southwestcrossroads.org/record. php?num=480 (accessed on July 20, 2011).

"Acoma Pueblo." *ClayHound Web.* http://www.clayhound.us/sites/acoma.htm (accessed on July 20, 2011).

"Acoma Pueblo." *New Mexico Magazine.* http://www.nmmagazine.com/native_ american/acoma.php (accessed on July 20, 2011).

"Acoma 'SkyCity'" *National Trust for Historic Preservation.*http://www. acomaskycity.org/ (accessed on July 20, 2011).

Haak'u Museum. http://museum.acomaskycity.org/ (accessed on July 20, 2011).

Halberstadt, Carol Snyder. "Traditional Acoma Pottery." *Migrations.* http:// www.migrations.com/traditionalacoma.html (accessed on July 20, 2011).

The Morgan Collection of Southwest Pottery. "Through the Eyes of the Pot: A Study of Southwest Pueblo Pottery and Culture: Acoma." *Lowell D. Holmes Museum of Anthropology, Wichita State University.* http://www.holmes. anthropology.museum/southwestpottery/acomapueblo.html (accessed on July 20, 2011).

National Museum of American History—Smithsonian Institution. "Pueblo Resistance: We Are Here." Video. *Mexico State Record Center and Archives.* http://www.newmexicohistory.org/filedetails.php?fileID=23042 (accessed on July 20, 2011).

Pueblo of Acoma. http://www.puebloofacoma.org/ (accessed on July 20, 2011).

"Simon Ortiz: Native American Poet." *The University of Texas at Arlington.* http://www.uta.edu/english/tim/poetry/so/ortizmain.htm (accessed on July 20, 2011).

Sky City Cultural Center. http://sccc.acomaskycity.org/ (accessed on July 20, 2011).

Weiser, Kathy. "New Mexico Legends: Acoma Pueblo—Ancient Sky City." *Legends of America.* http://www.legendsofamerica.com/nm-acoma.html (accessed on July 20, 2011).

Jemez Pueblo

Name

The people of the Jemez Pueblo (pronounced *HAY-mes PWEB-loh*, or traditionally as *HE-mish PWEB-loh*) call themselves *Hemes*, which in their language of Towa means "people." *Pueblo* is the Spanish word given to the stone and adobe, or mud-walled, villages inhabited by the various Pueblo peoples. The village where most tribal members reside is Walatowa, which means "this is the place."

Location

The Jemez Pueblo, a federal reservation, includes 90,000 acres of the tribe's former homeland in north-central New Mexico. It is located in the San Diego Canyon on the Jemez River about 55 miles (86 kilometers) northwest of Albequerque. Most of the Jemez people in the early twenty-first century live in the reservation town of Walatowa.

Population

In 1583, there were an estimated 30,000 Jemez Pueblo people. By 1630, there were only 3,000, and in 1706, only 300 survived. In the 1990 U.S. Census, 2,238 people identified themselves as Jemez. According to the 2000 census, 2,705 Jemez people lived in the United States. In 2001, the Bureau of Indian Affairs reported that tribal enrollment was 3,486 and, of that number, 58 percent lived on the reservation.

Language family

Tanoan.

Origins and group affiliations

Jemez oral history traces the tribe's origin to a lagoon near Stone Lake, New Mexico, now the site of the Jicarilla (pronounced *hee-kah-REE-yah*) Apache Reservation. Between 1250 and 1300, the Jemez moved from that site to the mountains of northern New Mexico in what is now part of the Santa Fe National Forest.

In 1838, the people from the Pecos Pueblo (see entry) joined the Jemez. The two groups merged as a legal entity in 1936, but each maintains its own identity.

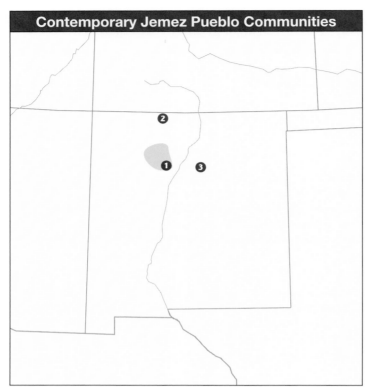

Contemporary Jemez Pueblo Communities

New Mexico
1. Walatowa (Jemez Reservation)
2. Jicarilla Apache Tribe
3. Pecos Pueblo

Shaded area
☐ Traditional lands of the Jemez Pueblo are located in the San Diego Canyon in present-day New Mexico

A map of contemporary Jemez Pueblo communities. MAP BY XNR PRODUCTIONS. CENGAGE LEARNING, GALE. REPRODUCED BY PERMISSION OF GALE, A PART OF CENGAGE LEARNING.

At the time the Jemez people first made contact with the Spanish, the Jemez Nation was one of the largest and most powerful in the region that is now the state of New Mexico. Their original homes, stone fortresses that sometimes contained more than two thousand rooms, are some of the largest ruins in the United States. Over the years, the people of the Jemez Pueblo, who were later joined by the Pecos Pueblo, have been able to withstand enormous outside pressures and still retain their traditional religion and culture.

HISTORY

Jemez make contact with the Spanish

During the fourteenth century, the Jemez made their home in the hills of San Diego Canyon, which has a fertile floor irrigated by the Jemez River. It was in this canyon that the first Spanish explorers of New Mexico came upon the Jemez people. The meeting took place in 1541, when Francisco Vásquez de Coronado (c. 1510–1554) led an expedition into the area. At that time, the pueblo had a population of more than thirty thousand.

Not until 1598 was there significant interaction between the Jemez and the Spanish. The association, lasting for a little more than eighty years, was fraught with difficulties and ended in a massive rebellion by the Native Americans.

Pueblo Revolt

The Spanish planned to convert the Jemez to the Catholic religion, by force if necessary. When the missionary priests first arrived, the Jemez were living either in small pueblos scattered throughout San Diego Canyon or on the surrounding large hills. These large hills had steep sides and flat tops and were called *mesas* (meaning "tables" in Spanish). The mesas offered protection against wandering raiders, such as the Apache and Comanche (see entries).

To make their work easier, Spanish priests and soldiers forced the Jemez and other Pueblo peoples down off the mesa tops. They took Jemez homes for themselves and ordered the people to build new villages and churches. The Spaniards made the Jemez pay taxes to the king in the form of crops, blankets, and pottery. They also forbid the tribe to practice their own religion, but many did so in secret. Finally, in 1680, the Jemez could take the mistreatment no longer and agreed to join in the Pueblo Revolt (see Pueblo entry). In spite of the superior weapons of the Spanish, the Pueblo peoples succeeded in casting the Spanish out of New Mexico.

Return of the Spanish

The Spanish were not gone for long. Between 1688 and 1692, they regained their power over Jemez land. They ordered the Pueblo peoples to pledge their support for Spain, but most Jemez refused to take such a vow. In 1694, the Jemez staged a raid against the Zia and Santa Ana tribes, who were supporters of the Spanish, taking their livestock and killing four men.

Important Dates

1680: The Pueblo Revolt, in which the Jemez people play a vital role, drives the Spanish from New Mexico.

1694: The Spanish recapture the San Diego Valley, home of the Jemez.

1696: Luis Cunixu, a Jemez war chief, tries to spark another Jemez rebellion, but he is later executed.

1838: The people of Pecos abandon their pueblo and join the Jemez at Walatowa.

1848: The United States takes control of New Mexico.

1936: The Jemez and Pecos peoples legally become one group.

2003: The Jemez Community Development Corporation (JCDC) is established to oversee business and economic development.

The Spaniards sent an expedition to punish the Jemez. In the bloody battle that followed, 381 Jemez women and children were captured, 84 people were killed, and villages were destroyed. Jemez crops and cattle were taken and distributed to Native allies of the Spaniards. The Spanish later pardoned and released most of the survivors. In 1696, the Jemez were commanded to leave their homes and live together in the small village of Walatowa.

Return to Jemez Pueblo

More bloodshed was to follow. In June 1696, a Spanish priest was found dead, and Jemez leader Luis Cunixu was accused of his murder. The Jemez, fearing vengeance from the Spanish, left the village and made plans to defend themselves. They requested help from the Acoma, Zuñi, and Navajo peoples (see entries), who obliged by sending some warriors. After a few battles, the tribes were forced to surrender. The Jemez scattered, and the other Native warriors returned home. By the early 1700s, matters had quieted down, and the people again began to settle at the Jemez Pueblo.

The Spanish retained control of the region until 1820. During that time, Spain's king assured the Jemez people of their rights to more than 17,000 acres of their traditional land. Although the Spanish persisted in trying to convert them and trampled on many sacred shrines and religious centers, the Jemez were able to stay together and preserve much of their culture.

Assured land rights

Pueblo territory passed into Mexican hands in 1820, and the Jemez lost much of their ancestral land. In 1838, the Pecos peoples, who were fleeing enemy raids and deadly epidemics (uncontrolled outbreaks of disease), joined the Jemez at Walatowa. Nearly one hundred years later, the two groups would legally become one.

Following America's victory in the Mexican-American War (1846– 48; a war in which Mexico lost about half of its national territory to the United States), the United States took over the Pueblo region from Mexico. The new government assured the Jemez that their rights to their land would be protected, but the United States failed to keep its promises. Settlers moved onto the land illegally. Throughout the twentieth century, the Jemez engaged in ongoing battles with U.S. courts to defend their land and water rights. They did achieve some victories, though, including the 1975 expansion of their land holdings to its present 90,000 acres.

Arson by Witches

To protect their privacy and sacred stories, the Jemez people normally do not share them with others. If they do tell a story, they omit parts of it—especially those that reveal information that should not be shared with outsiders. When anthropologist Elsie Parsons heard this tale, the teller explained that he left out certain parts, so the story is not complete as recorded.

> Dypolah. They were living at kyulaw-imu [a half-mile north of modern-day Taos], and at that time there were many people at Jemez. There was a boy visiting from setokwa. He was spending the night with one of his friends in the house where they were meeting. As he lay there still awake he overheard them say that they were going to burn the whole pueblo as far as setokwa. They said that all those who did not go into the water would be burned and all those who stepped into the water would be saved. The witches said that they would wrap pine gum in cedar bark and put it into the roof above people asleep. After he heard all this the boy left to tell his father. His father was ts'untawhi [chief of setokwa]. The boy said, "Father, something is going to happen tonight. I heard those bad people saying that they were going to fire the whole pueblo tonight. They are having a meeting at kyulawimu. So you had better do something to save your pueblo." "Yes, my son, I will try to." Then his father made prayer-sticks, and with them put canteens (babo) in a line, at black rocks [conspicuous boulders south of Taos]. While he was putting up the sticks he saw a big fire in the pueblo. It was burning as the wind blows, quickly. All of the people were burned, only those who went into the water were saved. The fire reached the place where the prayer-sticks were. When the fire touched the sticks they began to throw out water, and the fire stopped there, and that saved the pueblo. That is why there are witches now in Jemez, and that is why, because of that fire, we have only one pueblo. This happened in the beginning (kwaosho [a term descriptive of "anything of long ago"]). Qtsedaba.

SOURCE: Parsons, Elsie Clews. *The Pueblo of Jemez.* New Haven, CT: Yale University Press, 1925.

RELIGION

Very little is known about the traditional Jemez religion. Because they believe that their ceremonies will lose power if they are made public, the Jemez people hold all religious services in secret. They try to live in close harmony with nature. Their ceremonies are held to bring rain, help crops grow, and ensure abundant game supplies. When Jemez people tell tribal stories to outsiders, they sometimes leave out details that would reveal certain secrets about their traditions.

LANGUAGE

The Jemez language, Towa, is still spoken at Walatowa in combination with English and Spanish. Jemez law does not allow the language to be written down, because the people wish to keep outsiders from gaining knowledge about the tribe. Many elders also believe that because their language and history have been handed down orally since ancient times, it is important to respect and adhere to this tradition. Others disagree with this stance and want the language to be written down so it will not be lost to future generations. With most of the people still speaking the language into the early twenty-first century, the prospect of the language being lost was not an immediate concern.

GOVERNMENT

The Pueblo of Jemez is a sovereign nation, which means it is not subject to outside laws. Two types of government are in place: traditional and secular (nonreligious). The traditional government has two leaders who hold their positions for life. The most important of these, the *cacique,* is both a spiritual and a societal leader. He is served by the *opng-soma* (war captain), who enforces the religious rules and regulations. The secular government began during the time of the Spanish occupation. It consists of a governor and his staff, who are selected each year by the cacique, and a tribal council. (The council is composed of former governors.) The leadership includes two lieutenant governors, one each from the Jemez and the Pecos Pueblo peoples. The secular government maintains business relations with the outside world.

ECONOMY

For centuries, the Jemez relied on hunting, farming, and gathering to support the tribe. When the Spanish arrived, the Jemez sold them rabbit fur blankets and simple knee-length dresses called *mantas.* The Spanish introduced the Jemez people to new crops (chilies, wheat, grapes, and melons) and livestock (horses, donkeys, oxen, cattle, sheep, and goats). In time, most Jemez families owned a donkey. Grapes were harvested until World War II (1939–45; a war in which Great Britain, France, the

United States, and their allies defeated Germany, Italy, and Japan), when so many Jemez men went off to war that the vines withered from neglect.

In 1989, land on the reservation began producing oil and gas. In addition, the tribe earned funds by permitting the mining of sand and gravel on its territory. Also in the twentieth century, the Jemez began selling Ponderosa pine and Douglas fir from the reservation for use as timber and fuel. In 1999, they started the Walatowa Woodland initiative and partnered with several federal agencies to manage the land and reforest areas that were cut. The group owned a logging mill to produce a variety of wood products. Concern for the environment prompted the development of a Native Fish Aquarium with an interactive display so students could learn about the fish that were significant to their ancestors and remain important to the area.

From early times, the Jemez have been farmers or ranchers. Corn and chilies are their most important crops. Some people make and sell various arts and crafts such as ring baskets (round yucca-leaf baskets used to store food and wash wheat) and a red pottery developed in the 1950s. The Jemez also operate several service businesses and tourist attractions.

Many tribal members work for the Bureau of Indian Affairs, the U.S. Forest Service, local law enforcement agencies, and the tribal court system. Jemez officials are trying to secure permission for an off-site casino, which could fund many much-needed social programs and economic projects.

A ladder leans against a section of the Jemez Pueblo. © JEFFREY M. FRANK/SHUTTERSTOCK.COM.

DAILY LIFE

Buildings

The pueblo style of architecture (see Pueblo entry) was practiced by the Jemez from around 700 CE. They constructed and maintained large pueblos containing as many as four levels, with each level being smaller by one room than the level below it. They built roofs by laying whole log beams across two walls. Spaces between the logs were then filled in with grasses and plastered over with adobe (pronounced *uh-DOE-bee*; a sun-dried mud made of a mixture of clay, sand, and sometimes ashes, rocks, or straw).

The *kiva,* a room where ceremonies and sacred meetings take place, is also central to Jemez culture. One kiva is built for each tribal subdivision in a pueblo village. The kivas are usually built of stone.

Food

The Jemez lived and farmed at a higher elevation than any other Pueblo people. While the men farmed and hunted deer, antelope, or elk, the women gathered fruits, cactus, and other wild foods. They adopted the cultivation of chilies, melons, grapes, and wheat from the Spanish. To prepare wheat for grinding, they first winnowed it (separated it out), then washed it in an irrigation ditch in a ringbasket, and finally spread it on canvas to dry. Fields of corn, beans, squash, wheat, and chilies still fill the canyon floor at Walatowa, and agriculture and livestock represent a major source of livelihood on the reservation.

Education

In the mid-1800s, the government and the Presbyterian Church jointly established a school at the pueblo. One of their concerns was that no one could read or write, but they failed to take into account the fact that the Pueblo people do not believe in writing down their language (see "Language"), so the children had no need to learn these skills.

In modern times, the Jemez Pueblo offers Head Start classes for young children on the reservation. A Bureau of Indian Affairs day school and public elementary and secondary schools have been built there as well. Students have the option of attending charter schools, public schools, or a boarding school in Santa Fe. The Jemez was the first New Mexico tribe to operate its own charter school.

Healing practices

According to Jemez beliefs, supernatural creatures could either heal people or make them ill. The traditional Jemez relied on a curing society rather than a single shaman (pronounced *SHAH-mun* or *SHAY-mun*) to do the healing. Healing ceremonies took place before the whole community. To cure an individual or an entire community, the curing society called forth the supernatural forces—possibly spirits or even a witch within the pueblo—thought to be causing harm. In the early twenty-first century, the Jemez people made use of traditional healing practices in combination with modern methods.

ARTS

The Jemez traditions of pottery making and basket weaving date back to about 700. The people are known for five distinct types of pottery. The early styles were the "Jemez Black-on-White," as well as a cruder variation of that called "Jemez Black-on-White Rough," and "Jemez Plain Utility," an undecorated pottery style, with its variant, "Jemez Indented Corrugated," which was also plain but had indents in it. The Jemez stopped making the black-on-white pottery sometime during the eighteenth century, and they destroyed existing pots to keep them from the Spanish.

For two centuries, the Jemez used pottery from neighboring pueblos, particularly from the Pueblo of Zia. In the early 1900s, the Jemez resumed pottery making. Their new style incorporated some of the Zia designs, but they developed a unique type of pottery for which they gained recognition. These pots are black-on-red or black/red on tan.

In addition to their exquisite pottery and basketry, the people are known for their woven cloth, sculptures, and jewelry. Jemez artworks are sold at the Walatowa Visitor Center as well as around the world.

Eagle Dancers from the Jemez Pueblo perform at a festival.
© ERNESTO BURCIAGA/ALAMY.

CUSTOMS

Moieties

The Jemez have two tribal subdivisions, called moieties (pronounced *MOY-uh-teez*): the Turquoise and the Squash. These are not "clans," or groups of people descended from a common ancestor. Rather, they are tribal divisions that determine which group among the Jemez performs certain rites or ceremonies.

Festivals and ceremonies

Traditional celebrations The Jemez have a very complex organization for ceremonies, with twenty-three religious societies conducting various rites. Every Jemez male is a member of either the Eagle or Arrow society, but membership in the other groups is reserved for a select few who show some talent in curing, rainmaking, war, hunting, or other areas.

Dances are central to ceremonial and social life for the Jemez. The people perform many of their ritual dances and ceremonies, such as the Corn Dance, to gain the favor of the spirits. Traditionally, ceremonies and dances are shared among Pueblo peoples. For example, the Jemez learned the Pecos Bull Ceremony (see Pecos Pueblo entry) in 1838 after the remaining survivors of the Pecos Pueblo joined their tribe. The Corn Dance and Old Pecos Bull Ceremonyat Jemez are still held each August as part of the Saint Persingula Feast Day.

Feast days The celebration of feast days is a Catholic practice. Many Jemez identify themselves as Catholics and observe ceremonies of the Christian calendar, but they observe them in a traditional Pueblo way. For example, the celebration of a feast day displays Jemez reverence for foods—both animal and vegetable—provided by Mother Earth.

Families from different groups within the tribe are selected to host each feast day celebration. They provide a meal for all visitors, and in turn, the guests may bring an offering of food to be included with the meal. Part of the food preparation takes place outside in the tall adobe ovens, called "beehives," that are still present behind many Jemez homes. As a feast day progresses, ceremonial dances take place in the town square to give thanks for the bounty, which has been shared.

Modern festivals Other important feast days and festivals include the annual Jemez Red Rocks Arts & Crafts Show, St. Persingula Feast Day in August, Open Air Market, the San Diego Feast Day in November, and Our Lady of Guadalupe Feast Day, and the Walatowa Winter Arts & Crafts Show. The pueblo is open to the public only during selected special events. At all other times, the Jemez people wish to maintain their privacy and ask that visitors respect their closed village policy. Those who wish to visit at other times of the year may go to the Walatowa Visitor Center to learn more about the Jemez Pueblo and its people.

Track and field

Running is a longtime tradition at the Jemez Pueblo, which over the years has produced a number of world-class runners. The ancestors of the Jemez people often ran hundreds of miles to deliver messages. They endured the desert heat and the rough terrain of mesas and canyons. Now their descendants compete in local footraces as well as marathons, including the grueling one up Pikes Peak. Some have even made it to the Olympic trials.

CURRENT TRIBAL ISSUES

Land and water rights

The Jemez, who once inhabited the entire San Diego Canyon, have seen their land holdings dwindle since the Spanish arrived in their territory in the late 1500s. Four hundred years later, New Mexico courtrooms were hearing many cases regarding ongoing efforts to protect Jemez land rights.

Water rights are also a problem. With the increasing use of the Jemez River by people north of Walatowa, as well as the frequency of droughts in the area, Jemez farmers find it difficult to secure enough water for the irrigation of their crops. In 2007, New Mexico's Native nations backed legislation that provided funding for Native American water rights settlements, better education, language preservation efforts, and a minimum wage increase. Jemez Pueblo governor Raymond Gachupin, chairman of the Ten Southern Pueblos Council, asked for additional funds for health care services for Native people. In 2010, the Pueblo received $1 million from the U.S. Department of Agriculture Rural Utilities Service (USDA-RUS) to construct water and sewer utilities. This project needs to proceed with development of more housing and develop alternative energy sources.

Cultural preservation

Another concern of tribal elders is the spread of mainstream American cultural practices among the Jemez. Problems began when the plow replaced the traditional and sacred hoe. The elders thought that the use of modern technology would interfere with the religious nature of planting of corn and thereby anger the gods. As time went on, the plow was replaced by the tractor, and the horse was replaced by the pickup truck. In modern Walatowa, antennas protrude from pueblo rooftops and nearly every household has electricity and appliances. Experts in Native American studies disagree on whether these elements can coexist with traditional life or if they will someday will replace it altogether.

Along with the changes brought by outside culture, many Pueblo tribes have difficulties with tourists who do not respect their privacy. Taking pictures of ceremonies, recording prayers, or describing dances without the pueblo's permission is an invasion of the people's rights. Because of this, the Jemez Pueblo closed their reservation to outsiders except on special feast days, which they do not publicize in order to minimize the number of tourists who attend. The tribe's regular tourist attractions, such as Jemez Mountain Trail Scenic Byway and the Jemez Mountain National Recreation area, are still open to the public, as are their annual arts and crafts shows. The Jemez also run educational programs at their Walatowa Visitor Center.

CASINO CONSTRUCTION

The Jemez are working to get permission to construct an off-reservation casino. The Bureau of Indian Affairs denied their petition in 2008 because they said the casino location, which is about 300 miles from the reservation, would not provide any jobs for the Jemez people. Jemez officials pointed out that the income from the casino would fund many much-needed reservation programs. In 2011, the Obama administration agreed to review proposals for several off-reservation casinos. Jemez officials have gained the support of the eight Pueblo groups, including the Acoma and San Juan Pueblos (see entries), which have casinos of their own. The Jemez project, however, faces strong opposition from several other Native nations, particularly the Mescalero Apache, who operate the Inn of the

Mountain Gods Resort and Casino located 110 miles (180 kilometers) from the proposed Jemez site. The Apache believe it will draw away some of their business.

NOTABLE PEOPLE

Luis Cunixu, a Jemez leader (probably a war captain) who lived during the seventeenth century, refused to accept the Spaniards'return to his land when Spain reclaimed control over New Mexico in 1692. He fought to remove them, and he later fled to the Pecos Pueblo after being accused of killing a Spanish priest during an uprising in June 1696. Cunixu worked unsuccessfully to gain the support of the Pecos people, but he was turned over to the Spanish, who shot him to death in Santa Fe in front of the town church.

Other notable Jemez include the painter Jose Rey Toledo (1915–1994); the author, Pueblo historian, and educator Joe Sando (1923–2011), who wrote several books about the Pueblo people; and a legendary runner during the late 1800s, Tyila (Pablo Gachupin).

BOOKS

Bahti, Mark. *Pueblo Stories and Storytellers.* 3rd ed. Tucson, AZ: Rio Nuevo Publishers, 2010.

Carrillo, Charles M. *Saints of the Pueblos.* Albuquerque: LPD Press, 2008.

Isaacs, Judith Ann. *Jemez Valley Cookbook: The Food, the People, the Land.* Jemez Pueblo, NM: Butterfly & Bear Press, 1997.

Keegan, Marcia, and Regis Pecos. *Pueblo People: Ancient Traditions, Modern Lives.* Santa Fe, NM: Clear Light Publishers, 1999.

Mails, Thomas E. *Dancing in the Paths of the Ancestors: The Culture, Crafts, and Ceremonies of the Hopi, Zuni, Acoma, Laguna, and Rio Grande Pueblo Indians of Yesterday.* Berlin: Marlowe & Company, 1999.

Peaster, Lillian. *Pueblo Pottery Families: Acoma, Cochiti, Hopi, Isleta, Jemez, Laguna, Nambe, Picuris, Pojoaque, San Ildefonso, San Juan, Santa Clara, Santo Domingo, Taos, Tesuque, Zia, Zuni.*3rd ed. Atglen, PA: Schiffer Publishing, 2008.

Roberts, David. *The Pueblo Revolt: The Secret Rebellion that Drove the Spaniards Out of the Southwest.* New York: Simon & Schuster, 2005.

Sando, Joe S. *Life of PaaPeh: Reflections of a Pueblo Indian Elder.* Ithaca, NY: Clear Light Books, 2007.

Sando, Joe S. *Nee Hemish: A History of Jemez Pueblo.* Albuquerque: University of New Mexico Press, 1982.

Scully, Vincent. *Pueblo-Mountain, Village, Dance.* Chicago: University of Chicago Press, 1989.

Sweet, Jill Drayson, and Nancy Hunter Warren. *Pueblo Dancing*. Atglen, PA: Schiffer Publishing, 2011.

Trimble, Stephen. *Talking with the Clay: The Art of Pueblo Pottery in the 21st Century*. Santa Fe, NM: School for Advanced Research Press, 2007.

Wallace, Susan E. *The Land of the Pueblos*. Santa Fe, NM: Sunstone Press, 2006.

WEB SITES

"Jemez Pueblo." *ClayHound Web.* http://www.clayhound.us/sites/jemez.htm (accessed on July 20, 2011).

"Jemez Pueblo." *New Mexico Magazine.* http://www.nmmagazine.com/ native_american/jemez.php (accessed on July 20, 2011).

"Jemez Pueblos." *Four Directions Institute.* http://www.fourdir.com/jemez.htm (accessed on July 20, 2011).

Morgan Collection of Southwest Pottery. "Through the Eyes of the Pot: A Study of Southwest Pueblo Pottery and Culture: Jemez." *Lowell D. Holmes Museum of Anthropology, Wichita State University.* http://www.holmes. anthropology.museum/southwestpottery/jemezpueblo.html (accessed on July 20, 2011).

National Museum of American History—Smithsonian Institution. "Pueblo Resistance: We Are Here" (video). *Mexico State Record Center and Archives.* http://www.newmexicohistory.org/filedetails.php?fileID=23042 (accessed on July 20, 2011).

Pueblo of Jemez. http://www.jemezpueblo.org/ (accessed on July 20, 2011).

Redish, Laura, and Orrin Lewis. "Towa (Jemez) Language." *Native Languages of the Americas.* http://www.native-languages.org/towa.htm (accessed on July 20, 2011).

Walatowa Visitor Center. http://www.jemezpueblo.com/ (accessed on July 20, 2011).

Pecos Pueblo

Name

The name for the Pecos Pueblo (*PAY- kohs PWEB-loh*) came from the Keresanword *P'e'-a-ku'*, which was the name of their town. *Pueblo* is the Spanish word given to the stone and adobe (mud-walled) villages inhabited by the various Pueblo peoples. Early writers and explorers called the Pecos by many different names, including Cicuyé, Paquiah, Pekush, Peago, Peaku, and Peco.

Location

Pecos oral history indicated that the people originated in the north but later crossed the Rio Grande and lived in present-day San Jose, California, and Kingman, Arizona, before migrating into the Pecos River Valley of New Mexico. Traditional Pecos lands were located on the upper branch of Pecos River, about 30 miles (50 kilometers) southeast of Santa Fe. The largest of the pueblos, the Pecos Pueblo, occupied about 40 miles (65 kilometers) of valley lands from the north end of Cañon de Pecos to Anton Chico. By the time the Spanish arrived in 1540, most of the Pecos had gathered into one main pueblo, called Tshiquité, or Tziquité.

After 1838, the people moved to the Jemez Pueblo. Located in north-central New Mexico on the Jemez River, the present-day federal reservation of the two groups encompasses about 90,000 acres of the Jemez tribe's former homeland. The land is in the San Diego Canyon, about 55 miles (85 kilometers) northwest of Albuquerque. In the early twenty-first century, most of the Jemez and Pecos people lived in the reservation town of Walatowa.

Population

Before the Spanish arrived, estimates put the Pecos population at approximately 2,000 to 2,500. By 1760, that number had decreased to 599. In the early 1790s, Comanche raids killed almost every man, dropping the number of Pecos to 152. In 1805, the Pecos numbered 104, and in 1838, the remaining 17 survivors left their pueblo to join the Jemez. Beginning in 1838, the U.S. Census Bureau counted the Pecos as part of the Jemez Pueblo population. By the 1900s, only 25 blood-descendants of the Pecos were known to

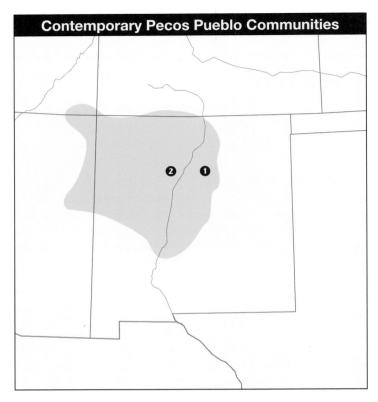

Contemporary Pecos Pueblo Communities

New Mexico
❶ Pueblo Tshiquite
❷ Walatowa (Jemez Reservation)

Shaded area
☐ Traditional lands of the Pueblo in present-day New Mexico, northeastern Arizona, southeastern Utah and southwestern Colorado

A map of contemporary Pecos Pueblo communities. MAP BY XNR PRODUCTIONS. CENGAGE LEARNING, GALE. REPRODUCED BY PERMISSION OF GALE, A PART OF CENGAGE LEARNING.

still be living, but some people on the Jemez reservation still claimed a Pecos heritage in the twenty-first century.

Language family
Tanoan.

Origins and group affiliations
The Pecos are descended from the ancient groups who lived in the Southwest. One of their ancestral groups, the *Hisatsinom,* or Ancestral Puebloans, also used cliff dwellings. The Pecos traded with the Apache and even protected them from the Jicarilla and the Comanche, but the Pecos later allied with the Spanish and sided against the Apache. The Comanche and Querecho remained enemies of the Pecos people. During the early 1800s, attacks from other tribes along with outbreaks of disease destroyed most of the Pecos

population. The few remaining people fled to the Jemez Pueblo in 1838. From that time on, the Pecos made their home with the Jemez Puebloans, who welcomed them warmly. The two groups became one official tribe in 1936, but each group still maintained its separate identity.

Once the largest and most populous pueblo, the Pecos were feared throughout the land, according to Spanish explorer Francisco Vásquez de Coronado (c. 1510–1554), who arrived in 1540. At that time, the Pecos people lived in two main four-story dwellings, each containing about 600 rooms. A farming community who irrigated their arid land, the Pecos occasionally hunted wild game. Raids by the Apache, Comanche (see entries), and Querecho decimated the Pecos population until only seventeen survivors remained in 1838. These Pecos moved to the Jemez pueblo, where the two groups officially merged in 1936.

Archaeologists excavate ancient Pueblo ruins at Pecos National Historic Park in 1916. © CORBIS.

Important Dates

800–950: The early Pecos built pit houses.

1539: The first Spaniard, Estevan, arrives in Pecos territory.

c. 1622: Spaniards found first church at the Pecos Pueblo.

1680: The Pueblo Revolt drives the Spanish from New Mexico.

1692: Pecos make peace with Spaniards, in spite of protests from some tribe members.

1838: The people of Pecos abandon their pueblo and join the Jemez at Walatowa.

1848: The United States takes control of New Mexico.

1936: The Jemez and Pecos peoples legally become one group.

1965: The Pecos National Monument is established to protect the archaeological ruins of the pueblo.

1990: An additional 5,500 acres is added to the monument grounds, and the site is renamed Pecos National Historical Park.

HISTORY

Ancient Pecos civilizations

For at least seven thousand years, people lived in the area around the Pecos pueblo. Some groups, such as the *Hisatsinom,* or Ancestral Puebloans (see Anasazi entry), used cliff dwellings like those of the Pecos Pueblo. The early Pecos lived in pit houses from about 800 to 950 CE; the people began building pueblos in the 1300s. Groups who lived in smaller communities came together, forming larger villages over the next two centuries. Buildings went through several phases until they reached multistory complexes, containing hundreds of rooms, around 1450.

Early Pecos peoples farmed the land but also made a living through trade. They bartered with other tribes, including the Plains Apache. The Pecos had many desirable goods—agricultural products, feathers, pottery, and cotton fabric and clothing—that they exchanged for tanned skins, buffalo hides, flint, shells, and slaves. The Pecos then swapped some of these items with other pueblos for turquoise, parrot feathers, and pottery. By the 1500s, the Pecos had become the most powerful tribe in the area and were both feared and respected.

Pecos encounter Spaniards

Soon after Spanish explorers entered New Mexico, they met the Pecos. The first Spaniard to enter Pecos territory, Estevan, arrived in 1539 as a member of the Fray Marcos de Niza (c. 1495–1558) expedition. The following year, Francisco Vásquez de Coronado (c. 1510–1554), along with more than 1,500 soldiers, reached the Zuni pueblo. The Pecos Puebloans were the only ones who agreed to meet with Coronado.

Under the leadership of a man the Spanish called Bigotes (Whiskers) for his long mustache, the Pecos brought gifts of headpieces, shields, and hides for the Europeans. In return, the Spanish gave them glass dishes, pearls, and small bells. An officer from the expedition, Hernando de Alvarado (c. 1518–1550), along with two hundred soldiers accompanied the Pecos back to their village, where the people greeted the Europeans

Message from the Eagle

When Coronado arrived in Zuni territory, only the Pecos sent a delegation to welcome the newcomers and bring them gifts. The people also greeted the Spanish troops warmly when Coronado's expedition arrived at the Pecos Pueblo. Perhaps their enthusiastic welcome stemmed from this story of this communication with an eagle.

> Upon one occasion, and before the Spaniards had settled in the country, a man and his little son went into the mountains to gather wood. The boy was startled at the sound of a voice, and asked his father who spoke to them, who replied that he did not hear any body, and they continued to pick up wood. In a few moments the voice was heard again, when the father looked up and saw a large eagle perched in the top of a high pine-tree. The bird now told the Indian that the king across the waters was sending people into the country to take care of the Pueblos, and that if he would come back to that spot in eight days, it could tell him when they would arrive. The eagle also directed him to inform his village what he had heard. When the Indian returned to the pueblo, he told the head men he had something to communicate, who assembled in the estufa to listen to him, when he related an account of the appearance of the eagle and what it had said to him. At the end of eight days he returned to the mountain, where he found the eagle awaiting him, which informed him that the men from across the waters would arrive in two days, and that all his people must go to meet them, and welcome them to the country, which was accordingly done.

SOURCE: Davis, W.W.H. *El Gringo; or, New Mexico and Her People.* New York: Harper & Brothers, 1857, pp. 154–55. Available online from *University of Arizona Library.* http://southwest.library.arizona.edu/elgr/body.1_div.6.html (accessed on July 20, 2011).

with music and gave them cloth and turquoise. When the Coronado expedition stopped at the Pecos pueblo, the people again demonstrated their generosity by giving Coronado and his men feather robes, animal skins, and cotton fabrics.

Breakdown of Spanish-Pueblo relations

A slave at the pueblo told Alvarado of great cities of gold in his homeland. The slave, whom the Spaniards called Turk, also claimed that the Pueblo had taken his gold bracelets when they captured him. After hearing Turk's story, Alvarado demanded these gold bracelets from Bigotes and the Pecos governor, an elderly man. When the Pecos leaders denied that the jewelry existed, Alvarado chained up both of them. The Pueblo people fought against this injustice, but the Spanish kept their prisoners for six months. From that point on, the Pueblo peoples no longer trusted the Spaniards. Alvarado also demanded three hundred pieces of fabric to clothe his soldiers. These same soldiers stopped people in the street and took from them any blankets or cloaks they wanted. The Pueblo people, who had a custom of generosity that called for each person to donate more than he or she had received, did not understand the Spanish demands, and relations became even more strained.

Other Spanish expeditions made their way to the pueblos during the late 1500s, but the next one to make a major impact on the Pecos was that of Gaspar Castaño de Sosa (1550–1593), who sent an advance guard to the pueblo in 1590. According to Spanish accounts, the Pecos initially welcomed the soldiers but later attacked and disarmed them. Then Castaño de Sosa attempted to bargain with the Pecos. When he did not succeed, he attacked the pueblo. As their town was shelled and people died, most of the Pecos fled. Castaño de Sosa's forces collected the goods the Pecos had left behind and moved on to another pueblo.

Attempts to convert the Pecos

Several years later, in 1598, Juan de Oñate (1552–1626), who would go on to become New Mexico's first governor, sent a priest to the pueblo after gaining an oath of loyalty from the Pecos. Several early missionaries sent to the pueblos had been killed, but the Pecos accepted Fray Francisco de San Miguel. The missionaries taught the Pecos new farming and animal husbandry practices, supplied tools, and preached the Catholic religion. A small church was built, but it was later replaced by La Mission de Nuestra Senora de Los Ángeles de Porciúncula in the 1620s. To construct this church, the Pecos had to make approximately 300,000 adobe bricks. (For more information on Pueblo labor on Spanish churches, see Pueblo entry.) When it was completed, the church was large enough to hold all 1,189 Pecos living at the pueblo.

The missionaries were determined to convert all Pueblos and began their task by destroying all Pecos religious items, which they termed idols. They believed they were following the bible's directives that said no images or items should be worshipped in place of God. They also forbid traditional ceremonies and rituals. Although many Pecos accepted the new religion, most still retained their old practices (see "Religion"). These they kept secret from the missionaries. Eventually, though, the Pueblos planned an uprising to rid themselves of Spanish domination.

A statue of Pueblo leader Popé, who led a revolt against the Spanish in 1680, stands in the Rotunda of the U.S. Capitol Building in Washington, D.C. © ROLL CALL/GETTY IMAGES.

Pueblo Revolt

In August 1680, the Pueblo people banded together to drive the Spaniards from their land. Led by Popé (died 1692), a religious leader from the San Juan Pueblo (see entry), the various Pueblo groups acted as a single force. In one day, they killed four hundred Spaniards, including twenty-one Catholic priests. The Pecos church that the people had labored to build was set on fire.

The Publoeans succeeded in driving the Spanish out of their homeland. Twenty percent of the Spaniards in the region died in the rebellion, and those who survived fled to Mexico. The Pueblo Revolt is sometimes called the "First American Revolution." It was the first and only successful attempt by Native North Americans to remove colonists from their lands.

Spanish reconquest

The Pueblo victory was short lived. A little more than a decade later, Don Diego de Vargas (1643–1704) began a quest to retake the Pecos villages. When de Vargas entered the Pecos Pueblo, he found it empty. The people had fled to the mountains. Using his captives from Jemez as messengers, de Vargas convinced the Pecos to surrender. He formally took possession of the Pecos Pueblo on October 17, 1692. Following that, around one-third of the people were baptized, and soldiers were stationed in the pueblo.

Decline of the Pecos

Over the next century, as the Spanish population increased, the number of Pecos dwindled. Records from 1694 show 736 Pecos living in the pueblo. By the 1790s, that figure had dropped to 152. Many died during raids or warfare with neighboring tribes. One of the worst attacks occurred in 1750 when the Comanche killed almost every man in the tribe. Diseases, such as the smallpox epidemic in 1788, took many lives.

By 1838, only seventeen Pecos were left. They walked 80 miles (130 kilometers) to the Jemez Pueblo (see entry), where the people welcomed them. Although the two groups merged in 1936, the Pecos still retained their culture, and they have a governor who is part of the traditional Jemez government.

The ruins of an adobe building stand at Pecos National Historic Park in New Mexico.
© TAYLORM/DREAMSTIME.

Selling of Pecos land

With the Pecos gone, settlers wanted to buy their land. Portions of the pueblo had been taken away beginning in 1824, when the Territorial Deputation of New Mexico granted plots on both sides of the Pecos River to non-Natives. The Pecos protested, but the government allowed any of their uninhabited land to be distributed. The best irrigated lands were given away, leaving the Pecos without good farming land. The new owners, according to Pecos accounts, killed their livestock and poisoned their waterholes. Soon most of their land was gone.

The land changed hands several times during the 1800s and early 1900s as private landowners and real estate speculators bought or claimed the land. Finally, in 1965, the government created Pecos National Monument to protect the pueblo and Spanish mission. In 1990, the area gained the status of a national historic park. Three years later, a donation from the R. K. Mellon Foundation comprising 5,500 acres of original Pecos lands enlarged the park to 5,865 acres, less than half of the 17,000 acres that had once belonged to the Pueblo. The National Park Service is currently in charge of caring for these historic buildings and sharing the history of the Pecos people.

Sacred Fire of Montezuma

The Pecos were the only ones of the Puebloans who watched for Montezuma. One early writer said it was not unusual to see a woman or a child staring off into the east with a dreamy expression. Perhaps they were hoping for Montezuma's return.

It is said that in the estufa (kiva) the sacred fire was kept constantly burning, having been originally kindled by Montezuma. It was in a basin of a small altar, and, in order to prevent its becoming extinguished, a watch was kept over it day and night. The tradition runs that Montezuma had enjoined upon their ancestors not to allow the fire to expire until he should return to deliver them from the Spaniards, and hence their watchful care over it. He was expected to appear with the rising sun, and every morning the Indians went upon the house-tops, and, with eyes turned toward the east, looked for the coming of their monarch. Alas for them, he never came; and when the smoldering embers had expired, they gave up all hope of deliverance, and sought new homes in a distant pueblo. The task of watching the sacred fires was assigned to the warriors, who served by turns for a period of two days and two nights at a time, without eating or drinking, while some say that they remained upon duty until death or exhaustion relieved them from their post. The remains of those who died from the effect of watching are said to have been carried to the den of a great serpent, which appears to have lived upon these delicacies alone.

SOURCE: Davis, W.W.H. *El Gringo; or, New Mexico and Her People.* New York: Harper & Brothers, 1857, pp. 152–3. Available online from *University of Arizona Library.* http://southwest.library.arizona.edu/elgr/body.1_div.6.html (accessed on July 20, 2011).

RELIGION

Religion was part of everyday life for the Pecos people. Most of their ceremonies were tied to the agricultural cycle. They performed ceremonies for good harvests, abundant rainfall, and warm weather. Rituals also ensured successful hunts.

Kivas, underground religious centers, could hold about thirty-four people. These circular buildings were used for religious ceremonies and for conducting village business. In the center of the kiva, a fire burned. The Pecos kept these sacred hot coals burning all the time because they said they had received special orders from Montezuma (see "Sacred Fire of Montezuma") to do so.

Catholicism

The Spaniards tried to convert all the Pueblo peoples to Christianity. The Pueblo killed the first missionaries, but in 1598, Juan de Oñate sent a priest, Fray Francisco de San Miguel, to the Pecos Pueblo. The Catholics destroyed all Puebloan religious items, because they termed them idols (see "History").

Although the Pecos converted to Catholicism, they practiced their own religion in secret. They reconstructed the idols the missionaries had destroyed and kept them hidden. At the same time, they participated in Christian rituals—baptisms, feast days, and masses. The priests named most pueblos for saints, and the pueblos still hold celebrations on the saints' feast days.

LANGUAGE

The Pecos people spoke Towa, a Tanoan language, as did the Jemez. Although the two dialects (varieties of a language) were similar, each group had its own. The Towa language is still spoken on the Jemez Pueblo, where the remaining Pecos people made their home. It is considered a strong language with many speakers; however, more adults than children use the language regularly.

The Puebloan languages are unique because the people do not believe in writing their language down. This has become a controversy between traditionalists, who want to maintain the oral language, and those who want to record the languages so they are preserved for future generations.

GOVERNMENT

In the past, important governmental decisions were made in the *estufa,* or kiva. The leader assembled a group of advisers who discussed the decision and voted on a final solution. One appointed official was the secret watch, who was in charge of preventing wrongdoing in the village. He caught people engaged in illegal behavior; the lawbreakers then faced the council. One of his most important duties was to be sure young people remained pure. If he discovered any teens having sexual relations, he brought them before the council, and they were ordered to marry (see "Childrearing" and "Marriage"). If they refused, they were kept apart by threat of whippings.

The present-day government at the Pueblo of Jemez is rooted in the traditions of both the Pecos and the Jemez. As in the past, two types of government are in place: traditional and secular (nonreligious). The traditional government has two leaders who hold their positions for life.

The most important of these, the *cacique,* is both a spiritual and a societal leader. The other is the *opng-soma,* or war captain, who enforces the religious rules and regulations. The secular government began during the time of the Spanish occupation. It consists of a governor and his staff, who are selected each year by the *cacique,* and a tribal council. (The council is composed of former governors.) The leadership includes two lieutenant governors, one each from the Jemez and the Pecos Pueblo peoples. The secular government maintains business relations with the outside world.

ECONOMY

The early Pecos people made their living by farming and trading. They formed relationships with many of the Great Plains nations, with whom they bartered for bison hides, tanned skins, mules, and slaves. In return, the Pecos supplied the Plains tribes with cotton cloth, crops, and pottery. The Pecos then bartered these goods with other pueblos.

Pecos agriculture supplied most of the people's daily diet. In addition to the staple foods of corn, beans, and squash, the Pecos planted and gathered many other crops, including cotton. They depended on the plants they grew for food, clothing, and medicine. They used dams and irrigation for watering their crops; their fields were so productive that they sold the extra produce. Although the Pecos rarely hunted, when they did, they used every part of the animal.

After 1838, the Pecos merged with the Jemez. Since that time, the economy has been based mainly on farming, ranching, and craft making. The sale of pottery, baskets, and other artworks provides a living for many artists. Many tribal members work for the Bureau of Indian Affairs, the U.S. Forest Service, local law enforcement agencies, and the tribal court system. Jemez officials are working to gain permission for an off-site casino, which could fund many much-needed social programs and economic projects.

DAILY LIFE

Buildings

In the early days, the Pecos people lived in many different pueblos that had two hundred to three hundred rooms each. Others built single-story houses that had between ten and fifty rooms each. By the 1300s, the

Spanish Description of the Pecos Pueblo (1596)

The explorer and writer Pedro de Castañeda, who recorded the events of the Coronado expedition, described the Pecos city the Spaniards called Cicuyé. This account is a translation of Castañeda's original account in Spanish, recopied in 1596.

> The village was very strong, because it was up on a rock out of reach, having steep sides in every direction, and so high that it was a very good musket that could throw a ball as high. There was only one entrance by a stairway built by hand, which began at the top of a slope which is around the foot of the rock. There was a broad stairway for about 200 steps, then a stretch of about 100 narrower steps, and at the top they had to go up about three times as high as a man by means of holes in the rock, in which they put the points of their feet, holding on at the same time by their hands. There was a wall of large and small stones at the top, which they could roll down without showing themselves, so that no army could possibly be strong enough to capture the village. On the top they had room to sow and store a large amount of corn, and cisterns to collect snow and water.

SOURCE: Castañeda, Pedro de. *Narrative of the Expedition of Coronado* in *Spanish Explorers in the Southern United States, 1528–1543,* Frederick W Hodge, ed. New York: C. Scribner's Sons, 1907. Available from *Early America Digital Archives of the University of Maryland.* http://mith.umd.edu/eada/html/display.php?docs=castaneda_account.xml&action=show (accessed on July 20, 2011).

small, scattered communities came together in larger pueblos. By the mid-1400s, most Pecos lived in one of two major pueblos.

The main Pecos pueblo, on top of a mesa, rose to four stories, or even five in places, and it had more than six hundred rooms. Shaped like a square, the town had a large courtyard dotted with *kivas.* Ceremonies and sacred meetings took place in these round underground rooms. The lower level of the huge pueblo did not have doors, so the Pecos used ladders to reach the upper stories of the pueblo. They could draw up the ladders to protect themselves from attack. The upper stories had interior corridors that allowed access to the rest of the pueblo. Each story was built farther from the edge than the one below it, so the roofs looked like giant steps. People on the upper levels used the roof of the floor below as a balcony. (For more information about pueblo construction, see "Buildings" in the Pueblo entry.)

Prior to European arrival, the Pecos were using stone held together with mortar to make their walls. Vertical logs in the masonry supported the four or five stories. The ground floor rooms were used for food storage and trash disposal.

The Pecos enclosed their pueblo with a low stone wall. They even had a spring inside to ensure them of a water supply. The security of the pueblo was important because the elderly, disabled, pregnant women, and spiritual leaders stayed there when the rest of the people moved to their seasonal homes or when the warriors went off to battle.

Clothing and adornment

Men wore a cotton loincloth (a piece of fabric that passes between the legs and is attached at the waist) topped with a blanket, buffalo robe, or a turkey-feather cloak when it was cold. Women wrapped fabric around themselves and tied it over one shoulder to form a dress. Children and unmarried women went naked in warm weather.

Writers of the early 1800s noted that the men wore deerskin jackets and leggings or a blanket wrapped at the waist. The women topped their beaded leggings with a fancy blanket or a cape. Many wore *tilmas*, dresses made of two pieces of fabric attached at the shoulders with slits for the arms and head. The cloth fell to the knees and was held in place with a woven belt or sash. Tilmas had dark backgrounds with bright woven designs.

The people later adopted Mexican-style clothing of cotton shirts and pants. Missionaries pressured the women to dress more modestly, so many donned blouses under their one-shoulder dresses.

Food

The early Pecos raised the "three sisters"—beans, corn, and squash—because these crops grew well together. They also raised cotton and, later, wheat. After the Spanish came, the Pueblo people raised pumpkins, frijoles and habos (types of beans), chili peppers, herbs, red and green peppers, onions, and peas. Fruits included apples, plums, peaches, apricots, muskmelons, watermelons, and grapes. The Pecos based most of their diet on the crops they raised. On occasion, the men hunted deer, elk, antelope, or rabbits. They sometimes killed a bison on the plains, but meat was not a large part of their daily meals.

The Pecos made many meals from dried corn ground with a stone metate (grinding stone). Some food items, such as the tortilla, were adopted from the Mexicans. Others, such as *guayave,* were their own creations. This thin tortilla-like bread was made from a paste of cornmeal that was swiped onto hot flat stones in a thin layer. It was quickly peeled off and stacked into layers. The Pecos rolled up the layers and took the rolls of *guayave* on their journeys.

Education

In the mid-1800s, the government and the Presbyterian Church jointly established a school at the Jemez Pueblo, where the Pecos were living by then. One of the educator's concerns was that no one could read or write, but they failed to take into account the fact that the Pueblo people did not believe in writing down their language, so the children had no reason to learn these skills. An Indian agent's report in 1883 about the Jemez Pueblo said that schools had been established there and at two other pueblos, but the agent noted that the teachers complained the students did not apply themselves.

In modern times, the Jemez Pueblo offers Head Start classes for young children on the reservation. A Bureau of Indian Affairs day school and public elementary and secondary schools also operate there as well. Students have the option of attending charter schools, public schools, or a boarding school in Santa Fe. The Jemez-Pecos people were the first New Mexico tribe to operate its own charter school.

Healing practices

The Pecos were absorbed into Jemez society, where traditional healing relied on a curing society rather than a single shaman (pronounced *SHAH-mun* or *SHAY-mun*) or healer. Curing ceremonies took place before the whole community. To heal an individual or an entire community, the curing society called forth the supernatural forces—possibly spirits or even a witch within the pueblo—thought to be causing harm. One way to identify witches was to look for people whose eyes were red and tired, because the Pueblo people believed that witches did not to sleep at night, but instead they turned themselves into animals and roamed the world while others slept.

With their skill in farming, the Pecos could use their knowledge of plants and herbs for healing. In the early twenty-first century, the Pecos and Jemez people make use of traditional healing practices in combination with modern methods.

ARTS

Traditionally, the Pueblo people used woven cotton to make blankets and fabrics, but the quality of the cloth declined after the Europeans arrived. By the 1800s, the Puebloan were only weaving coarse blankets.

Pecos pottery, which was in demand, was painted before it was fired. In the early years, potters used baskets to hold the drying clay; patterns from the basket weave impressed onto the surface. Women painted designs on white pots with black mineral paint; in time, the paint was made from plant materials. The designs show some influence of northeastern peoples. Later pottery was red, cream, beige, orange, or a mix of colors. Some Pecos pottery had a runny black glaze called Pecos glaze polychrome that made their pottery unusual.

Pecos basket weaving was extremely tight, and the baskets were specially treated in order to be watertight. The people even wove canteens to carry water when they were traveling.

CUSTOMS

Social organization

The Pecos were divided into several clans, and clan relationships were traced through the mother's lineage. Marriages could not take place between two people from the same clan.

In addition to clans, both women and men belonged to societies, some of which were restricted to a single sex. Leaders of these groups were called "fathers," and they took charge of certain ceremonies. Some societies were responsible for war, hunting, curing, and weather.

All Pueblo peoples are divided into Summer and Winter people, also sometimes known as the Squash and Turquoise People. These two divisions oversee ceremonies during their time of year. Most often, they have a *cacique* (see "Government"), or leader.

Childrearing

Mothers wrapped their babies in lengths of cotton fabric and slipped them onto a cradleboard. The mothers could then carry the cradleboard, set it on the floor, or hang it from the rafters.

Parents taught their children to be hard workers and to tell the truth. As they grew older, teens were expected to be chaste. The Pueblo even appointed a secret watchman (see "Government") who made sure that people behaved properly. If he caught teens having intercourse, they were brought before the tribal council, where they were ordered to marry. If the man refused, the couple had to stay away from each other. If they did not, they were told they would have to face a whipping.

Marriage and Divorce

Pueblo marriages were initiated by the girl. After she told her father which man she wanted to marry, her father approached the parents of the boy. The boy's family paid for the father's loss of his daughter; the amount of payment depended on the wealth and status of the family. The bride made the wedding feast, and friends gathered to enjoy music and dancing.

Most people married someone within their own village. People married only one spouse, but couples could separate. If they did, the grandparents took the children. The spouses were free to marry again, but divorce was rare.

Death and burial

The Pecos buried their dead in shallow graves. They placed the corpse face down in a flexed position, surrounded by the dead person's possessions.

War rituals

The pueblos that the Pecos built protected their homes from attack (see "Buildings"). With no entrances to the first floor and ladders they could pull up, the Pecos effectively prevented enemies from gaining access to the upper levels of their homes. One early writer noted that the Pecos used the terraces formed by their roofs to store their weapons. They laid out bows and arrows, spears, shields, and war clubs on these balcony-like structures.

Festivals and ceremonies

One of the rituals the Pecos introduced to the Jemez when they moved to the Jemez Pueblo was that of the Pecos Bull; the Jemez and the Pecos still celebrate the feast day of Porcingula with the Pecos Bull Ceremony and the Corn Dance. After a secret-four day rite in the kivas, the men are spiritually prepared for the event. Women spend the final day baking bread and sweeping outside their houses. Then a man enters the plaza clad in a bull costume made of a willow-rib frame covered with black cloth dotted with white rings. As he dances through the streets, the men and boys who belong to the Pecos Eagle Watchers Society chase him, pretending to be bullfighters. Dressed in black long-tailed coats and top hats with their faces and hands painted white, they clown around and play tricks. Afterward the bull collects bread or food from a house, and the boys take it to the house of Porcingula, the patron saint of the Pecos mission.

Next, six priests chant as they walk around the plaza followed by the war captain, who calls the dancers to the kiva. They are dressed all in white, with red headbands, sashes, and moccasins. The boys return to chasing the bull until they lasso it. The next morning, after the bull appears, it is caught and tied to a ladder by Porcingula's house. Then women wearing fancy headscarves and traditional dresses and buckskin leggings balance baskets of food on their heads and offer it to the bull. As the boys sit and eat, the bull tries to spill the food.

The priest then sings a mass to honor Porcingula, and he carries her shrine to the plaza. A feast follows. Soon dancers from the Squash kiva emerge to participate in the Corn Dance. They are painted yellow. Dancers from the Turquoise kiva, painted blue, emerge to participate in the Corn Dance.

CURRENT TRIBAL ISSUES

In the early 1900s, archaeologist Alfred V. Kidder excavated the abandoned Pecos Pueblo. He gathered a great deal of data about the early inhabitants, including some artifacts from more than two thousand years ago. During his work, he sent more than 10,000 pottery fragments and artifacts as well as almost 2,000 human remains to the Robert S. Peabody Museum of Archaeology in Andover, Massachusetts. After the Native American Graves Protection and Repatriation Act passed in 1990, museums were required to return human remains and grave goods to the Native nations to which they belonged. With the help of Jemez Pueblo tribal archaeologist William J. Whatley, who searched records for almost a decade to trace the remains and artifacts Kidder had taken from the Pecos Pueblo, the Pecos people were able to regain their ancestors' bones and grave goods. In 1999, they ritually reburied them at Pecos National Historic Park, where their former pueblo is now on view as part of the National Park Service.

After 1838, the lives of the Pecos Puebloans were intricately tied to those of the Jemez with whom they lived, so any problems affecting the modern-day Jemez also affect the Pecos (see Jemez Pueblo entry, "Current Tribal Issues"). Some ongoing concerns are water rights, the loss of traditional culture, and the need for sustainable sources of income for the residents of the pueblo. One effort to secure more money and to fund tribal business and social initiatives was the proposed Jemez casino in Anthony, New Mexico. Opposition to the project originally came from the Bureau of Indian Affairs, who declared that the casino would be too far from the reservation to provide jobs for the Pecos and Jemez. The Mescalero Apache, who operate the Inn of the Mountain Gods Resort and Casino located 110 miles (180 kilometers) from the proposed Jemez site, also protested because they believed it would draw away some of their business. A major setback to casino construction occurred in 2011 when the U.S. Bureau of the Interior rejected the plan.

BOOKS

Bahti, Mark. *Pueblo Stories and Storytellers.* 3rd ed. Tucson, AZ: Rio Nuevo Publishers, 2010.

Carrillo, Charles M. *Saints of the Pueblos.* Albuquerque: LPD Press, 2008.

Decker, Carol Paradise. *Pecos Pueblo People Through the Ages: "—And We're Still Here": Stories of Time and Place.* Santa Fe, NM: Sunstone Press, 2011.

Fergusson, Erna. *Dancing Gods.* New York: A.A. Knopf, 1931. Available online at http://www.sacred-texts.com/nam/sw/dg/dg04.htm.

Knudten, Cory. *Crossroads of Change: An Environmental History of Pecos National Historical Park.* Boulder: Colorado State University, 2008.

Morgan, Michèle E. *Pecos Pueblo Revisited.* Cambridge, MA: Peabody Museum of Archaeology and Ethnology, Harvard University, 2010.

Sweet, Jill Drayson, and Nancy Hunter Warren. *Pueblo Dancing.* Atglen, PA: Schiffer Publishing, 2011.

PERIODICALS

Reff, Daniel T. "An Alternative Explanation of Subsistence Change during the Early Historic Period at Pecos Pueblo." *American Antiquity* 58, no. 3 (July 1993): 563–64.

WEB SITES

Baca, Jimmy Santiago. "Invasions." *Southwest Crossroads.* http://southwestcrossroads.org/record.php?num=21 (accessed on July 20, 2011).

Bowden, J.J. "Pueblo of Pecos Grant." *New Mexico State Record Center and Archives.*

Castañeda, Pedro de. *Narrative of the Expedition of Coronado.* Original Source: Hodge, Frederick W., ed. *Spanish Explorers in the Southern United States, 1528–1543.* New York: C. Scribner's Sons, 1907. Available from *Early America Digital Archives of the University of Maryland* (2002). http://mith.umd.edu/eada/html/display.php?docs=castaneda_account.xml&action=show (accessed on July 20, 2011).

Flint, Richard, and Shirley Cushing Flint. "Castaño de Sosa, Gaspar." *New Mexico State Record Center and Archives.* http://www.newmexicohistory.org/filedetails_docs.php?fileID=463 (accessed on July 20, 2011).

Flint, Richard, and Shirley Cushing Flint. "Cicuique (Pecos Pueblo)."*New Mexico State Record Center and Archives.* http://www.newmexicohistory.org/filedetails.php?fileID=489 (accessed on July 20, 2011).

National Museum of American History—Smithsonian Institution. "Pueblo Resistance: We Are Here." Video, 14:34. *Mexico State Record Center and Archives.* http://www.newmexicohistory.org/filedetails.php?fileID=23042 (accessed on July 20, 2011).

Nordby, Larry. "The Prehistory of the Pecos Indians." *Rozylowicz.* http://www.rozylowicz.com/pdf-files/pecos-ruins2.pdf (accessed on November 23, 2011).

"Pecos Indian Tribe History." *Access Genealogy.* http://www.accessgenealogy.com/native/tribes/pecos/pecoshist.htm(accessed on July 20, 2011).

"Pecos National Historical Park." *Desert USA.* http://www.desertusa.com/pecos/pnpark.html (accessed on July 20, 2011).

"Pecos Pueblos." *Four Directions Institute.* http://www.fourdir.com/pecos.htm (accessed on July 20, 2011).

"People of Pecos." *National Park Service.* http://www.nps.gov/peco/historyculture/peple-of-pecos.htm (accessed on July 20, 2011).

Pueblo of Jemez. http://www.jemezpueblo.org/ (accessed on July 20, 2011).

Walatowa Visitor Center. http://www.jemezpueblo.com/ (accessed on July 20, 2011).

Walters, Scott. "Archaic Indians of the Lower Pecos." *Archaic Indians.* http://www.archaicindians.net/ (accessed on July 20, 2011).

Weiser, Kathy. "PuebloRevolt—Rising Up against the Spanish." *Legends of America.* http://www.legendsofamerica.com/na-pueblorevolt.html (accessed on July 20, 2011).

OTHER

Spirits of the Canyon: Ancient Art of the Pecos Indians. DVD. Produced by Sylvia Komatsu. New York: Films Media Group, 2001.

San Juan Pueblo (Ohkay Owingeh)

Name

San Juan Pueblo (pronounced *sahn HWAHN PWEB-loh*). The Spanish term "pueblo," which means "town," refers to both the Pueblo people and the pueblos (cities) where they live. In the Tewa language of the San Juan people, their pueblo is called *Oke Owingeh*. In 1598, the Spanish gave the village the name San Juan Bautista (sometimes also called San Juan de los Caballeros) in honor of St. John the Baptist, a Christian saint. In November 2005, the people changed their pueblo's name back to their original, pre-Spanish name of *Ohkay Owingeh,* meaning "place of the strong people." In addition to the common name, the pueblo also has a ceremonial name, which means "village of the dew-bedecked corn structure."

Location

The San Juan Pueblo, a federal reservation of more than 2,000 acres, is located about 30 miles (50 kilometers) north of Santa Fe in north-central New Mexico, northeast of where the Rio Grande meets the Rio Chama.

Population

In 1680, there were an estimated 300 San Juan Pueblo. In the 1990 U.S. Census, 1,081 people identified themselves as San Juan Pueblo. Although the 2000 census showed a total of 6,748 people living on the reservation, only 1,438 people in the United States classified themselves as San Juan Pueblo. Statistics in 2001 from the Bureau of Indian Affairs indicated the San Juan Pueblo had 2,723 members enrolled.

Language family

Tanoan.

Origins and group affiliations

San Juan oral history traces the tribe's origin to a land in the north where the first people emerged from beneath a lake. From this place, the people migrated to the Rio Grande, the river that separates Mexico from the state of

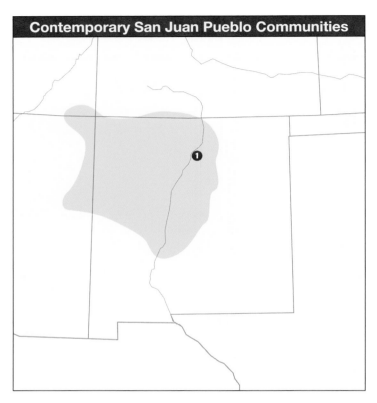

Contemporary San Juan Pueblo Communities

New Mexico
1 San Juan Pueblo

Shaded area
☐ Traditional lands of the Pueblo in present-day New Mexico, northeastern Arizona, southeastern Utah and southwestern Colorado

A map of contemporary San Juan Pueblo communities. MAP BY XNR PRODUCTIONS. CENGAGE LEARNING, GALE. REPRODUCED BY PERMISSION OF GALE, A PART OF CENGAGE LEARNING.

Texas and stretches throughout central New Mexico. They eventually created seven pueblo communities, of which six still exist.

The San Juan Pueblo's closest allies have always been the other Tewa-speaking communities: Santa Clara, San Ildefonso, Nambé, Pojoaque, and Tesuque. The six groups share a common ancestry and similar mythologies and customs. The San Juan also had mostly friendly relations with the other pueblos in New Mexico and with the Jicarilla (pronounced *hee-kah-REE-yah*) Apache.

The people of San Juan, the northernmost of the pueblos containing Tewa speakers, called their pueblo the "Mother Village." They have lived and cultivated crops on the reservation's flat farmlands for at least seven hundred years. The San Juan group has carefully adopted the parts of mainstream American culture that are most useful to them while maintaining the most meaningful of their traditional ways.

HISTORY

Spanish persecution

The Tewa-speaking peoples first made contact with Europeans in 1541, when men from the Spanish expedition of Francisco Vásquez de Coronado (c. 1510–1554) traveled through the area looking for food. Fearful of these strangers, the people retreated to easily defended villages in the mountains. In 1591, Don Juan de Oñate (1552–1626) and his group made their way to the lands of the Tewa-speaking people to establish a permanent Spanish settlement.

Throughout the seventeenth century, the people of San Juan and other pueblos endured religious persecution at the hands of Spanish Catholics and were forced to work for the benefit of Spanish settlers. This oppressive situation sparked a spirit of revolution among the Pueblos that fueled the Pueblo Revolt of 1680 (see Pueblo entry). One of the leaders of the rebellion was a San Juan man named Popé (c. 1630–1692).

Important Dates

1541: Spanish expedition headed by Francisco Vásquez de Coronado enters Tewa territory.

1591: Spanish colonization of Pueblo land begins.

1680: The Pueblo Revolt pushes the Spanish from the area for twelve years.

1846–48: Mexican-American War is fought; San Juan lands become part of U.S. territory.

1924: Pueblo Lands Act reduces size of San Juan reservation.

2005: The tribe changes its name back to its original, pre-Spanish name of *Ohkay Owingeh.*

Pueblo rebellions

Popé, a medicine man, had been among forty-seven Pueblo religious leaders jailed in Santa Fe in 1675. Because the Spaniards considered the Pueblo religion a form of idolatry, they forbid all traditional spiritual practices. To punish those who disobeyed that rule, Spanish officials whipped the Pueblo religious leaders and hanged four of them. After his release from prison, Popé moved to the Taos Pueblo (see entry). There, with the support of the other pueblos, he planned to rid the Pueblo homelands of Spaniards.

In August 1680, the Pueblo people acted as a single force. In one day, they killed four hundred Spaniards, including twenty-one Catholic priests. They set fire to Catholic churches and missions. Twenty percent of the Spaniards in the region died in the rebellion, and those who survived fled to Mexico. The Pueblo Revolt of 1680 is sometimes called the "First American Revolution." It was the first and only successful attempt by Native North Americans to remove colonists from their lands.

A second Pueblo Rebellion in June 1696 involved several groups, including the San Juan, Taos, Picuris, Santo Domingo, and Cochiti Pueblos. Several of their former allies, such as the Pecos Pueblo (see entry), declined to participate. This time the rebels killed five missionaries and twenty-one settlers and soldiers. They also burned several more mission churches and then fled into the nearby mountains.

Alliances with the Spanish

The Pueblo revolts drove the Spanish from the region for only twelve years. The rebellions failed to bring the peace and prosperity sought by the people of the pueblos. Drought, famine, and attacks by the Apache (see entry) compounded problems. In time, the alliances among the San Juan and other Native groups that had been formed during the revolt weakened.

The Spanish returned to the area in 1692, but this time, some of their leaders took an attitude of greater tolerance and moderation. Because San Juan was centrally located for the Spanish, it became a religious and trade center for the area. Throughout the 1700s, the Pueblo peoples and Spanish settlers supported one another in the face of attacks by the

Ruins of the Pueblo Bonito.
© CAITLIN MIRRA/
SHUTTERSTOCK.COM.

U•X•L Encyclopedia of Native American Tribes, 3rd Edition

Apache and the Comanche (see entry). The Spanish and the people of the pueblos sometimes held joint ceremonies to celebrate their victories in battle, and in this way, their friendship was cemented.

Facing U.S. expansion

When Mexico gained its independence from Spain in 1821 members of the San Juan Pueblo were given Mexican citizenship. About twenty-five years later, following the Mexican-American War (1846-48; a war in which Mexico lost about one-half of its national territory to the United States), San Juan Pueblo was made part of the United States. Like other pueblos, San Juan soon faced settlers claiming their land in an ever-expanding United States.

The San Juan Pueblo was made a reservation in 1858. The U.S. government claimed it recognized the rights of the San Juan to their homelands, but its actions over time proved otherwise. For example, the Pueblo Lands Act of 1924 reduced the size of the San Juan reservation from 17,544 acres to 12,234 acres. Over the course of the twentieth century, the land and water rights of the San Juan were the subject of a number of disputes. In 1995, the governor of New Mexico appointed a Special Assistant on Indian Water Resources to settle water rights issues without costly legal battles. By the early 2000s, state funds were available for providing water to reservations.

RELIGION

Traditional San Juan religious beliefs are linked to all aspects of everyday life. In fact, there is no Tewa word for "religion"; native religious practices are simply known as the "Indian Way."

The whole tribe takes part in ceremonial dances, prayer retreats, and games, which are all considered important spiritual events. The San Juan use ceremonies and rituals to thank the Creator for good fortune and to ask for his blessings.

Highly honored groups within the tribe are called *sodalities* (pronounced *soh-DAL-uh-teez*). Members of sodalities organize and carry out the major social and religious rituals of the San Juan people. Tribal members who are accepted into these special sodalities are known as the *Pa Towa*, or "Made People."

Most modern-day San Juan people are Roman Catholic, but they typically combine their Christian faith with important aspects of their traditional tribal religion. For example, marriage ceremonies and naming/baptism ceremonies have both Catholic and Native elements, and the celebration of the Catholic San Antonio's Day (St. Anthony's Day; June 13) features a traditional Corn Dance.

LANGUAGE

The San Juan people speak a dialect (variety) of the Tewa language, part of the Tanoan language family. Tewa speakers originally spoke several languages and could communicate with the other pueblos and neighboring tribes. When the Spanish took charge of the area, the San Juan began using the Spanish language as their primary means of communication. English later replaced Spanish as the tribe's main language.

Some Native children continue to learn Tewa at home, but doing so has become increasingly difficult. The population of Tewa speakers is aging, and most grandparents no longer live in the same house with their grandchildren. The youngest generation of San Juan Indians is therefore not exposed to their native language on a regular basis. To remedy this, all children at the Ohkay Owingeh Community School (grades K–8) are taught Tewa.

GOVERNMENT

Unlike most other Native American tribes, the San Juan government operates with no constitution. Three types of government leaders are in place: civil (nonreligious) officers, tribal religious leaders, and officers of the Catholic Church.

The civil government dates back to the time of Spanish rule in the early 1600s. It includes a governor, two lieutenant governors, a sheriff, and a tribal council. Officers are appointed to one-year terms by the tribal religious leaders, but they may serve an unlimited number of terms. The tribal council is composed of the serving governor, lieutenant governors, a sheriff, all former governors, and the heads of the religious societies of the village. Active religious leaders select other officers, as well as civil and Catholic officers. A tribal court was established in 1976. In the early twenty-first century, San Juan served as the headquarters of the Eight Northern Indian Pueblos Council, a group that unites the various pueblos in an effort to improve life for the people on their reservations.

ECONOMY

Emergence of wage labor

For centuries, the San Juan people relied mostly on farming, cattle raising, and trade to make their living. All members of the community once shared farming efforts and crops, but in modern times working for wages has become more common.

In 1965, a tribal program was introduced to help the pueblo gain federal funding for construction projects. Those monies allowed the people to construct a youth center, a senior center, a tribal office, a tribal court, a warehouse, and a post office. The tribe's bingo facility provided modest profits and employment for tribal members. Among the other facilities owned by the tribe were a service station, the Blue Rock Office Complex, and a variety of service and tourism businesses. Some mining of sand, gravel, and adobe (pronounced *uh-DOE-bee*; a sun-dried mud made of a mixture of clay, sand, and sometimes ashes, rocks, or straw) building materials added to the tribe's income.

Growth in arts, tourism, professions

Several pueblo women established the Oke-Oweenge Arts & Crafts Cooperative to showcase locally produced art of all kinds. More than one hundred artists earn at least part of their income from the sales of San Juan pottery, which has earned the praise of art experts (see "Arts"). The Okhay Casino Resort offers Las Vegas style gaming action and brings the pueblo additional income. Ceremonial dances attract visitors to the pueblo throughout the year, although the San Juan people also hold dances that are not open to the public.

By the start of the twenty-first century, a growing number of San Juan people were graduating from high school, attending college, and working in business, health care, science, or tribal government.

Planning for the future

The San Juan Agricultural Cooperative formed in 1992 to bring farming back to pueblo lands. At that time the tribe had about 2,000 acres of farmland, but only 200 acres were being used. In 1995, this co-op, along with Sandia National Laboratories, installed a solar oven on the pueblo. Capable of baking forty loaves of bread at once or of drying large quantities of food, the oven could take the place of the horno, the large traditional wood-fired oven the community has always used. In addition to saving fuel, which is scarce, the oven encouraged greater crop growth for preservation and increased sales of prepackaged foods under its brand name of Pueblo Harvest Foods.

In 2000, the San Juan Pueblo initiated a variety of programs for community planning and economic growth. Their Master Land Use Plan presented designs for housing and retail/commercial buildings using traditional-style architecture. In 2003, they completed the first project: a forty-unit development that included a community center and a mix of full-price homes and low-income housing. The Environmental Protection Agency (EPA) in 2004 awarded them the Small Communities Smart Growth Achievement Award. Since then, the people have continued to move forward with their long-term planning for economic growth and expansion.

DAILY LIFE

Buildings

The San Juan Pueblo once consisted of two-story adobe structures built around public squares. Individual two- to four-room homes shared common walls to form adjoining "apartments." Because the buildings were

People make their way along a street at San Juan Pueblo in 1927. © BUYENLARGE/GETTY IMAGES.

made of bricks of mud, the village blended in with its surroundings and was only visible from a few hundred feet away, making it more difficult for enemies to find and attack.

Much of this original pueblo still exists, although the second stories have disappeared. Maintaining the village is an expensive proposition, and many modern-day families live in American-style homes or trailers. During the 1950s and 1960s, a relocation program moved some San Juan people to various western cities, but within twenty to thirty years, many of these families moved back to the pueblo. By the late 1990s, a program had been launched to renovate (fix up) the adobe homes around the pueblo's central square, and families continued to occupy the old village during ceremonial periods.

Clothing and adornment

Although most San Juan people now wear modern dress, the tribe maintains traditional ceremonial costumes. Large headdresses worn by the men for the Deer Dance are made of a fan of painted split cane, antlers, and turkey feathers. Cotton leggings complete the outfit. Women wear lavishly embroidered dresses with woven belts.

Food

The tribe's thousands of acres of fertile, well-watered land have been cultivated for centuries. The San Juan people raised corn, beans, squash, and chilies and made use of wild plant foods such as asparagus, mint, and amaranth, an edible plant with colorful leaves and tassel-like flowers They also collected pine nuts from the surrounding hills and mountains.

The Spanish introduced many new crops to San Juan—wheat, melons, apricots, apples, and onions among them. At first, these crops were grown merely to trade with the Spanish, but in time, they became staples of the San Juan Pueblo diet. Likewise, the Spanish introduced the idea of raising livestock such as goats, sheep, cows, horses, chickens, and pigs. These animals provided the tribe with a new source of meat and proved useful for plowing, harvesting, and transportation.

During the 1990s, residents and returning retirees began to do more farming at San Juan. Additional crops raised on the pueblo included a variety of vegetables, chilies, alfalfa, and orchard fruit. The tribe also owned cattle.

Education

At a very early age, San Juan children learn the importance of responsible behavior. Formal schooling starts at the preschool level, with three- and four-year-olds attending a Head Start program. Students can also attend public school or one operated by the Bureau of Indian Affairs (BIA). Junior and senior high school students may attend public schools in several nearby towns or a boarding school in Santa Fe.

In 1996, the tribe established the Pueblo of Ohkay Owingeh Department of Education to oversee their students' schooling. Some of the projects they implemented were getting grants to install high-speed Internet in the reservation schools and in many homes, providing scholarships to college-bound students, holding leadership institutes, paying for students to attend conferences, and overseeing the education of pueblo students.

In the early twenty-first century, the Ohkay Owingeh Community School (OOCS) was set up to provide students in grades K–8 with a curriculum based on Native traditions. The school's motto is "Don't teach me my culture, use my culture to teach me!" In keeping with this philosophy, the school instituted programs to teach children their native language, Tewa. The school also planned summer programs taught by tribal elders to pass on such traditional skills as pottery-making, farming, and cooking as well as academic subjects and arts appreciation.

Healing practices

Traditional San Juan believed that illnesses were caused by evil spirits or witches called *chuge*. People often used charms to protect themselves from harm and disease.

In early times, members of the Bear Medicine Society were responsible for curing the sick. Modern-day San Juan people obtain health care at a hospital in Santa Fe. A community health program on the pueblo offers some services, and the New Moon Lodge provides treatment for alcohol abuse.

CUSTOMS

Worldview

Since ancient times, the San Juan people have divided the physical world into three parts. The first part is comprised of the village and adjoining areas, which belong to the women and are marked by four sacred objects indicating the directions north, south, east, and west. The second part is made up of the mesas (pronounced *MAY-sas*; a Spanish word meaning "tables"; mesas are large hills with steep sides and flat tops). They surround San Juan Pueblo and are open to men, women, and children, but they are under male authority. The third part of the physical world is the outside world, beyond the mesas. Belonging solely to the men of the tribe, the outside world is the place where they hunt, defend their people when necessary, and seek spiritual guidance.

Childhood and adult rites

The San Juan people observe a series of rituals to bring a child into the community. A "water-giving" rite makes the child a member of a moiety (see "Moieties") during the first year of life. A "water-pouring" rite takes place between ages six and nine. An initiation rite officially accepts an adolescent into the Tewa religion. Other rites are associated with sex, marriage, community offices, and membership in various groups.

Moieties

Every San Juan family belongs to one of two social groups known as moieties (pronounced *MOY-uh-teez*). Membership in the Winter and Summer moieties determines the roles played by individuals in religious, political, and economic matters of the pueblo. For example, the annual schedule of religious dances is divided between the moieties. Winter events are usually associated with hunting and trade, whereas summer rituals are related to farming and gathering wild plant foods.

ARTS

In 1968, several craftspeople from the San Juan Pueblo opened the Oke-Oweenge Crafts Cooperative. The co-op expanded to allow artists from the eight northern pueblos sell their wares. Most Jemez craftspeople are known for their redware pottery. They create these distinctive pieces from clay native to the pueblo. The artists cut geometric pattern into each vessel. When the pieces are fired, they have an inner glow and luster that make them unique. Other craftspeople also do weaving, painting, stone and wood carvings, and jewelry-making.

Members of the San Juan Pueblo perform the Deer Dance at the Intertribal Indian Ceremonial event in Gallup, New Mexico.
© AP IMAGES/CHRIS LAMASTER.

Festivals

During the 1700s, when the Spanish and the Pueblo people were on friendly terms, festive dances were held to celebrate their victories over raiding other Native nations. The dances were called "Scalp Dances" or "Chief Dances." At these events, a male dancer dressed up as a chief; a female dancer followed him as he danced. The family of the male dancer gave a variety of gifts to the female dancer, and baskets full of household goods and fruit were tossed into the crowd. Other couples followed them, also dancing and distributing gifts to give thanks for their warriors' safe return.

Buffalo, Animal, and Deer Dances are still held each February in the San Juan Pueblo, and each one is regarded as a significant occasion. The Deer Dance, for example, is performed to assure prosperity for the coming year. Deer dancers often poke fun at Apache-type hunters, stalking the other dancers and pretending to hunt them down with sunflower-stalk arrows. Clowns are major features at other dances held throughout the year.

Additional San Juan celebrations include the June feast days of San Antonio and San Juan and the Harvest Dances in September. The Turtle Dance is an important winter ceremony, marking the end of one year and the beginning of the next. The Matachine dance, which depicts Spanish oppression, is held in December. Some festivities are open only to tribal members, and certain aspects of the celebrations are kept secret.

CURRENT TRIBAL ISSUES

A proud and honorable people, the San Juan are increasingly concerned about the way their culture has been portrayed by outsiders. Since the late 1800s, many scholars have visited the pueblo and later published articles about the tribe's "dying way of life." The San Juan object to the nature of such commentary and are making efforts to review and approve the content of future articles.

Maintaining the tribe's centuries-old right to water is a critical issue at San Juan. Water is needed for farming and for the development of projects such as the San Juan Lakes Recreation Area, which attracts tourists and provides funds for the tribe. At the end of the twentieth century, the state of New Mexico was seeking legal means to limit tribal water rights. In 2007, the Ten Southern Pueblos Council endorsed legislation to provide $10 million for Native American water rights settlements, greater education and health-care opportunities, more substance abuse programs, and a minimum wage increase. Their efforts were backed by Jemez Pueblo governor Raymond Gachupin, chairman of the group. In 2011, the Ohkay Owingeh (formerly San Juan) Pueblo was in the midst of a lawsuit with the state of New Mexico over land ownership and water rights in the Santa Cruz watershed.

NOTABLE PEOPLE

Popé (c. 1630–1692) was born at San Juan but moved to the Taos Pueblo during the 1670s. In 1680, he led the most successful Native American uprising in United States history. His forces drove the Spanish from New Mexico and worked to return the Pueblo to their earlier religion and traditions. After his death, the Spanish reconquered Pueblo lands, but they were never again as strong a force as they had been.

Alfonso Alex Ortiz (1939–1998), an author, received his Ph.D. from the University of Chicago and went on to teach anthropology at the University of New Mexico. Ortiz's works include *American Indian Myths and Legends, New Perspectives on the Pueblos, North American Indian Anthropology,* and *The Tewa World: Space, Time, Being, and Becoming in a Pueblo Society.*

Esther Martinez (1912–2006), author and storyteller, received many awards. In 1996, she was named a Living Treasure of New Mexico. In 1999, the National Congress of American Indians chose her Woman of the Year, and in 1999, New Mexico honored her for her contributions to the arts. Her books include *The San Juan Pueblo Tewa Dictionary, The Naughty Little Rabbit and Old Man Coyote,* and *My Life in San Juan Pueblo: Stories of Esther Martinez.*

BOOKS

Agoyo, Herman, and Joe S. Sando, eds. *Po'pay: Leader of the First American Revolution.* Santa Fe, NM: Clear Light Publishing, 2005.

Bahti, Mark. *Pueblo Stories and Storytellers.* 3rd ed. Tucson, AZ: Rio Nuevo Publishers, 2010.

Carrillo, Charles M. *Saints of the Pueblos.* Albuquerque: LPD Press, 2008.

Jacobs, Sue-Ellen, and Josephine Binford, eds. *My Life in San Juan Pueblo: Stories of Esther Martinez.* Urbana: University of Illinois Press, 2004.

Ortiz, Alfonso. "San Juan Pueblo." In *Handbook of North American Indians,* Vol. 9: *Southwest,* edited by Alfonso Ortiz. Washington, DC: Smithsonian, 1979.

Ortiz, Alfonso. *The Tewa World: Space, Time, Being, and Becoming in a Pueblo Society.* Chicago: University of Chicago Press, 1969.

Peaster, Lillian. *Pueblo Pottery Families: Acoma, Cochiti, Hopi, Isleta, Jemez, Laguna, Nambe, Picuris, Pojoaque, San Ildefonso, San Juan, Santa Clara, Santo Domingo, Taos, Tesuque, Zia, Zuni.* 3rd ed. Atglen, PA: Schiffer Publishing, 2008.

Roberts, David. *The Pueblo Revolt: The Secret Rebellion That Drove the Spaniards Out of the Southwest.* New York: Simon & Schuster, 2005.

Sando, Joe S. *Pueblo Nations: Eight Centuries of Pueblo Indian History.* Santa Fe: Clear Light, 1992.

Sweet, Jill Drayson, and Nancy Hunter Warren. *Pueblo Dancing.* Atglen, PA: Schiffer Publishing, 2011.

Trimble, Stephen. *Talking with the Clay: The Art of Pueblo Pottery in the 21st Century.* Santa Fe, NM: School for Advanced Research Press, 2007.

Wallace, Susan E. *The Land of the Pueblos.* Santa Fe, NM: Sunstone Press, 2006.

WEB SITES

Aquino, Pauline. "Ohkay Owingeh: Village of the Strong People" (video). *New Mexico State Record Center and Archives.* http://www.newmexicohistory.org/filedetails.php?fileID=22530 (accessed on July 20, 2011).

"Arlene Archuletta: Oke-Oweenge Crafts Cooperative." *Greater Española Valley Community Development Corporation.* http://www.goespanola.com/Profiles/archuletta_profile (accessed on July 20, 2011).

Eight Northern Indian Pueblos Council. http://www.enipc.org/ (accessed on July 20, 2011).

The Morgan Collection of Southwest Pottery. "Through the Eyes of the Pot: A Study of Southwest Pueblo Pottery and Culture: San Juan." *Lowell D. Holmes Museum of Anthropology, Wichita State University.* http://www.holmes.anthropology.museum/southwestpottery/sanjuanpueblo.html (accessed on July 20, 2011).

National Museum of American History—Smithsonian Institution. "Pueblo Resistance: We Are Here." Video 14:34. *Mexico State Record Center and Archives.* http://www.newmexicohistory.org/filedetails.php?fileID=23042 (accessed on July 20, 2011).

"Ohkay Owingeh." *Indian Pueblo Cultural Center.* http://www.indianpueblo.org/19pueblos/ohkayowingeh.html (accessed on July 20, 2011).

"Past and Future Meet in San Juan Pueblo Solar Project." *Solar Cookers International.* http://solarcooking.org/sanjuan1.htm (accessed on July 20, 2011).

"San Juan Pueblo Pottery." *ClayHound Web.* http://www.clayhound.us/sites/sanjuan.htm (accessed on July 20, 2011).

"San Juan Pueblo." *New Mexico Magazine.* http://www.nmmagazine.com/native_american/san_juan.php (accessed on July 20, 2011).

"San Juan Pueblo O'Kang." *Indian Pueblo Cultural Center.* http://www.indianpueblo.org/19pueblos/ohkayowingeh.html (accessed on July 20, 2011).

Weiser, Kathy. "Pueblo Revolt—Rising Up against the Spanish." *Legends of America.* http://www.legendsofamerica.com/na-pueblorevolt.html (accessed on July 20, 2011).

Wroth, William H. "Ohkay Owingeh." *New Mexico State Record Center and Archives.* http://www.newmexicohistory.org/filedetails.php?fileID=510 (accessed on July 20, 2011).

Taos Pueblo

Name

Taos Pueblo (pronounced *TAH-ohs PWEB-loh*). The term *Taos* comes from a Spanish word meaning "in the village." The Spanish term *pueblo,* which means "town," is used to refer to both the people and the buildings in which they live. The Taos referred to themselves as "the people." In the Tiwa language the Taos Pueblo are called *Tua-tah,* meaning "our village."

Location

The Taos Pueblo, a federal reservati on, is located in northeastern New Mexico. It sits on a plateau at the base of Mount Wheeler in the Sangre de Cristo Mountains, approximately 70 miles (110 kilometers) north of Santa Fe.

Population

In 1680, there were an estimated 2,000 Taos Pueblo. In 1864, there were only 361. By 1930, the count had risen to 694. In the 1990 U.S. Census, 1,875 people identified themselves as Taos Pueblo. The 2000 census showed 1,877 Taos Puebloans. According to the Bureau of Indian Affairs, tribal enrollment in 2001 reached 2,443. In 2011, only about 150 people lived in the ancient pueblo, but more than 1,900 had homes on Taos Pueblo lands.

Language family

Tanoan.

Origins and group affiliations

The origin of the Taos people is uncertain, but it may be traced back to the Ancestral Puebloans (see Anasazi entry) or Chaco peoples. The language of the Taos is most closely related to that spoken by the Picuris, Isleta, and Sandia Pueblos. The Taos have maintained generally good relations with neighboring Pueblo peoples, as well as with the Ute, Apache, and Navajo tribes.

The Taos Pueblo may be the most photographed and most easily recognized pueblo in the world because of its beauty and perfectly preserved condition. Since the arrival of the Spaniards in the sixteenth century,

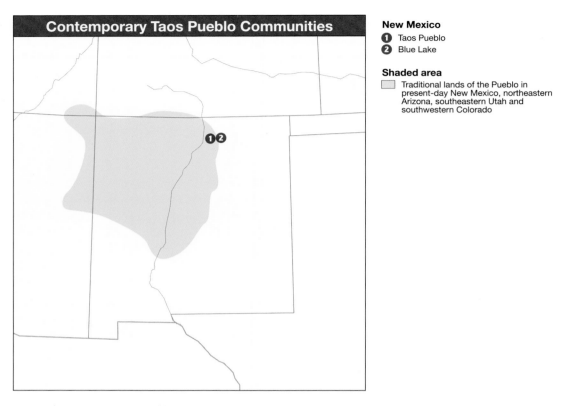

Contemporary Taos Pueblo Communities

New Mexico
① Taos Pueblo
② Blue Lake

Shaded area
Traditional lands of the Pueblo in present-day New Mexico, northeastern Arizona, southeastern Utah and southwestern Colorado

A map of contemporary Taos Pueblo communities. MAP BY XNR PRODUCTIONS. CENGAGE LEARNING, GALE. REPRODUCED BY PERMISSION OF GALE, A PART OF CENGAGE LEARNING.

when the Taos people were raising cattle and doing limited farming, the pueblo has been subject to periods of Spanish, Mexican, and American rule. Its people have been at the forefront of revolts against outside domination and have twice rebuilt their city when parts of it were burned by outsiders. The strong sense of community and interdependence among the Taos people has helped them preserve their traditional way of life with only minor changes through the centuries.

HISTORY

Emerges as trading center

Although little is known about the history of the Taos Pueblo before the coming of Europeans, their oral history tells of a long period when the tribe roamed the plains near New Mexico's Sangre de Cristo Mountains.

Archaeologists (scientists who study ancient cultures by examining the things they left behind) estimate the tribe arrived in the area some one thousand years ago. The first pueblo may have been built in the mid-1300s, less than a mile north of its present-day site.

By the time the Spanish explorer Francisco Vá de Coronado (c. 1510–1554) arrived in 1540, Taos was already a thriving trading center. Coronado wrote then of the wonders he saw. The many-storied adobe (pronounced *uh-DOE-bee*) buildings, large circular places of worship, a low adobe wall encircling the original village— all of these things still exist in Taos. (Adobe is a sun-dried mud made of a mixture of clay, sand, and sometimes ashes, rocks, or straw.)

Many other Pueblo peoples and members of several different tribes, including the Comanche, the Apache, and the Navajo (see entries), traveled to Taos to trade animal hides, meat, blankets, and vegetables. Long after the Spanish arrived, these trade fairs continued to flourish. In later years, non-Natives also took part in the fairs.

Important Dates

1540: Spanish explorer Francisco de Coronado arrives in Pueblo country.

1598: Juan de Oñate sets up a Spanish colony and builds San Geronimo Mission at Taos Pueblo.

1680: The Pueblo Revolt pushes the Spaniards from the region for twelve years.

1847: Another Pueblo rebellion leads to the assassination of the American territorial governor. In retaliation U.S. troops destroy the mission at Taos Pueblo, killing 150 Taos Indians.

1970: The U.S. government returns the sacred Blue Lake to Taos Pueblo.

1996: The Taos people receive 764 acres in Wheeler Park Wilderness, including a trail connecting the pueblo with the Blue Lake Wilderness.

Catholic religion by force

In 1598, the Spanish explorer Juan de Oñate (1552–1626) arrived in the Pueblo area, intent on making the Native people part of a Spanish colony. When he established his headquarters barely 50 miles (80 kilometers) south of Taos, a long, difficult, and often violent period in Pueblo history began.

One of Oñate's goals was to convert the Native peoples to Christianity. Mission San Geronimo was established at Taos, and a Catholic priest took up residence there. Anyone caught participating in Native rituals was punished and fined. While Taos residents adopted many Catholic rituals, they secretly practiced their own traditions as well.

Natives overthrow Spanish for a time

Drawn together by religious oppression and other threats to their ancestral way of life, the various Pueblo tribes began the Pueblo Revolt of 1680 (see Pueblo and San Juan Pueblo entries). Popé (c. 1630–1692),

San Geronimo Church serves the large Catholic community among the Taos Pueblo, where people blend Catholicism with Native religious practices. © ROLF RICHARDSON/ALAMY.

a medicine man from San Juan Pueblo, had earlier fled from the Spanish oppressors and sought refuge at Taos, where he planned the revolt. At dawn on August 10, 1680, all of the Pueblo groups struck at once. The Taos burned the mission on their pueblo and killed more than seventy settlers, including two priests. The Spaniards left the area and did not return for twelve years.

The Spanish reestablished their colonies in the Pueblo region in 1692. The Taos Pueblo resisted and staged another revolt in 1696, but the success of 1680 was not repeated. The Spanish military quickly forced the Taos to surrender, thus beginning an uneasy peace between the Native Americans and the colonizers that extended over the next 150 years.

Death and destruction

During that time control of the region passed from Spain to Mexico and then, after the Mexican-American War (1846–48; a war in which Mexico lost about one-half of its national territory to the United States), to the United States. The Mexicans were unhappy with this transfer of power and persuaded the Pueblo peoples to help them stage a revolt. The Revolt of 1847, which originated at Taos, led to the assassination of the American territorial governor. The U.S. Army responded swiftly.

Upon learning that the American Army was approaching, more than seven hundred Taos Pueblo barricaded themselves inside the San Geronimo Mission. U.S. troops, unable to break through the walls of the mission, bombarded it with gunfire and set fire to the roof. In the resulting bloodbath more than 150 Taos Pueblo lost their lives, and the mission was destroyed. The next day Taos surrendered, and the long process of rebuilding the pueblo began.

The battle for Blue Lake

Since that time the battles fought in Taos have been legal, rather than military, ones. The most famous was the battle for Blue Lake, the spiritual home and sacred ceremonial site of the Taos people. In 1906, Congress seized much of the Taos homeland, including Blue Lake, and made it part of Carson National Forest. Tourists visiting the site prevented the Taos people from making their annual pilgrimages to the lake.

The Taos reacted to this threat to their religion with a court battle that lasted for fifty years. It finally ended in 1970 when the U.S. Senate voted to return Blue Lake to the Taos people. The settlement marked the first time that land—not money—was returned to an American Indian tribe upon the completion of a court case over lost territory.

In 1996, the Taos gained 764 additional acres in the Wheeler Park Wilderness. This area contained a trail, called Path of Life, from the pueblo to Blue Lake Wilderness. The tribe also purchased Moreno Ranch, adding 16,000 acres to their holdings.

RELIGION

The traditional Native religion continues at Taos Pueblo in modern times, but it is cloaked in secrecy. The Taos Indians forbid any disclosure of their religious practices, and very little information has been published

Taos Names for the Moons

Most Native Americans looked to the moon to tell passage of time. Each moon was named after a specific event that occurred during that time of year. January, for example, was called the "Man Moon" because men bathed in frigid streams and exercised outdoors during this cold month to strengthen and toughen their bodies. December is the Taos "Night Moon" because the nights are the longest at that time of year.

January: Man Moon
February: Winter Moon
March: Wind Strong Moon
April: Ashes Moon
May: Corn Planting Moon
June: Corn-tassel Appear Moon
July: Sun House Moon
August: Autumn Moon
September: Leaf Yellow Moon
October: Corn Ripe Moon
November: Corn Harvest Moon
December: Night Moon

about them. Scholars say that a lot of the written information about the religion is unreliable.

Most of the pueblo members consider themselves Catholic, and many attend church services regularly. There has been much blending of the Catholic and Native religions over time, but they are still considered separate. The church and *kiva* (circular adobe structures partially below ground used in Pueblo religion) hold equally prominent places in the village, and the Taos people see no conflict in practicing both religions.

The spiritual leader of the Taos tribe is the *cacique* (pronounced *kuh-SEEK*), who is also a society leader. Only a man can hold this lifelong position. Other important religious leaders are the chiefs of the six kivas. Kiva groups run ceremonies, dances, and seasonal rituals. Though women may belong to kivas, only men participate in the sacred practices.

LANGUAGE

Tiwa is the native language of Taos Pueblo. It is a dialect (variety) of the Tanoan language family. Other pueblos that speak Tiwa are the Picuris Pueblo, Sandia Pueblo, and Isleta Pueblo, but the language varies at each location.

Most pueblo residents spoke English by the end of the twentieth century, but many of the elders still spoke Tiwa, and it is also used in Taos ceremonies. Still an unwritten language, Tiwa has been passed down orally for generations. The pueblo's day school is engaged in efforts to teach Tiwa to Taos youth. Classes are conducted by those who still know the language.

GOVERNMENT

Taos Pueblo is an independent, self-governed nation. The government is run by a tribal council, a governor, and the office of the war chief. The tribal council, the highest authority, has more than fifty male elders who serve for life. Council members include major religious leaders and all former governors, lieutenant governors, the war chief, and the lieutenant war chief. The governor, the war chief, and their staffs are appointed by the tribal council and serve one-year terms of office.

The members of the governor's staff carry on the day-to-day affairs of the pueblo and deal with village and church matters, law and order, roads and water issues, and non-Native relations. The war chief and his staff members deal with land and natural resources, hunting and grazing, crop and boundary control, and protecting the mountains and lands outside the pueblo walls. As part of the government, the tribal council founded a central management system to handle any federal programs and funds that are not overseen by the governor's or war chief's offices.

ECONOMY

In early times

The Taos Pueblo sits at a high altitude in the New Mexican mountains and has a short growing season. The tribe based its early economy primarily on hunting and gathering, with limited farming. The people hunted deer, bear, turkey, antelope, elk, and buffalo regularly and conducted massive rabbit drives, which required the participation of every man who knew how to shoot with a bow and arrow.

The Taos reservation has about 10,000 acres of land that can be irrigated. The people raise hay, alfalfa, and vegetables in addition to the cattle and horses that graze on the rangeland. The 16,000-acre Moreno Ranch was set up to raise bison. For the most part, though, the cattle raising and farming of earlier years has been replaced by work for wages and income from government grants and self-help projects.

In modern times

Tourism is now the main source of income for the Taos economy. Because it has been declared a National Historical Landmark and a World Heritage Site, many people travel to see the pueblo every year. The tribe charges entrance and parking fees as well as fees for taking photographs. Tribal members serve as paid tour guides. A plaza of shops and restaurants gives tourists opportunities to buy traditional foods and crafts. The Taos Indian Horse Ranch provides tours and horseback riding. For more than twenty years, the people have held an annual Taos Pueblo Powwow,

People assemble at the Taos Pueblo near Taos, New Mexico. © SCOTT WARREN/AURORA PHOTOS.

which includes traditional singing and dancing. Other dances and ceremonies are also open to the public each year.

The Taos Pueblo Enterprises promotes tribal economic development and manages tribally owned businesses. Small businesses owned by tribal members produce such handcrafted items as deer horn sculptures, pottery, silver and turquoise jewelry, blankets, tanned buckskin moccasins, and drums. Taos Mountain Casino opened in late 1997.

Although tribal lands are rich in game and forest products, the tribe considers them and the mountains surrounding them as sacred. They do not allow timbering, mining, or grazing on most of the lands, preferring to keep them as a religious sanctuary. At one time, the tribe allowed gold mining, but by the mid-2000s, the only mining was for adobe materials (sand and gravel) and stone for building. In 2004, they received almost $250,000 from the U.S. Fish and Wildlife Service to improve game management on their lands.

A family gathers in its living quarters at Taos Pueblo in the 1800s. © NORTH WIND PICTURE ARCHIVES.

DAILY LIFE

Buildings

The buildings that lie on both sides of the Rio Pueblo are classic examples of pueblo architecture, and some families still reside there. But the majority of people live in single-family homes located outside the pueblo wall. Built with modern materials, these houses have stucco (cement-plastered) exteriors to make them look like traditional adobe buildings.

Clothing and adornment

Although Taos Indian dress has changed considerably since Spanish colonial days, some traditional elements remain. Men still wear the *mantas* (blanketlike cloaks) that were first observed by the Spaniards. At one time, the people made mantas from buffalo hide, but by the 1900s, white cotton was preferred. In modern times, machine-made blankets are commonly worn.

Men used to wear rough cloth leggings fastened to the waist by a cord. They wore them with a cotton loincloth (flaps of material that covered the front and back and were suspended from the waist). When Western-style pants were first introduced, Taos men cut out the seats to turn them into leggings.

As they still do, Taos men wore their hair in two braids, one behind each ear. Many Taos women still wear their hair in the traditional style, long and loose with eyebrow length bangs. Older women twist their hair into chignons (buns).

Women wore traditional pueblo dress, consisting of a sleeveless print dress attached over one shoulder and worn over a long-sleeved white cotton garment. They fastened a thick woven belt around their waists and wore buckskin boots that often reached mid-thigh. Both men and women also wore heelless shoes.

Food

The Taos ate traditional Pueblo foods, but by 1936, their principal crops were corn and wheat, which the men cultivated, while the women tended small vegetable gardens. To supplement their food supply, they raised livestock, including chickens, cattle, and pigs.

In the late 1990s, the Taos grew beans and pumpkins, tended fruit trees, and raised a small herd of buffalo, but they relied heavily on store-bought groceries as well. The people of the pueblo have, however, maintained the tradition of using outdoor adobe ovens called *hornos* to bake bread.

Education

The pueblo has a Head Start Program and an elementary day school operated by the Bureau of Indian Affairs. Students may also attend public and private schools in the nearby town of Taos, New Mexico, or an Indian boarding school in Santa Fe. The University of New Mexico opened a campus at Taos, and students who go on to college receive tribal scholarships.

Healing practices

Unlike most Pueblo tribes, the Taos did not have curing societies. Instead, they relied on individual healers. Working for four days at the patient's home, the healer sang medicine songs, brushed eagle feathers over the patient, and sucked out disease-causing foreign objects from the body. Because witchcraft was considered the source of sickness, it was part of the healer's job to figure out who sent the sickness and to spit a special type of medicine to ward off witches. Healers used plants and animal blood to make medicine.

Modern-day Taos receive their medical care at a health center or nearby hospitals. Special clinics offer information about diabetes and other health issues.

ARTS

The Taos are known for their skilled use of leather in crafting boots, moccasins, clothing, and drums. They also create unusual pottery flecked with mica and fashion jewelry from silver. Many craftspeople add modern touches to the traditional arts to create unique designs. The tribally owned Pueblo of Tesuque Flea Market, the Santa Fe Indian Market, and the Eight Northern Pueblos Arts & Crafts Show provide outlets for artists to sell their crafts.

Oral literature

The Taos have always enjoyed telling tales during the long winter evenings. They typically begin the stories by naming a character and stating where he lives. Some of the most popular characters are Yellow Corn girl, Blue Corn girl, Magpie-tail boy, and Coyote, the trickster, but the people often adopt stories from other cultures. Adults tell these tales to the youngsters, so that someday they will relate them to their own children.

CUSTOMS

Secrecy

The Pueblo people have always been very secretive about the social organization and customs of their tribe, because harsh punishment traditionally resulted from speaking too freely in front of outsiders. Religious ceremonies are closed to outsiders, and photography is not allowed at public dances or in sacred areas. The annual pilgrimages to Blue Lake are private; no non-Native is known to have ever participated.

Naming

Historians say that formal rituals to find the proper name for a child were never observed at Taos. Rather, any friend or relative could suggest a name for an infant. Once the name was determined, a male relative would present the child to the sun and/or the moon and pray for good

Testing for the Baby's Father

Many Taos tales star the trickster, Coyote, or the other characters found in this tale. Because the Pueblo language is not written, stories must be shared orally if they are to be passed down to the next generations. In addition to the traditional storytelling venues, many reservation schools now have elders tell these stories to students in their native Tiwa language.

Magpie-tail boy was living with his daughters, Blue Corn girl and Yellow Corn girl, and the people [of Taos] were living. And people asked them to marry, but they would not take them. Blue Corn girl was the elder. She got a baby without anybody knowing her. The people said to look for the father of the little boy who was growing very fast. So the people called her to find out the father of the child. They called Magpie-tail boy, too, with his two daughters and they asked him who was the father of the child. Magpie-tail boy said he did not know how she got the baby. They sat all around and they told Blue Corn girl to put the child in the middle to see which man he would go to. The boy paid no attention to the men, he just played in the middle. Just when the sun came up he ran to the place the sun shone on. When he ran they all said, "He is the son of our father the Sun." The little boy began to sing and it began to rain. While he was singing, he was dressed up nicely in buckskin. The rain filled up the house and the men said, "Please, our son, make the rain stop." But he would not listen. And they stood up because the house was full of water. He kept on singing and he began to climb up the ladder, and the house was full of water and drowned those people who had been mean to his mother. And from those who survived come the people who are living now.

SOURCE: Parsons, Elsie Clews. *Taos Tales*. New York: The American Folklore Society, J. J. Augustin, 1940.

luck and long life for the child. All infants were dedicated to one of the six kivas (places of worship). A short time after the birth, a member of that kiva would arrive to give the child its kiva name. This ceremonial name was only used during the sacred activities of the kiva.

Adolescence

Kiva spiritual training took place when a boy was between eight and ten years old. His initiation period lasted for eighteen months and ended with a pilgrimage to Blue Lake. During training, the boy was required to live within the walls of the kiva.

A Taos dancer performs at the Intertribal Indian Ceremonial in Gallup, New Mexico. © AP IMAGES/JOHN A. BOWERSMITH.

Although girls were also dedicated to a kiva, they did not undergo initiation. Instead, they participated in an adolescence ritual that began with their first menstrual period. The girl was confined for four days in the ground-floor room of her home, required to grind corn in silence, and was not allowed to be touched by sunlight. On the fourth day the childhood braid was removed from her hair and her bangs were cut. After this ritual had occurred, the girl—at this point eligible for marriage—could also go to Blue Lake.

Festivals

Various annual festivals and dances are important to the Taos way of life. These community events have continued mostly unchanged for centuries. They include the Deer Dance, Christmas festivities in December followed by Three Kings Day in January, the Feast of San Diego in November, and the Corn Dance in the summer. Festivals often feature dancing, relay races, and pole-climbing competitions, which visitors may attend. But the sacred rituals associated with the festivals are open only to tribal members.

The 1970 return of Blue Lake inspired the Taos people and made them even more determined to preserve their traditional religion and culture. The tribe's most important ritual is the August pilgrimage to Blue Lake. Blue Lake is believed to be the earth's navel, from which the Taos people emerged. It is a sacred site that provides more than just water; it has great spiritual meaning as the source of life.

Marriage

Until recently members of the Taos Pueblo were forbidden to marry anyone but other pueblo residents, a practice meant to preserve pure bloodlines. Most people who marry outside the tribe choose to reside off the reservation, often many miles away. Marriages are either nonreligious or are performed in accordance with the Roman Catholic Church. Divorces, once almost nonexistent, have become easier to obtain in modern times.

Funerals

Traditionally Taos held burials the morning after death. Following the burial, family members remained in the house of the deceased for four days to prevent the person's spirit from returning to the home. After the fourth day, mourners placed ritual offerings—feathers, food, and moccasins—to the north just beyond the edge of town. They offered a bit of food to the spirits of the dead at mealtimes. As they still are today, the dead were buried at the ruins of the old Taos mission with their heads toward the south.

CURRENT TRIBAL ISSUES

The people of Taos Pueblo still work to preserve the old ways. For example, it was not until 1971 that the Pueblo Council allowed electricity to be installed on the reservation, and electricity and running water are still not used within the old pueblo walls. Every able-bodied adult is expected to perform duties for the community. These include projects such as cleaning irrigation ditches, repairing fences, and plastering buildings, as well as performing ceremonial-linked activities. Activities such as these—and the teaching of the Tiwa language to their children—are community events that reinforce tribal traditions.

The Taos Pueblo is organized into a wilderness zone, religious and ceremonial zones, housing and cropland zones, commercial zones, recreational zones, and range management zones. The Taos Pueblo Environmental Office trains tribal members to manage Taos environmental lands and helps to protect and preserve the tribe's natural resources.

In 2006, after many struggles with the surrounding communities and the state of New Mexico over water rights, the Taos committee reached an agreement with the government and other interested parties that was fair to everyone involved. Governor James Lujan Sr. summed up the results of the joint effort: "This is a good day, and this is a fair settlement. When it's completed it will resolve the Pueblo's water rights claims as well as long-standing water sharing disputes between Pueblo and non-Native American irrigators, and it will provide the basic rules for groundwater production in the valley without injuring surface water supplies or overburdening the aquifer." This agreement was finally signed into law at the end of 2010. The final Taos Pueblo (Abeyta case) settlement gave the people water rights from another long-standing lawsuit along with settlement funds of $124 million to purchase additional water rights and construct projects to manage groundwater, improve water quality, and increase water use efficiency.

NOTABLE PEOPLE

Phillip Doren Lujan (c. 1948–), a Kiowa-Taos Pueblo Indian, has served as an attorney for various Native legal organizations, as director of the Native American Studies Program at New Mexico State University, and as professor of communications at the University of Oklahoma in Norman, where he specialized in intercultural communication and the study of tribal governments. He also has held positions in various tribal court systems.

Other notable Taos Pueblo include painters Albert Looking Elk (1888–1940), Vicente Mirabal (1918–1944), and Pop Chalee (1906–1993).

BOOKS

Bahti, Mark. *Pueblo Stories and Storytellers.* 3rd ed. Tucson, AZ: Rio Nuevo Publishers, 2010.

Bodine, John. "Taos Pueblo." *Handbook of North American Indians,* Vol. 9: *Southwest.* Ed. Alfonso Ortiz. Washington DC: Smithsonian Institution, 1979.

Bodine, John J. *Taos Pueblo: A Walk Through Time.* Tucson, AZ: Rio Nuevo, 2006.

Curtis, Edward. "Taos." In *The North American Indian (1907–1930).* Vol. 26. Reprint. New York: Johnson Reprint Corporation, 1970.

Grant, Blanche Chloe. *Taos Indians.* 1925 ed. Santa Fe: Sunstone Press, 2007.

Keegan, Marcia. *Taos Pueblo and Its Sacred Blue Lake.* Santa Fe: Clear Light Publishers, 2010.

Martinez Martinez, Deborah. *Trade on the Taos Mountain Trail.* Pueblo, CO: Vanishing Horizons, 2010.

Parsons, Elsie Clews. *Pueblo Indian Religion.* Chicago: University of Chicago Press, 1939.

Parsons, Elsie Clews. *Taos Pueblo.* Menasha, WI: George Banta Publishing Company, 1936.

Parsons, Elsie Clews. *Taos Tales.* New York: Dover Publications, 1996.

Peaster, Lillian, and Guy Berger. *Pueblo Pottery Families: Acoma, Cochiti, Hopi, Isleta, Jemez, Laguna, Nambe, Picuris, Pojoaque, San Ildefonso, San Juan, Santa Clara, Santo Domingo, Taos, Tesuque, Zia, Zuni.* 3rd ed. Atglen, PA: Schiffer, 2008.

Sweet, Jill Drayson, and Nancy Hunter Warren. *Pueblo Dancing.* Atglen, PA: Schiffer Publishing, 2011.

Warm Day, Jonathan. *Taos Pueblo: Painted Stories.* Santa Fe, NM: Clear Light Publishing, 2004.

Weber, David J. *The Taos Trappers: The Fur Trade in the Far Southwest, 1540–1846.* Norman: University of Oklahoma Press, 2005.

WEB SITES

Eight Northern Indian Pueblos Council. http://www.enipc.org/ (accessed on July 20, 2011).

The Morgan Collection of Southwest Pottery. "Through the Eyes of the Pot: A Study of Southwest Pueblo Pottery and Culture: Taos." *Lowell D. Holmes Museum of Anthropology, Wichita State University.* http://www.holmes.anthropology.museum/southwestpottery/taospueblo.html (accessed on July 20, 2011).

Muenker, Rose. "Taos Pueblo: Cultural Traditions Enrich Ancient Indian Village." *UNESCO World Heritage Sites.* http://www.muenkermedia.com/owh/site-Taos.shtml (accessed on July 20, 2011).

National Museum of American History—Smithsonian Institution. "Pueblo Resistance: We Are Here" (video). *Mexico State Record Center and Archives.* http://www.newmexicohistory.org/filedetails.php?fileID=23042 (accessed on July 20, 2011).

Taos Pueblo. http://www.taospueblo.com/ (accessed on July 20, 2011).

"Taos Pueblo." *Bluffton University.* http://www.bluffton.edu/~sullivanm/taos/taos.html (accessed on July 20, 2011).

"Taos Pueblo." *New Mexico Magazine.* http://www.nmmagazine.com/native_american/taos.php (accessed on July 20, 2011).

"Taos Pueblo: A Thousand Years of Tradition." *Taos Pueblo.* http://taospueblo.com/ (accessed on July 20, 2011).

"Taos Pueblo Pottery." *ClayHound Web.* http://www.clayhound.us/sites/taos.htm (accessed on July 20, 2011).

Weiser, Kathy. "Taos Pueblo—1,000 Years of History." *Legends of America.* http://www.legendsofamerica.com/nm-taospueblo.html (accessed on July 20, 2011).

Zuñi Pueblo

Name

The Zuñi (pronounced *ZOON-yee* or *ZOO-nee*) call themselves *A'shiwi,* or "the flesh." Their pueblo bears the name *Itiwana,* or "middle place," because in the tribe's origin story, it is the place to which their ancestors came after they emerged from the underworld. The Spanish word *pueblo* means "town" and refers to both the Pueblo people and the pueblos (cities) where they live.

Location

The main site of the 408,404-acre Zuñi Pueblo, a federal reservation, is 35 miles (56 kilometers) south of Gallup, in west-central New Mexico. The tribe's property consists of several parts: the main portion in west-central New Mexico, which includes the tribe's farming and grazing areas, and smaller sites in New Mexico and Arizona that are sacred to the tribe.

Population

In 1540, there were an estimated 6,000 Zuñi. In the late 1700s, the count had dropped to 1,600 to 1,900. In 1850, a census counted about 1,300 Zuñi. In the 1990 U.S. Census, 8,281 people identified themselves as Zuñi Pueblo. At the time of the 2000 census, that number had risen to 9,311. The Bureau of Indian Affairs reported a tribal enrollment of 9,554 in 2001.

Language family

Zuñian.

Origins and group affiliations

According to Zuñi oral history, their earliest ancestors came into the world with webbed feet, long ears, hairless tails, and moss-covered bodies. They acquired a human form only after bathing in the waters of a sacred spring. The Zuñi may be descendants of the Mogollon Indians who, over time, mixed with other groups.

The Pueblo of Zuñi is now one of the largest of the Pueblo nations in terms of both population and land ownership. The reservation has many

Contemporary Zuñi Pueblo Communities

The Zuñi Reservation

1 Zuñi property consists of the 400,000-acre reservation with five villages in west central New Mexico and three small sacred sites in New Mexico and Arizona.

Shaded area

Traditional Zuñi lands in present-day New Mexico and Arizona

A map of contemporary Zuñi Pueblo communities. MAP BY XNR PRODUCTIONS. CENGAGE LEARNING, GALE. REPRODUCED BY PERMISSION OF GALE, A PART OF CENGAGE LEARNING.

attractive features, including a strong sense of community, the availability of good health care, and a highly developed cultural life. Because of its desirable lifestyle, almost all tribal members have chosen to remain on the reservation, and those who leave to take jobs often return when their employment ends.

HISTORY

Spanish visit trading center

For more than two thousand years, the Zuñi people have occupied the Zuñi and Little Colorado River valleys of the Southwest. By around 1250, Zuñi was a major trading center for a region that stretched from California to the Great Plains and into Mexico. Items such as corn, salt, turquoise, cotton cloth, and jewelry were exchanged at the pueblo for macaw feathers, seashells, coral, and copper.

In 1539, a man known as Esteban, or Estevanicio, led a party of Spaniards on a quest to find the fabled, gold-paved "Seven Cities of Cíbola," thought to be on Zuñi land. During the trip, Esteban entered the Zuñi village of Hawikuh and demanded gifts of turquoise and women. Some Zuñi men became angry at Esteban's attitude and threats;they killed him, so he could not reveal their location to his allies. His companions retreated without entering the village.

In 1540, a second Spanish group led by Francisco Vásquez de Coronado (c. 1510–1554) reached Hawikuh. Coronado's timing could not have been worse; he arrived during a sacred ceremony. The bow priests (see "Government"), who were in charge of the pueblo, drew a line on the ground and told Coronado his party could not cross it while the ritual continued. However, the Spaniards disregarded the order and proceeded to cross the line. In the bloody battle that followed, twenty Zuñi were killed.

Retreat from invaders

In Hawikuh, Coronado found a well-ordered community rich in tradition but not in gold or treasures. Disappointed, he stayed in Hawikuh-for a while before traveling on in search of riches. The Zuñi kept their feelings to themselves and encouraged the foreigners to explore other regions. When confrontations with the Spanish seemed unavoidable, the Zuñi retreated to a temporary settlement atop Thunder Mountain, a thousand-foot-high mesa. A mesa (the Spanish word for "table") is a large hill with steep sides and a flat top.

During the fifteenth and sixteenth centuries, all the villages of the Zuñi were destroyed when the Navajo, Apache (see entries), and other tribes overran the area. After the Pueblo Revolt of 1680 (see Pueblo entry), in which the Spanish were expelled from the region, the Zuñi moved to Thunder

Important Dates

1250: Zuñi Pueblo is an important trading center for Native peoples from California, Mexico, and the American Southwest.

1540: Spanish expedition under Francisco Vásquez de Coronado spends four months at the main Zuñi village of Hawikuh.

1600s: All Zuñi villages are destroyed by raiding tribes.

1692: The Zuñi build a new village atop the old site of Halona.

1846: The United States assumes control of Zuñi lands.

1877: Zuñi reservation is established.

1978: The U.S. government returns ownership of the sacred Zuñi Salt Lake to the tribe.

1984: The U.S. government restores the tribe's ownership of the sacred area known as "Zuñi Heaven" in eastern Arizona.

1990: The Zuñi Land Conservation Act passes and provides a trust fund to assist in sustainable resource development.

Mountain. The Spanish returned in 1692 and reclaimed the area for Mexico. Diego de Vargas (1643–1704), governor of the region, convinced the Zuñi to accept Spanish authority, and the people came down from Thunder Mountain and built a new pueblo atop the abandoned village of Halona.

Spanish leave the Zuñi alone

When Catholic missionaries went to Zuñi Pueblo to reestablish the Spanish mission there, they were accompanied by three Spanish officials who planned to set up a nonreligious government office, but the Zuñi killed the three in 1703. Some accounts say the officials mistreated the Pueblo people. For more than one hundred years, the Zuñi were largely left alone by the Spanish and lived their lives in their traditional manner.

In 1820, the Spanish missionaries left Zuñi Pueblo for good, unable to overcome tribal resistance to Christianity. The Spanish could no longer endure the constant Apache and Navajo raids in the Southwest, and they feared a planned Mexican revolt against Spain. The missionaries left behind little evidence of nearly three centuries of influence: the use of a few metal tools, the introduction of new crops and animals, and several religious ideas the Zuñi adopted into their belief system.

Taken over by Mexico, then by United States

Mexico's revolt against Spain was successful, but Mexico could not afford to send soldiers to oversee the "northern frontier," which included Zuñi land. The Zuñi began trading with the United States, and within twenty-five years, the United States conquered the region with no opposition.

In accordance with U.S. policy toward Native peoples, a reservation was set up for the Zuñi in 1877. From 1879 until 1883, Frank Hamilton Cushing (1857–1900), an American ethnologist (a scholar who studies the cultures of various peoples), lived among the Zuñi and learned their language and customs. He deeply offended them when he later published information about their most sacred ceremonies and spiritual beliefs. The Zuñi people felt he had violated their trust.

Beginning in the 1870s, the influence of American society on the pueblo was profound. A railroad was constructed in the region, which made it possible to ship animals. The Zuñi became involved in raising and selling sheep and cattle. By the late 1890s, many non-Natives lived in the Zuñi Pueblo, including teachers, missionaries, traders, and some government officials.

A century of hardships

Outsiders brought strange diseases, and many Zuñi died from a series of smallpox epidemics that swept through their homelands. By the end of the nineteenth century, the Zuñi had lost much of their land to trespassing settlers and the railroads. The people were no longer able to sustain themselves by raising crops and livestock. To survive, many Zuñi turned to making silver jewelry, a skill they learned from the Navajo (see entry) people.

Life improves

At the beginning of the twentieth century, the Zuñi suffered severe health problems and struggled with land claims and the question of educating their children. Conditions began to improve for the tribe by the end of the century. With the availability of better health care, the population finally surpassed the level it had been at the time the tribe first encountered the Spanish. Since 1978, the tribe has regained ownership of its sacred Zuñi Salt Lake, as well as an area known as "Zuñi Heaven," where the spirits of the Zuñi people are believed to reside after death. In 1980, the reservation established its own public school district, thereby assuming full responsibility for educating its children.

RELIGION

Although the Zuñi recognized many gods, their Supreme Being was the Sun, the source of all life. They admired the keen senses, sharp teeth, claws, talons, cleverness, and quickness of animals and believed animals were closer to the spirit world than people were.

In modern times, the traditional religion of the Zuñi remains very important, but many of them also belong to one of the various Christian churches that were established after the Spanish converted many Zuñi to Christianity. As late as the 2000s, certain elements of the traditional religion remained secret.

Fetishes

Fetishes, tiny animals carved from stone, have great spiritual importance to the tribe and are featured in the jewelry they make. Most are carved from bone, shell, wood, or stone in the shapes of certain important

Zuñi Words

awite	"four"
ha'i	"three"
kohanna	"white"
ky'awe	"water"
kwinna	"black"
makyi	"woman"
shillowa	"red"
tapa	"one"
watsita	"dog"
yachunne	"moon"
yatakya	"sun"

creatures such as the wildcat, falcon, coyote, eagle, mole, wolf, or ground owl. Fetish stones found in nature, rather than carved, are believed to be more powerful.

Often the maker attaches shells, turquoise beads, arrowheads, feathers, or bones to the fetish. Some fetishes have lines painted or etched on them. These may look like bird's feathers or be designs similar to those used for ceremonial masks or clothing. Many have a "heartline arrow," a line from the animal's mouth to its heart. This arrow, with its point touching the heart, represents the breath or life of the animal spirit.

Most people keep sets of fetishes in clay jars lined with down; the outsides are often dusted with turquoise bits before firing. The jar has a hole in the side, but its top opening is covered with hide. Owners care for their jars by washing them regularly.

Each set of fetishes usually consists of three to seven figures and has a special purpose—for example, healing the sick or initiating the person into a religious order. The Zuñi hold a special ceremony once a year called "The Day of the Council of Fetishes" (see "Festivals").

Effigies

Effigies, carvings in the images of war gods made from lightning-struck trees, are worshiped at a special ceremony every year. In 1990, the Zuñi Tribal Council contacted museums and collectors that possessed these Zuñi figures and requested that they be returned to the tribe. Within two months, the Zuñi had received thirty-eight effigies from twenty-four different collections.

LANGUAGE

Although their cultures are similar, no other Pueblo tribe speaks Zuñi. Many linguists (scientists who study language) have concluded that Zuñi is an isolated language and is unrelated to any other present-day languages. A few others disagree and believe it is related to Penutian, a language spoken by some tribes along the West Coast.

Although most Zuñi now speak English, the Zuñi language is the basis of their culture and the primary language of most tribal members. Programs now exist in the public schools to help Zuñi children learn their language in written form. In the early twenty-first century, about six thousand people spoke the language.

GOVERNMENT

For centuries the Zuñi pueblo was run by men called bow priests, who were in charge of the priestly council. During the 1890s, the United States put bow priests in jail to do away with the tribe's ancient religious and political system. By 1934, the Zuñi could no longer choose their governor and tribal council by traditional means. Over the several decades that followed, a switch from a religious to a nonreligious democratic government took place. By 1970, the tribe had passed a constitution, and today the Zuñi Tribal Council acts as the governing body for the reservation.

Since 1974, the Zuñi have held elections for the offices of governor, lieutenant governor, and their six-member tribal council. The government includes legislative, executive, and judicial branches. In addition to this constitutional government, the tribe maintains the traditional system of matrilineal clans (groups of related families that trace their ancestry through the mother of the family), six kiva (worship) societies, ten medicine societies (groups that cure illnesses), and two priesthoods.

ECONOMY

Decline of agriculture

The economy once depended on farming. After the move to the reservation, the Zuñi population was restricted to a smaller land area than their ancestors, and it was difficult for them to grow enough crops to sustain themselves.

Hoping to increase farming efficiency, the Bureau of Indian Affairs constructed an irrigation system on the Zuñi reservation in the early 1900s, but the major dam collapsed immediately after it was completed. Over the years the tradition of community farms became unworkable, so between 1911 and 1988, the number of acres farmed at the Zuñi pueblo declined by 83 percent. Although some of the tribe still maintain traditional peach orchards, by the late 1990s, only about 1,000

A Zuñi family plants crops.
© NORTH WIND PICTURE
ARCHIVES.

acres were farmed, whereas 95 percent of the tribal land was used for grazing livestock.

Employment in modern times

By the 1960s, 90 percent of the tribe's members were involved in the silver-making craft at least part-time. By the early 2000s, the Zuñi had also become famous as firefighters. They were the first group of Native Americans trained as firefighting experts, and the U.S. Forest Service frequently transports them to extinguish the worst forest fires in the United States.

Since the 1960s, the tribe has received nearly $50 million in settlements for court cases involving land claims. The Zuñi have used these funds to increase individual income and educational opportunities and to improve living conditions on the reservation.

In the late twentieth century, sheep production was a major source of income on the reservation, and the tribe's herd numbered around fourteen thousand by the turn of the century. The Zuñi also tended peach orchards and raised cattle, as well as hogs, pigs, fowl, horses, and goats.

The tribal government is the major employer on the reservation. Most of the small businesses on the reservation focus on arts and crafts. Crafters work in hundreds of mini-workshops to produce jewelry, fetishes, pottery, paintings, and beadwork. Often families work together to fashion jewelry. Their designs "belong" to them and are passed down from generation to generation. The Zuñi Craftsman Cooperative Market sells works by Zuñi artists. Many people also held jobs in retail, education, manufacturing, service business, construction, or tourism, but more than one-third of the population lived in poverty in 2011.

DAILY LIFE

Responsibilities of men and women

According to Zuñi tradition, men were farmers, herdsmen, and hunters, who provided the food for women to prepare. They were responsible for keeping the gods happy, whereas women were responsible for the family and the tribe. Women blessed newborn babies and presented them to the Sun Father, prepared food offerings for the gods, presented food offerings to ancestors at each meal, greeted the sunrise, and prepared bodies for burial. Men made the prayer sticks (carved and painted sticks adorned with feathers and shells) that they offered to the gods. Men also organized the annual cycle of ceremonies and impersonated the spirits during ritual dances.

Buildings

As recently as the late 1800s, most Zuñi lived in typical pueblo "apartment" houses that stood five stories high. Zuñi is one of the few pueblos that used rectangular rooms inside their homes as kivas (places of worship), rather than building separate, circular facilities for this purpose.

In modern times, many Zuñi live in single-family homes. They may be modern in architectural style, but they are often built using the same stone the people have used for centuries. Some structures survive from ancient Halona and are now the ceremonial heart of the pueblo.

Clothing and adornment

Zuñi men wore breechcloths (flaps of material that covered the front and back) with fringed edges and a tassel at each corner, which they tied over the hips. They sometimes added long robes of feathers or the skins of hares, or cotton blankets. Women wore the traditional Pueblo *mantas* (pronounced *MAHN-tuhs*), dresses formed by wrapping a dark blue or black rectangular piece of cotton around the body, passing it under the left arm, and tying it above the right shoulder. A sash encircled the waist. After the Spanish introduced sheep herding to the region, wool became a popular material for mantas. Women wore boot-like moccasins topped with leggings formed by spiraling strips of deerskin around the leg.

Food

The Zuñi are known for their sophisticated irrigation techniques. For centuries, they constructed small dams and canals that directed rainwater to the crops but protected them from the destructive torrents that often occurred during storms. They even developed a method to protect their crops from birds. They strung cactus leaves on lines crisscrossing the fields. The leaves waved in the wind and frightened scavengers. When this system was not enough, children and elderly people were posted in the fields to make noise and throw stones.

Corn was the major crop; the people thought of it as the flesh of the mystical Corn Maidens. They may have cultivated as many as 10,000 acres of corn at a time. In a good year, they produced enough surplus to feed the people for two years in case of a drought or other disaster. The Zuñi supplemented the corn, beans, and various garden vegetables they raised by hunting wild game such as rabbit, deer, and bear. They also fished and gathered wild nuts and fruits.

In modern times, the Zuñi are taking steps to protect certain varieties of long-lasting traditional seeds, including corn, beans, squash, melons, chilies, and peaches, so they can be enjoyed by future generations.

Education

The Zuñi manage their own school system. The schools teach language and cultural history, and they support tribal customs in various ways. For example, students who are restricted to a special diet because they are undergoing initiation rites are provided with special lunches, and classes are canceled during the important Sha'lak'o festival.

Begun in 1992, the Zuñi bookmobile program brings library books to outlying areas three times a week. The tribe received funding in 2005 to replace their broken-down van, and a new van was put into service in 2006. The Zuñi Public Library is the only Native library in New Mexico with a bookmobile.

Healing practices

Both men and women are permitted to become lifelong members of Zuñi medicine societies, groups that heal people from various ailments. Some societies approach curing from a spiritual standpoint, whereas others use medicinal methods. Members learn how plants, roots, massage, and healing rituals work.

In earlier times, some Zuñi medicine societies staged displays to show their power and to bring good health to the whole community. These exhibitions featured performers who swallowed fire or swords or danced unharmed over hot coals. Many ailments were thought to be caused by spirits and witches, either as punishment or out of cruelty. According to Zuñi healers, curing such an ailment might require removing a pebble, feather, or wood particle that had been "shot" inside the body by the supernatural being.

ARTS

The Zuñi love of color is seen in the beautiful jewelry they produce, which is made of turquoise, shell, and jet, and set into silver in intricate patterns. Known for their fine beadwork, tribal members make belts, necklaces, and even figures out of beads. They also carve animals from translucent shells. The most popular Zuñi pottery is white with a reddish-brown design.

CUSTOMS

Clans

Every Zuñi is born into a clan, a group that traces its ancestry to the same person. An individual's clan membership comes from the mother, but families also retain ties to the father's clan. Zuñi clans are in a constant state of change, as some die out while others grow larger.

Birth and naming

After a baby is born, the child is secluded with its mother and kept in the dark until he or she is presented to the sun. On the eighth day before daybreak, the baby's aunts from the father's side of the family wash the child's head. Then they place cornmeal in the infant's hand and take the child outside facing east toward the sunrise. The baby's paternal grandmother (the father's mother) says a prayer as the sun rises.

A procession marks the arrival of the ceremonial Shalako at Zuñi Pueblo. © NORTH WIND PICTURE ARCHIVES.

Festivals

A traditional Zuñi ritual is "The Day of the Council of Fetishes," which was held every year near the winter solstice. Everyone arranges their fetishes around the altar in the council chamber. Animals that walk are set in slats on the floor so they stand upright. Those that fly are hung in the air on strings. People sing and chant through most of the night, and at the end of prayers or stanzas they imitate animal sounds and movements. The day ends with a feast that is shared with the fetishes, and then the leftover food is buried.

The Sha'lak'o Ceremony

The most spectacular annual Zuñi ceremony involves the Sha'lak'o. They are men dressed as ten- to twelve-foot-tall messenger birds who dramatize the annual visit of the birds to bring blessings to the Zuñi people.

Each year on a late winter afternoon, the Zuñi hear the cries of the approachingSha'lak'os as they begin crossing the small river that runs through the pueblo. The crowds of people who have gathered in the Zuñi village square fall silent. Rhythmic jingles in the distance grow louder, and finally, the majestic Sha'lak'o stride into the square.

These commanding, colorful creatures have wide eyes, buffalo horns, and ruffs of raven feathers beneath their domed-shaped, beaked heads. They wear brilliant masks of bright red, turquoise, and black, as well as beautiful jewelry, rattles, ankle bells, and pine boughs. Some of the most important gods being impersonated are Sayatasha, the rain god of the north; Shulawitsi, the little fire god; and Yamukato, a frightful warrior who uses green yucca leaves to swat any observers who fall asleep during the all-night celebration.

Through their prayers, the Sha'lak'o honor all things in the universe, living and nonliving. As the creatures encircle the village square, masked singers chant, and the air rings with the rhythmic sounds of drums, bells, rattles, and the clacking of wooden bird beaks as they open and close. Then the Sha'lak'o bend their knees and begin their classic back-and-forth dancing. They dance to awaken Earth and stir the clouds, in hopes of bringing on the rain that is so vital to the parched land of the Zuñi.

Visitors were formerly welcome to watch the Sha'lak'o ceremony, but they were asked not to record their observations. In recent times, the large crowds of visitors prevented the Zuñi from entering the new houses in the pueblo and carrying out their blessing ritual. As a result, this event has been closed to non-Natives since 1995.

All pueblo businesses are closed for four days twice a year in June and December during Deshkwi, or "Fasting." As part of this observance, the Zuñi do not spend money, build fires, eat greasy food, touch others, or toss litter.

The most dramatic annual event at the Zuñi Pueblo is the Sha'lak'o ceremony, which is held to celebrate the new year and to bless new houses. It is not open to the public, but visitors can attend several other annual events, such as the June Rain Dance, the McKinley County Fair, and the many Zuñi arts markets.

Courtship and marriage

Zuñi courtship was a rather complicated undertaking. When a young man became interested in marrying a young woman, he let her know of his admiration and asked if she shared that feeling. If she did, she discussed his suitability as a mate with her mother. If her family approved of the match, the young couple met several times in secret to decide if they wanted to wed. During this time, either party could call off the relationship. If the woman called it off, there were no negative consequences for her, but if the man called it off, he had to pay a "bride price" to her family. If the woman refused the bride price, she could "go public" with her intentions to marry him.

Going public meant that the young woman went to the young man's home during the daylight hours so everyone could see what was happening. She presented his mother with a gift. If the mother liked the young woman, she presented the bride-to-be with wedding finery: the traditional black dress, moccasins, shawl, and beads. If at this point the man had a change of heart, he returned to the girl's home with her. If he still would not marry her, she could choose to move into his household and stay until he changed his mind or she became ashamed. At that point, she gave the wedding finery back to his mother and retreated to her family home.

If, from the first, the couple decided to marry, the woman ground corn as a gift for her mother-in-law. The man then presented his wife to his mother, who gave her the wedding finery. The couple went back to

Zuñi Pueblo conduct a burial ceremony, circa 1800s.
© NORTH WIND PICTURE ARCHIVES.

the bride's home, and the man spent the night, leaving in daylight so the new relationship was known to all.

Death

A body was buried the day after death, but the spirit was thought to remain in the home for four days. When a person died, he or she was no longer mentioned by name, but silent prayers could be said in his or her memory. In contrast, the people who replaced deceased religious men, called rain priests, prayed to them by name.

CURRENT TRIBAL ISSUES

Middle Village in danger of collapse

Buildings that make up the old "Middle Village" rest on ruins that extend as deep as 36 feet (10 meters) below the currently inhabited buildings. Because they have not been maintained for centuries, the old structures have been crumbling, causing walls to crack and floors to slope in the occupied rooms above.

This area of the pueblo is where ceremonial dances take place. Hundreds of people climb on walls and sit on rooftops to watch, which adds to the pressures on the decaying foundation. As a result, a number of homes and kivas are in danger of collapsing. Strengthening the foundations requires extensive work. Repairs are complicated by the fact that the pueblo is listed on the National Register of Historic Places, an organization that has strict rules for reconstruction.

Return of religious sites

The Zuñi have achieved the return of two of their major religious sites, Zuñi Salt Lake and Zuñi Heaven. They have also received cash settlements from the federal government for tribal lands that were illegally sold to non-Natives or were damaged by federal mismanagement. The money has allowed the tribe to begin a major project to restore damaged lands.

For twenty years, the Zuñi fought against federal and state approval of a 9,000-acre coal mine that would be located only 12 miles (19 kilometers) from Zuñi Salt Lake. Despite their argument that the mine would pollute the sacred lake, the plan was approved in 1996, but after years of lawsuits, the project was dropped.

Conservation award

For centuries, the Zuñi adopted eagles and treated them with respect. Some birds lived with Zuñi families for more than fifty years. In this way, the tribe both respected the animals and obtained feathers for their prayer offerings and ceremonies when the birds molted.

When the U.S. government passed laws protecting eagles, it became illegal for the Zuñi to have eagle feathers. In 1987, however, American Indian Religious Freedom Act passed, allowing the people to keep molted eagle feathers. In 1999, the pueblo became the first Native tribe to open a bird sanctuary. The Zuñi Eagle Sanctuary protects twenty species that might otherwise have become endangered. The sanctuary also enables the Zuñi to follow their religious beliefs of treating all animals, especially the eagle, with kindness and respect and continues to supply them with feathers so they can conduct their ceremonies. The Zuñi hold educational programs open to the public and have trained their teens to care for the birds.

NOTABLE PEOPLE

Edmund Ladd (1926–1999), whose grandfather once served as tribal governor, was the first Zuñi to earn a college degree. In the paper he wrote for his PhD, he explored the roles played by birds and feathers in Zuñi mythology and religion. He worked as an archaeologist for the National Park Service and was an official at the Museum of New Mexico in Santa Fe. He also published several papers on Hawaiian archaeology.

Other notable Zuñi include the painter Kai Sa (1918–1974), also known as Percy Sandy; the jewelry designer Rod Kaskalla (1955–); and Roger Tsabetsaye (1941–), an artist who worked with President Lyndon B. Johnson (1908–1973; served 1963–69) on his social welfare program called the War on Poverty in the 1960s.

BOOKS

Bonvillain, Nancy. *The Zuñi.* New York: Chelsea House Publishers, 2011.

Button, Bertha P. *Friendly People: The Zuñi Indians.* Santa Fe, NM: Museum of New Mexico Press, 1963.

Cushing, Frank H. *Zuñi Folk Tales.* Charleston, SC: Kessinger Publishing, 2011)

Hart, E. Richard, ed. *Zuñi and the Courts: A Struggle for Sovereign Land Rights.* Lawrence: University Press of Kansas, 1995.

Hicks, Terry Allan. *The Zuñi.* New York: Marshall Cavendish Benchmark, 2010.

Jones, Hester. *Zuñi Shalako Ceremony.* Charleston, SC: Kessinger Publishing, 2011.

Lanmon, Dwight P. and Francis H. Harlow. *The Pottery of Zuñi Pueblo.* Santa Fe: Museum of New Mexico Press, 2008.

McManis, Kent. *Zuñi Fetishes and Carvings.* 2nd ed. Tucson, AZ: Rio Nuevo Publishers, 2010.

Roberts, David. *The Pueblo Revolt: The Secret Rebellion That Drove the Spaniards out of the Southwest.* New York: Simon and Schuster, 2005.

Ryan, Marla Felkins, and Linda Schmittroth. *Tribes of Native America: Zuñi Pueblo.* San Diego: Blackbirch Press, 2002.

Sando, Joe S. *Pueblo Nations: Eight Centuries of Pueblo Indian History.* Santa Fe, NM: Clear Light Publishers, 1992.

Stevenson, Matilda Coxe. *The Zuñi Indians and Their Uses of Plants.* Charleston, SC: Kessinger Publishing, 2011.

Stevenson, Tilly E. *The Religious Life of the Zuñi Child.* Charleston, SC: Kessinger Publishing, 2011.

Trimble, Stephen. *The People: Indians of the American Southwest.* Santa Fe, NM: School of American Research Press, 1993.

Wallace, Susan E. *The Land of the Pueblos.* Santa Fe, NM: Sunstone Press, 2006.

Wright, Barton. *Classic Hopi and Zuñi Kachina Figures.* Santa Fe: Museum of New Mexico Press, 2006.

WEB SITES

The Morgan Collection of Southwest Pottery. "Through the Eyes of the Pot: A Study of Southwest Pueblo Pottery and Culture: Zuñi." *Lowell D. Holmes Museum of Anthropology, Wichita State University.* http://www.holmes.anthropology.museum/southwestpottery/zunipueblo.html (accessed on July 20, 2011).

National Museum of American History—Smithsonian Institution. "Pueblo Resistance: We Are Here" (video). *Mexico State Record Center and Archives.* http://www.newmexicohistory.org/filedetails.php?fileID=23042 (accessed on July 20, 2011).

Pueblo of Zuñi. http://www.ashiwi.org/(accessed on July 20, 2011).

Smithsonian Folkways. "Rain Dance (Zuñi)." *Smithsonian Institution.* http://www.folkways.si.edu/TrackDetails.aspx?itemid=16680 (music track) and http://media.smithsonianfolkways.org/liner_notes/folkways/FW06510.pdf (instructions for dance). (accessed on July 20, 2011).

Weiser, Kathy. "The Zuñi—A Mysterious People." *Legends of America.* http://www.legendsofamerica.com/na-zuni.html (accessed on July 20, 2011).

"Zuñi." *Northern Arizona University.* http://www.cpluhna.nau.edu/People/zuni.htm (accessed on July 20, 2011).

"Zuñi." *Southwest Crossroads.* http://southwestcrossroads.org/record. php?num=2&hl=zuni (accessed on July 20, 2011).

"Zuñi Pueblo." *New Mexico Magazine.* http://www.nmmagazine.com/native_ american/zuni.php (accessed on July 20, 2011).

"Zuñi Pueblos (Ashiwi)." *Four Directions Institute.* http://www.fourdir.com/ zuni.htm (accessed on July 20, 2011).

Tohono O'odham

Name

The name Tohono O'odham (pronounced *to-HO-no oh-O-tahm*) means "desert people." The tribe was formerly known as the Papago, a name the Spanish called them that came from a mispronunciation of a Pima word meaning "bean people" or "bean-eaters."

Location

The Tohono O'odham describe their territory as stretching south from the Gila River in Arizona to the Sonora River in the northwestern part of the Mexican province of Sonora, and from the Colorado River in the west to the San Pedro River in the east. They lived in hilly areas away from the rivers occupied by the Pima. In modern times, most tribal members live in the United States and are members of the Tohono O'odham Nation, which is made up of four reservations located in Arizona. Others share the Ak-Chin Reservation with the Pima. There are a few scattered communities in Sonora, Mexico.

Population

In 1680, there were an estimated 6,000 Tohono O'odham. In the 1990 U.S. Census, 16,876 people identified themselves as Tohono O'odham, making them the fifteenth-largest tribe in the United States. At that time about 200 Tohono O'odham lived in Caborca, Sonora, Mexico. By 2000, the census counted 17,466 Tohono O'odham in the United States, and a total of 20,087 people who had some Tohono O'odham heritage. Of that number, 10,787 lived on the reservation. In 2004, the Tohono O'odham Nation tribal enrollment showed 25,940 members in the United States and 1,800 in Mexico. The 2010 census counted 19,522 Tohono O'odham, with 23,478 people claiming some Tohono O'odham ancestry. By 2011, total tribal enrollment had reached nearly 28,000.

Language family

Uto-Aztecan.

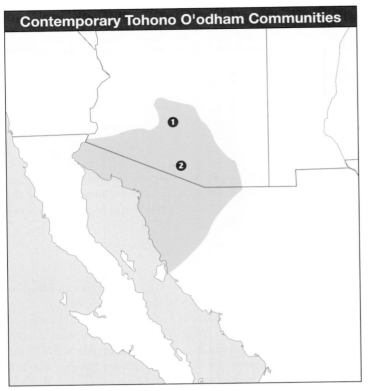

Contemporary Tohono O'odham Communities

Arizona

❶ Ak Chin Indian Community
❷ Tohono O'odham Nation, composed of
four reservations: Tohono O'odham, Sells,
Gila Bend, and San Xavier

Shaded area

☐ Traditional Tohono O'odham lands in
present-day Arizona and the
Sonoran Desert in Mexico

A map of contemporary Tohono O'odham communities. MAP BY XNR PRODUCTIONS. CENGAGE LEARNING, GALE. REPRODUCED BY PERMISSION OF GALE, A PART OF CENGAGE LEARNING.

Origins and group affiliations

Some historians believe the Tohono O'odham are descendants of the oldest known Native American culture of the area: the Hohokam, whose culture faded about 1450. The Spanish grouped the Tohono O'odham with the Pima, but they were different people. The Tohono O'odham were bitter enemies of the Apache. In fact, the Tohono O'odham word for "enemy" (*ob*) is also their ancient name for Apache.

The Tohono O'odham were a sociable, desert-dwelling people. Because of the unusual climate and geography of their Arizona-Mexico homeland, they were both farmers and hunter-gatherers. Although they cooperated with the Spanish who overran their territory beginning in the late 1600s, they refused to be dominated by them or by the Americans who came later. In the early twenty-first century, they maintain a vibrant cultural life, incorporating old and new elements, and their numbers have increased dramatically since the days when the Spanish arrived in their territory.

HISTORY

Minimal early contact with Spanish

For hundreds of years before the Spanish came, the Tohono O'odham divided their time between their winter villages and their summer villages, either growing or searching for food. From time to time, they endured severe water shortages, which required them to move in with their neighbors so they could work together, but the people adapted to and lived successfully in their desert homeland.

The first Europeans to see the Tohono O'odham were Spanish explorers, who entered tribal territory as early as 1539. The Spanish called the people "Papabotus," which means "bean people," because their diet relied heavily on beans. This name was mispronounced "Papago" by outsiders, and that is the name by which the tribe was called for the next four hundred years.

For a time, the Spanish ignored the Tohono O'odham, believing the land to be barren and the people to be savages. Spanish attitudes toward the land changed when they discovered silver at the San Miguel River in the 1640s. The Spanish began building permanent settlements among the Tohono O'odham, whom they now viewed as perfect candidates to work in their silver mines.

Important Dates

1687: Father Eusebio Kino begins missionary work among the Tohono O'odham.

1853: The Gadsden Purchase brings Tohono O'odham lands under the control of the United States.

1874: The San Xavier Reservation is established.

1876: The Tohono O'odham make a lasting peace with their traditional enemy, the Apache.

1882: The Gila Bend Reservation is established.

1916: The Sells Reservation (later Papago; now Tohono O'odham), the second-largest Native American reservation in the United States, is established.

1976: The U.S. government awards the Tohono O'odham $26 million for lost lands and restores mineral rights.

1986: The people, until now called Papago, vote to legally adopt their own name for themselves—Tohono O'odham, or "desert people," to distinguish them from the Pima, or "river people."

Father Kino's innovations

In 1687, the Catholic missionary priest Eusebio Francisco Kino (1645–1711) arrived to work among the Tohono O'odham. Father Kino hoped to win the people as converts to his religion. To do that, he had to gain their confidence and their love, which he did by protecting them from the Spanish miners who wanted to make them slaves. Father Kino took great pains to make sure his future converts were not bothered by the miners. He succeeded so well that by 1689, he had performed more than eight hundred baptisms.

Father Kino introduced the Tohono O'odham to European livestock (horses and cattle) and to crops such as wheat and barley. The Tohono O'odham believed the Spanish missionaries were good men, but their relations with Spanish soldiers and settlers were troubled. Still, the Spanish came to respect the bravery of Tohono O'odham warriors, especially when they cooperated in punishing the Apache (see entry) who raided Spanish settlements. The Tohono O'odham were not displaced by Spanish settlers because the king of Spain placed them under his protection and granted them legal title to their lands.

In 1768, missionary priests launched an ambitious construction program. Father Juan Bautista Velderrain (died 1790) led the Tohono O'odham in building San Xavier de Bac, a church that still stands and is considered an architectural and artistic gem. Although the church's architect, painters, and sculptors were Spaniards, the paid laborers who laid the stone foundations, molded and fired the bricks, raised the walls, and constructed the arches and vaulted and domed roof were Tohono O'odham.

Mexico takes over the land

Mexico gained its independence from Spain in 1821. Without the protection of the king of Spain, the Tohono O'odham found their lands taken over by Mexican settlers. These invasions led to open violence and occasional warfare. The conflicts often involved disputes over water holes. Natives and, occasionally, Mexicans were killed. This fighting, which became especially intense in the early 1830s, continued sporadically throughout the century. Meanwhile, Apache raiding increased, especially between the 1830s to 1850s.

During this time, the Natives' relationship with Mexican settlers changed. Some Tohono O'odham traveled to Mexico to help settlers with the harvests. They returned with goods and money and continued to maintain homes in their traditional villages, far from their employers. At the same time, however, Mexican settlers and ranchers moved farther and farther into Tohono O'odham lands, and hostilities increased.

The Gadsden Purchase (1853) lessened the tension between the Tohono O'odham and the Mexicans. This Mexican-U.S. agreement transferred portions of Arizona, California, and New Mexico to the United States and fixed the present borders between the United States and Mexico. Some Tohono O'odham territory came under the authority of the United States, but part was left in Mexican hands. Tohono O'odham warriors quickly found employment with the U.S. Army as scouts against Apache raiders. By 1865, the Tohono O'odham had formed a standing army of their own to retaliate against Apache attackers.

In 1871, Tohono O'odham warriors helped Arizona settlers carry out the Camp Grant Massacre against their longtime enemies, the Aravaipa band of Apaches on the San Pedro River. About five hundred members of the Aravaipa band had gone to Camp Grant for protection and to make peace. On April 30, 1871, a so-called public safety committee made up of 140 Anglo-Americans, Mexicans, and Tohono O'odham went into the camp and murdered 125 Aravaipa Apache, mostly women and children, and kidnapped 27 children and sold them into slavery.

Land disputes begin

The legal title to Tohono O'odham lands granted by the king of Spain had been guaranteed by the U.S. government. This did not stop settlers from trespassing. Finally, the federal government resolved the land disputes by establishing two reservations for the Tohono O'odham. San Xavier Reservation was established in 1874, and Gila Bend Reservation in 1882. The greater part of the Tohono O'odham homeland, however, was left unprotected from settlers.

The Tohono O'odham still living in Mexico at the end of the nineteenth century were not in much better condition than their relatives in the United States. The Mexican government proved as unable or unwilling as its northern counterpart to protect Tohono O'odham lands from trespassers. In 1898, the hostility between Tohono O'odham and Mexicans erupted in violence. The Tohono O'odham raided the mining town of El Ploma in northern Sonora, and several of the attackers were killed. After this incident many Mexican Tohono O'odham left their lands and moved to Arizona. The Mexican Army destroyed the homes of many in 1908 and 1927. By 1980, fewer than two hundred Tohono O'odham were living in Sonora.

Another small reservation, Ak-Chin, was established in 1912 for Pima (see entry) and Tohono O'odham people. A large reservation was

Mission San Xavier de Bac in Tucson, Arizona, was originally built by the Tohono O'ohdham people in the late 1790s. COURTESY OF THE METROPOLITAN TUCSON CONVENTION & VISITORS BUREAU.

established in 1916 as the Papago Reservation, but by then, many settlers and business interests had already claimed land in the area. Tohono O'odham territory was not fully restored until 1926. The agreement reached at that time, however, did not grant the people rights to any minerals on their land. It took another fifty years to resolve that issue.

RELIGION

The religion practiced by the Tohono O'odham before the Spanish came has been almost entirely lost. Most members of the tribe are Catholics, remaining in the religion brought to them by Father Kino more than three hundred years ago. Their Catholicism is so deeply rooted that it has become a major part of their present-day culture. The first of their four reservations centered on the church of San Xavier de Bac, thanks in part to the efforts of the U.S. government Indian agent R. A. Wilbur. Wilbur declared that it would be a terrible thing "to take them away from the church which their ancestors built … and which owes its present state of remarkable preservation to their care and interest alone. … They built, and have protected the old mission church, which is now one of the wonders of past ages." Since 1993, Tohono O'odham workers have been restoring the building, learning preservation techniques from masters around the world.

LANGUAGE

Most speakers of the Tohono O'odham language are over the age of twenty-five, and some children do not speak it at all. In reservation schools, however, students now learn the language from the elementary grades through high school.

The language of the Tohono O'odham has been thoroughly studied because, unlike some other Native languages, many people still speak it regularly. It is a very complex language. For example, the Tohono O'odham have no tense system; their language cannot indicate the future, present, or past in the same way that English can. Things are not in the future or the past; they are close (in time), or far away (in time) to the speaker. This reveals several things about the way the ancient Tohono O'odham thought about their world. Based on their language, the ancestors of the Tohono O'odham had a non-Western concept of time; they saw time as less important than the great distances they covered in their land.

Tohono O'odham Words

cheoj	"man"
chuk	"black"
umpe	"water"
gogs	"dog"
judumi	"bear"
kawiyu	"a horse"
mashath	"moon"
oks	"woman"
shuhthagi	"water"
tash	"sun"
toha	"white"

GOVERNMENT

The Tohono O'odham lived in small, independent communities where decisions were made by the group as a whole. Each village had a headman or chief who was the center of public life. He was responsible for making public announcements, keeping the cycle of ceremonies intact, and running public functions.

In 1934, the Tohono O'odham voted to form a tribal government. In 1986, a major reorganization occurred when the tribe approved a new constitution and changed its name from Papago to Tohono O'odham Nation. The new constitution set up a government consisting of executive, legislative, and judicial branches. Eligible adult members of the community elect the chairperson and council that govern the tribe. Elections are structured so that small communities can be as well represented as large ones. Although they call themselves a nation, many Tohono O'odham people continue to think of themselves as members of separate communities.

ECONOMY

Early economy

The Tohono O'odham had a close relationship with the Pima. The two tribes exchanged food from their different environments—wild desert produce in exchange for cultivated crops. In times of drought, when they had little to trade, the Tohono O'odham worked for the Pima and other tribes as farm laborers, earning a share of the crop in exchange for their work. After the Spanish arrived, the Tohono O'odham changed their economy from one based on hunting and gathering to one based on farming.

The people still collected food from the desert, but by the late twentieth century, the Tohono O'odham economy was mainly based on the cattle business introduced by Father Kino in 1696. Ranching became successful after the U.S. government dug deep wells on the reservations and water was more easily available. Father Kino had also introduced European-style crops, but this produce was sensitive to the lack of rain and sometimes refused to grow in the dry climate.

Members of the tribe who still follow a traditional way of life live in widely scattered villages in southern Arizona and northern Sonora, Mexico. Their major source of income is through cattle ranching, although they occasionally hire out as agricultural laborers. By the 1990s, however, most Tohono O'odham lived or worked in larger Arizona towns or cities.

More recent economy

In the twentieth century, the Tohono O'odham adopted a money-based economy. They derived income from the mineral rights to their lands (mineral rights were granted in 1976) and from working as laborers in mines or on cattle ranches. The Tohono O'odham have also established themselves as one of the primary producers of extra long staple cotton in Arizona.

In 1995, the Ak-Chin Reservation, home to a small number of Tohono O'odham and Pima, became America's first Native community to open a gaming facility in partnership with the well-known Harrah's casino operations. In modern times, most of the Tohono O'odham Nation's income comes from its three Desert Diamond casinos. Money from gaming funds the tribe's fire department and supports many social service programs. The income, however, is not sufficient to meet the many pressing needs on the reservations, such as housing, health care, and education. Every few years, the casinos distribute their excess profits to the adults in the tribe. In the past, people have each received $2,000 payments.

This amount, however, is not enough to offset the poverty level of the tribe. With almost 25 percent of its population unemployed in the early 2000s, the Tohono O'odham were working to develop more sources of income. In 1996, they started Tohono O'odham Community Action (TOCA), an organization to revitalize the culture, improve community health, and support business development. One difficulty the tribe faces as they work to improve their economy is their isolated location.

DAILY LIFE

Education

At the beginning of the twentieth century, government agents sent Tohono O'odham children away to boarding schools far from home, but the Tohono O'odham did not tolerate this policy for long. In 1911, they set aside land for day schools. Today, most children are educated at reservation schools whose foundations were laid by Catholic missionaries in 1912. Other educational options include a Bureau of Indian Affairs boarding school and a day or boarding school for disabled students.

The Tohono O'odham Community College began as a two-year school but now provides all levels of college education in partnership with the Career Center. Pima Community College and the University of Arizona are nearby. The Nation consults with the University of Arizona to support higher education efforts of tribe members.

Buildings

The buildings used by the Tohono O'odham have changed greatly over time. The Hohokam, believed to be their ancestors, dug pit houses in the desert soil and built walls and roofs of mud. The Tohono O'odham did not have access to the same water resources as the Hohokam, so they did not use mud as a building material. Instead they made simple shelters from desert materials such as brush. These dwellings, with or without roofs, consisted of a round area enclosed by brush walls. Other buildings in the community included enclosed kitchens, an open-walled sunshade, special buildings for storing food, a corral for livestock, and a brush hut in which menstruating women were isolated.

Every community centered on the meeting house, or "smoking house," so called because "smoking" really meant "to have a meeting." The meetings were actually held outside the building, in an open area covered by a sunshade and containing a fireplace for night meetings. The meeting house was in a central location, so that even the most distant house of the village could hear the headman's announcements. The headman was also responsible for the material stored in the meeting house, which could include ceremonial wine and other ritual items. Present-day meeting houses are also called *o-las kis* (round houses), because they are the only buildings still constructed in the old round style.

Food

The Tohono O'odham were originally a nomadic desert people. They acquired about 75 percent of their food from wild sources, mostly desert plants and animals such as deer, rabbit, elk, and birds. They base their thirteen-month lunar calendar on desert cycles; the year begins in June, with the ripening and harvest of saguaro cactus fruits. Other months designate the time the rains begin (July), the coldest months (the "Inner Backbone Moon" of December), the "Time the Animals Mate" (January to February), and the "Time the Flowers Bloom" (April).

The remaining 25 percent of the traditional Tohono O'odham diet came from agricultural produce: corn, squash, and several kinds of beans. Some of this they raised themselves, but to obtain the rest, they traded with other tribes.

The fruit of the saguaro (pronounced *suh-WHAR-oh*), a very large cactus, is traditionally a tribal favorite. Children are taught from an early age to respect the saguaro fruit, because it stores water and provides delicious food even during times of drought. From the saguaro fruit, the Tohono O'odham make syrup, jam, and wine for use in ceremonies and prayers for rain. In the early twenty-first century, the Tohono O'odham people have harvesting rights in Saguaro National Park.

Corn and such desert foods as acorns and cactus fruits and flowers were dried, ground into meal, and stored. They were later made into tortillas (pronounced *tor-TEE-yas*) or *atole* (*uh-TOW-lay*), a drink made from dried corn and water.

The Spanish introduced pigs and cattle, as well the technique of frying food instead of the healthier way of baking or roasting formerly used by the tribe. Living on reservations during the twentieth and twenty-first centuries, the people ate more store-bought products and government handouts of foods high in fat. American teachers in government-run schools taught the people that their traditional diet was primitive and uncivilized. The Tohono O'odham attribute current problems with obesity to these unhealthy changes in their diet.

Clothing and adornment

The Tohono O'odham wore clothing appropriate for the desert. Men usually wore nothing more than a simple deerskin loincloth, a garment with front and back flaps that hung from the waist. Women wore skirts or aprons made of a single hide or two hides joined together. Their skirts might also be made of willow bark or cloth. Both men and women wrapped themselves in rabbit-skin blankets when it was cold. Sandals could be made of fiber or of hide. The people tattooed and painted their bodies, wore turquoise earrings, and kept their hair long.

After the Catholic missionaries arrived, the tribe adopted European-style dress. Some modern Tohono O'odham women continue to wear the skirts and blouses typical of Mexican peasants of the nineteenth and early twentieth centuries.

Tools

In the 1830s, the Tohono O'odham began to use calendar sticks on which they carved circles and dot to mark important events. To record nonreligious happenings they cut notches into the stick. Other tools they found useful were *kuibits,* special long poles that were handy for dislodging saguaro fruit from a cactus.

Healing practices

Healers called shamans (pronounced *SHAH-munz* or *SHAY-munz*) could both cause and cure sickness, and they could put spells on enemies or predict rainfall. In the old days, the Tohono O'odham regarded shamans with some suspicion, and from time to time, they killed those they blamed for epidemics (terrible outbreaks of sicknesses). The shaman was often a lonely person, shunned because of his powers. Christianity discouraged belief in the power of shamans, but the Tohono O'odham continued to treat them with a combination of respect and fear.

Tohono O'odham shamans divided disease into two different types: "wandering" sickness and "staying" sickness. The "wandering" sicknesses

A Tohono O'ohdham woman makes a basket, a traditional skill that has been important to the tribe's economy.
© AURORA PHOTOS/ALAMY.

were infectious diseases such as the ones Europeans brought with them into the New World. They were called "wandering" sicknesses because others brought them, they were infectious and passed from person to person, and they came and went. "Wandering" sicknesses had to be cured by Western medicine.

Only the Tohono O'odham came down with "staying" sicknesses. They never spread to other races, and they were never completely eliminated. "Staying" sicknesses resulted from not respecting animals, plants, lightning, wind, or the ocean. If such a sickness went untreated for too long, the patient could die. The shaman diagnosed the sickness by blowing smoke over the victim and calling on the spirits to make sure of his diagnosis. The actual process of curing the victim was turned over to specialists in ritual, who knew the songs that were needed to remove the sick-making spirit and make peace with it. The songs acted like prayers and sometimes brought almost immediate relief to the sufferers.

By the 1970s, the rituals and cures of the shamans were falling into disuse, and the only role left for them was that of naming the illness. Curing was left to experts at modern hospitals and clinics. Many Tohono O'odham today value the abilities of shamans because they provide a connection to the past; they also encourage people to reconsider the way they have been living.

ARTS

Basket making

An important Tohono O'odham custom that is still successful in modern times is making traditional baskets. Except for the storage of food, the Tohono O'odham did not use clay pottery like other southwestern tribes because it was too heavy to be carried from winter to summer villages. Instead, they made baskets from desert plants, including green yucca, beargrass, devil's claw, and white willow. Burden baskets were designed to be carried by women, but in the 1880s, the Tohono O'odham began manufacturing them for the tourist trade.

During the Great Depression (1929–41; the period, following the stock market crash in 1929, of depressed world economies and high unemployment), the federal government set up the Papago Arts and Crafts Board to market (advertise and sell) these baskets. Many were "novelty" items—baskets in the shape of cacti, dogs, or humans—but others were beautiful works of art, and they helped support the tribe during a long period of drought and poverty.

Popular music

Waila, or chicken scratch music, is popular dance music among the Tohono O'odham people. *Waila* comes from the Spanish word *baile,* meaning "dance," and is a version of country-western dance and music. It probably came across the Mexican border in the mid-1800s, and the Tohono O'odham musicians were also influenced by the polka music brought to Texas by German settlers. Chicken scratch music makes use of guitars, saxophones, and the accordion-like instrument called a concertina.

CUSTOMS

Childrearing

Parents taught their children to be calm, modest, hardworking, giving, and quiet. Children were not to express anger or get into fights. Being generous and soft-spoken were traits the Tohono O'odham valued; in fact, they looked for these traits in their village headmen, who were also expected to have a sense of humor.

Marriage and divorce

Tohono O'odham couples married young. A girl's parents arranged her marriage after puberty; young men married at about age sixteen. The newlyweds usually moved in with the husband's parents until they had children, at which time they built a house of their own. Both husbands and wives could have more than one spouse, and divorce was easy to obtain, even for a cause such as a bad temper.

Death and burial customs

When warriors died, they were cremated, but other people, dressed in their finery, were buried in caves or stone houses along with their possessions. After a person died, the Tohono O'odham destroyed the person's house and killed the horses.

Traditional Tohono O'ohdham youth dancers participate in a fiesta at Tumacacori National Monument in Arizona.
© TOM BEAN/CORBIS.

Festivals and ceremonies

Traditional rituals Tohono O'odham life was rich with ceremonies, and many of them are still practiced. Among the major ceremonies and celebrations are Chelkona, the cleansing ceremony, the Prayerstick Festival, Saguaro Festival, and salt pilgrimages.

The Chelkona ceremony is a dance performed by boys and girls. They ask for rain and fertile fields and carry symbols representing rainbows, lightning, birds, and clouds. The winter hunting season opens with a cleansing ceremony, in which the people kill a deer and cook it along with items from the recent harvest. Participants sing, dance, and give speeches. This cleansing ceremony is still performed in Mexico, ten days before the Prayerstick Festival.

The Prayerstick Festival is a joyous occasion in which the people ask the spirits to bring rain and keep the world orderly for another year.

As part of the festivities, people sprinkle corn-meal around, corn dancers perform, and clowns, singers, and musicians entertain. Prayersticks, carved and painted sticks adorned with feathers and shells, are made and passed out to all the participants.

The Saguaro festival opens the rainy season. All the women of a village gather to make cactus wine, and there is much singing, dancing, and reciting of poems.

Salt pilgrimages were annual trips young men made to the Gulf of California. Pilgrims made the trip four years in a row with little food, water, or sleep on the way. Upon reaching their destination, the participants made offerings of prayersticks and cornmeal, before running into the gulf. Sometimes they experienced visions while performing this ritual, and the visions gave them guidance on how to lead their lives.

Catholic celebrations The Tohono O'odham observe many Catholic feast days. Their celebra-tion honoring the memory of Patron Saint Francis Xavier at San Xavier Mission dates back to the mission's founding in 1692. Such festivities are a way of maintaining contact with other members of the tribe. Other major festivals are San Juan's Day (June 24); a pilgrimage to Magdalena, Sonora (Mexico), on the Feast of St. Francis (October 4); and the annual rodeo and craft festival.

Village People

The groups of Pima people who shared a common language called themselves *o'odham*, meaning "the people." They distinguished themselves and each other by their three different lifestyles. The Tohono O'odham were "Two Villagers"; they spent half the year in one village, then during the second half of the year they moved to another place for new food resources. In times of extreme drought or famine, they joined the Akimel O'odham (Pima), the "River People," and helped them harvest their crops in return for food and water.

The Akimel O'odham lived in river valleys where there was a relatively constant supply of water, and had no need to move to find fresh food supplies. Because they stayed in one place year round, they were called "One Villagers."

The third group was the Hiac'ed O'odham, sometimes called the Sand Papagos. They practiced an entirely nomadic lifestyle, mov-ing from place to place in search of whatever food the desert had to offer. As more and more people moved into southern Arizona at the beginning of the twentieth century, the Hiac'ed O'odham found that they could no longer follow their traditional way of life. They settled down and were absorbed into other Native populations.

CURRENT TRIBAL ISSUES

Health problems

Many Tohono O'odham suffer from health problems such as obesity and alcoholism. Like the Pima, they have a high rate of diabetes, a serious disorder in which the body does not make enough insulin. Many tribe members participate in medical studies to help doctors determine the causes and possible cures for this disease. The Tohono O'odham are ideal candidates for medical studies because researchers can study several generations of a family at one time to find hereditary causes. The people themselves have been changing their diets and lifestyles to help lower their risk of diabetes.

U.S.-Mexico border

Because the U.S. reservation shares a border with Mexico and about 2,000 tribal members live south of that border, the Tohono O'odham Nation opposed the Secure Fence Act, passed in 2006. The government planned to close the border off with triple fences to prevent illegal immigrants from crossing into the United States. However, that also would have eliminated Tohono O'odham access. The Tohono O'odham north of the border attend festivals in Mexico, and Mexican Tohono O'odham often come north for health care and other services.

Illegal border crossings pose additional problems for the Tohono O'odham; tribal police detain as many as six thousand immigrants per year. The police also have to deal with dead bodies on tribal land; many of those attempting the border crossing are in poor health, and the deprivations of the trip are too much for them. The Tohono O'odham estimate that dealing with the immigration problem costs them millions every year, an expense the Nation funds through casino profits.

One additional problem for some of the Tohono O'odham is the fact that they do not have U.S. documentation. Because the reservation is a sovereign (independent) nation rather than a part of the United States, the people do not get U.S. birth certificates. Guards at border crossings often stop them, believing they are illegal immigrants. People living near the border also face dangers from smugglers, who may be heavily armed, and from desperate and starving immigrants who steal food or money to survive. Crime rates in the border area have increased rapidly, especially car thefts.

Preserving sacred sites

Since 1950, the Tohono O'odham have leased their sacred mountain, Iolkam, to Kitt Peak National Observatory. The observatory has twenty-three telescopes and is the largest in the world. In 2005, the Tohono O'odham Nation sued the National Science Foundation to prevent them from building VERITAS, or the Very Energetic Radiation Imaging Telescope Array System, in the Gardens of the Sacred Spirit I'itoi. The

Tohono O'odham felt their rights were violated because the project was initiated without consulting them, and as owners, they want to approve any additional installations on the land.

Court cases

Because they believed the Bureau of Indian Affairs mismanaged tribal funds, the Tohono O'odham filed two lawsuits against the federal government, but in 2010 a case was dismissed; the tribe was told it could not pursue two cases at the same time. That decision affects not only the Tohono O'odham, but many other Native nations seeking restitution. Also in 2010, the government offered a settlement of $3.4 billion to be divided among all the Native nations whose money had been mismanaged. The nations must choose whether they want to take the settlement or continue their lawsuits against the government.

Other lawsuits involving the Tohono O'odham Nation are ones that have been filed to prevent them from constructing another casino. The city where they hoped to build their gaming facility is determine to stop them; the state even gave the city permission to annex the land, which the Tohono O'odham say is unlawful. In addition, the state of Arizona and the Gila River Indian Community also introduced lawsuits in 2011 to block the casino; they contend that the Tohono O'odham facility will violate an agreement the state made in 2002 with various tribes who already own casinos in Arizona.

NOTABLE PEOPLE

Ofelia Zepeda (1954–) is a language scholar who has done much to preserve O'odham culture. She was one of seven children and the first member of her family to graduate from high school and enter college. Zepeda vividly recalled her two reasons for seeking higher education in an interview for *Notable Native Americans*: "It is sort of a philosophy that we have in O'odham culture … a lot of responsibility made sense. My second reason for attending college was to avoid working as a farm laborer. It was hard work, work that children were required to do. More than any of my other siblings, I was disinclined [unwilling] to do farm labor work." Zepeda's highly regarded O'odham language dictionary, *A Papago Grammar,* was published in 1983. She also wrote other books, including *Ocean Power: Poems from the Desert* and *Home Places: Contemporary Native American Writing from Sun Tracks.*

Thomas Segundo (1921–1971) was born on the Papago Reservation in southern Arizona, but he left as a young man to settle in California. He returned to his homeland in 1946 and found so many in need among his people that he stayed to help. He was elected tribal chairperson in 1951, becoming the youngest Native chief in the United States. Segundo worked to revive the tribal government and increase tribal income. After seven terms as tribal chairperson, he went to the University of Chicago for courses in law and social science and then returned to his home with high hopes of improving conditions there. Segundo introduced conservation measures to increase rangeland for cattle ranchers and improve irrigation programs for farmers. He knew, though, that even after reservation land was productive, one-third of the Tohono O'odham people would have to find work off the reservation. He tried to provide the training and education they needed for these careers. Segundo also proposed the construction of boarding schools for children and expanded public health facilities.

Another notable Tohono O'odham is the dancer and painter Michael Chicago (1946–). He danced at the World's Fair in 1964 and also received national recognition for his art. In 1997, he illustrated the picture book, *Singing Down the Rain*.

BOOKS

Bahr, Donald. *How Mockingbirds Are: O'odham Ritual Orations.* Albany: State University of New York Press, 2011.

Erickson, Winston P. *Sharing the Desert: The Tohono O'Odham in History.* Tucson: University of Arizona Press, 2003.

Jacoby, Karl. *Shadows at Dawn: A Borderlands Massacre and the Violence of History.* New York: Penguin Press, 2008.

Marshall, Ann. *Rain: Native Expressions from the American Southwest.* Phoenix, AZ: Heard Museum, 2000.

McIntyre, Allan J. and the Arizona Historical Society. *The Tohono O'odham and Pimeria Alta.* Charleston, SC: Arcadia Publishing, 2008.

Underhill, Ruth. *The Papago Indians of Arizona and Their Relatives the Pima.* Whitefish, MT: Kessinger Publishing, 2010.

Zepeda, Ofelia. *Where Clouds Are Formed: Poems.* Tucson: University of Arizona Press, 2008.

PERIODICALS

Carroll, Susan. "Tribe Fights Kitt Peak Project." *The Arizona Republic.* March 24, 2005. Available online at http://www.nathpo.org/News/Sacred_Sites/News-Sacred_Sites109.htm (accessed on July 20, 2011).

WEB SITES

Ak-Chin Indian Community. http://www.ak-chin.nsn.us/ (accessed on July 20, 2011).

"Ak-Chin Indian Reservation." *Northern Arizona University.* www.cba.nau.edu/caied/tribepages/AkChin.asp (accessed on July 20, 2011).

"A Coyote's Tales—Tohono O'odham." *First People: American Indian Legends.* http://www.firstpeople.us/FP-Html-Legends/A_Coyotes_Tales-TohonoOodham.html (accessed on July 20, 2011).

Field Division of Education. "Material Culture of the Pima, Papago, and Western Apache." *National Park Service.* http://www.cr.nps.gov/history/online_books/berkeley/beals1/beals1i.htm (accessed on July 20, 2011).

Gross, Greg. "Triple Fence along Border Would Split Indian Nation." *SignOnSanDiego.com,* October 22, 2006. Available online at http://www.signonsandiego.com/news/nation/20061022-9999-1n22tohono.html (accessed on July 20, 2011).

"Ha:sañ Bak: The Saguaro Harvest." *StoryTrail.com.* http://storytrail.com/pages/Saguaroharvest.html (accessed on July 20, 2011).

Kitt Peak National Observatory. "Tohono O'odham." *Association of Universities for Research in Astronomy.* http://www.noao.edu/outreach/kptour/kpno_tohono.html (accessed on July 20, 2011).

Meeks, Heather, Michael Mensah, and Ashley Cobb. "Waila Music." *University of Arizona.* http://parentseyes.arizona.edu/msw/waila/index.html (accessed on July 20, 2011).

"O'odham (O'odham ñiok)." *Omniglot.* http://www.omniglot.com/writing/oodham.htm (accessed on July 20, 2011).

"Pima-Papago—Religion and Expressive Culture." *Countries and Their Cultures.* http://www.everyculture.com/North-America/Pima-Papago-Religion-and-Expressive-Culture.html (accessed on July 20, 2011).

Redish, Laura, and Orrin Lewis. "Tohono O'odham (Papago) and Akimel O'odham (Pima)." *Native Languages of the Americas.* http://www.native-languages.org/papago.htm (accessed on July 20, 2011).

Tohono O'odham Community Action. www.tocaonline.org/ (accessed on July 20, 2011).

"Tohono O'odham (Papago)." *Four Directions Institute.* http://www.fourdir.com/tohono_o'odham.htm (accessed on July 20, 2011).

"Tohono O'Odham Pottery." *ClayHound Web.* http://www.clayhound.us/sites/tohono.htm (accessed on July 20, 2011).

Yaqui

Name

The name Yaqui (pronounced *YAH-kee*) came from the river called Rio Yaqui, along which the people lived. Rio Yaqui most likely meant "chief river." The tribe has also been called *Cáhita,* which is the name of their language. They refer to themselves as *Yoeme* (sometimes spelled *Yueme*). The plural form of their name, *Yoemem,* means "the people."

Location

The Yaqui lived along the Yaqui River in Sonora, present-day northwestern Mexico. They claimed about 6,000 square miles (15,500 square kilometers) around what later became the Mexican cities of Sonora, Guaymas, and Ciudad Obregón. In the early twenty-first century, the Yaqui reside in Mexico and on the Pascua Yaqui Reservation in southern Arizona. Some Yaqui still live in the Tucson area, although the city took over their original village in 1952. Arizona Yaqui reside in four communities in the Tucson area in addition to Penjamo in Scottsdale, Guadalupe in Tempe, and High Town in Chandler.

Population

Prior to European arrival there may have been as many as 30,000 Yaqui. In 1760 about 62,000 Yaqui lived in the Sonora and Yaqui River areas. That number dropped significantly to 11,501 by 1822. It reached a low of between 7,000 to 9,000 in 1932. In the 2000 U.S. Census, 15,632 people identified themselves as Yaqui only, while 23,414 claimed some Yaqui heritage. About 16,000 Yaqui resided in Mexico in 1993. In 1995, combined census figures reported 74,518 Yaqui in the two countries. In 2004, tribal sources reported an enrollment of 3,002 for the Pascua Yaqui Tribe of Arizona In the 2010 U.S. Census, 21,679 Yaqui were counted, and 32,595 people claimed some Yaqui ancestry.

Language family

Uto-Aztecan.

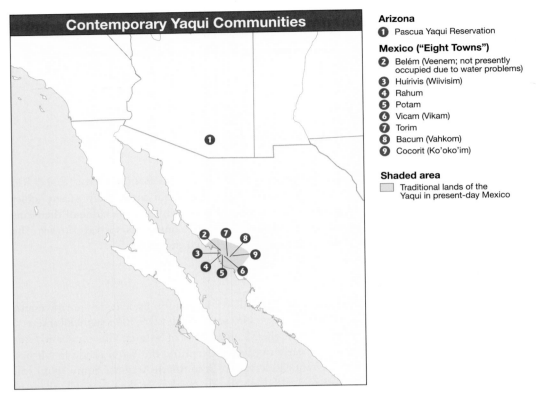

Contemporary Yaqui Communities

Arizona
1. Pascua Yaqui Reservation

Mexico ("Eight Towns")
2. Belém (Veenem; not presently occupied due to water problems)
3. Huírivis (Wiivisim)
4. Rahum
5. Potam
6. Vicam (Vikam)
7. Torim
8. Bacum (Vahkom)
9. Cocorit (Ko'oko'im)

Shaded area
Traditional lands of the Yaqui in present-day Mexico

A map of contemporary Yaqui communities. MAP BY XNR PRODUCTIONS. CENGAGE LEARNING, GALE. REPRODUCED BY PERMISSION OF GALE, A PART OF CENGAGE LEARNING.

Origins and group affiliations

Descendants of the Toltec, the Yaqui traded with tribes throughout northern Mexico and the south-central United States, including the Comanche, Pima, Shoshone, Pueblo, and Aztecs. The Yaqui, along with many other groups in the Sonora area, spoke a dialect of Cáhita. During the 1700s many of these Cáhita-speaking tribes were absorbed into the Yaqui and Mayo communities.

Although the Yaqui are classified as a Southwest tribe, their lifestyle more closely resembled that of Native tribes to the north. They hunted and foraged, but they also cultivated fields. They believed their land to be sacred. According to their oral history, the singing of angels (*batnaataka*) had defined the boundaries in ancient times, so the Yaqui fought to protect their land from invasion. Known for their independence, they refused to be dominated and thus maintained their culture. They did, however, incorporate many Catholic beliefs and rituals into their traditional religious life.

Yaqui Indians in traditional costumes and animal masks are chased by others dressed in Euro-American clothing as part of a ceremony depicting hunting rituals in the early 1900s. LIBRARY OF CONGRESS.

HISTORY

Early Yaqui society

By 552, the tribe, descendants of the Toltecs, lived in small family groups from the Yaqui River in present-day Sonora, Mexico, to the Gila River. In addition to hunting and gathering, they grew vegetables and traded with other tribes. They traveled through what is now northern Mexico and the south-central United States to exchange goods with other tribes in those areas. Sometimes they even lived among these groups, but by 1414, they had become a distinct and united tribe.

Before the Europeans arrived, the Yaqui lived in rancherías (small clusters of huts) scattered along the banks of the lower Yaqui River. These eighty rancherías were spread over a distance of approximately 60 miles (100 kilometers). Most settlements had fewer than 250 people who lived in dome-shaped houses close to the edge of the river.

Resistance to outside rule

In 1533, the first Spaniards entered the area led by conquistador Nuño de Guzmán (c. 1490–1544). The Yaqui asserted their rights to their territory by drawing a line in the dirt and insisting they would fight anyone

Important Dates

1533: Spaniards led by Nuño de Guzmán enter Yaqui territory.

1609–10: Spanish and Native Americans attack Yaqui three different times; the Yaqui sign a peace treaty with Spain.

1740: The Yaqui revolt.

1821: Mexico gains its independence from Spain.

1880s: The Mexican government deports the Yaqui to work on plantations in the Yucatán.

1886: Almost four thousand Yaqui are captured by the Mexican army in the Battle of Buatachive.

1927: Another Yaqui uprising results in a settlement, and the tribe gains the rights to land along the Yaqui River.

1952: The original forty-acre Pascua Village becomes the property of the city of Tucson, Arizona.

1964: The U.S. government grants 202 acres to the Pascua Yaqui in Arizona.

1978: The Pascua Yaqui Tribe of Arizona receives federal recognition.

1982: The Yaqui tribe receives 690 additional acres.

1988: The Pascua Yaqui Constitution is signed by the Bureau of Indian Affairs.

1994: The Casino of the Sun opens.

who crossed it. The Spanish ignored the warning but turned back when they lost many men. Over the next centuries, the Yaqui continued to defend their land.

Beginning in 1609, a small force of Spanish soldiers, aided by approximately four thousand Native peoples, attacked the Yaqui. When that attempt failed, they tried twice more. Each time, the Yaqui were successful in repelling the stronger forces. Nevertheless, they agreed to sign a peace treaty with Spain in 1610.

Lifestyle changes

Soon the Catholics built missions, creating the "Eight Towns." The missionaries convinced the Yaqui to move to the vicinities around the eight churches and form permanent settlements. Adobe buildings were constructed, and the Yaqui changed from ranchería dwellers to pueblo, or town, people. (Adobe, pronounced *uh-DOE-bee,* is sun-dried mud made of a mixture of clay, sand, and sometimes ashes, stones, twigs, and straw.) They also accepted the Jesuits' religious instruction. Although outwardly tribe members appeared to be Catholic, they continued to practice their own religion and kept their traditional customs. They also did not consider themselves subject to Spanish rule.

When a Yaqui prospector, Antonio Siraumea, discovered silver in 1736, miners flocked to the area. Siraumea filed a claim, and the court decided he had a legal right to the land. Still more people joined the Silver Rush; many settled on sacred Yaqui land. By 1740, the Yaqui had banded with a neighboring tribe, the Mayo, to defend their land. These battles were to continue for almost two centuries as the Yaqui fought first the Spanish, then the Mexicans.

Yaqui leadership

During these ongoing clashes, several strong Yaqui leaders emerged. The first, Juan Banderas (c. 1795–1833), attempted to unite the Opata, Mayo, and Pima (see entry) with the Yaqui to form their own nation. For two years, he gathered a force around him and succeeded in pushing the Mexican capital south, but he was captured and killed in 1833.

War took a heavy toll on the tribe. In 1868, a large group of Yaqui men, women, and children were disarmed and locked in a church. All night long the Mexicans fired on the church, killing 120 to 150 of the 600 people inside. That and a smallpox epidemic dropped the tribe's numbers to 4,000. Still the Yaqui continued to fight.

Cajemé (1837–1887) followed in Banderas's footsteps and encouraged the Yaqui to unite and declare their independence. A Mexican military leader and a Yaqui, Cajemé was honored with the post of alcalde mayor, and used his position to fight for Yaqui rights. He insisted that he would not recognize the Mexican government unless his people could rule themselves.

After his home was burned and his family terrorized, he retaliated by attacking ranches, the railroad, and ships in port. In response, the Mexicans, under president Porfirio Diaz (1830–1915), began a campaign against the Yaquis. Tens of thousands of Yaqui were sold as slaves to work on Yucatán plantations; a large number of the people fled to Arizona. They continued to support their relatives in Mexico, though, by sending guns and supplies. In 1886, almost four thousand Yaquis were captured during the Battle of Buatachive.

Cajemé was apprehended and executed in 1887, and the Mexican army occupied Yaqui land. The government sent surveyors to divide the land, but the Yaqui, who believed in holding all land in common, rebelled. Their knowledge of the rugged terrain of that area allowed them to hold off their better-equipped attackers.

Short-lived peace

In 1897, the Yaqui signed a peace treaty with Mexico, but not all of the people agreed with this action. More than four hundred of them went into the Bacatete Mountains to defy the government. Within a few years, the Sonoran governor, Izabal, ordered Yaquis arrested. Men, women, and children were rounded up. If the prisoners gave information on the rebels, they were set free, but their fellow Yaquis despised them. Those

Congressman Morris Udall of Arizona speaks during the Democratic National Convention in 1988. © BILL PIERCE/ TIME LIFE PICTURES/GETTY IMAGES.

who had no information or refused to comply were divided into three groups. One group was shot, one deported, and one set free.

Between 1902 and 1908, approximately eight thousand to fifteen thousand of the thirty thousand Yaqui were deported. Again many Yaqui took refuge in the United States. A few years later, other families moved to Arizona to avoid the bloodshed during the Mexican Revolution (1910–20).

In 1916, Sonora's governor, Adolfo de la Huerta (1881–1955), who was part Yaqui, attempted to restore Yaqui land and resolve differences. The nation's next president, Alvaro Obregón (1880–1928), reversed those decisions, and fighting began again. The Yaqui's final battle occurred in 1927 at Cerro del Gallo (Hill of the Rooster). Mexico set up military posts in all the Yaqui villages. Although the Yaqui ceased fighting, they still say they were undefeated.

Changes for the better

In 1939, Mexican president Lázaro Cárdenas (1895–1970) instituted many reforms. In addition to outlawing capital punishment (which in Mexico consisted of firing squads) and building roads, he changed the policies toward the Yaqui. He not only granted the tribe official recognition, he gave them title to their land.

In the United States, thanks to the urging of Congressman Morris Udall (1922–1998), the Pascua Yaquis were given 202 acres of desert land in 1964. On September 18, 1978, the Pascua Yaqui Tribe of Arizona received federal recognition. This meant that they became an independent nation and that they were also eligible for federal funding and benefits. This improved life for the Yaquis.

The Yaquis, however, are trying to get both the United States and Mexico to honor treaties that allow the people free access between the two countries. Because ties between the Yaqui in both countries are strong, the people often travel from one country to the other to visit relatives or attend festivals. Present border policies make this difficult.

RELIGION

Creation story

The Yaqui believe the Creator made ocean animals first; some of these moved onto the land and became humans called *Surem.* At first, these Yaqui ancestors dwelt in peace, but then God, speaking through a small tree, warned the people of future troubles. When the Surem heard that invaders would try to take their land, some turned themselves into a tall, strong people called Yo'emem, or Yaquis, and trained themselves to fight. The Surem who chose not to fight returned to live inside the mountain. Some say they turned into ants.

Yaqui beliefs

Early Yaqui lived in the world of *Huya Aniya* (or *anía*), the realm of timeless events. This world was divided into four parts: the world of animals, the world of flowers, the world of people, and the world of death. None of this changed when the Jesuit missionaries arrived and converted the people to Christianity.

Prior to the arrival of the missionaries, the Yaquis had been sun worshipers, so when Christian missionaries pointed to the sky in reference to God in Heaven, they thought the missionaries were speaking of *Itom Achai Taa'a,* "Our Father Sun." Thus, the Yaquis accepted the Jesuits and integrated Catholic beliefs into their ceremonies and dances, among them the Deer, Pascola, Coyote, Raccoon, and Naji (Water-fly) Dances. In modern times, they retain many of these traditions, but their dances revolve around Christian holy days. The goal of these rituals is to improve the world and eliminate harm or evil. Most Yaqui believe that their yearly Easter rituals play a major role in sustaining the world.

Yaqui Words

The Yaqui often use sounds or gestures to make their intent clear as some words have more than one meaning. They also have many words for relatives. Names that describe kin on the mother's side are different from those on the father's. Males and females use different terms for most family members.

When greeting each other, the Yaqui are very formal, even with close friends. Four ways to say "hello" are listed below under "Greetings." Some common Yaqui words are also included.

Greetings

Aman ne tevote em yevihnewi	"I extend my greetings."
Lios em chania	"God preserve you."
Lios em chiokoe	"God pardons you."
Empo allea	"May you rejoice."

Other Yaqui Words

o'ow	"man"
hamut	"woman"
halla'i	"friend"
maaso	"deer"
taa'a	"sun"
meecha	"moon"
vaa'am	"water"

LANGUAGE

About fifteen thousand Yaqui speak their original language, Cáhita, part of the Uto-Aztecan family. Quite a few people are trilingual (speak three languages). Many Yaqui who live near the U.S.-Mexican border speak Spanish and English in addition to their native language. Many vowels and several consonants in the Yaqui language are pronounced similarly to Spanish.

One unusual feature of the language is called *sound symbolism.* The way Yaqui speakers pronounce certain vowels reveals how they feel about something. The pronunciation can show approval or disapproval. Certain words can also have opposite meanings; watching a speaker's hands is the only way to tell what he or she intends to say. For example, *laute* is used for both "slow" and "fast." Rapid hand movements indicate "quickly," while leisurely motions mean "slowly."

GOVERNMENT

The Sonora Yaquis still use the traditional form of government. Important issues are discussed at a village council, called a *junta.* Council members include five *kobanaom* (governors), the *pueplo yo'owe* (former governors or elders), the *sontaom* (military society), church officials, and members of ceremonial societies. This group makes all tribal decisions.

Problems that arise between members of different pueblos are solved through joint meetings of the councils of both towns. The opinion of the elders is always respected. Ritual and prayers are a part of every meeting. Traditional punishments included being put in stocks or receiving lashes from a rawhide whip that an official, called the *alawasin,* carried around his waist.

In 1934, the Pascua tribe organized under the Indian Reorganization Act and now has a eleven-member elected tribal council that includes a chairperson, vice chairperson, treasurer, and secretary. In 1988, they adopted a constitution. Biweekly council meetings and community meetings occur regularly in the council chambers in Tucson.

ECONOMY

Early economy

In the early days, the Yaqui were farmers who grew corn, beans, and squash. Like the Pima (see entry) they also raised cotton and made cloth products. The people exchanged food, fur, shells, salt, and other goods with many of the Southwestern tribes as well as the Aztecs. Many who lived along the rivers also fished. In addition, for much of their history, they served as skillful warriors.

Pascua Yaqui economy

At the start of the twenty-first century, the three major sources of employment for the Pascua Yaqui included tribal government, gaming, and tourism. Tribal government is the largest employer on the reservation. In the 1990s, the Yaqui opened a bingo hall and casino. Since 2001, the Casino of the Sun has netted the tribe more income than any other enterprise; it also employs quite a few Yaqui people. Income from the casino funds many educational and social programs.

To attract businesses to the reservation, the tribe offers tax incentives in addition to the state of Arizona's special job training funds. They also operate several businesses of their own, including a plant nursery, a pet lodge, a smoke shop, a gas station, and a plant that manufactures adobe bricks.

In spite of the strides they have made, the unemployment rate in 2000 was 18 percent. This was lower than that of many other reservations but still much higher than the rest of the United States. Per capita income was only $5,921 compared to the average national income of $21,587.

In 2006, the Pascua Yaqui worked out a Strategic Economic Development Plan to strengthen the economy. One of the components of that plan was instituting a Tribal Enterprise Corporation (TEC) to encourage business development.

A Yaqui Indian girl. LIBRARY OF CONGRESS.

Mexican Yaqui economy

Most Mexican Yaqui retain their traditional farming lifestyle. Many grow wheat in addition to the three staple crops—corn, beans, and squash. Most also raise livestock. Making and selling bamboo mats, willow baskets, or pottery adds to their income. Some receive government support. The largest expenses most Yaqui have are the costs of their lavish ceremonies (see "Religion" and "Festivals").

DAILY LIFE

Families

Several generations often live in the same house. The oldest person in the household is the head of the family, and everyone respects the opinions and decisions of these elders. In addition to parents, every child also has godparents, who are part of the religious ceremonies surrounding a child's birth (see "Birth and naming"). All of these people form a mutual circle of support that make up the larger extended family.

Buildings

The Yaqui lived in rancherías, small clusters of houses, along the banks of the Rio Yaqui (Yaqui River). One of the most important features of their homes were the ramadas, or *hekka*, which were porches open on three sides. Posts held up a roof made of matting or thatch. Ramadas provided shade from the sun and a cool place to sleep on hot nights. The Yaqui built rectangular homes using mesquite poles. The walls were either cane mats or plaited cane coated with mud. Mesquite rafters supported layers of cane to form the roof. Inside, the people had cooking platforms, shelves, and storage bins. Many Yaqui also had cages for pet birds such as parakeets or doves. Most houses had two or three rooms.

After the Spanish arrived, the Jesuits encouraged the people to abandon their rancherías and live in pueblos (villages). The church, built of adobe, was at the center of each town, giving it a place of prominence. In modern times, many people have cross-shaped porches in front of their homes to serve as a reminder of the importance of religion in their lives.

Clothing and adornment

Before European influence, the men may have worn pieces of cloth wrapped around their lower bodies, sometimes secured to look like pants, like the costumes many of them wear now during religious dances. Soon, however, they adopted the typical Spanish dress of that time.

Men wore cotton clothes in a style similar to that of Sonora farmers, but they often carried knives, pistols, or ammunition pouches on their leather belts. They tied colored handkerchiefs around their necks. A sombrero (wide-brimmed straw hat) and cowhide sandals completed their outfits. In Arizona, many men adopted the American custom of wearing boots and ten-gallon hats.

Women wore brightly colored cotton blouses and long, full skirts. Over them, they wore rebozos (lengths of cloth used as shawls). They usually draped a cloth over their heads as well. They braided their long hair and often decorated it with colored ribbons. In the early twenty-first century, many women wear blouses embroidered with beautiful floral designs. These are a reminder to the Yaqui of the importance of the flower world (see "Religion").

Food

As farmers, the Yaqui depended on their crops for survival. Corn, beans, and squash were their staple foods. The Jesuits taught them to grow a variety of fruits, such as figs, peaches, mangoes, and pomegranates, in addition to wheat, sweet potatoes, and spices. Other crops included garlic, onion, melon, and tomatoes. The people also depended on foods that grew naturally—cactus fruit, bean pods, seeds, and wild greens.

Because the Yaqui lived near the water, fish was their main source of meat. Those who lived near the ocean added shellfish to their diets; oysters and swordfish were especially popular. Men rarely hunted, but if they did, they generally went after small game such as rats or rabbits, or sometimes a deer. After the Spanish introduced them to raising livestock, the Yaqui had ready supplies of cattle, sheep, and goats for both meat and milk.

Education

Traditionally, Yaqui children were trained to be cooperative and think first of the group. The students' culture and beliefs often conflicted with what they were taught once they attended public schools. For example, whereas schools stressed competition, the Yaqui believed in working for the benefit of others. Cultural differences caused difficulties for many Yaqui students. In 1985, a group of educational researchers identified some of these problems, and many schools adapted their teaching methods to accommodate Yaqui learning styles.

On the Pascua Yaqui Reservation, students in grades K–12 attend Tucson public schools. Younger children have a preschool or Head Start program. Adult and continuing education classes are also available. In addition, the Yaqui have support services for those who need help or tutoring, scholarship programs for college, and a computer lab where community members can access the Internet and take classes to improve their knowledge. The tribe also has language development programs to pass on tribal knowledge and history to the next generation.

Healing practices

Yaqui healers used both herbs and prayers to cure illness. They also needed to be skilled in identifying witches. Healers used dreams to do this, then held the proper ceremonies to cure the village or person who had been afflicted.

Some Yaqui today still use the ancient healing methods, which may date back as far as 2000 BCE. According to one present-day healer, however, most of this sacred knowledge has been kept secret since the Spanish arrived and was only passed down privately in oral traditions. Although modern healers do not rule out surgery or medicine as last resorts, they believe most illnesses, including emotional and mental problems, can be cured with plants.

This science of healing is based on a reverence for and understanding of plants. Grandfather Kachora, a Yaqui healer, explained in an interview posted on the Web site for the Wisdom Traditions Institute that plants "are living things full of energy of many kinds. They are filled with information and knowledge. It is possible to listen to a plant in such a way that this knowledge is imparted to one and assists one."

Along with the benefits of herbs, Yaqui healers also depend on spiritual assistance from the Great Spirit. Purifying the body and mind is an important step in the healing process. A sweat lodge, or *temescal,* is a building for this purpose. Water is poured over hot rocks to create steam. Inner cleansing may also be practiced by fasting (not eating or drinking).

Many Yaqui in modern times rely on both traditional and modern treatments for illness. On the Pascua reservation, the Yaqui Healer's House combines an alternative medicine program with community health services such as diabetes programs, mental health services, substance abuse programs, and a dialysis center. In addition to a health clinic, they have hospitals operated through the Indian Health Service.

ARTS

Along with the intricate and brightly colored floral designs embroidered on their clothing and their pottery making, the Yaqui are known for making masks. These masks are worn during religious ceremonies. Made from wood or paper, they are decorated in a variety of ways to represent different animals (butterflies, bulls, goats, owls, bats, and rabbits) or characters. Others have stylized designs. Although these are works of art, there are certain taboos associated with them. Masks are sacred and should never be given away or sold. They also may not be touched by other people, nor should they be stared at closely.

Music, dance, and drama are an important part of these ceremonies as well. As with many things in the Yaqui culture, music reflects their dual heritage. People may sing *alabanzas* (Spanish word for hymns) and use European instruments, such as the harp or violin. Yet the songs of the Deer Singers and the accompanying instruments—*tenevoim* (strings of rattles made by sewing pebbles into cocoons of the giant silk moth), deer hooves, *tampaleo* (a small water drum played with one stick)—are clearly from a more ancient time. Their drama and dance also merge traditional beliefs with Catholism (see "Festivals").

CUSTOMS

Birth and naming

Godparents had a very important part in Yaqui society. Although this idea is partially based in Catholic tradition, godparents had a much larger role in the tribe. A person could have many different godparents, and it was customary for godparents to take on the responsibility of caring for at least three children in the same family. This practice of having multiple godparents began after the Yaqui fled to Arizona during their ongoing battles with the Mexican government. Some have suggested it came about because people had separated from their families, so they created new ones through the godparent relationship. Another possibility may have been that, with so many Yaqui being killed and deported, a child might lose many godparents over the years.

Marriage

The bride's *pascola* ("old man of the celebration," who acts as host) wears a pink scarf and ties his hair up with a pink ribbon. The musicians at the groom's home are similarly adorned. The pascola, pretending he is a girl crying about leaving her parents' home, carries a basket of toiletries as the procession walks to the groom's home. Other family members carry bundles and baskets of food—tamales, tortillas, sweet bread, and *vannaim* (pudding).

At the groom's home they place the food on a blanket on the front lawn by the patio cross, which is decorated with paper flowers and ribbons. The groom's family stands behind the cross; the bride's family, in front. A sister-in-law tells the bride this is the patio she will sweep. She also shows her where she will cook and wash dishes. The mother-in-law shows the bride where to grind corn.

Then the bride is taken to the room where the groom is waiting. They stay there and eat, while the rest of the party dines outside. Afterward, the couple goes outside to be counseled and advised. The pascolas (entertainers) continue all afternoon (see "Easter Ceremony Participants" sidebar).

Festivals

Deer Dancer On important occasions such as religious holidays, weddings, funerals, and death anniversaries, a *pahko* is held. A pahko is a *fiesta,* or celebration, usually lasting from dusk until dawn. The central part of these festivities is the Deer Dance. Long ago this dance was held before the people went out to hunt deer. Its purpose was to ask the deer's forgiveness for killing it and to thank it for providing food.

The *Maaso,* or Deer Dancer, wears a white cloth covering his hair with a deer head mounted on top. Shaking gourd rattles, he dances to music from rasping sticks and a water drum. The Maaso dances alone, although other performers surround him. Some of these performers include the *Moro* (master of ceremonies); *pahkolam* ("old men of the fiesta" who give sermons, joke with the audience, and act like clowns); a violinist and harpist; a *tampaleo* (musician who plays the drum and flute

The Deer Dance

In this story, Walking Man is traveling through Seye Wailo, the wilderness where people go when they dream. The Yaqui believed the best songs came to people from *Seye Wailo*, or the Flower World.

One day, as Walking Man was out, he heard a sound from a hilltop. It was like a sound he had heard before at the time of year when the deer are mating. It was the clattering of antlers. He knew that the bucks would fight in this way during the mating time, striking their antlers together. But it was not that time of year and this sound was different. It was a softer sound and its rhythm was like that of a song. He went to look, but he could see nothing.

The next morning Walking Man rose before the sun came up and went back to that hilltop. He sat quietly on a fallen tree and waited as the sun rose. He began to hear that sound again, and he looked carefully. There not far from him were two big deer. They had huge antlers and, as they stood facing each other, they rattled their antlers together. Near them was a young deer. As Walking Man watched, he saw that young deer lift its head and lower it. It ran from side to side, leaping up and down. It seemed happy as it did this. Walking Man knew what he was seeing. He was seeing the deer do their own special dance. Though he had his weapons with him, he did not try to kill them. He watched them dance for a long time.

When Walking Man went down that hill, he had a thought in his mind. There were songs coming into his mind. When he rose the next morning, he went out to walk and as he walked he found a newborn fawn where its mother had left it hidden among the flowers. He made a song for that fawn. Then he went to the village and gathered some of his friends.

"I am going to make songs for the deer," he said.

He took two sticks and put notches on one of them so that he could make the sound of the deer's antlers. He showed one of the boys in the village how the young deer danced and had the boy dance that way as they played the deer song and sang.

So it was that the Deer Dance came to the Yaqui people, a gift from the deer, a gift from Seye Wailo.

SOURCE: Bruchac, Joseph. "Native American Animal Stories." In *Keepers of the Animals,* by Michael J. Caduto and Joseph Bruchac. Golden, CO: Fulcrum Publishing, 1992.

at the same time); and deer singers (usually three men, one of whom plays the water drum, which represents the deer's heartbeat).

Pascola, or Easter Ceremony Each Friday in Lent (the weeks before Easter when people prepare for the holiday by giving up certain foods or bad habits), the participants go to the church for prayers and services. On Palm Sunday (one week before Easter), children playing the part of soldiers called *Fariseos* and *Caballeros* go door to door to collect money and food for the fiesta.

Rituals and church services occur every day during the week leading up to Easter, each one symbolizing the life and death of Jesus. The players enact all of the important events including the crucifixion and resurrection.

On Holy Saturday (the day before Easter), the *Maestro* and male singers set up in the fiesta ramada (a roofed shelter with one open side) along with the *Pascolas* and the Deer Dancer. After they have opened the ceremony, the *Matachinis* alternate dancing with rest periods and perform throughout the night. A straw Judas (the man who betrayed Jesus) is hung, and people throw flowers or confetti to "kill" the Fariseos.

To conclude the drama, the Fariseos are draped in black, and their faces are covered with black scarves. *Chapayekas* wave their swords, bells are rung, Pascolas throw flowers, and everyone sings and dances. The Fariseos rush around trying to get into the church, but they are repelled each time. Finally, they run to the straw Judas, who is set on fire. They all throw their masks and weapons into the flames. Their godparents then throw coats over their heads and take them to the church altar to rededicate them to Jesus. Everyone else dances in celebration and then forms a circle around the church cross to listen to the Maestro's sermon.

Other festivals Each town and church holds a Saint's Day Fiesta to honor the patron saint for whom it is named. These celebrations are run like a pahko (fiesta or party) and include feasting, clowning, Pascola dancers, Deer Dancers, and an enactment of a drama.

The Arizona Yaqui remember their history on Tribal Recognition Day on September 18, the date they became a federally recognized tribe. Since 1999, the people have also hosted an annual Harvest Festival at which they sell crafts, produce they have harvested, baked goods, and traditional foods. Live entertainment is also part of this gathering, which is open to public. Other major celebrations throughout the year are saint's feast days.

Easter Ceremony Participants

Two ceremonial societies—the *Fariseos* (foot soldiers) and *Caballeros* (usually horsemen)—take charge of the Easter Ceremony and do all the preparation and clean up. Fariseos represent the people who persecuted Jesus; their leader is called Pilate. Common soldiers, *Cahpayekas*, wear masks with long ears, short horns, and a long nose. They perform all acts left-handed and backwards and mock the other players. Because they are playing the part of evildoers, they hold crosses in their mouths so evil does not enter their hearts. They carry weapons and shake their belts of deer- and pig-hoof rattles, but cannot speak.

The church group plays the parts of Jesus (boys) and Mary (girls); their leaders are the *Maestros*, who preside over the religious services. Many women take part in these—women singers, altar women, girl flag bearers, and bearers of figures of Mary. Young children serve as angels.

Another important society is the *Matachin* dance society, composed of young boys who wear long skirts, embroidered shirts, ribbons sashes, and beads. They wear peaked cane caps with streamers attached to the top called *sewa* (flower). They carry gourd rattles and a feather to represent flowers. They serve as the soldiers of Mary, and their dance on Holy Saturday helps defeat the evil Fariseos.

Other festival dancers are the *Pascolas*, who wear bead necklaces ending in a cross and a cotton blanket around their hips and fastened below their knees. They tie their hair on top of their heads with red ribbon to look like a flower and have cocoon rattles, bells, and a carved wood mask with a long, white horse-hair beard. The Deer Dancer performs with them. To close the fiesta, a Pascola gives a sermon.

CURRENT TRIBAL ISSUES

One problem the Yaqui face is that their tribe lives in two countries. In spite of that, the people have maintained close ties with family members and friends on each side of the border. They like to visit frequently and attend festivals in both Mexico and the United States. This freedom was assured years ago, but with the increase of border patrols, many people now have difficulty crossing the border. They are sometimes mistaken for illegal aliens. To comply with U.S. Homeland Security requirements, the tribe developed the first ETC (Enhanced Tribal Card) that meets all the requirements of the Western Hemisphere Travel Initiative. This card, first used in 2011, takes the place of a passport or birth certificate.

In addition to border crossing difficulties, the Yaqui of Sonora, Mexico, are facing high rates of cancer and birth defects. Even very young people have been dying of cancer, and babies are being born with deformities. Doctors have linked these deaths to the dangerous pesticides and chemicals used to spray the wheat and corn crops. Because many Yaqui work as farm laborers, they have been exposed to these cancer-producing agents on a regular basis. Most of these toxic chemicals have been banned in other countries, but Mexico does not have any import regulations to prevent them from being sold. Members of the tribe began holding educational seminars to inform people of the dangers of working with these pesticides, and the Yaqui issued a declaration that anyone using their land had to submit information on the pesticides they planned to use. Other points in the document forbid aerial spraying, and demanded that the government ensure that the Yaqui communities have drinkable water that is not contaminated by pesticides. They also wanted coverage for medical expenses incurred due to pesticide exposure.

NOTABLE PEOPLE

Juan Ignacio Jusacamea (c. 1795–1833), also called Juan Banderas—*bandera* means "flag" in Spanish—was a Yaqui leader. His flag was designed based on a vision. This vision also inspired him to lead the Yaqui to unite the Native tribes of northwest Mexico. He hoped to create an independent people, but the Yaqui lost to Mexico in 1832, and Banderas was executed the following year.

José María Leyva (or José María Leiba Peres; 1837–1887) is one of the revered Yaqui heroes from Sonora, Mexico. Leyva joined the Mexican army as a young man. He was nicknamed Cajemé, "He Who Does Not Drink," because he could go for long periods of time without water. He moved up to captain and later was appointed governor. As a leader, he stood up for his people's rights, and eventually went to war with Mexico. Historical sources note that Cajemé never tried to expand his territory, only defend it. He led the Yaquis in their fight against Mexico for many years until 1887, when he died in front of a firing squad.

Juan Maldonado (1867–1901) continued defending the Rio Yaqui territory after Cajemé was executed. People called him Tetabiate (or Tetaviakte), meaning "Rolling Stone." He negotiated the peace agreement between Mexico and the Yaqui in 1897. Each year a celebration is held in his honor in July.

BOOKS

Barker, George C. *The Yaqui Easter Ceremony at Hermosillo.* Los Angeles: University of California Press, 1957.

Bogan, Phebe M. *Yaqui Indian Dances of Tucson Arizona: An Account of the Ceremonial Dances of the Yaqui Indians at Pascua.* Whitefish, MT: Kessinger Publishing, 2011.

Erickson, Kirstin C. *Yaqui Homeland and Homeplace.* Tucson: University of Arizona Press, 2008.

Evers, Larry, and Felipe S. Molina. *Yaqui Deer Songs, Maso Bwikam: A Native American Poetry.* Tucson: University of Arizona Press, 1987.

Giddings, Ruth Warner. *Yaqui Myths and Legends.* Charleston, SC: BiblioBazaar, 2009.

Painter, Muriel Thayer. *Faith, Flowers and Fiestas: The Yaqui Indian Year, A Narrative of Ceremonial Events.* Tucson: University of Arizona Press, 1962.

Painter, Muriel Thayer. *With Good Heart: Yaqui Beliefs and Ceremonies in Pascua Village,* edited by Edward Holland Spicer. Tucson: University of Arizona Press, 1986.

Philip, Neil, ed. *A Braid of Lives: Native American Childhood.* New York: Clarion Books, 2000.

Savin, Adolfo. *Yaqui.* Edited by Manuel Aleman. Lawrence, MA: CBH Books, 2010.

Shorter, David Delgado. *We Will Dance Our Truth: Yaqui History in Yoeme Performances.* Lincoln: University of Nebraska Press, 2009.

PERIODICALS

Chilcott, John H. "Yaqui Worldview and the School: Conflict and Accomodation." *Journal of American Indian Education* 24, no. 1 (January 1985).

WEB SITES

"Cahita Indian Tribe History." *Access Genealogy.* http://www.accessgenealogy.com/native/tribes/c/cahita_indian_tribe_history.htm (accessed on July 20, 2011).

Giddings, Ruth Warner. "Yaqui Myths and Legends Index." *1959. Internet Sacred Text Archive.* http://www.sacred-texts.com/nam/sw/yml/index.htm (accessed on July 20, 2011).

"The Great Yaqui Nation." *Manataka American Indian Council.* http://www.manataka.org/page129.html (accessed on July 20, 2011).

"The Pasqu Yaqui Connection." *Through Our Parents' Eyes: History and Culture of Southern Arizona.* http://parentseyes.arizona.edu/pascuayaquiaz/ (accessed on July 20, 2011).

The Pascua Yaqui Tribe. http://www.pascuayaqui-nsn.gov/ (accessed on July 20, 2011).

Redish, Laura, and Orrin Lewis. "Yaqui Indian Language (Yoeme)." *Native Languages of the Americas.* (accessed on July 20, 2011).

"Seyewailo: The Flower World, Yaqui Deer Songs." *Words & Place: Native Literature from the American Southwest.* http://parentseyes.arizona.edu/wordsandplace/seyewailo.html (accessed on July 20, 2011).

"Vachiam Eecha: Planting the Seeds." *Hemispheric Institute of Performance and Politics.* http://hemi.nyu.edu/cuaderno/yoeme/content.html (accessed on July 20, 2011).

"Yaqui." *Four Directions Institute.* http://www.fourdir.com/yaqui.htm (accessed on July 20, 2011).

"Yaqui and Mayo Indian Easter Ceremonies." *RimJournal.* http://www.rimjournal.com/arizyson/easter.htm (accessed on July 20, 2011).

"Yaqui Sacred Traditions." *Wisdom Traditions Institute.* http://www.wisdomtraditions.com/yaqui2.html (accessed on July 20, 2011).

Zoontjens, Linda and Yaomi Glenlivet. "A Brief History of the Yaqui and Their Land." *Sustained Action.* http://www.sustainedaction.org/Explorations/history_of_the_yaqui.htm (accessed on July 20, 2011).

Yuman

Name

Yuman (pronounced *YOO-muhn*). The name may have Spanish roots and might be related to the people's habit of building large fires to attract rain. *Umo* in Spanish means "smoke." It could also come from the Papago (now Tohono O'odham) word *yuumi*. Although many different tribes of the Southwest are called by the name *Yuman,* the word actually refers to a branch of the Hokan language.

Location

The Yuman once lived along the Colorado and Gila rivers, and their territory stretched from western Arizona to southern California in the United States as well as along the Baja Peninsula and into northwestern Sonora in Mexico. In the early twenty-first century, most Yuman live on reservations in Arizona, Nevada, and California and on several reserves in Mexico.

Population

In 1909, there were 3,700 Yuman. The 2000 U.S. Census indicated that 7,972 Yuman lived in the United States; many of those belonged to different tribes. A total of 9,833 people claimed to have some Yuman heritage. According to statistics from the 2000 Mexican census, 1423 Yuman resided there. The 2010 U.S. Census counted 7,727 Yuman, with 10,089 people claiming some Yuman ancestry.

Language family

Hokan.

Origins and group affiliations

Although united by a common language, many Yuman tribes fought among themselves; others allied to fight common enemies. For example, the Yuma headed the Quechan (pronounced *KWUH-tsan*) League, a group that included the Mohave, Paiute, and several other tribes who fought against the Maricopa, Cocopá, and Pima. Other Yuman enemies were the Papago (now Tohono O'odham) and Apache.

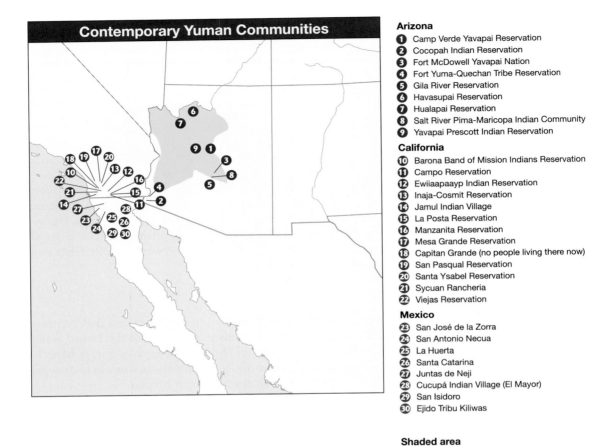

Contemporary Yuman Communities

Arizona
1. Camp Verde Yavapai Reservation
2. Cocopah Indian Reservation
3. Fort McDowell Yavapai Nation
4. Fort Yuma-Quechan Tribe Reservation
5. Gila River Reservation
6. Havasupai Reservation
7. Hualapai Reservation
8. Salt River Pima-Maricopa Indian Community
9. Yavapai Prescott Indian Reservation

California
10. Barona Band of Mission Indians Reservation
11. Campo Reservation
12. Ewiiaapaayp Indian Reservation
13. Inaja-Cosmit Reservation
14. Jamul Indian Village
15. La Posta Reservation
16. Manzanita Reservation
17. Mesa Grande Reservation
18. Capitan Grande (no people living there now)
19. San Pasqual Reservation
20. Santa Ysabel Reservation
21. Sycuan Rancheria
22. Viejas Reservation

Mexico
23. San José de la Zorra
24. San Antonio Necua
25. La Huerta
26. Santa Catarina
27. Juntas de Neji
28. Cucupá Indian Village (El Mayor)
29. San Isidoro
30. Ejido Tribu Kiliwas

Shaded area
Traditional lands of the tribes of the Yuman in present-day Arizona

A map of contemporary Yuman communities. MAP BY XNR PRODUCTIONS. CENGAGE LEARNING, GALE. REPRODUCED BY PERMISSION OF GALE, A PART OF CENGAGE LEARNING.

In modern times, Yuman languages are spoken by the following tribes: Paipai (Akwa'ala), Cocopá (Cocopah, Cucupá), Kumeyaay (Kumiai, Diegueño), Havasupai, Kiliwa (Kiliwi), Maricopa, Mohave, Walapai (Hualapai, Hualpai), Yavapai, and Quechan (formerly Yuma). Although the Cochimí language is extinct, some Kumeyaay (Kumiai) identify themselves as Cochimí.

Many tribes are classified as Yuman, but they are distinct and separate from each other, connected mainly by a shared family of languages. Over the centuries, some of these tribal groups have disappeared or been absorbed into the ten tribes that exist in the early twenty-first century. For much of their history, the Yuman-speaking peoples have fought with each other as well as outsiders. They were skilled warriors who had two other advantages: their isolation and the hot, arid climate. This combination deterred Europeans from colonizing tribal lands until the late 1700s. Even then, the Yuman struggled to preserve their land and culture. In modern times, the tribes maintain their individuality but share many similar customs and traditions.

HISTORY

Earliest history

From about 700 to 1550, the Patayan, possible ancestors of the River and Delta Yuman people, occupied present-day Arizona and California. They roamed the Colorado Valley, the Grand Canyon, and Baja California, Mexico, in nomadic bands. They farmed the floodplains but mainly relied on hunting and gathering. As a division of the Hakatayan culture, they were, along with the Mogollon, Hohokam, and Anasazi (see entry), one of the early subcultures in the Southwest.

Early European contact

Several Spanish explorers passed through Yuman territory during the 1500s, including Hernando de Alarcón, who first saw the Yuman in 1540. The Europeans, however, did not establish permanent settlements in the area for more a century.

The first Spanish colonization of Yuman land began in the early 1600s. Sebastián Vizcaíno (c. 1548–c. 1624) arrived on the Baja Peninsula, Mexico, where eight hundred Yuman warriors waited to defend their territory. Nevertheless, Vizcaíno built a fort at La Paz. The

Important Dates

1540: Hernando de Alarcón first encounters the Yuman.

1687: Father Eusebio Francisco Kino establishes the first of twenty-eight missions in Yuman territory.

1769: Junipero Serro founds the San Diego Mission.

1775: The Kumeyaay revolt and burn the San Diego Mission.

1840: The Kiliwa and Paipai burn the Santa Catalina Mission; the Spanish retaliate by killing five hundred Native people and forcing prisoners to work at other missions.

1850: The U.S. Army builds Fort Yuma.

1857: The Maricopa and Pima help the United States defeat the Quechan Confederacy in the Battle of Maricopa Wells.

1863: Natives lose Walapai Wars.

1872: Many Natives die in Skeleton Cave Massacre.

1875: The U.S. Army forces the Yavapai and Apache to march to the San Carlos Apache Reservation; 115 die along the way.

1975: The Havasupai regain 188,077 acres of former tribal land in the Grand Canyon area.

1978: The U.S. government returns 25,000 acres of Quechan land to the tribe.

Yuman succeeded in driving him off. Not until 1683 did Spain again try to colonize the area. Admiral Isidro Atondo y Antillón soon deserted the settlement due to conflicts with the Natives. The next post established in 1685 was also abandoned.

Mission era

Father Eusebio Francisco Kino (1645–1711), a Jesuit, was one of the first to venture into Yuman territory and stay. He established his first mission in 1687 in present-day Mexico. Kino mapped the Baja Peninsula in 1701 and explored north of the border. During that time he encountered many tribes, including the Pima (see entry) and Yuman. He taught the Pima advanced farming techniques and founded twenty-seven more missions in the area. Most of the missions were built by Native laborers using adobe (pronounced *uh-DOE-bee*; sun-dried mud made of a mixture of clay, sand, and sometimes ashes, stones, twigs, and straw).

Many Native people were attracted to the mission by the food, clothes, and supplies the priests offered. Some of the tribes, such as the Cochimí, readily converted to Christianity. To keep the new converts close to the church and to ensure a steady supply of labor, the priests encouraged the people to live in small settlements near the mission called *rancherías*. Unfortunately, the close quarters caused the rapid spread of European diseases to which the Native Americans had no immunity. The worst outbreak of disease was the typhus epidemic of 1742–44, which killed about eight thousand Native people. This and other epidemics completely wiped out many smaller tribes and left others struggling to survive.

In 1767, the king of Spain removed all the Jesuit missionaries. Dominican missionaries came instead, and they concentrated their efforts on the Yuman tribes, particularly the Cochimí, Kiliwa, Paipai, and Kumeyaay. Almost a century after Father Kino had started his first mission, Junipero Serro (1713–1784) founded the San Diego Mission in 1769.

Mission revolts

Although some Kumeyaay in the area converted, others resented the missionaries, who were living in their territory and insisting the people change their lifestyle. Many also blamed the Europeans for the diseases that were killing their people and resented being forced to build missions. In 1775, they revolted, killing the priest and burning the mission.

Around this time the Quechan chief, Salvador Palma, embraced Christianity. He converted and asked the priest, Father Francisco Garcés (1738–1781), to establish a mission in their area. Garcés agreed and requested the necessary help from Spain, but it was slow in coming. When the group finally arrived years later, the Quechan were disappointed. They had been expecting a large settlement party with multitudes of soldiers, horses, cattle, and expensive goods. Instead two priests, twelve soldiers, and a few others arrived. The lavish gifts they had been expecting also did not arrive.

In 1780, against the advice of Father Garcés, the Spanish established two missions in the area. Palma and his people rebelled. In 1781, they burned both missions, killed most of the men, and took women and children captive. Initially, at Palma's urging, the priest's life was spared, but a few days later, the priest, too, was clubbed to death.

Following the attack, the Spanish military both fought and negotiated with the Quechan for the return of the prisoners. Neighboring enemy tribes, including the Pima and Maricopa, joined the fray, killing the Quechan and burning their villages. A short while later the Spanish withdrew, and no missions were ever built in that area.

In other places, the establishment of new missions and the arrival of more Spanish settlers also led to increasing hostility. In 1840, the Kiliwa and Paipai burned the Santa Catalina Mission. The Spanish retaliated and killed five hundred Natives. They took prisoners and forced them to work at other missions. The remaining Paipai hid in the canyons, while the Kiliwa fled to Arroyo Leon.

American presence

After the Mexican-American War (1846–48; a war in which Mexico lost about one-half of its national territory to the United States), the Baja Peninsula was divided. The lower half of the peninsula still belonged to Mexico, but the northern portion came under American control. The Mexican portion then split into two separate *partidos* (political districts), which later became Mexican states. The new governments of both countries drew borders through Yuman territory and considered tribal lands their property.

The discovery of gold in the region brought floods of miners to the area, and soon settlements sprang up around the region. The U.S. Army established Fort Yuma to protect the new arrivals from Native attacks, and American settlement increased. Some tribes, such as the Pima and Maricopa, allied themselves with the Americans.

Yuman battles

The Quechan and Mohave (see entry) had dominated the lower Colorado River Valley for centuries. Their warriors, *kwanami,* fought off the Spanish as well as other tribes who entered their lands. Although they resented the Americans entering their territory, they also prospered by transporting gold seekers and their livestock across the Colorado River. As more settlers moved in and cities grew, however, the tribes' control over their traditional lands diminished.

In 1857, several hundred Quechan, Mohave, and Yavapai warriors crossed more than 160 miles (260 kilometers) of desert on foot to attack the Maricopa. The Maricopa and Pima, with aid from their American allies, fought back. The Quechan league lost more than one hundred warriors. This war, called the Battle of Maricopa Wells, was the last major battle the River Yuman fought. The Maricopa and Pima may have won, but their victory was short-lived. Two years later, they were the first of the Yuman tribes to be moved to a reservation.

Several years after that U.S. prospectors killed the Walapai leader, Wauba Yuma. The tribe took revenge, and the Walapai Wars began in 1863. After several battles, the Americans defeated the Walapai in 1869 and sent them to a camp. They were later forcibly removed to the Colorado River Reservation. Over the next year, many grew sick and died, and tribe members fled back to their original homeland only to find that settlers had taken over their territory. Some Walapai found jobs as miners; others were moved to a reservation in 1883.

Moved to reservations

For more than a century, the United States moved the various Yuman tribes from their lands onto reservations. The Maricopa and Pima were the first to be sent to the Gila River Reservation in 1859. In 1871, the U.S. Army had orders to force all Apaches (see entry) onto a reservation in Middle Verde Valley. Resisters were to be shot. The military also rounded up the Yavapai. Soldiers killed one hundred Yavapai men, women, and children who had taken refuge in the Salt River Canyon. This later came to be called the Skeleton Cave Massacre.

The Yavapai and Apache prospered during their two years on the reservation. American settlers, however, pressured the government to move them elsewhere. The 1,500 surviving Yavapai and Apaches were marched to the San Carlos Apache Reservation during the winter of

1875, a distance of more than 180 miles (290 kilometers). Along the way 115 people died. Because of its similarity to the forced march the Cherokees endured in 1838, this removal, too, became known as a "Trail of Tears."

Other Yuman tribes were put on reservations over the next few years. Between 1875 and 1883, the Kumeyaay, Havasupai, and Hualapai all lost large portions of their lands and were confined to reservations. Mohave, Apache (see entries), and Yavapai who had escaped the removals stayed in their traditional territory, but when minerals were discovered there in the 1890s, they were sent to reservations too.

Twentieth century and beyond

Under the Indian Reorganization Act of 1934, many tribes wrote constitutions and started tribal councils to govern their reservations. By the mid-1900s, most Yuman-speaking people lived on or near the reservations. Many struggled to adjust to life on small parcels of land when they had been used to a nomadic lifestyle. Hunters and gatherers now attempted to farm arid soil. Some left the reservations to find jobs. Others worked in the mines or for nearby farmers or ranchers. By the start of the twenty-first century, many communities had opened casinos or started other businesses to improve their economies (see "Economy").

RELIGION

Traditional beliefs

Although each community had its own beliefs and stories, all believed in a Great Spirit, or Creator. Most tribes did not have the elaborate rituals of other Southwest peoples, but they did emphasize the importance of dreams. Instead of a creation story, their main religious stories explained natural phenomena or told of the first cremation. Many tribes also had an origin story of twins, or two forces, representing good and evil. Other tales described the formation of the Colorado River and the sacred mountain.

The sacred mountain was the site where shamans (pronounced *SHAH-munz* or *SHAY-munz*) dreamed before they were born. Most people dreamed of the future, but a shaman could dream of the past— even as far back as creation. Dreams gave people the power to conceive children, cure diseases, cast spells, defeat enemies, or serve as leaders.

All special abilities and supernatural powers came from dreaming. Luck, good or bad, resulted from dreams. Even a child in a mother's womb could dream, so there were pregnancy taboos (see "Childbirth and naming").

Songs, another important part of Yuman religion, also came from dreams. If members of the tribe became upset or were in deep emotional distress, they went to a secluded area for a time until they received new songs. Singing was an important part of a shaman's skill in curing the sick.

Some tribes, such as the Cocopá, believed in ghosts. Certain shamans contacted the spirits of the dead. For this ceremony the shaman wore a cape made of the hair of dead virgins.

The *Karuk,* or Mourning Ceremony, was important to most Yuman tribes (see "Death rituals"). In their dry climate, rainmaking ceremonies were considered vital. Fires to encourage rainfall may have been what earned them their name from the Spanish *uma,* meaning "smoke".

Christian influences

Jesuit missionaries arrived in the late 1600s to convert the people. Some tribes, such as the Cochimí, wholeheartedly adopted Christian beliefs and ceremonies, whereas others rejected them. The Cochimí gave up their traditional beliefs and tried to live as the Jesuits suggested. By living close to the mission, the tribe was decimated by diseases brought by the Europeans. By the time the Dominicans replaced the Jesuits in 1768, few Cochimí still survived.

Presbyterians converted many Maricopa and Yavapai during the late 1800s and early 1900s. Some Yavapai continue to hold traditional ceremonies along with their Christian practices. In the mid-1900s other churches—Baptist, Mormon, Seventh-Day Adventists, and Pentecostals—brought their beliefs to the tribes.

Other religions

Some groups, such as the Walapai, resisted Christianity, preferring instead to practice the Ghost Dance religion (see Paiute entry). Followers danced in the hope that it would rid the land of whites and bring back the buffalo and dead Native ancestors. On the Fort McDowell Reservation, many Yavapai attend the Holy Ground Church, started in the 1920s by a White Mountain Apache (see entry), because it honors their traditions.

A more recent development in the Havasupai and Walapai tribes is the Rastafari movement and reggae music. Many of the people relate to the song lyrics that speak of oppression and misuse of the land. One Native reggae fan explained, as quoted in the book *Understanding the Connections Between Black and Aboriginal Peoples*:

> We are struggling and striving as much as the black people who have been afflicted by the governments that have taken over their homelands. I feel that the same afflictions and prejudice that have happened to black people have happened to the American Indian people. Reggae music brings our people, the black and American Indian people together.

LANGUAGE

All the languages spoken by the Yuman tribes are part of the Hokan language family. Experts believe that the separation of the language into different dialects (varieties) may have occurred as far back as 2,500 years ago. Today, each language falls into one of four subdivisions: Delta-California Yuman (Kumeyaay and Cocopá); River Yuman (Quechan, Maricopa, and Mohave); Pai (Upland Yuman—Yavapai, Hualapai or Walapai, and Havasupai dialects—and Paipai); and Kiliwa.

Many Yuman languages are endangered and spoken by only a few hundred tribe members, mostly the elderly. The Cochimí language became extinct in the 1800s, but some Kumeyaay (Kumiai) in the early twenty-first century are sometimes called Cochimí, which often causes confusion. In Mexico about half the tribes speak their Native languages. In the United States, the Havasupai and Walapai have large populations that still speak those dialects. Several reservations have programs for children to ensure that the tribe's language and culture are passed down to the next generations.

GOVERNMENT

Traditional leadership

Although the clans or bands of each tribe were spread out over a large area, they saw themselves as united. Together they fought common enemies and followed similar customs. Some tribes, like the Kumeyaay, however, consisted of many autonomous groups, each with its own leader.

Most bands had only one chief who presided over the whole tribe, usually the headman of the strongest village. His position was hereditary, but sometimes tribes chose a leader by his speaking ability or skill in battle. Most of the time the chief's position was advisory, and a council of elders assisted with tribal decisions.

Other leaders in the tribe claimed their positions because of their dreams. Shamans, song and dance leaders, directors of funerals and mourning ceremonies, orators, Brave Men (war leaders), and Scalp-Keepers all received their positions after dreaming about them.

Present-day government

In the early twenty-first century, most Yuman communities are governed by a tribal council elected by the people. Councils are usually headed by a chairperson or president and a vice chairperson or vice president, who are elected to their positions. Some councils also have a secretary and treasurer. Many serve staggered four-year terms, although others serve two years. An exception is the Yavapai-Prescott Reservation, which has a board of directors.

On the Gila River Reservation, a Youth Council made up of twenty-one young adults, ranging in age from fourteen to twenty-one, are elected by others their own age. Begun in 1988, this Akimel O'odham/Pee-Posh

Neon lights welcome gamblers to the Gila River Casino in Casa Blanca, Arizona. © AP IMAGES/MATT YORK.

Youth Council advises the tribal council on youth issues, institutes programs to promote understanding, and acts as a spokesperson for their peers. Council members are elected to two-year terms.

ECONOMY

Subsistence lifestyle

The River Yuman subsisted mainly on farming, whereas Upland Yuman lived by hunting and gathering. The people moved often to find food, to foil enemies, or because floods washed away their campsites. Many tribes traded with each other and with neighboring tribes; some traveled great distances to barter.

Modern-day economy

Many present-day Yuman make their livings by farming, ranching, mining, construction, manufacturing, or artwork. Some tribes lease land; others own industrial parks, service stations, campgrounds, fisheries, and corporations that provide jobs and income for the tribe.

The majority of the tribes have opened casinos to bring in additional income. Profits from gaming finance many social, educational, and health programs on most reservations. Under a policy begun in 2005, the Camp Verde Reservation gives each member ten percent of casino profits.

Because most reservations are located in areas of historical interest, tourism is a big business. Recreational vehicle parks, hotels, restaurants, shopping malls, big game hunting, and other services that cater to tourists bolster tribal economies. The tribes living in the Grand Canyon area operate river rafting, helicopter and mule rides, and guide services.

Even with these business opportunities, the Hualapai (Walapai) suffered from high unemployment. Their casino did not generate enough funds, and forty percent of the people were out of work. To increase tribal income, they opened a glass skywalk at the Grand Canyon in 2007. People pay to walk out on a 4-inch thick (10-centimeter) glass shelf to peer down at the canyon below.

Mexican economy today

Many Yuman in Mexico make their living by selling crafts (baskets and pottery), raising livestock, farming, fishing, digging stone and gravel, and providing seasonal labor in nearby communities. Others have moved off the reservations to find work. Some have even sold their land to non-Natives to survive. In the past, people gathered herbs, jojoba, piñon, and wildflower seeds to sell to supplement tribal income, but now harvesting these plants is more difficult because it requires expensive permits.

DAILY LIFE

Families

Extended families (parents, children, grandparents, and other relatives) formed the basis of social and political life. Most families formed bands and migrated together. Some joined other groups in their region, but there were no social classes. Everyone was equal, and prestige was earned by skill, hard work, and good behavior.

Two Yuman women and a man wear typical tribal clothing.
© BETTMANN/CORBIS.

Buildings

While most early homes were dome-shaped, later ones were rectangular. Houses were partially underground and made from a frame of posts linked by rafters that supported flat, thatched roofs. Walls of arrowweed (a tall shrub with lance-shaped leaves) were held in place by willow branches woven through the thatch. Many walls and roofs were also covered with dirt. Most houses had ramadas, open-sided shelters covered by a roof, useful for shade during the day and for sleeping during hot weather. When it was cold, some people dug a hole, scraped ashes from a fire into it, and lay down on top to stay warm.

Most Yuman lived in *rancherías,* a Spanish name for these small settlements. rancherías usually had homes for several hundred people as well as a large meeting house, a storage building for grain, a small hut for purification and menstruation (see "Puberty"), and an open-air kitchen made from a screen of weeds near a cooking fire.

Some tribes used caves as shelter. Others, such as the Walapai, used wickiups or made simple shelters by piling branches against a tree. After the Walapai moved to the reservation, they built hogans and sweat lodges.

In the 1930s, *jacals* became popular. These Mexican-style houses had adobe between the posts; roof beams were covered with sticks, brush, and dirt. Later, log homes, and then cement block homes, were often built.

Clothing and adornment

Many of the Yuman went naked, especially children. Some men wore breechcloths, a piece of fabric that passed between their legs and attached to their belts. Apronlike flaps woven of willow bark hung to their knees in the front and back. Other men tied blankets around their waists, then pulled the folds up between their legs with cord to make pantaloons (short, puffy-legged pants).

Women wore small aprons made from the inner bark of cottonwood or willow trees. Some tied a deerskin around their waists; others donned skirts of fringed fabric strips. In cooler weather, most people draped blankets or rabbit-skin capes over their shoulders.

Most tribes went barefoot, but some, like the Kiliwa, wore agave (pronounced *uh-GAH-vee*; a plant with spiny, sword-shaped leaves) fiber sandals. The Cocopá made sandals from cowhide with the fur on top. The Kiliwa wore reed caps, and Kumeyaay wore coiled basketry hats. To dress up for dances, people washed their hair, then men tied feathers in their hair and painted their faces and bodies with red, yellow, and white clay. Women wore necklaces and bracelets made of beads.

Both sexes pierced their ears. In many tribes, men also pierced their noses; they inserted a shell pendant, a plug, or a bone through the hole. Tattoos done with cactus spines and charcoal were common. Babies often had their heads flattened, which was thought to make them more beautiful. Most tribes wore their hair long; some used a lotion made of mesquite (pronounced *me-SKEET* or *MES-keet*) to prevent the sun from bleaching their hair.

Food

Early Yuman tribes survived by hunting and gathering. Men shot larger game such as deer, pronghorn antelope, bighorn sheep, and mountain lion. The tribe worked together to drive smaller game such as jackrabbits and quail into nets. In addition to hunting for moles, wood rats, lizards, caterpillars, and birds, the men of some tribes also caught fish, shellfish, and reptiles.

Plants they harvested in the wild included acorns, seeds, prickly pears, apples, pine nuts, cactus fruits, yucca, berries, onion, and garlic. Agave and mesquite beans were important foods. Mesquite also served as medicine, paint, and hair treatment. Women usually spent all day picking mesquite beans, while men hunted nearby to protect them.

Mesquite beans could be dried and stored for later use. Women pounded green ones and mixed them, with their uncracked seeds, in water to drink. Beans that were not good enough to store or drink were ground into flour, which they sifted by shaking a traylike basket and letting the lighter flour fall onto a blanket on the ground. Women then dug deep, oval-shaped holes in the ground and wet the dirt. They poured a layer of mesquite flour into it and sprinkled water over it. They repeated the process until the hole was filled. After covering it with dirt, they let the flour set. The next day, they removed the hard cake called *hapa'ndj*. Most women prepared at least twenty cakes at a time. To use them, they broke off chunks and put them in water to drink or boiled them with other ground seeds.

As did the majority of the Southwest tribes, most Yuman learned to grow maize (corn), beans, and squash, although some traded goods for Mexican wheat. Other crops that grew well in this area were pumpkins, gourds, watermelons, and cowpeas. Later some tribes learned to gather wild honey. Treks were also made to the coast to collect salt.

Education

In most Yuman tribes, mothers, grandmothers, and siblings taught younger children. Little pressure was put on children to learn because the people believed skills and talents came from dreams. Children spent most of their time playing, often imitating adult behavior.

In modern times, most Yuman children attend public schools. Others go to reservation schools, private schools, or boarding schools. Many reservations have Head Start programs and tribal colleges. At the Fort McDowell Reservation, the tribe funded their own school so students could take classes that include language study and culture.

Healing practices

After people dreamed of being a healer, they paid an experienced shaman to teach them. These healers used herbs, rubbing, and singing. They also used tobacco smoke and sucking to cure patients. Dreams helped them identify symptoms and suggested treatment. In addition, shamans were said to have the power to bring lost souls back, a skill they had learned before they were born.

Some tribes also feared shamans, who had the power to cause illnesses as well as cure them. If a medicine person failed to heal a patient or was suspected of being a witch and causing evil, the people might kill him.

ARTS

The ancestors of some Yuman tribes, the Patayan, may have created the geoglyphs along the rivers in California, Arizona, and Nevada. These huge landscape constructions look like humans or mountain lions. Others are geometric shapes. Many are over 30 feet (9 meters) long; one is even 300 feet (90 meters) in length. To make them, the artists removed the darker top layer of soil, so the lighter soil underneath showed.

Baskets and Pottery

The Upland Yuman were known for basketry, whereas tribes like the Maricopa earned a reputation for their pottery. Girls as young as age five learned pottery-making from their mothers. They used a paddle to beat a small ball of clay into shape over another vessel, then pinched up the sides and dried the bowls in sun. They coated the bowls with hematite to give them their distinct red color and hardened them in mesquite-fired ovens.

Quechan, Kumeyaay, Mohave, and Kamia (a tribe later absorbed into the others) were also known for their pottery. Some of these nations shaped their vessels with paddles like the Maricopa did; others used coils to build their pots. Potters made many different kinds of pots or jars, called *ollas*. The tribe sometimes buried these partially underground, leaving only a small portion showing to serve as traps for small animals. Large lidded vessels for storage were filled with food, then sealed with pitch or unfired clay.

Different tribes made figurines with eyes shaped like coffee beans as well as miniature containers, possibly for funerals. Although groups made narrow-necked jars, the Maricopa only made wide-mouthed jars. The most interesting and hardest to make pieces were large, flat bowls, many over three feet (one meter) in diameter. Women put babies or possessions in these, then swam across the water, pushing the bowls ahead of them.

Calendars

The Maricopa also used calendar sticks like the Tohono O'odham and Pima (see entries). They cut notches to mark each year along with symbols to help them remember certain events. Some historians believe this custom began in 1833 to record a meteor shower, but the tribe's oral history seems to indicate it may be a much older tradition.

CUSTOMS

Birth and naming

Because they believed babies had important dreams even before they were born, expectant parents had many taboos. A mother was not to lie on her back, because it might cause the baby to be born facing the wrong direction. Nor should she touch a rattlesnake, or her child might lack bones like the snake. Both parents avoided looking at dead animals, because it was thought to put the baby at risk of being paralyzed; when fathers hunted, they avoided looking at what they had killed. Diet, too, was important. If a mother got too fat, it was thought that her baby might choke, and once the baby was born, neither parent was allowed to eat salt or fat.

Births took place in a menstrual hut or special circular lodge with a fire in the center. A woman's mother and another female relative (one who had had a short delivery) typically assisted at the birth. The woman sat facing east, with her back against a post in the west. In front of her was a sand-filled hollow lined with rabbitskin or soft cloth for the baby. If labor lasted too long, other women came and sat in the hut with her. As a last resort, they called in a shaman. Her husband or other male relative might also help.

Puberty

For many boys, the puberty ceremony involved nose piercing and long periods of seclusion. Elders taught them about tribal history and culture. A girl went to a special hut when her first menstruation began. Different tribes observed different customs, but this seclusion typically lasted four days and included taboos such as not touching the face or body.

Marriage

Most tribes did not have any special ceremonies for marriage. Some had trial marriages, where couples lived with a few different partners before deciding on a spouse. In other communities, a man went to stay with a woman; if she accepted him, they were considered married. Having more than one wife was acceptable in many groups, and a divorce could be obtained by walking out on a spouse.

Games and sports

Many Yuman excelled in running, wrestling, and swimming, but these sports, too, required a dream. Runners jogged or raced to trade with tribes on the Gulf of California or the Pacific coast, then took shells or coastal products to inland tribes to trade for additional goods.

Festivals

Yuman dances were mostly social events. The few rituals included special dances at harvest times, war and scalp celebrations, and funeral or mourning rites (see "Death rituals"). Girls' puberty rites were often celebrated in many tribes. Singing was also important to the tribe. During times of poverty, the Maricopa sometimes sang for the Pima in exchange for food.

Dances were held in the open during a full moon. The Yuman often invited neighboring tribes to join them. One person sang his dream songs and accompanied himself with a gourd rattle. He might also beat on a basket or scrape it to make additional sounds. Dancers formed a circle around the singer, with men and women alternating, and they hopped or shuffled in a counterclockwise direction.

War etiquette

Yuma and Mohave warriors marched out in formation. Prior to a battle they might watch their leaders fight a duel. Dreams were important to prowess on the battlefield, as only men who had had dreams could take scalps. Those who scalped an enemy had to be purified in a four-day rite. When the tribes took prisoners, the captives also had to be purified before they became slaves or were killed.

Death rituals

Sometimes when a shaman could not cure a patient with singing, he changed his songs to speed the person on to the next world. Before the elderly died, an orator gave a speech; he also gave one at the funeral to encourage the relatives to be happy in spite of their loss.

The Visit of the Dead

Many Yuman tribes believed that dead spirits could come back to take the living along with them. To prevent that and to hurry the spirits along to the afterlife, they burned the dead person's possessions.

An Halchidhoma family was coming to visit the people at kwa'akamat [Gila Bend]. They got half way and camped for the night. They built a fire. Late in the evening, they sat around it. As they sat there they saw the dead people gather and talk to them. The dead threw corn to them and brought melons. But the humans did not say anything. They recognized the faces of those long dead. The dead said, "Hurry up and eat your melons. Let us dance; there is a dance going on." The humans were afraid to go to sleep: they kept the fire going all night. Toward morning the woman went to sleep: she died. But the husband held a little baby in his arms. Whenever the baby fell asleep, he pinched it hard to wake it. The reason the baby was saved was because he pinched it all night long. He arrived at kwa'akamat with only the baby. He told them he had come with the baby alone. It is always said if you go beyond the mountains to that place, and lie there, you will hear all kinds of noises. If you should fall asleep, you will die.

SOURCE: Spier, Leslie. *Yuman Tribes of the Gila River.* New York: Dover Publications, 1978.

When someone died, an elderly friend of the family usually combed the hair, painted the face, and wrapped the body in a cloth that was tied three places—above the head, at the waist, and below the feet. Cremation occurred within a day or less. A person's possessions were burned with the body to discourage the spirit from remaining on Earth. Many tribes also tore down or burned the deceased's home and engaged in ritual wailing.

CURRENT TRIBAL ISSUES

Water supplies

From 1976 to 1981, the Yavapai fought to prevent the Central Arizona Project from building the Orme Dam where the Salt and the Verde Rivers meet. The dam would have flooded more than half of their reservation. They won their court case, and the dam was not built. In 1990, they won another water settlement with the U.S. government, which allotted the tribe 36,000 acre-feet of water every year, enough to supply the tribe's needs and water their crops, including the eighty thousand pecan and citrus trees they had planted. During the early 2000s, the tribe leased some of its extra water to the growing city of Phoenix. The Salt River Project also agreed to keep enough water in the Verde River to sustain the wildlife, particularly the bald eagle.

Water is also a concern for the Mexican Yuman. Many settlements do not have water supplies, and people must rely on water collected in hand-dug water basins; some of these collection basins have cement sides, whereas others do not. All water needs to be boiled before it is used. Another difficulty is that toxic waste is contaminating the lakes and rivers where the people fish. They also have trouble with squatters and poachers on their land.

Oil and mining concerns

Concern about the Arizona Clean Fuels plan to build an oil refinery on 1,460 acres of land in Yuma County prompted the Quechan to file suit in 2007 to halt the transfer of the land. Although the land is no longer tribal land, it is culturally significant to the people. They also have concerns about the impact of the refinery. The court denied their request, so the project continued to move forward in spite of the tribe's concerns, and the refinery, originally slated to open in 2009, moved the projected date into 2012 after difficulties in securing an air-quality permit.

The Quechan supported a bill to avoid or lessen mining damages to Native American sacred places, which the California governor vetoed in 2002. He did sign a bill requiring mining companies to completely back-fill open pit mines near sacred locations. One of the tribe's main concerns was their ongoing fight to protect ancient sites that would be damaged by the Glamis Imperial Mine's cyanide heap leach goldmine at Indian Pass. The Quechan continued to press for action to halt the mine, and after six years of studies, the Department of the Interior denied a permit to the mining company owners, who sued the U.S. government to recover the loss of their investment, a case they lost in 2009. The mine would have affected fifty-five archaeological sites as well as rare desert plants and animals. It would also have used up 389 million gallons of water each year in a desert area where water is scarce. The issue was not settled, however, because the following year the decision was overturned, which allowed the mining permit to be reconsidered, resulting in additional legal challenges and court battles.

Around that same time, the Quechan decided to build a new casino at Pilot Knob. That project was challenged by some tribal elders and an archaeologist who claimed the land was sacred and contained remains and artifacts from ten thousand years ago. Some of the people joined a protest march, the Long Walk 2, from California to Washington, D.C., hoping to stop the construction and save other Native sites from destruction, but the project continued in spite of their efforts.

NOTABLE PEOPLE

Carlos Montezuma (1866–1923), a Yavapai, was stolen by Pimas when he was a child and sold to an American photographer, who educated the boy in Chicago. Montezuma was one of the first Native Americans to get a medical degree and later became an advocate for Native rights.

BOOKS

Austin, Alfredo Lopez, and Leonardo Lopez Lujan. *Mexico's Indigenous Past*. Norman: University of Oklahoma Press, 2001.

Densmore, Frances. *American Indians and Their Music*. Kila, MN: Kessinger Publishing, 2010.

Dub, Raging Blakkindian. *Understanding the Connections Between Black and Aboriginal Peoples*. Bloomington: Fire This Time/1st Books Library, 2002.

Euler, Robert C., and Carma Lee Smithson. *Havasupai Legends: Religion and Mythology of the Havasupai Indians of the Grand Canyon*. Salt Lake City: University of Utah Press, 2002.

Halpern, A. M. *Karuk: Native Accounts of the Quechan Mourning Ceremony*. Berkeley: University of California, 1997.

Hayes, Allan, and Carol Hayes. *The Desert Southwest: Four Thousand Years of Life And Art*. Berkeley, CA: Ten Speed Press, 2006.

Hirst, Stephen. *I Am the Grand Canyon: The Story of the Havasupai People*. Grand Canyon, AZ: Grand Canyon Association, 2006.

Iliff, Flora Gregg. *People of the Blue Water: My Adventures among the Walapai and Havasupai Indians*. Tuscon: University of Arizona Press, 2001.

Keller, Jean A., and Lorene Sisquoc. *Boarding School Blues: Revisiting American Indian Educational Experiences*. Lincoln: University of Nebraska Press, 2006.

McGinty, Brian. *The Oatman Massacre: A Tale of Desert Captivity and Survival*. Norman: University of Oklahoma Press, 2005.

Santiago, Mark. *Massacre at the Yuma Crossing: Spanish Relations with the Quechans, 1779–1782*. Tucson: University of Arizona Press, 2010.

Sauder, Robert. *The Yuma Reclamation Project*. Santa Fe: University of Nevada Press, 2009.

Secrest, William B. *When the Great Spirit Died: The Destruction of the California Indians, 1850–1860*. Sanger, CA: Word Dancer Press, 2003.

Smith, White Mountain. *Indian Tribes of the Southwest*. Kila, MN: Kessinger Publishing, 2005.

Speroff, Leon. *Carlos Montezuma, M.D.: A Yavapai American Hero—The Life and Times of an American Indian, 1866–1923*. Portland, OR: Arnica Publishing, 2005.

WEB SITES

Cocopah Indian Tribe. http://www.cocopah.com/ (accessed on July 20, 2011).

Fort McDowell Yavapai Nation. http://www.ftmcdowell.org/ (accessed on July 20, 2011).

"Fort Yuma-Quechan Tribe." *Inter-Tribal Council of Arizona, Inc*. http://www.itcaonline.com/tribes_quechan.html (accessed on July 20, 2011).

"Kumeyaay Culture." *Kumeyaay Info*. http://www.kumeyaay.info/culture/ (accessed on July 20, 2011).

Kumeyaay.com. http://www.kumeyaay.com (accessed on July 20, 2011).

Liggett, Lori. "1890s America: A Chronology: Ghost Dance Religion." *Bowling Green State University.* http://www.bgsu.edu/departments/acs/1890s/woundedknee/WKghost.html (accessed on July 20, 2011).

Schmal, John P. "History of Mexico: Indigenous Baja." *Houston Institute for Culture.* http://www.houstonculture.org/mexico/baja.html (accessed on July 20, 2011).

Yavapai Prescott Indian Tribe. http://www.ypit.com/ (accessed on July 20, 2011).

"Yuma (Quechan)." *Four Directions Institute.* http://www.fourdir.com/yuma.htm (accessed on July 20, 2011).

Yuman Indian Tribe History." *Access Genealogy.* http://www.accessgenealogy.com/native/tribes/yuman/yumanfamilyhist.htm (accessed on July 20, 2011).

Where to Learn More

Books

Abel, Kerry. *Drum Songs: Glimpses of Dene History.* Montreal, Quebec: McGill–Queen's University Press, 1993.

Adams, Richard C. *A Delaware Indian Legend and the Story of Their Troubles.* Whitefish, MT: Kessinger Publishing, LLC, 2006.

Adamson, Thelma, ed. *Folk-tales of the Coast Salish.* Lincoln: Bison Books, 2009.

Aderkas, Elizabeth, and Christa Hook. *American Indians of the Pacific Northwest.* Oxford: Osprey Publishing, 2005.

Adil, Janeen R. *The Northeast Indians: Daily Life in the 1500s.* Mankato, MN: Capstone Press, 2006.

Agonito, Joseph. *Lakota Portraits: Lives of the Legendary Plains People.* Guilford, CT: TwoDot, 2011.

Agoyo, Herman, and Joe S. Sando, eds. *Po'pay: Leader of the First American Revolution.* Santa Fe, NM: Clear Light Publishing, 2005.

Akers, Donna L. *Culture and Customs of the Choctaw Indians.* Santa Barbara, CA: Greenwood, 2012.

The Aleut Relocation and Internment during World War II: A Preliminary Examination. Anchorage, AK: Aleutian/Pribilof Islands Association, 1981.

Alexander, Annie Lou. *Blood Is Red…So Am I.* New York: Vantage Press, 2007.

Alexie, Sherman. *The Absolutely True Diary of a Part-Time Indian.* Waterville, ME: Thorndike Press, 2008.

Alfred, Agnes. *Paddling to Where I Stand: Agnes Alfred, Kwakwaka'wakw Noblewoman.* Seattle: University of Washington Press, 2005.

Alger, Abby L. *In Indian Tents: Stories Told by Penobscot, Passamaquoddy and Micmac Indians.* Park Forest, IL: University Press of the Pacific, 2006.

Allen, John W. *Legends and Lore of Southern Illinois.* Carbondale: Southern Illinois University Press, 2010.

Andersen, Raoul R., and John K. Crellin. *Mi'sel Joe: An Aboriginal Chief's Journey.* St. John's, Newfoundland: Flanker Press, 2009.

Anderson, Jeffrey D. *One Hundred Years of Old Man Sage: An Arapaho Life.* Lincoln: University of Nebraska Press, 2003.

Andersson, Rani-Henrik. *The Lakota Ghost Dance of 1890.* Lincoln: University of Nebraska Press, 2008.

Angell, Tony, and John M. Marzluff. *In the Company of Crows and Ravens.* New Haven, CT: Yale University Press, 2007.

Anthony, Alexander E., Jr., David Neil Sr., and J. Brent Ricks. *Kachinas: Spirit Beings of the Hopi.* Albuquerque, NM: Avanyu Publishing, 2006.

Archer, Jane. *The First Fire: Stories of the Cherokee, Kickapoo, Kiowa, and Tigua.* Dallas, TX: Taylor Trade, 2005.

Arnold, Caroline, and Richard R. Hewett. *The Ancient Cliff Dwellers of Mesa Verde.* New York: Clarion Books, 2000.

Aron Crowell, ed. *Living Our Cultures, Sharing Our Heritage: The First Peoples of Alaska.* Washington, DC: Smithsonian Institution, 2010.

Augaitis, Daina, Lucille Bell, and Nika Collison. *Raven Travelling: Two Centuries of Haida Art.* Seattle: University of Washington Press, 2008.

Ayagalria, Moses K. *Yupik Eskimo Fairy Tales and More.* New York: Vantage Press, 2006.

Bahti, Mark. *Pueblo Stories and Storytellers.* 3rd ed. Tucson, AZ: Rio Nuevo Publishers, 2010.

Bahti, Mark, and Eugene Baatsoslanii Joe. *Navajo Sandpaintings.* 3rd ed. Tucson, AZ: Rio Nuevo Publishers, 2009.

Bailey, Garrick, ed. *Traditions of the Osage: Stories Collected and Translated by Francis la Flesche.* Albuquerque: University of New Mexico Press, 2010.

Baker, Wendy Beth. *Healing Power of Horses: Lessons from the Lakota Indians.* Irvine, CA: BowTie Press, 2004.

Ball, Eve, Nora Henn, and Lynda A. Sánchez. *Indeh: An Apache Odyssey.* Reprint. Norman: University of Oklahoma Press, 1988.

Ballantine, Betty, and Ian Ballantine, eds. *The Native Americans: An Illustrated History.* Atlanta: Turner Publishing, 1993.

Bancroft-Hunt, Norman. *People of the Totem: The Indians of the Pacific Northwest.* Photographs by Werner Forman. New York: Putnam, 1979.

Barbeau, Marius. *Huron and Wyandot Mythology.* Ottawa, Ontario: Government Printing Bureau, 1915.

Barbour, Jeannie, Amanda J. Cobb, and Linda Hogan. *Chickasaw: Unconquered and Unconquerable.* Ada, OK: Chickasaw Press, 2006.

Barker, James H., and Ann Fienup-Riordan. *Yupiit Yuraryarait = Yup'ik Ways of Dancing.* Fairbanks: University of Alaska Press, 2010.

Barkwell, Lawrence J. *Women of the Metis Nation.* Winnipeg, Manitoba: Louis Riel Institute, 2009.

Barnett, James F., Jr. *The Natchez Indians: A History to 1735.* Jackson: University Press of Mississippi, 2007.

Barrett, Samuel Alfred. *Ceremonies of the Pomo Indians and Pomo Bear Doctors.* University of California Publications in American Archeology and Ethnology. 1917. Reprint. Whitefish, MT: Kessinger Publishing, 2010.

— — —. *The Washo Indians.* 1917. Reprint. Charleston, SC: Kessinger Publishing, 2010.

Barron, Donna Gentle Spirit. *The Long Island Indians and their New England Ancestors: Narragansett, Mohegan, Pequot and Wampanoag Tribes.* Bloomington, IN: AuthorHouse, 2006.

Bartram, William, and Gregory A. Waselkov. *William Bartram on the Southeastern Indians.* Lincoln: University of Nebraska Press, 2002.

Basel, Roberta. *Sequoyah: Inventor of Written Cherokee.* Minneapolis, MN: Compass Point Books, 2007.

Bastedo, Jamie. *Reaching North: A Celebration of the Subarctic.* Markham, Ontario: Red Deer Press, 2002.

Bauerle, Phenocia, ed. *The Way of the Warrior: Stories of the Crow People.* Lincoln: University of Nebraska Press, 2003.

Bean, Lowell John, ed. "Introduction." In *The Ohlone Past and Present: Native Americans of the San Francisco Bay Region.* Menlo Park, CA: Ballena Press, 1994.

Bean, Lowell John, and Florence C. Shipek. "Luiseño." In *Handbook of North American Indians.* Vol. 8: *California,* edited by Robert F. Heizer. Washington, DC: Smithsonian Institution, 1978.

Bean, Lowell, Frank Porter, and Lisa Bourgeault. *The Cahuilla.* New York: Chelsea House, 1989.

Beasley, Richard A. *How to Carve a Tlingit Mask.* Juneau: Sealaska Heritage Institute, 2009.

Becenti, Karyth. *One Nation, One Year: A Navajo Photographer's 365-Day Journey into a World of Discovery, Life and Hope.* Los Ranchos, NM: Rio Grande Books, 2010.

Beck, Mary G. *Heroes and Heroines: Tlingit-Haida Legend.* Anchorage: Alaska Northwest Books, 2003.

Beckwourth, James. *The Life and Adventures of James P. Beckwourth, Mountaineer, Scout, and Pioneer, and Chief of the Crow Nation of Indians.* Paris, France: Adamant Media Corporation, 2005.

Behnke, Alison. *The Apaches.* Minneapolis, MN: Lerner Publications, 2006.

Behrman, Carol H. *The Indian Wars.* Minneapolis, MN: Lerner Publications, 2005.

Belting, Natalia. *Whirlwind Is a Spirit Dancing: Poems Based on Traditional American Indian Songs and Stories.* New York: Milk and Cookies Press, 2006.

Bergon, Frank. *Shoshone Mike.* New York: Viking Penguin, 1987.

Berleth, Richard. *Bloody Mohawk: The French and Indian War and American Revolution on New York's Frontier.* Hensonville, NY: Black Dome, 2009.

Betty, Gerald. *Comanche Society: Before the Reservation.* College Station: Texas A&M University Press, 2005.

Bial, Raymond. *The Chumash.* New York: Benchmark Books, 2004.

— — —. *The Cree.* New York: Benchmark Books, 2006.

— — —. *The Delaware.* New York: Benchmark Books, 2006.

— — —. *The Menominee.* New York: Marshall Cavendish Benchmark, 2006.

— — —. *The Tlingit.* New York: Benchmark Books, 2003.

Bibby, Brian. *Deeper than Gold: A Guide to Indian Life in the Sierra Foothills.* Berkeley: Heyday Books, 2004.

Bielawski, Ellen. *In Search of Ancient Alaska: Solving the Mysteries of the Past.* Anchorage: Alaska Northwest Books, 2007.

Birchfield, D.L., and Helen Dwyer. *Apache History and Culture.* New York: Gareth Stevens, 2012.

Biskup, Agnieszka. *Thunder Rolling Down the Mountain: The Story of Chief Joseph and the Nez Percé.* Mankato, MN: Capstone Press, 2011.

Bjorklund, Ruth. *The Cree.* Tarrytown, NY: Marshall Cavendish, 2009.

— — —. *The Hopi.* Tarrytown, NY: Marshall Cavendish Benchmark, c. 2009.

Blackbird, Andrew J. *History of the Ottawa and Chippewa Indians of Michigan.* Charleston, SC: Nabu Press, 2010.

Bodine, John. "Taos Pueblo." *Handbook of North American Indians,* Vol. 9: *Southwest.* Ed. Alfonso Ortiz. Washington DC: Smithsonian Institution, 1979.

— — —. *Taos Pueblo: A Walk Through Time.* Tucson, AZ: Rio Nuevo, 2006.

Bodinger de Uriarte, John J. *Casino and Museum: Representing Mashantucket Pequot Identity.* Tucson: University of Arizona Press, 2007.

Bogan, Phebe M. *Yaqui Indian Dances of Tucson Arizona: An Account of the Ceremonial Dances of the Yaqui Indians at Pascua.* Whitefish, MT: Kessinger Publishing, 2011.

Bonvillain, Nancy, and Ada Deer. *The Hopi.* Minneapolis, MN: Chelsea House Publications, 2005.

— — —. *The Nez Percé.* New York: Chelsea House, 2011.

— — —. *The Zuñi.* New York: Chelsea House Publishers, 2011.

Boule, Mary Null. *Mohave Tribe.* Vashon, WV: Merryant Publishers Inc., 2000.

Bourque, Bruce J., and Laureen A. LaBar. *Uncommon Threads: Wabanaki Textiles, Clothing, and Costume.* Augusta: Maine State Museum in association with University of Washington Press, 2009.

Bowes, John P. *The Choctaw.* New York: Chelsea House, 2010.

Bradley, Donna. *Native Americans of San Diego County, CA.* Mt. Pleasant, SC: Arcadia, 2009.

Bragdon, Kathleen J. *The Columbia Guide to American Indians of the Northeast.* New York: Columbia University Press, 2005.

Braje, Todd J., and Torben C. Rick, eds.*Human Impacts on Seals, Sea Lions, and Sea Otters: Integrating Archaeology and Ecology in the Northeast Pacific.* Berkeley: University of California Press, 2011.

Bray, Kingsley M. *Crazy Horse: A Lakota Life.* Norman: University of Oklahoma Press, 2006.

Breen, Betty, and Earl Mills, Sr. *Cape Cod Wampanoag Cookbook: Wampanoag Indian Recipes, Images & Lore.* Santa Fe, NM: Clear Light Books, 2001.

Brehm, Victoria. *Star Songs and Water Spirits: A Great Lakes Native Reader.* Tustin, MI: Ladyslipper Press, 2010.

Brimner, Larry Dane. *Pocahontas: Bridging Two Worlds.* New York: Marshall Cavendish Benchmark, 2009.

Bringhurst, Robert. *A Story as Sharp as a Knife: The Classical Haida Mythtellers and Their World.* 2nd ed. Vancouver, BC: Douglas & McIntyre, 2011.

Bringing the Story of the Cheyenne People to the Children of Today. Northern Cheyenne Curriculum Committee. Helena, MT: Office of Public Instruction, 2009.

Broker, Ignatia, *Night Flying Woman: An Ojibway Narrative.* St. Paul: Minnesota Historical Society Press, 1983.

Brown, Dee. *Bury My Heart at Wounded Knee: An Indian History of the American West.* New York: Holt, Rinehart, and Winston, 1970.

Brown, James W., and Rita T. Kohn, ed. *Long Journey Home: Oral Histories of Contemporary Delaware Indians.* Bloomington: Indiana University Press, 2008.

Brown, John A., and Robert H. Ruby. *The Chinook Indians: Traders of the Lower Columbia River.* Norman: University of Oklahoma Press, 1988.

Brown, Joseph. *The Spiritual Legacy of the American Indian: Commemorative Edition with Letters while Living with Black Elk.* Bloomington, IN: World Wisdom, 2007.

Brown, Tricia, and Roy Corral. *Children of the Midnight Sun: Young Native Voices of Alaska.* Anchorage: Alaska Northwest Books, 2006.

— — —. *Silent Storytellers of Totem Bight State Historical Park.* Anchorage: Alaska Geographic Association, 2009.

Brown, Virginia Pounds, Laurella Owens and Nathan Glick. *The World of the Southern Indians: Tribes, Leaders, and Customs from Prehistoric Times to the Present.* Montgomery, AL: NewSouth Books, 2011.

Browner, Tara, ed. *Music of the First Nations: Tradition and Innovation in Native North America.* Urbana: University of Illinois Press, 2009.

Bruchac, Joseph. *Flying with the Eagle, Racing the Great Bear: Tales from Native North America.* Golden, CO: Fulcrum, 2011.

Bruemmer, Fred. *Arctic Visions: Pictures from a Vanished World.* Toronto, Ontario: Key Porter Books, 2008.

Brugge, Doug, Timothy Benally, and Esther Yazzie-Lewis. *The Navajo People and Uranium Mining.* Albuquerque: University of New Mexico Press, 2006.

Bullchild, Percy. *The Sun Came Down: The History of the World as My Blackfeet Elders Told It.* Lincoln: University of Nebraska Press, 2005.

Burgan, Michael. *The Arapaho.* Tarrytown, NY: Marshall Cavendish Benchmark, 2009.

— — —. *Inuit History and Culture.* New York: Gareth Stevens, 2011.

Burke, Heather, et al, eds. *Kennewick Man: Perspectives on the Ancient One.* Walnut Creek, CA: Left Coast Press, 2008.

Burns, Louis F. *A History of the Osage People.* Tuscaloosa: University of Alabama Press, 2004.

— — —. *Osage Indian Customs and Myths.* Tuscaloosa: University of Alabama Press, 2005.

Button, Bertha P. *Friendly People: The Zuñi Indians.* Santa Fe, NM: Museum of New Mexico Press, 1963.

Calloway, Colin G. *The Shawnees and the War for America.* New York: Viking, 2007.

Carbone, Elisa. *Blood on the River: James Town 1607.* New York: Viking, 2006.

Carlos, Ann M. *Commerce by a Frozen Sea: Native Americans and the European Fur Trade.* Philadelphia: University of Pennsylvania Press, 2010.

Carlson, Paul H., and Tom Crum. *Myth, Memory, and Massacre: The Pease River Capture of Cynthia Ann Parker.* Lubbock: Texas Tech University Press, 2010.

Carlson, Richard G., ed. *Rooted Like the Ash Trees: New England Indians and the Land.* Naugatuck, CT: Eagle Wing Press, 1987.

Carpenter, Cecelia Svinth, Maria Victoria Pascualy, and Trisha Hunter. *Nisqually Indian Tribe.* Charleston, SC: Arcadia, 2008.

Carter, John G. *The Northern Arapaho Flat Pipe and the Ceremony of Covering the Pipe.* Whitefish, MT: Kessinger Publishing, 2007.

Cashin, Edward J. *Guardians of the Valley: Chickasaws in Colonial South Carolina and Georgia.* Columbia, SC: University of South Carolina Press, 2009.

Cassidy, James J., Jr., ed. *Through Indian Eyes: The Untold Story of Native American Peoples.* Pleasantville, NY: Reader's Digest Association, 1995.

Cassinelli, Dennis. *Preserving Traces of the Great Basin Indians.* Reno, NV: Jack Bacon & Company, 2006.

Castillo, Edward D. *The Pomo.* Austin: RaintreeSteck-Vaughn, 1999.

Chalcraft, Edwin L. *Assimilation's Agent: My Life as a Superintendent in the Indian Boarding School System.* Lincoln: University of Nebraska Press, 2007.

Champagne, Duane, ed. *The Native North American Almanac.* Detroit: Gale, 1994.

Charles, Nicholas and Maria. *Messenger Spirits: Yup'ik Masks and Stories.* Anchorage, AK: N & M, 2009.

Chatters, James C. *Ancient Encounters: Kennewick Man and the First Americans.* New York: Simon and Schuster, 2001.

Chaussonnet, Valerie, ed. *Crossroads Alaska: Native Cultures of Alaska and Siberia.* Washington, DC: Arctic Studies Center, National Museum of Natural History, Smithsonian Institution, 1995.

Chehak, Gail, and Jan Halliday. *Native Peoples of the Northwest: A Traveler's Guide to Land, Art, and Culture.* Seattle: Sasquatch Books, 2002.

Chenoweth, Avery, and Robert Llewellyn. *Empires in the Forest: Jamestown and the Making of America.* Earlysville, VA: Rivanna Foundation, 2010.

Childs, Craig. *House of Rain: Tracking a Vanished Civilization across the American Southwest.* 2nd ed. New York: Back Bay Books, 2008.

Clark, Cora, and Texa Bowen Williams. *Pomo Indians: Myths and Some of Their Sacred Meanings.* Reprint. Charleston, SC: Literary Licensing, 2011.

Clark, Ella E. *Indian Legends of the Pacific Northwest.* Berkeley: University of California Press, 2003.

Clark, Jerry E. *The Shawnee.* Lexington: University Press of Kentucky, 2007.

Clow, Richmond L., ed. *The Sioux in South Dakota History: A Twentieth-Century Reader.* Pierre, SD: South Dakota State Historical Society Press, 2007.

Cobb, Amanda J. *Listening to Our Grandmothers' Stories: The Bloomfield Academy for Chickasaw Females, 1852–1949.* Lincoln: University of Nebraska Press, 2007.

— — —. *Massacre at Camp Grant: Forgetting and Remembering Apache History.* Tucson: University of Arizona Press, 2007.

Cone, Marla. *Silent Snow: The Slow Poisoning of the Arctic.* New York: Grove Press, 2005.

Confederated Salish and Kootenai Tribes. *Bull Trout's Gift: A Salish Story about the Value of Reciprocity.* Lincoln: University of Nebraska Press, 2011.

Cook, Franklin A. "Nunapitchuk, Alaska: A Yup'ik Eskimo Village in Western Alaska." *Anna Tobeluk Memorial School, Nunapitchuk, Alaska.* Lincoln: University of Nebraska Press, 2005.

Cook, R. Michael, Eli Gifford, and Warren Jefferson, eds. *How Can One Sell the Air?: Chief Seattle's Vision.* Summertown, TN: Native Voices, 2005.

Corwin, Judith Hoffman. *Native American Crafts of the Northwest Coast, the Arctic, and the Subarctic.* New York: Franklin Watts, 2002.

Costa, David J. *Narratives and Winter Stories.* Oxford, OH: Myaamia Publications, 2010.

Coté, Charlotte. *Spirits of Our Whaling Ancestors: Revitalizing Makah, and Nuu-chah-nulth Traditions.* Seattle: University of Washington Press, 2010.

Coyote, Bertha Little, and Virginia Giglio. *Leaving Everything Behind: The Songs and Memories of a Cheyenne Woman.* Norman: University of Oklahoma Press, 1997.

Cozzens, Peter. *The Army and the Indian.* Mechanicsburg, PA: Stackpole Books, 2005.

Crediford, Gene J. *Those Who Remain.* Tuscaloosa: University of Alabama Press, 2009.

Crompton, Samuel Willard. *The Mohawk.* Edited by Paul C. Rosier. New York: Chelsea House Publishers, 2010.

Medicine Crow, Joseph. *Counting Coup: Becoming a Crow Chief on the Reservation and Beyond.* Washington, DC: National Geographic, 2006.

— — —. *From the Heart of the Crow Country: The Crow Indians' Own Stories.* Lincoln: University of Nebraska Press, 2000.

Crowell, Aron L. *Living Our Cultures, Sharing Our Heritage: The First Peoples of Alaska.* Washington, DC: Smithsonian Books, 2010.

Croy, Anita. *Ancient Pueblo: Archaeology Unlocks the Secrets of America's Past.* Washington, DC: National Geographic, 2007.

Cunningham, Kevin, and Peter Benoit. *The Wampanoag.* New York: Children's Press, 2011.

Curtin, Jeremiah. *Myths of the Modocs.* Whitefish, MT: Kessinger Publishing, 2006.

— — —. "The Yanas." In *Creation Myths of Primitive America.* Boston, MA: Little, Brown, and Company, 1903.

Curtain, Jeremiah, and Roland B. Dixon, eds. *Achomawi and Atsugewi Myths and Tales.* Reprint. Sandhurst, UK: Abela Publishing, 2009.

— — —. *The Plains Indian Photographs of Edward S. Curtis.* Lincoln: University of Nebraska Press, 2001.

— — —. "Salishan Tribes." In *The North American Indian.* Vol. 7. Edited by Frederick Webb Hodge. Norwood, MA: The Plimpton Press, 1911. Available online from http://curtis.library.northwestern.edu/curtis/viewPage.cgi?showp=1&size=2&id=nai.07.book.00000075&volume=7 (accessed on August 11, 2011).

— — — "Taos." In *The North American Indian (1907–1930).* Vol. 26. Reprint. New York: Johnson Reprint Corporation, 1970.

— — —. "Umatilla." In *The North American Indian,* edited by Fredrick Webb Hodge. Vol. 8. 1911. Available online from http://curtis.library.northwestern.edu/curtis/viewPage.cgi?showp=1&size=2&id=nai.08.book.00000129.p&volume=8#nav (accessed on August 11, 2011).

— — —. "The Washoe." In *The North American Indian*. Vol. 15. Edited by Frederick Webb Hodge. Norwood, MA: The Plimpton Press, 1926: 89–98. Available online from Northwestern University. http://curtis.library.northwestern.edu/curtis/viewPage.cgi?showp=1&size=2&id=nai.15.book.00000141&volume=15 (accessed on August 15, 2011).

Cushing, Frank H. *Zuñi Folk Tales*. Charleston, SC: Kessinger Publishing, 2011)

Cwiklik, Robert. *King Philip and the War with the Colonists*. Englewood Cliffs, NJ: Silver Burdette Press, 1989.

Dahlin, Curtis A., and Alan R. Woolworth. *The Dakota Uprising: A Pictorial History*. Edina, MN: Beaver's Pond Press, 2009.

Damas, David, ed. *Handbook of North American Indians,* Vol. 5: *Arctic*. Washington, DC: Smithsonian Institution, 1984.

Dangberg, Grace, translator. *Washo Tales*. Reprint. Carson City: Nevada State Museum, 1968.

De Angulo, Jaime. *Indian Tales*. Santa Clara, CA: Heyday Books, 2003.

De Capua, Sarah. *The Shawnee*. New York: Marshall Cavendish Benchmark, 2008.

De Laguna, Fredericæ. "Tlingit." In *Handbook of North American Indians: Northwest Coast*. Vol. 7, edited by Wayne Suttles. Washington, DC: Smithsonian Institution, 1990, pp. 203–28.

Decker, Carol Paradise. *Pecos Pueblo People through the Ages: "—And We're Still Here": Stories of Time and Place*. Santa Fe, NM: Sunstone Press, 2011.

Decker, Peter R. *"The Utes Must Go!": American Expansion and the Removal of a People*. Golden, CO: Fulcrum Publishing, 2004.

DeJong, David H. *Forced to Abandon Our Fields: The 1914 Clay Southworth Gila River Pima Interviews*. Salt Lake City: University of Utah Press, 2011.

Deloria, Vine, Jr. *Red Earth, White Lies: Native Americans and the Myth of Scientific Fact*. New York: Scribner, 1995.

Dempsey, L. James. *Blackfoot War Art: Pictographs of the Reservation Period, 1880–2000*. Norman: University of Oklahoma Press, 2007.

Denetdale, Jennifer. *The Long Walk: The Forced Navajo Exile*. New York: Chelsea House, 2008.

— — —. *The Navajo*. New York: Chelsea House, 2011.

Densmore, Frances. *American Indians and Their Music*. Kila, MN: Kessinger Publishing, 2010.

DeRose, Cat. *Little Raven: Chief of the Southern Arapaho*. Palmer Lake, CO: Filter Press, 2010.

Dial, Adolph L., and David K. Eliades. *The Only Land I Know: A History of the Lumbee Indians*. Syracuse: Syracuse University Press, 1996.

Dickey, Michael E. *The People of the River's Mouth: In Search of the Missouria Indians*. Columbia: University of Missouri, 2011.

Ditchfield, Christin. *Northeast Indians.* Chicago: Heinemann Library, 2012.

— — —. *Plateau Indians.* Chicago: Heinemann Library, 2012.

Doak, Robin S. *Arctic Peoples.* Chicago: Heinemann Library, 2012.

— — —. *Subarctic Peoples.* Mankato, MN: Heinemann-Raintree, 2011.

Doherty, Craig A. *California Indians.* New York: Chelsea House Publications, 2007.

— — —. *Northeast Indians.* Broomall, PA: Chelsea House Publications, March 2008.

— — —. *Southeast Indians.* Minneapolis, MN: Chelsea House, 2007.

Doherty, Craig A., and Katherine M. Doherty. *Arctic Peoples.* New York: Chelsea House, 2008.

— — —. *Great Basin Indians.* Minneapolis, MN: Chelsea House, 2010.

— — —. *Plains Indians.* New York: Chelsea House, 2008.

— — —. *Plateau Indians.* New York: Chelsea House, 2008.

— — —. *Southwest Indians.* Minneapolis, MN: Chelsea House, 2007.

Dolan, Edward F. *The American Indian Wars.* Brookfield, CT: Millbrook Press, 2003.

Donlan, Leni. *Cherokee Rose: The Trail of Tears.* Chicago, IL: Raintree, 2007.

Downum, Christian E. Hisatsinom: *Ancient Peoples in a Land without Water.* Santa Fe: School for Advanced Research Press, 2011.

Dresser, Thomas. *The Wampanoag Tribe of Martha's Vineyard: Colonization to Recognition.* Charleston, SC: History Press, 2011.

Driver, Harold E., and Walter R. Goldschmidt. *The Hupa White Deerskin Dance.* Whitefish, MT: Kessinger Publishing, 2007.

Drury, Clifford M., ed. *Nine Years with the Spokane Indians: The Diary, 1838–1848, of Elkanah Walker.* Glendale, CA: Arthur H. Clark Company, 1976.

DuBois, Cora. *The 1870 Ghost Dance.* Reprint. Lincoln: University of Nebraska, 2007.

Duncan, Kate C. *Northern Athapaskan Art: A Beadwork Tradition.* Seattle: University of Washington Press, 1989.

Dunn, Jacob Piatt. *Massacres of the Mountains: A History of the Indian Wars of the Far West 1815–1875.* Whitefish, MT: Kessinger Publishing, 2006.

Dutton, Bertha P. *Indians of the American Southwest.* Englewood Cliffs, NJ: Prentice-Hall, 1975.

Duval, Kathleen. *The Native Ground: Indians and Colonists in the Heart of the Continent.* Philadelphia: University of Pennsylvania Press, 2006.

Dwyer, Helen, ed. *Peoples of the Southwest, West, and North.* Redding, CT: Brown Bear Books, 2009.

Dwyer, Helen, and D. L. Birchfield. *Cheyenne History and Culture.* New York: Gareth Stevens, 2012.

Dwyer, Helen, and Mary A. Stout. *Nez Percé History and Culture.* New York: Gareth Stevens, 2012.

Eastman, Charles A. *The Essential Charles Eastman (Ohiyesa), Revised and Updated Edition: Light on the Indian World.* Michael Oren Fitzgerald, ed. Bloomington, IN: World Wisdom, 2007.

— — —. *From the Deep Woods to Civilization.* Whitefish, MT: Kessinger Publishing, 2006.

— — —. *The Soul of the Indian.* New York: Dodo Press, 2007.

Eaton, William M. *Odyssey of the Pueblo Indians: An Introduction to Pueblo Indian Petroglyphs, Pictographs and Kiva Art Murals in the Southwest.* Paducah, KY: Turner Publishing Company, 2001.

Ember, Melvin, and Peter N. Peregrine, eds. *Encyclopedia of Prehistory,* Vol. 2: *Arctic and Subarctic.* New York: Kluwer Academic/Plenum Publishers, 2001.

Englar, Mary. *The Iroquois: The Six Nations Confederacy.* Mankato, MN: Capstone Press, 2006.

Erb, Gene, and Ann DeWolf Erb. *Voices in Our Souls: The DeWolfs, Dakota Sioux and the Little Bighorn.* Santa Fe: Sunstone Press, 2010.

Erdoes, Richard. *The Sun Dance People: The Plains Indians, Their Past and Present.* New York: Random House, 1972.

Erickson, Kirstin C. *Yaqui Homeland and Homeplace.* Tucson: University of Arizona Press, 2008.

Erickson, Winston P. *Sharing the Desert: The Tohono O'Odham in History.* Tucson: University of Arizona Press, 2003.

Erikson, Patricia Pierce. *Voices of a Thousand People: The Makah Cultural and Research Center.* Lincoln: University of Nebraska Press, 2005.

Ezell, Paul H. "History of the Pima." In *Handbook of North American Indians,* Volume 10: *Southwest,* edited by Alfonso Ortiz. Washington, DC: Smithsonian Institution Press, 1983.

Falconer, Shelley, and Shawna White. *Stones, Bones, and Stitches: Storytelling through Inuit Art.* Toronto, Ontario: Tundra Books, 2007.

Fariello, Anna. *Cherokee Basketry: From the Hands of Our Elders.* Charleston, SC: History Press, 2009.

Field, Ron. *The Seminole Wars, 1818–58.* New York: Osprey, 2009.

Fitzgerald, Judith, and Michael Oren Fitzgerald, eds. *The Spirit of Indian Women.* Bloomington, IN: World Wisdom, 2005.

Forczyk, Robert. *Nez Percé 1877: The Last Fight.* Long Island City, NY: Osprey, 2011.

Foreman, Grant. *Indian Removal.* Norman: University of Oklahoma Press, 1972.

Foster, Martha Harroun. *We Know Who We Are: Métis Identity in a Montana Community.* Norman: University of Oklahoma Press, 2006.

Foster, Sharon Ewell. *Abraham's Well: A Novel.* Minneapolis, MN: Bethany House, 2006.

Fowler, Loretta. *The Columbia Guide to American Indians of the Great Plains.* New York: Columbia University Press, 2005.

Fradin, Dennis B. *The Pawnee.* Chicago: Childrens Press, 1988.

Frank, Andrew. *The Seminole.* New York: Chelsea House, 2011.

Freedman, Russell. *The Life and Death of Crazy Horse.* New York: Holiday House, 1996.

Gagnon, Gregory O. *Culture and Customs of the Sioux Indians.* Westport, CT: Greenwood, 2011.

Garfinkel, Alan P., and Harold Williams. *Handbook of the Kawaiisu.* Kern Valley, CA: Wa-hi Sina'avi, 2011.

Geake, Robert A. *A History of the Narragansett Tribe of Rhode Island: Keepers of the Bay.* Charleston, SC: History Press, 2011.

Geronimo. *The Autobiography of Geronimo.* St. Petersburg, FL: Red and Black Publishers, 2011.

Giago, Tim A. *Children Left Behind: Dark Legacy of Indian Mission Boarding Schools.* Santa Fe, NM: Clear Light Publishing, 2006.

Gibson, Karen Bush. *The Chumash: Seafarers of the Pacific Coast.* Mankato, MN: Bridgestone Books, 2004.

— — —. *The Great Basin Indians: Daily Life in the 1700s.* Mankato, MN: Capstone Press, 2006.

— — —. *New Netherland: The Dutch Settle the Hudson Valley.* Elkton, IN: Mitchell Lane Publishers, 2006.

Giddings, Ruth Warner. *Yaqui Myths and Legends.* Charleston, SC: BiblioBazaar, 2009.

Gipson, Lawrence Henry. *The Moravian Indian Mission on White River: Diaries and Letters, May 5, 1799, to November 12, 1806.* Indianapolis: Indiana Historical Bureau, 1938.

Girdner, Alwin J. *Diné Tah: My Reservation Days 1923–1938.* Tucson: Rio Nuevo Publishers, c2011.

Glancy, Diane. *Pushing the Bear: After the Trail of Tears.* Norman: University of Oklahoma Press, 2009.

Goddard, Pliny Earle. *Hupa Texts.* Reprint. Charleston, SC: BiblioBazaar, 2009.

— — —. *Life and Culture of the Hupa.* Reprint. Charleston, SC: Nabu Press, 2011.

— — —. *Myths and Tales from the San Carlos Apache.* Whitefish, MT: Kessinger Publishing, 2006.

———. *Myths and Tales of the White Mountain Apache.* Whitefish, MT: Kessinger Publishing, 2011.

Goodman, Linda J. *Singing the Songs of My Ancestors: The Life and Music of Helma Swan, Makah Elder.* Norman: University of Oklahoma Press, 2003.

Goodwin, Grenville. *Myths and Tales of the White Mountain Apache.* Whitefish, MT: Kessinger Publishing, 2011.

Gordon, Irene Ternier. *A People on the Move: The Métis of the Western Plains.* Surry, British Columbia: Heritage House, 2009.

Grafe, Steven L. ed. *Lanterns on the Prairie: The Blackfeet Photographs of Walter McClintock.* Norman: University of Oklahoma Press, 2009.

Grant, Blanche Chloe. *Taos Indians.* 1925 ed. Santa Fe: Sunstone Press, 2007.

Grant, Campbell. *Rock Paintings of the Chumash: A Study of a California Indian Culture.* Reprint. Santa Barbara, CA: Santa Barbara Museum of Natural History/EZ Nature Books, 1993.

Gray-Kanatiiosh, Barbara A. *Cahuilla.* Edina, MN: ABDO, 2007.

———. *Modoc.* Edina, MN: ABDO, 2007.

———. *Paiute.* Edina, MN: ABDO Publishing, 2007.

———. *Yurok.* Edina, MN: ABDO, 2007.

Graymont, Barbara. *The Iroquois.* New York: Chelsea House, 1988.

Green, Michael D., and Theda Perdue. *The Cherokee Nation and the Trail of Tears.* New York: Viking, 2007.

———. *The Columbia Guide to American Indians of the Southeast.* New York: Columbia University Press, 2001.

Grinnell, George Bird. *Blackfeet Indians Stories.* Whitefish, MT: Kessinger Publishing, 2006.

———. *The Cheyenne Indians: Their History and Lifeways.* Bloomington, IN: World Wisdom, 2008.

Guigon, Catherine, Francis Latreille, and Fredric Malenfer. *The Arctic.* New York: Abrams Books for Young Readers, 2007.

Gunther, Vanessa. *Chief Joseph.* Greenwood, 2010.

Guthridge, George. *The Kids from Nowhere: The Story behind the Arctic Education Miracle.* Anchorage: Alaska Northwest Books, 2006.

Hagan, William T. *The Sac and Fox Indians.* Norman: University of Oklahoma Press, 2008.

Hahn, Elizabeth. *The Pawnee.* Vero Beach, FL: Rourke Publications, Inc., 1992.

Haig-Brown, Roderick. *The Whale People.* Madeira Park, BC: Harbour Publishing, 2003.

Hancock, David A. *Tlingit: Their Art and Culture.* Blaine, WA: Hancock House Publishers, 2003.

Handbook of North American Indians, Vol. 6: *Subarctic.* Ed. June Helm. Washington, DC: Smithsonian Institution, 1981.

Harpster, Jack, and Ken Stalter. *Captive!: The Story of David Ogden and the Iroquois.* Santa Barbara, CA: Praeger, 2010.

Harrington, Mark Raymond. *Certain Caddo Sites in Arkansas.* Charleston, SC: Johnson Press, 2011.

Hayes, Allan, and Carol Hayes. *The Desert Southwest: Four Thousand Years of Life And Art.* Berkeley, CA: Ten Speed Press, 2006.

Hearth, Amy Hill. *"Strong Medicine Speaks": A Native American Elder Has Her Say: An Oral History.* New York: Atria Books, 2008.

Hebner, William Logan. *Southern Paiute: A Portrait.* Logan: Utah State University Press, 2010.

Heinämäki, Leena. *The Right to Be a Part of Nature: Indigenous Peoples and the Environment.* Rovaniemi, Finland: Lapland University Press, 2010.

Heizer, R. F., ed. *Handbook of North American Indians.* Vol. 8: *California.* Washington, DC: Smithsonian Institution, 1978.

Hessel, Ingo. *Inuit Art: An Introduction.* Vancouver, British Columbia: Douglas & McIntyre, 2002.

Hicks, Terry Allan. *The Chumash.* New York: Marshall Cavendish Benchmark, 2008.

— — —. *The Zuñi.* New York: Marshall Cavendish Benchmark, 2010.

Hill, George, Robert H. Ruby, and John A. Brown. *The Spokane Indians: Children of the Sun.* Norman: University of Oklahoma Press, 2006.

Himsl, Sharon M. *The Shoshone.* San Diego, CA: Lucent Books, 2005.

Hirst, Stephen. *I Am the Grand Canyon: The Story of the Havasupai People.* Grand Canyon, AZ: Grand Canyon Association, 2006.

Hobson, Geary. *Plain of Jars and Other Stories.* East Lansing: Michigan State University Press, 2011.

Hodge, Frederick Webb. "Dwamish." *Handbook of American Indians North of Mexico.* New York: Pageant Books, 1959.

Hogeland, Kim, and L. Frank Hogeland. *First Families: Photographic History of California Indians.* Berkeley: Heyday Books, 2007.

Holm, Bill. *Spirit and Ancestor: A Century of Northwest Coast Indian Art in the Burke Museum.* Seattle: Burke Museum; University of Washington Press, 1987.

Hooper, Lucile. *The Cahuilla Indians.* Kila, MN: Kessinger Publishing, 2011.

Hoover, Alan L. *Nuu-chah-nulth Voices, Histories, Objects, andJourneys.* Victoria: Royal British Columbia Museum, 2000.

Hopping, Lorraine Jean. *Chief Joseph: The Voice for Peace.* New York: Sterling, 2010.

Houston, James A. *James Houston's Treasury of Inuit Legends.* Orlando, FL: Harcourt, 2006.

Hungrywolf, Adolf. *Tribal Childhood: Growing Up in Traditional Native America.* Summertown, TN:Native Voices, 2008.

Hyde, Dayton O. *The Last Free Man: The True Story behind the Massacre of Shoshone Mike and His Band of Indians in 1911.* New York: Dial Press, 1973.

Hyde, George E. *Indians of the Woodlands: From Prehistoric Times to 1725.* Norman: University of Oklahoma Press, 1962.

Indians of the Northwest Coast and Plateau. Chicago: World Book, 2009.

Indians of the Southwest. Chicago: World Book, 2009.

Inupiaq and Yupik People of Alaska. Anchorage: Alaska Geographic Society, 2004.

Jacknis, Ira. *The Storage Box of Tradition: Kwakiutl Art, Anthropologists, and Museums, 1881–1981.* Washington, DC: Smithsonian Institution Press, 2002.

Jackson, Helen Hunt. *The Indian Reform Letters of Helen Hunt Jackson, 1879–1885.*Edited by Valerie ShererMathes. Norman: University of Oklahoma Press, 1998.

— — —. *Ramona.* New York: Signet, 1988.

James, Cheewa. *Modoc: The Tribe That Wouldn't Die.* Happy Camp, CA: Naturegraph, 2008.

Jastrzembski, Joseph C. *The Apache.* Minneapolis: Chelsea House, 2011.

— — —. *The Apache Wars: The Final Resistance.* Minneapolis: Chelsea House, 2007.

Jenness, Aylette, and Alice Rivers. *In Two Worlds: A Yu'pik Eskimo Family.* New York: Houghton Mifflin, 1989.

Jennys, Susan. *19th Century Plains Indian Dresses.* Pottsboro, TX: Crazy Crow, 2004.

Jensen, Richard E., ed. *The Pawnee Mission Letters, 1834-1851.* Lincoln: University of Nebraska Press, 2010.

Jeter, Marvin D. *Edward Palmer's Arkansaw Mounds.* Tuscaloosa: University of Alabama Press, 2010.

Johansen, Bruce E. *The Iroquois.* New York, NY: Chelsea House, 2010.

Johnsgard, Paul A. *Wind through the Buffalo Grass: A Lakota Story Cycle.* Lincoln, NE: Plains Chronicles Press, 2008.

Johnson, Jerald Jay. "Yana." In *Handbook of North American Indians.* Vol. 10: *Southwest,* edited by Alfonso Ortiz. Washington, DC: Smithsonian Institution, 1983.

Johnson, Michael. *American Indians of the Southeast.* Oxford: Osprey Publishing, 1995.

— — —. "Duwamish." *The Native Tribes of North America.* New York: Macmillan, 1992.

— — —. *Native Tribes of the Northeast.* Milwaukee, WI: World Almanac Library, 2004.

Johnson, Michael, and Jonathan Smith. *Indian Tribes of the New England Frontier.* Oxford: Osprey Publishing, 2006.

Johnson, Thomas H., and Helen S. Johnson. *Also Called Sacajawea: Chief Woman's Stolen Identity.* Long Grove, IL: Waveland Press, 2008.

— — —. *Two Toms: Lessons from a Shoshone Doctor.* Salt Lake City: University of Utah Press, 2010.

Jonaitis, Aldona. *Art of the Northwest Coast.* Seattle: University of Washington Press, 2006.

Joseph, Frank. *Advanced Civilizations of Prehistoric America: The Lost Kingdoms of the Adena, Hopewell, Mississippians, and Anasazi.* Rochester, VT: Bear & Company, December 21, 2009.

Josephson, Judith Pinkerton. *Why Did Cherokees Move West? And Other Questions about the Trail of Tears.* Minneapolis: Lerner Publications, 2011.

Josephy, Alvin M., Jr. *500 Nations: An Illustrated History of North American Indians.* New York: Knopf, 1994.

— — —. *Nez Percé Country.* Lincoln: University of Nebraska Press, 2007.

Kallen, Stuart A. *The Pawnee.* San Diego: Lucent Books, 2001.

Kaneuketat. *I Dreamed the Animals: Kaneuketat: the Life of an Innu Hunter.* New York: Berghahn Books, 2008.

Kavasch, E. Barrie. *Enduring Harvests: Native American Foods and Festivals for Every Season.* Old Saybrook, CT: The Globe Pequot Press, 1995.

Keegan, Marcia. *Pueblo People: Ancient Tradition, Modern Lives.* Santa Fe, NM: Clear Light Publishers, 1999.

— — —. *Taos Pueblo and Its Sacred Blue Lake.* Santa Fe: Clear Light Publishers, 2010.

Keegan, Marcia, and Regis Pecos. *Pueblo People: Ancient Traditions, Modern Lives.* Santa Fe, NM: Clear Light Publishers, 1999.

Kegg, Maude. *Portage Lake: Memories of an Ojibwe Childhood.* Edmonton: University of Alberta Press, 1991.

Kennedy, J. Gerald. *Life of Black Hawk, or Ma-ka-tai-me-she-kia-kiak. Dictated by Himself.* New York: Penguin Books, 2008.

King, David C. *The Blackfeet.* New York: Marshall Cavendish Benchmark, 2010.

— — —. *First People.* New York: DK Children, 2008.

— — —. *The Inuit.* New York: Marshall Cavendish Benchmark, 2008.

— — —. *The Nez Percé.* New York: Benchmark Books, 2008.

— — —. *Seminole.* New York: Benchmark Books, 2007.

Kiowa and Pueblo Art: Watercolor Paintings by Native American Artists. Mineola, NY: Dover Publications, 2009.

Kirkpatrick, Katherine. *Mysterious Bones: The Story of Kennewick Man.* New York: Holiday House, 2011.

Kissock,Heather, and Jordan McGill. *Apache: American Indian Art and Culture.* New York: Weigl Publishers, 2011.

Kissock, Heather, and Rachel Small. *Caddo: American Indian Art and Culture.* New York: Weigl Publishers, 2011.

Koyiyumptewa, Stewart B., Carolyn O'Bagy Davis, and the Hopi Cultural Preservation Office. *The Hopi People.* Charleston, SC: Arcadia Publishing, 2009.

Kristofic, Jim. *Navajos Wear Nikes: A Reservation Life.* Albuquerque: University of New Mexico Press, 2011.

Kroeber, Theodora. *Ishi in Two Worlds: A Biography of the Last Wild Indian in North America.* Berkeley: University of California Press, 2004.

Krupnik, Igor, and Dyanna Jolly, eds. *The Earth Is Faster Now: Indigenous Observations of Arctic Environmental Change.* Fairbanks, Alaska: Arctic Research Consortium of the United States, 2002.

Kuiper, Kathleen, ed. *American Indians of California, the Great Basin, and the Southwest.* New York: Rosen Educational Services, 2012.

— — —. *American Indians of the Northeast and Southeast.* New York: Rosen Educational Services, 2012.

— — —. *American Indians of the Plateau and Plains.* New York: Rosen Educational Services, 2012.

— — —. *Indigenous Peoples of the Arctic, Subarctic, and Northwest Coast.* New York: Rosen Educational Services, 2012.

Lacey, T. Jensen. *The Blackfeet.* New York: Chelsea House, 2011.

— — —. *The Comanche.* New York: Chelsea House, 2011.

Lankford, George E., ed. *Native American Legends of the Southeast: Tales from the Natchez, Caddo, Biloxi, Chickasaw, and Other Nations.* 5th ed. Tuscaloosa: University of Alabama Press, 2011.

Lanmon, Dwight P. and Francis H. Harlow. *The Pottery of Zuñi Pueblo.* Santa Fe: Museum of New Mexico Press, 2008.

Larsen, Mike, Martha Larsen, and Jeannie Barbour. *Proud to Be Chickasaw.* Ada, OK: Chickasaw Press, 2010.

Lenik, Edward J. *Making Pictures in Stone: American Indian Rock Art of the Northeast.* Tuscaloosa: University of Alabama Press, 2009.

Levine, Michelle. *The Delaware.* Minneapolis, MN: Lerner Publications, 2006.

— — —. *The Ojibway.* Minneapolis, MN: Lerner Publications, 2006.

Levy, Janey. *The Wampanoag of Massachusetts and Rhode Island*. New York: PowerKids Press, 2005.

Liebert, Robert. *Osage Life and Legends: Earth People/Sky People*. Happy Camp, California: Naturegraph Publishers, 1987.

Life Stories of Our Native People: Shoshone, Paiute, Washo. Reno, NV: Intertribal Council of Nevada, 1974.

Liptak, Karen. *North American Indian Ceremonies*. New York: Franklin Watts, 1992.

Little, Kimberley Griffiths. *The Last Snake Runner*. New York: Alfred A. Knopf, 2002.

Lloyd, J. William. *Aw-aw-tam Indian Nights: The Myths and Legends of the Pimas*. Westfield, NJ: The Lloyd Group, 1911. Available online from http://www.sacred-texts.com/nam/sw/ain/index.htm (accessed on July 20, 2011).

Lobo, Susan, Steve Talbot, and Traci L. Morris, compilers. *Native American Voices: A Reader*. 3rd ed. Upper Saddle River, NJ: Prentice Hall, 2010.

Lourie, Peter. *The Lost World of the Anasazi: Exploring the Mysteries of Chaco Canyon*. Honesdale, PA: Boyds Mills Press, 2007.

Macdougall, Brenda. *One of the Family: Metis Culture in Nineteenth-Century Northwestern Saskatchewan*. Vancouver, British Columbia: UBC Press, 2010.

Mann, John W.W. *Sacajawea's People: The Lemhi Shoshones and the Salmon River Country*. Lincoln, NE: Bison Books, 2011.

Margolin, Malcolm. *The Ohlone Way*. Berkeley, CA: Heyday Books, 1981.

— — —. *The Way We Lived: California Indian Stories, Songs, and Reminiscences*. Reprint. Heyday Books, Berkeley, California, 2001.

Marriott, Alice, and Carol K. Rachlin. *Plains Indian Mythology*. New York, NY: Thomas Y. Crowell, 1975.

Marshall, Ann, ed. *Home: Native People in the Southwest*. Phoenix, AZ: Heard Museum, 2005.

Marshall, Bonnie. *Far North Tales: Stories from the Peoples of the Arctic Circle*. Edited by Kira Van Deusen. Santa Barbara, CA: Libraries Unlimited, 2011.

Marsi, Katie. *The Trail of Tears: The Tragedy of the American Indians*. New York: Marshall Cavendish Benchmark, 2010.

McDaniel, Melissa. *Great Basin Indians*. Des Plaines, IL: Heinemann, 2011.

— — —. *The Sac and Fox Indians*. New York: Chelsea Juniors, 1995.

— — —. *Southwest Indians*. Chicago: Heinemann Library, 2012.

Mcmullen, John William. *Ge Wisnemen! (Let's Eat!): A Potawatomi Family Dinner Manual*. Charleston, SC: CreateSpace, 2011.

Melody, Michael E., and Paul Rosier. *The Apache*. Minneapolis: Chelsea House, 2005.

Merriam, C. Hart. *The Dawn of the World: Myths and Tales of the Miwok Indians of California.* Kila, MN: Kessinger Publishing, 2010.

Michael, Hauser. *Traditional Inuit Songs from the Thule Area.* Copenhagen: Museum Tusculanum Press, 2010.

Miles, Ray. "Wichita." *Native America in the Twentieth Century, An Encyclopedia.* Ed. Mary B. Davis. New York: Garland Publishing, 1994.

Miller, Debbie S., and Jon Van Dyle. *Arctic Lights, Arctic Nights.* New York: Walker Books for Young Readers, 2007.

Miller, Frederic P., Agnes F. Vandome, and John McBrewster, eds. *Nuu-chah-nulth People.* Beau Bassin, Mauritius: Alphascript Publishing, 2011.

Miller, Raymond H. *North American Indians: The Apache.* San Diego: KidHaven Press, 2005.

Milner, George R. *The Moundbuilders: Ancient Peoples of Eastern North America.* New York: Thames & Hudson, 2005.

Mooney, James. *Calendar History of the Kiowa Indians.* Whitefish, MT: Kessinger Publishing, 2006.

— — —. *Myths of the Cherokee.* New York: Dover Publications, 1996.

Mosqueda, Frank, and Vickie Leigh Krudwig. *The Hinono'ei Way of Life: An Introduction to the Arapaho People.* Edited by Susan Scott Hill. Concho, OK: Cheyenne and Arapaho Tribes of Oklahoma, 2008.

— — —. *The Prairie Thunder People: A Brief History of the Arapaho People.* Edited by Susan Scott Hill. Concho, OK: Cheyenne and Arapaho Tribes of Oklahoma, 2008.

Mossiker, Frances. *Pocahontas: The Life and the Legend.* New York: Alfred A. Knopf, 1976.

Mundell, Kathleen. *North by Northeast: Wabanaki, Akwesasne Mohawk, and Tuscarora Traditional Arts.* Gardiner, ME: Tilbury House, Publishers, 2008.

Myers, Albert Cook, ed. *William Penn's Own Account of the Lenni Lenape or Delaware Indians.* Somerset, NJ: Middle Atlantic Press, 1970.

Myers, Arthur. *The Pawnee.* New York: Franklin Watts, 1993.

Myers, James E. "Cahto." In *Handbook of North American Indians.* Vol. 8: *California,* edited by R. F. Heizer. Washington, D.C.: Smithsonian Institution, 1978: 244–48.

Neeley, Bill. *The Last Comanche Chief: The Life and Times of Quanah Parker.* New York: Wiley, 1996.

Nelson, Sharlene, and Ted W. Nelson. *The Makah.* New York: Franklin Watts, 2003.

Nez, Chester, and Judith Schiess Avila. *Code Talker.* New York: Berkley Caliber, 2011.

Nichols, Richard. *A Story to Tell: Traditions of a Tlingit Community.* Minneapolis: Lerner Publications Company, 1998.

Nowell, Charles James. *Smoke from their Fires: The Life of a Kwakiutl Chief.* Hamdon, CT: Archon Books, 1968.

O'Neale, Lila M. *Yurok-Karok Basket Weavers.* Berkeley, CA: Phoebe A. Hearst Museum of Anthropology, 2007.

Opler, Morris Edward. *Myths and Tales of the Chiricahua Apache Indians.* Charleston, SC: Kessinger Publishing, 2011.

Ortega, Simon, ed. *Handbook of North American Indians.* Vol. 12: *The Plateau.* Washington, DC: Smithsonian Institution, 1978.

Ortiz, Alfonso, ed. *Handbook of American Indians.* Vols. 9–10. *The Southwest.* Washington, DC: Smithsonian Institution, 1978–83.

Owings, Alison. *Indian Voices: Listening to Native Americans.* New Brunswick, N.J.: Rutgers University Press, 2011.

Page, Jake, and Susanne Page. *Indian Arts of the Southwest.* Tucson, AZ: Rio Nuevo Publishers, 2008.

Page, Susanne and Jake. *Navajo.* Tucson, AZ: Rio Nuevo Publishers, 2010.

Paige, Amanda L., Fuller L. Bumpers, and Daniel F. Littlefield, Jr. *Chickasaw Removal.* Ada, OK: Chickasaw Press, 2010.

Palazzo-Craig, Janet. *The Ojibwe of Michigan, Wisconsin, Minnesota, and North Dakota.* New York: PowerKids Press, 2005.

Peltier, Leonard. *Prison Writings: My Life Is My Sun Dance.* New York: St. Martin's, 2000.

Penny, Josie. *So Few on Earth: A Labrador Métis Woman Remembers.* Toronto, Ontario: Dundurn Press, 2010.

Peoples of the Arctic and Subarctic. Chicago: World Book, 2009.

Perritano, John. *Spanish Missions.* New York: Children's Press, 2010.

Philip, Neil, ed. *A Braid of Lives: Native American Childhood.* New York: Clarion Books, 2000.

Pierson, George. *The Kansa, or Kaw Indians, and Their History, and the Story of Padilla.* Charleston, SC: Nabu Press, 2010.

Pijoan, Teresa. *Pueblo Indian Wisdom: Native American Legends and Mythology.* Santa Fe: Sunstone Press, 2000.

Pritzker, Barry, and Paul C. Rosier. *The Hopi.* New York: Chelsea House, c. 2011.

Riddell, Francis A. "Maidu and Concow." *Handbook of North American Indians.* Vol. 8: *California.* Edited by Robert F. Heizer. Washington DC: Smithsonian Institution, 1978.

Rielly, Edward J. *Legends of American Indian Resistance.* Westport, CT: Greenwood, 2011.

Riordan, Robert. *Medicine for Wildcat: A Story of the Friendship between a Menominee Indian and Frontier Priest Samuel Mazzuchelli.* Revised by

Marilyn Bowers Gorun and the Sinsinawa Dominican Sisters. Sinsinawa, WI: Sinsinawa Dominican Sisters, 2006.

Rollings, Willard H. *The Comanche.* New York: Chelsea House Publications, 2004.

Rosoff, Nancy B., and Susan Kennedy Zeller. *Tipi: Heritage of the Great Plains.* Seattle: Brooklyn Museum in association with University of Washington Press, 2011.

Ruby, Robert H., John A. Brown, and Cary C. Collins. *A Guide to the Indian Tribes of the Pacific Northwest.* Norman: University of Oklahoma Press, 2010.

Russell, Frank. *The Pima Indians.* Whitefish, MT: Kessinger Publishing, 2010.

Ryan, Marla Felkins, and Linda Schmittroth. *Tribes of Native America: Zuñi Pueblo.* San Diego: Blackbirch Press, 2002.

— — —. *Ute.* San Diego: Blackbirch Press, 2003.

Rzeczkowski, Frank. *The Lakota Sioux.* New York: Chelsea House, 2011.

Seton, Ernest Thompson. *Sign Talk of the Cheyenne Indians.* Mineola, NY: Dover Publications, 2000.

Sherrow, Victoria. *The Iroquois Indians.* New York: Chelsea House, 1992.

Shipek, Florence Connolly. "Luiseño." In *Native America in the Twentieth Century: An Encyclopedia,* edited by Mary B. Davis. New York: Garland Publishing, 1994.

Shipley, William. *The Maidu Indian Myths and Stories of Hanc'Ibyjim.* Berkeley: Heyday Books, 1991.

Shull, Jodie A. *Voice of the Paiutes: A Story About Sarah Winnemucca.* Minneapolis, MN: Millbrook Press, 2007.

Simermeyer, Genevieve. *Meet Christopher: An Osage Indian Boy from Oklahoma.* Tulsa, OK: National Museum of the American Indian, Smithsonian Institution, in association with Council Oak Books, 2008.

Simmons, Marc. *Friday, the Arapaho Boy: A Story from History.* Albuquerque: University of New Mexico Press, 2004.

Sita, Lisa. *Indians of the Northeast: Traditions, History, Legends, and Life.* Milwaukee, WI: Gareth Stevens, 2000.

— — —. *Pocahontas: The Powhatan Culture and the Jamestown Colony.* New York: PowerPlus Books, 2005.

Slater, Eva. *Panamint Shoeshone Basketry: An American Art Form.* Berkeley: Heyday Books, 2004.

Smith, White Mountain. *Indian Tribes of the Southwest.* Kila, MN: Kessinger Publishing, 2005.

Snell, Alma Hogan. *A Taste of Heritage: Crow Indian Recipes & Herbal Medicines.* Lincoln: University of Nebraska Press, 2006.

Sneve, Virginia Driving Hawk. *The Cherokee*. New York: Holiday House, 1996.

———. *The Cheyenne*. New York: Holiday House, 1996.

———. *The Iroquois*. New York: Holiday House, 1995.

———. *The Nez Percé*. New York: Holiday House, 1994.

———. *The Seminoles*. New York: Holiday House, 1994.

Snyder, Clifford Gene. *Ghost Trails: Mythology and Folklore of the Chickasaw, Choctaw, Creeks and Other Muskoghean Indian Tribes*. North Hollywood, CA: JES, 2009.

———. *The Muskogee Chronicles: Accounts of the Early Muskogee/Creek Indians*. N. Hollywood, CA: JES, 2008.

Solomon, Madeline. *Koyukon Athabaskan Songs*. Homer, AK: Wizard Works, 2003.

Sonneborn, Liz. *The Choctaws*. Minneapolis, MN: Lerner Publications, 2007.

———. *The Creek*. Minneapolis: Lerner Publications, 2007.

———. *The Chumash*. Minneapolis, MN: Lerner Publications, 2007.

———. *The Navajos*. Minneapolis, MN: Lerner Publications, 2007.

———. *Northwest Coast Indians*. Chicago: Heinemann Library, 2012.

———. *The Shoshones*. Minneapolis, MN: Lerner Publications, 2006.

———. *Wilma Mankiller*. New York: Marshall Cavendish Benchmark, 2010.

Spalding, Andrea. *Secret of the Dance*. Orca, WA: Orca Book Publishers, 2006.

Spence, Lewis. *Myths and Legends of the North American Indians*. Whitefish, MT: Kessinger Publishing, 1997.

Spragg-Braude, Stacia. *To Walk in Beauty: A Navajo Family's Journey Home*. Santa Fe: Museum of New Mexico Press, 2009.

Sprague, DonovinArleigh. *American Indian Stories*. West Stockbridge, CT: Hard Press, 2006.

———. *Choctaw Nation of Oklahoma*. Chicago, IL: Arcadia, 2007.

———. *Old Indian Legends: Retold by Zitkala--Sa*. Paris: Adamant Media Corporation, 2006.

———. *Standing Rock Sioux*. Charleston, SC: Arcadia, 2004.

St. Lawrence, Genevieve. *The Pueblo And Their History*. Minneapolis, MN: Compass Point Books, 2006.

Stanley, George E. *Sitting Bull: Great Sioux Hero*. New York: Sterling, 2010.

Stern, Pamela R. *Daily Life of the Inuit*. Santa Barbara, CA: Greenwood, 2010.

Sterngass, Jon. *Geronimo*. New York: Chelsea House, 2010.

Stevenson, Matilda Coxe. *The Zuñi Indians and Their Uses of Plants.* Charleston, SC: Kessinger Publishing, 2011.

Stevenson, Tilly E. *The Religious Life of the Zuñi Child.* Charleston, SC: Kessinger Publishing, 2011.

Stewart, Philip. *Osage.* Philadelphia, PA: Mason Crest Publishers, 2004.

Stirling, M.W. *Snake Bites and the Hopi Snake Dance.* Whitefish, MT: Kessinger Publishing, 2011.

Stone, Amy M. *Creek History and Culture.* Milwaukee: Gareth Stevens Publishing, 2011.

Stout, Mary. *Blackfoot History and Culture.* New York: Gareth Stevens, 2012.

— — —. *Hopi History and Culture.* New York: Gareth Stevens, 2011.

— — —. *Shoshone History and Culture.* New York: Gareth Stevens, 2011.

Strack, Andrew J. *How the Miami People Live.* Edited by Mary Tippman, Meghan Dorey and Daryl Baldwin. Oxford, OH: Myaamia Publications, 2010.

Straub, Patrick. *It Happened in South Dakota: Remarkable Events That Shaped History.* New York: Globe Pequot, 2009.

Sullivan, Cathie, and Gordon Sullivan. *Roadside Guide to Indian Ruins & Rock Art of the Southwest.* Englewood, CO: Westcliffe Publishers, 2006.

Sullivan, George. *Geronimo: Apache Renegade.* New York: Sterling, 2010.

Suttles, Wayne, and Barbara Lane. "Southern Coast Salish." *Handbook of North American Indians.* Vol. 7: *Northwest Coast.* Edited by Wayne Suttles. Washington, DC: Smithsonian Institution, 1990.

Swanton, John R., and Franz Boas. *Haida Songs; Tsimshian Texts (1912).* Vol. 3. Whitefish, MT: Kessinger Publishing, 2010.

Sweet, Jill Drayson, and Nancy Hunter Warren. *Pueblo Dancing.* Atglen, PA: Schiffer Publishing, 2011.

Tenenbaum, Joan M., and Mary Jane McGary, eds. *Denaina Sukdua: Traditional Stories of the Tanaina Athabaskans.* Fairbanks: Alaska Native Language Center, 2006.

Tiller, Veronica E. Velarde. *Culture and Customs of the Apache Indians.* Santa Barbara, CA: ABC-CLIO, 2011.

Underhill, Ruth. *The Papago Indians of Arizona and their Relatives the Pima.* Whitefish, MT: Kessinger Publishing, 2010.

Van Deusen, Kira. *Kiviuq: An Inuit Hero and His Siberian Cousins.* Montreal: McGill-Queen's University Press, 2009.

Vanderwerth, W. C. *Indian Oratory: Famous Speeches by Noted Indian Chieftains.* Norman: University of Oklahoma Press, 1979.

Vaudrin, Bill. *Tanaina Tales from Alaska.* Norman: University of Oklahoma Press, 1969.

Viola, Herman J. *Trail to Wounded Knee: The Last Stand of the Plains Indians 1860–1890.* Washington, DC: National Geographic, 2004.

Von Ahnen, Katherine. *Charlie Young Bear.* Minot, CO: Roberts Rinehart Publishers, 1994.

Wade, Mary Dodson. *Amazing Cherokee Writer Sequoyah.* Berkeley Heights, NJ: Enslow, 2009.

Wagner, Frederic C. III. *Participants in the Battle of the Little Big Horn: A Biographical Dictionary of Sioux, Cheyenne and United States Military Personnel.* Jefferson, NC: McFarland, 2011.

Waldman, Carl. "Colville Reservation." In *Encyclopedia of Native American Tribes.* New York: Facts on File, 2006.

— — —. *Encyclopedia of Native American Tribes.* New York: Facts on File, 2006.

Wallace, Mary. *The Inuksuk Book.* Toronto, Ontario: Maple Tree Press, 2004.

— — —. *Make Your Own Inuksuk.* Toronto, Ontario: Maple Tree Press, 2004.

Wallace, Susan E. *The Land of the Pueblos.* Santa Fe, NM: Sunstone Press, 2006.

Ward, Jill. *The Cherokees.* Hamilton, GA: State Standards, 2010.

— — —. *Creeks and Cherokees Today.* Hamilton, GA: State Standards, 2010.

Warm Day, Jonathan. *Taos Pueblo: Painted Stories.* Santa Fe, NM: Clear Light Publishing, 2004.

Waters, Frank. *Book of the Hopi.* New York: Viking Press, 1963.

White, Bruce. *We Are at Home: Pictures of the Ojibwe People.* St. Paul, MN: Minnesota Historical Society Press, 2007.

White, Tekla N. *San Francisco Bay Area Missions.* Minneapolis, MN: Lerner, 2007.

Whitehead, Ruth Holmes. *The Micmac: How Their Ancestors Lived Five Hundred Years Ago.* Halifax, Nova Scotia: Nimbus, 1983.

Whiteman, Funston, Michael Bell, and Vickie Leigh Krudwig. *The Cheyenne Journey: An Introduction to the Cheyenne People.* Edited by Susan Scott-Hill. Concho, OK: Cheyenne and Arapaho Tribes of Oklahoma, 2008.

— — —. *The Tsististas: People of the Plains.* Edited by Susan Scott-Hill. Concho, OK: Cheyenne and Arapaho Tribes of Oklahoma, 2008.

Wiggins, Linda E., ed. *Dena—The People: The Way of Life of the Alaskan Athabaskans Described in Nonfiction Stories, Biographies, and Impressions from All Over the Interior of Alaska.* Fairbanks: Theata Magazine, University of Alaska, 1978.

Wilcox, Charlotte. *The Iroquois.* Minneapolis, MN: Lerner Publishing Company, 2007.

— — —. *The Seminoles.* Minneapolis: Lerner Publications, 2007.

Wilds, Mary C. *The Creek.* San Diego, CA: Lucent Books, 2005.

Wiles, Sara. *Arapaho Journeys: Photographs and Stories from the Wind River Reservation.* Norman: University of Oklahoma Press, 2011.

Williams, Jack S. *The Luiseno of California.* New York: PowerKids Press, 2003.

———. *The Modoc of California and Oregon.* New York: PowerKids Press, 2004.

———. *The Mojave of California and Arizona.* New York: PowerKids Press, 2004.

Wilson, Darryl J. *The Morning the Sun Went Down.* Berkeley, CA: Heyday, 1998.

Wilson, Elijah Nicholas. *The White Indian Boy: The Story of Uncle Nick among the Shoshones.* Kila, MN: Kessinger Publishing, 2004.

Wilson, Frazer Ells. *The Peace of Mad Anthony: An Account of the Subjugation of the Northwestern Indian Tribes and the Treaty of Greeneville.* Kila, MN: Kessinger Publishing, 2005.

Wilson, Norman L., and Arlean H. Towne. "Nisenan." In *Handbook of North American Indians.* Vol. 8: *California.* Edited by Robert F. Heizer. Washington DC: Smithsonian Institution, 1978.

Winnemucca, Sarah. *Life among the Paiutes: Their Wrongs and Claims.* Privately printed, 1883. Reprint. Reno: University of Nevada Press, 1994.

Wolcott, Harry F. *A Kwakiutl Village and School.* Walnut Creek, CA: AltaMira Press, 2003.

Wolfson, Evelyn. *The Iroquois: People of the Northeast.* Brookfield, CT: The Millbrook Press, 1992.

Woolworth, Alan R. *Santee Dakota Indian Tales.* Saint Paul, MN: Prairie Smoke Press, 2003.

Worl, Rosita. *Celebration: Tlingit, Haida, Tsimshian Dancing on the Land.* Edited by Kathy Dye. Seattle: University of Washington Press, 2008.

Wright, Muriel H. *A Guide to the Indian Tribes of Oklahoma.* Norman: University of Oklahoma Press, 1951.

Wyborny, Sheila. *North American Indians: Native Americans of the Southwest.* San Diego: KidHaven Press, 2004.

Wynecoop, David C. *Children of the Sun: A History of the Spokane Indians.* Wellpinit, WA, 1969. Available online from http://www.wellpinit.wednet.edu/shorthistory (accessed on August 11, 2011).

Wyss, Thelma Hatch. *Bear Dancer: The Story of a Ute Girl.* Chicago: Margaret K. McElderry Books, 2010.

Zepeda, Ofelia. *Where Clouds Are Formed: Poems.* Tucson: University of Arizona Press, 2008.

Zigmond, Maurice L. *Kawaiisu Mythology: An Oral Tradition of South-Central California.* Banning, CA: Malki-Ballena Press, 1980.

— — —. "Kawaiisu." In *Handbook of North American Indians, Great Basin.* Vol. 11. Edited by Warren L. D'Azavedo. Washington, DC: Smithsonian Institution, 1981, pp. 398–411.

Zimmerman, Dwight Jon. *Tecumseh: Shooting Star of the Shawnee.* New York: Sterling, 2010.

Zitkala-Sa, Cathy N. Davidson, and Ada Norris. *American Indian Stories, Legends, and Other Writings.* New York: Penguin, 2003.

Periodicals

Barrett, Samuel Alfred, and Edward Winslow Gifford. "Miwok Material Culture: Indian Life of the Yosemite Region" *Bulletin of Milwaukee Public Museum* 2, no. 4 (March 1933).

Barringer, Felicity. "Indians Join Fight for an Oklahoma Lake's Flow." *New York Times.* April 12, 2011, A1. Available online from http://www.nytimes.com/2011/04/12/science/earth/12water.html (accessed on June 18, 2011).

Beck, Melinda. "The Lost Worlds of Ancient America." *Newsweek* 118 (Fall–Winter 1991): 24.

Bourke, John Gregory. "General Crook in the Indian Country." *The Century Magazine,* March 1891. Available online from http://www.discoverseaz.com/History/General_Crook.html (accessed on July 20, 2011).

Bruchac, Joseph. "Otstango: A Mohawk Village in 1491," *National Geographic* 180, no. 4 (October 1991): 68–83.

Carroll, Susan. "Tribe Fights Kitt Peak Project." *The Arizona Republic.* March 24, 2005. Available online at http://www.nathpo.org/News/Sacred_Sites/News-Sacred_Sites109.htm (accessed on July 20, 2011).

Chief Joseph. "An Indian's View of Indian Affairs." *North American Review* 128, no. 269 (April 1879): 412–33.

Collins, Cary C., ed. "Henry Sicade's History of Puyallup Indian School, 1860 to 1920." *Columbia* 14, no. 4 (Winter 2001–02).

Dalsbø, E.T., "'We Were Told We Were Going to Live in Houses': Relocation and Housing of the Mushuau Innu of Natuashish from 1948 to 2003." *University of Tromsø,* May 28, 2010. Available from http://www.ub.uit.no/munin/bitstream/handle/10037/2739/thesis.pdf?sequence=3 (accessed on May 26, 2011).

Dixon, Roland B. "Achomawi and Atsugewi Tales." *Journal of American Folklore* 21. (1908): 159–77.

Dold, Catherine. "American Cannibal." *Discover* 19, no. 2 (February 1998): 64.

Duara, Nigel. "Descendants Make Amends to Chinook for Lewis and Clark Canoe Theft." *Missourian.* (September 23, 2011). Available online from http://www.columbiamissourian.com/stories/2011/09/23/descendants-make-amends-chinook-lewis-clark-canoe-theft/ (accessed on November 2, 2011).

Elliott, Jack. "Dawn, Nov. 28, 1729: Gunfire Heralds Natchez Massacre." *Concordia Sentinel.* November 5, 2009. Available from http://www.concordiasentinel.com/news.php?id=4321 (accessed on June 27, 2011).

Eskin, Leah. "Teens Take Charge. (Suicide Epidemic at Wind River Reservation)." *Scholastic Update,* May 26, 1989: 26.

Et-twaii-lish, Marjorie Waheneka. "Indian Perspectives on Food and Culture." *Oregon Historical Quarterly,* Fall 2005.

Griswold, Eliza. "A Teen's Third-World America." *Newsweek.* December 26, 2010. Available online from http://www.thedailybeast.com/articles/2010/12/26/a-boys-third-world-america.html (accessed on July 20, 2011).

ICTMN Staff. "Washoe Tribe's Cave Rock a No-go for Bike Path" *Indian Country Today Media Network,* February 10, 2011. Available online at http://indiancountrytodaymedianetwork.com/2011/02/washoe-tribes-cave-rock-a-no-go-for-bike-path/ (accessed on August 15, 2011).

Johnston, Moira. "Canada's Queen Charlotte Islands: Homeland of the Haida." *National Geographic,* July 1987: 102–27.

Jones, Malcolm Jr., with Ray Sawhill. "Just Too Good to Be True: Another Reason to Beware False Eco-Prophets." *Newsweek.* (May 4, 1992). Available online at http://www.synaptic.bc.ca/ejournal/newsweek.htm (accessed on November 2, 2011).

June-Friesen, Katy. "An Ancestry of African-Native Americans." *Smithsonian.* February 17, 2010. Available online from http://www.smithsonianmag.com/history-archaeology/An-Ancestry-of-African-Native-Americans.html#ixzz1RN1pyiD1 (accessed on June 21, 2011).

Kowinski, William Severini. "Giving New Life to Haida Art and the Culture It Expresses." *Smithsonian,* January 1995: 38.

Kroeber, A. L. "Two Myths of the Mission Indians." *Journal of the American Folk-Lore Society* 19, no. 75 (1906): 309–21. Available online at http://www.sacred-texts.com/nam/ca/tmmi/index.htm (accessed on August 11, 2011).

Lake, Robert, Jr. "The Chilula Indians of California." *Indian Historian* 12, no. 3 (1979): 14–26. Available online fromhttp://www.eric.ed.gov/ERICWebPortal/search/detailmini.jsp?_nfpb=true&_&ERICExtSearch_SearchValue_0=EJ214907&ERICExtSearch_SearchType_0=no&accno=EJ214907

Parks, Ron. "Selecting a Suitable Country for the Kanza." *The Kansas Free Press.* June 1, 2011. Available online from http://www.kansasfreepress.com/2011/06/selecting-a-suitable-country-for-the-kanza.html (accessed on June 17, 2011).

Rezendes, Michael. "Few Tribes Share Casino Windfall." *Globe.* December 11, 2000. Available online from http://indianfiles.serveftp.com/TribalIssues/Few%20tribes%20share%20casino%20windfall.pdf(accessed on July 4, 2011).

Roy, Prodipto, and Della M. Walker. "Assimilation of the Spokane Indians." *Washington Agricultural Experiment Station Bulletin.* No. 628.

Pullman: Washington State University, Institute of Agricultural Science, 1961.

Shaffrey, Mary M. "Lumbee Get a Win, But Not without Stipulation." *Winston-Salem Journal* (April 26, 2007).

Shapley, Thomas. "Historical Revision Rights a Wrong." *Seattle Post-Intelligencer.* (December 18, 2004). Available online from http://www.seattlepi. com/local/opinion/article/Historical-revision-rights-a-wrong-1162234. php#ixzz1WBFxoNiw (accessed on August 15, 2011).

"Q: Should Scientists Be Allowed to 'Study' the Skeletons of Ancient American Indians?" (Symposium: U.S. Representative Doc Hastings; Confederated Tribes of the Umatilla Indian Reservation Spokesman Donald Sampson). *Insight on the News* 13, no. 47 (December 22, 1997): 24.

Siegel, Lee. "Mummies Might Have Been Made by Anasazi." *Salt Lake Tribune,* April 2, 1998.

Stewart, Kenneth M. "Mohave Warfare." *Southwestern Journal of Anthropology* 3, no. 3 (Autumn 1947): 257–78.

Trivedi, Bijal P. "Ancient Timbers Reveal Secrets of Anasazi Builders." *National Geographic Today,* September 28, 2001. Available online at http://news. nationalgeographic.com/news/2001/09/0928_TVchaco.html (accessed on June 29, 2007).

Trumbauer, Sophie. "Northwest Tribes Canoe to Lummi Island." *The Daily.* (August 1, 2007). Available online at http://thedaily.washington.edu/article/2007/8/1/northwestTribesCanoeToLumm (accessed on November 2, 2011).

Van Meter, David. "Energy Efficient." *University of Texas at Arlington,* Fall 2006.

Wagner, Dennis. "Stolen Artifacts Shatter Ancient Culture." *The Arizona Republic,* November 12, 2006.

Warshall, Peter. "The Heart of Genuine Sadness: Astronomers, Politicians, and Federal Employees Desecrate the Holiest Mountain of the San Carlos Apache." *Whole Earth* 91 (Winter 1997): 30.

Win, WambliSina. "The Ultimate Expression of Faith, the Lakota Sun Dance." *Native American Times.* July 4, 2011. Available online from http://www.nativetimes.com/index.php?option=com_ content&view=article&id=5657:the-ultimate-expression-of-faith-the-lakota-sun-dance&catid=46&Itemid=22 (accessed on July 4, 2011).

Web Sites

"Aboriginal Fisheries Strategy." *Fisheries and Oceans Canada.* http://www. dfo-mpo.gc.ca/fm-gp/aboriginal-autochtones/afs-srapa-eng.htm (accessed on August 15, 2011).

"Aboriginal Peoples: The Métis." *Newfoundland and Labrador Heritage.* http://www.heritage.nf.ca/aboriginal/metis.html (accessed on August 4, 2011).

"About the Hopi." Restoration. http://hopi.org/about-the-hopi/ (accessed on July 20, 2011).

"Acoma Pueblo." *ClayHound Web.* http://www.clayhound.us/sites/acoma.htm (accessed on July 20, 2011).

"Acoma Pueblo." *New Mexico Magazine.* http://www.nmmagazine.com/native_american/acoma.php (accessed on July 20, 2011).

"Acoma'Sky City'" *National Trust for Historic Preservation.* http://www.acomaskycity.org/ (accessed on July 20, 2011).

"Address of Tarhe, Grand Sachem of the Wyandot Nation, to the Assemblage at the Treaty of Greeneville, July 22, 1795." *Wyandotte Nation of Oklahoma.* http://www.wyandotte-nation.org/history/tarhe_greenville_address.html (accessed May 12, 2011).

"The Adena Mounds." *Grave Creek Mound State Park.* http://www.adena.com/adena/ad/ad01.htm (accessed June 7, 2011).

Adley-SantaMaria, Bernadette. "White Mountain Apache Language Issues." *Northern Arizona University.* http://www2.nau.edu/jar/TIL_12.html (accessed on July 20, 2011).

Akimoff, Tim. "Snowshoe Builders Display Their Craft at the Anchorage Museum." *KTUU.* May 5, 2011. http://www.ktuu.com/news/ktuu-snowshoe-builders-display-their-craft-at-the-anchorage-museum-20110505,0,7760220.story (accessed on June 6, 2011).

Alamo Chapter. http://alamo.nndes.org/ (accessed on July 20, 2011).

Alaska Native Collections. *Smithsonian Institution.* http://alaska.si.edu/cultures.asp (accessed on August 15, 2011).

— — —. "Unangan." *Smithsonian Institution.* http://alaska.si.edu/culture_unangan.asp(accessed on August 15, 2011).

"Alaska Native Language Center." *University of Alaska Fairbanks.* http://www.uaf.edu/anlc//anlc/languages/ (accessed on June 4, 2011).

Alaska Yup'ik Eskimo. http://www.yupik.com (accessed on August 15, 2011).

All Indian Pueblo Council. http://www.20pueblos.org/ (accessed on July 20, 2011).

Allen, Cain. "The Oregon History Project: Toby Winema Riddle." *Oregon Historical Society.* http://www.ohs.org/education/oregonhistory/historical_records/dspDocument.cfm?doc_ID=000A9FE3-B226-1EE8-827980B05272FE9F (accessed on August 11, 2011).

"Alutiiq and Aleut/Unangan History and Culture." *Anchorage Museum.* http://www.anchoragemuseum.org/galleries/alaska_gallery/aleut.aspx (accessed on August 15, 2011).

Aluttiq Museum. http://alutiiqmuseum.org/ (accessed on August 15, 2011).

"Anasazi: The Ancient Ones." *Manitou Cliff Dwellings Museum.* http://www. cliffdwellingsmuseum.com/anasazi.htm (accessed on July 20, 2011).

"Anasazi Heritage Center: Ancestral Pueblos." *Bureau of Land Management Colorado.* http://www.co.blm.gov/ahc/anasazi.htm (accessed on July 13, 2011).

"The Anasazi or 'Ancient Pueblo.'" *Northern Arizona University.* http://www. cpluhna.nau.edu/People/anasazi.htm (accessed on July 20, 2011).

"Ancient Architects of the Mississippi." *National Park Service, Department of the Interior.* http://www.cr.nps.gov/archeology/feature/feature.htm (accessed on July 10, 2007).

"Ancient DNA from the Ohio Hopewell." *Ohio Archaeology Blog,* June 22, 2006. http://ohio-archaeology.blogspot.com/2006/06/ancient-dna-from-ohio-hopewell.html (accessed on July 10, 2007).

"Ancient Moundbuilders of Arkansas." *University of Arkansas.* http://cast.uark.edu/ home/research/archaeology-and-historic-preservation/archaeological-interpretation/ ancient-moundbuilders-of-arkansas.html (accessed on June 10, 2011).

"Ancient One: Kennewick Man." *Confederated Tribes of the Umatilla Reservation.* http://www.umatilla.nsn.us/ancient.html (accessed on August 11, 2011).

Anderson, Jeff. "Arapaho Online Research Resources." *Colby College.* http:// www.colby.edu/personal/j/jdanders/arapahoresearch.htm (accessed on July 2, 2011).

"Anishinaabe Chi-Naaknigewin/Anishinabek Nation Constitution." *Anishinabek Nation.* http://www.anishinabek.ca/uploads/ANConstitution.pdf (accessed on May 16, 2011).

"Antelope Valley Indian Peoples: The Late Prehistoric Period: Kawaiisu." *Antelope Valley Indian Museum.* http://www.avim.parks.ca.gov/people/ ph_kawaiisu.shtml (accessed on August 15, 2011).

"Apache Indian History." *Access Genealogy.* http://www.accessgenealogy.com/ native/tribes/apache/apachehist.htm (accessed on July 15, 2011).

"Apache Indians." *AAA Native Arts.* http://www.aaanativearts.com/apache (accessed on July 15, 2011).

"Apache Nation: Nde Nation." *San Carlos Apache Nation.* http://www. sancarlosapache.com/home.htm (accessed on July 15, 2011).

"Apache Tribal Nation." *Dreams of the Great Earth Changes.* http://www. greatdreams.com/apache/apache-tribe.htm (accessed on July 15, 2011).

"The Apsáalooke (Crow Indians) of Montana Tribal Histories." *Little Big Horn College.* http://lib.lbhc.edu/history/ (accessed on July 5, 2011).

Aquino, Pauline. "Ohkay Owingeh: Village of the Strong People" (video). *New Mexico State Record Center and Archives.* http://www.newmexicohistory.org/ filedetails.php?fileID=22530 (accessed on July 20, 2011).

"The Arapaho Tribe." *Omaha Public Library.* http://www.omahapubliclibrary. org/transmiss/congress/arapaho.html (accessed on July 2, 2011).

Arctic Circle. http://arcticcircle.uconn.edu/Museum/ (accessed on June 10, 2011).

"Arctic Circle." *University of Connecticut.* http://arcticcircle.uconn.edu/VirtualClassroom/ (accessed on August 15, 2011).

"The Arctic Is...." *Stefansson Arctic Institute.* http://www.thearctic.is/ (accessed on August 15, 2011).

Arctic Library. "Inuit" *Athropolis.* http://www.athropolis.com/library-cat.htm#inuit (accessed on August 15, 2011).

"Arikira Indians." *PBS.* http://www.pbs.org/lewisandclark/native/ari.html (accessed on June 19, 2011).

"Arkansas Indians: Arkansas Archeological Survey." *University of Arkansas.* http://www.uark.edu/campus-resources/archinfo/ArkansasIndianTribes.pdf (accessed on June 12, 2011).

Arlee, Johnny. *Over a Century of Moving to the Drum: Salish Indian Celebrations on the Flathead Reservation.* Helena: Montana Historical Society Press, 1998. Available online from http://www.archive.org/stream/historicalsketch00ronarich/historicalsketch00ronarich_djvu.txt (accessed on August 11, 2011).

Armstrong, Kerry M. "Chickasaw Historical Research Page." *Chickasaw History.* http://www.chickasawhistory.com/ (accessed on June 16, 2011.

"Art on the Prairies: Otoe-Missouria." *The Bata Shoe Museum.* http://www.allaboutshoes.ca/en/paths_across/art_on_prairies/index_7.php (accessed on June 20, 2011).

"Assiniboin Indian History." *Access Genealogy.* http://www.accessgenealogy.com/native/tribes/assiniboin/assiniboinhist.htm (accessed on June 7, 2011).

"Assinboin Indians." *PBS.* http://www.pbs.org/lewisandclark/native/idx_ass.html (accessed on June 7, 2011).

"Assiniboine History." *Fort Belknap Indian Community.* http://www.ftbelknap-nsn.gov/assiniboineHistory.php (accessed on June 6, 2011).

"Athabascan." Alaska Native Heritage Center Museum. http://www.alaskanative.net/en/main_nav/education/culture_alaska/athabascan/ (accessed on June 6, 2011).

Banyacya, Thomas. "Message to the World." *Hopi Traditional Elder.* http://banyacya.indigenousnative.org/ (accessed on July 20, 2011).

Barnett, Jim. "The Natchez Indians." *History Now.* http://mshistory.k12.ms.us/index.php?id=4 (accessed on June 27, 2011).

Barry, Paul C. "Native America Nations and Languages: Haudenosaunee." *The Canku Ota—A Newsletter Celebrating Native America.* http://www.turtletrack.org/Links/NANations/CO_NANationLinks_HJ.htm (accessed on June 5, 2011).

"Before the White Man Came to Nisqually Country." *Washington History Online.* January 12, 2006. http://washingtonhistoryonline.org/treatytrail/teaching/before-white-man.pdf (accessed on August 15, 2011).

Big Valley Band of Pomo Indians. http://www.big-valley.net/index.htm (accessed on August 11, 2011).

Bishop Paiute Tribe. http://www.bishoppaiutetribe.com/ (accessed on August 15, 2011).

"Black Kettle." *PBS.* http://www.pbs.org/weta/thewest/people/a_c/blackkettle.htm (accessed on July 4, 2011).

"Blackfeet." *Wisdom of the Elders.* http://www.wisdomoftheelders.org/program208.html (accessed on July 2, 2011).

"Blackfoot History." *Head-Smashed-In Buffalo Jump Interpretive Centre.* http://www.head-smashed-in.com/black.html (accessed on July 2, 2011).

Blackfeet Nation. http://www.blackfeetnation.com/ (accessed on July 2, 2011).

Boyer, Ruth McDonald, and Narcissus Duffy Gayton. "Apache Mothers and Daughters: Four Generations of a Family. Remembrances of an Apache Elder Woman." *Southwest Crossroads.* http://southwestcrossroads.org/record.php?num=825&hl=Apache (accessed on July 20, 2011).

British Columbia Archives. "First Nations Research Guide." *Royal BC Museum Corporation.* http://www.royalbcmuseum.bc.ca/BC_Research_Guide/BC_First_Nations.aspx (accessed on August 15, 2011).

Bruchac, Joe. "Storytelling." *Abenaki Nation.* http://www.abenakination.org/stories.html (accessed on June 5, 2011).

Brush, Rebecca. "The Wichita Indians." *Texas Indians.* http://www.texasindians.com/wichita.htm (accessed on June 9, 2011).

"Caddo Indian History." *Access Genealogy.* http://www.accessgenealogy.com/native/tribes/caddo/caddohist.htm (accessed on June 12, 2011).

"Cahto (Kato)." *Four Directions Institute.* http://www.fourdir.com/cahto.htm (accessed on August 11, 2011).

"Cahto Tribe Information Network." *Cahto Tribe.* http://www.cahto.org/ (accessed on August 11, 2011).

"Cahuilla." *Four Directions Institute.* http://www.fourdir.com/cahuilla.htm (accessed on August 11, 2011).

Cahuilla Band of Mission Indians. http://cahuillabandofindians.com/ (accessed on August 11, 2011).

"California Indians." *Visalia Unified School District.* http://visalia.k12.ca.us/teachers/tlieberman/indians/ (accessed on August 15, 2011).

California Valley Miwok Tribe, California. http://www.californiavalleymiwoktribe-nsn.gov/ (accessed on August 11, 2011).

Cambra, Rosemary, et al. "The Muwekma Ohlone Tribe of the San Francisco Bay Area." http://www.islaiscreek.org/ohlonehistcultfedrecog.html (accessed on August 11, 2011).

"Camp Grant Massacre—April 30, 1871." *Council of Indian Nations.* http://www.nrcprograms.org/site/PageServer?pagename=cin_hist_campgrantmassacre (accessed on July 20, 2011).

Campbell, Grant. "The Rock Paintings of the Chumash." *Association for Humanistic Psychology.* http://www.ahpweb.org/articles/chumash.html (accessed on August 11, 2011).

Canadian Heritage Information Network. "Communities& Institutions: Talented Youth." *Tipatshimuna.* http://www.tipatshimuna.ca/1420_e.php (accessed on May 19, 2011).

Carleton, Kenneth H. "A Brief History of the Mississippi Band of Choctaw Indians." *Mississippi Band of Choctaw.* http://mdah.state.ms.us/hpres/A%20Brief%20History%20of%20the%20Choctaw.pdf (accessed on June 12, 2011).

Central Council: Tlingit and Haida Indian Tribes of Alaska. http://www.ccthita.org/ (accessed on November 2, 2011).

Cherokee Nation. http://www.cherokee.org/ (accessed on June 12, 2011).

"Cheyenne Indian." *American Indian Tribes.* http://www.cheyenneindian.com/cheyenne_links.htm (accessed on July 4, 2011).

"Cheyenne Indian History." *Access Genealogy.* http://www.accessgenealogy.com/native/tribes/cheyenne/cheyennehist.htm (accessed on July 4, 2011).

"Chickasaw Indian History." *Access Genealogy.* http://www.accessgenealogy.com/native/tribes/chickasaw/chickasawhist.htm (accessed on June 16, 2011).

The Chickasaw Nation. http://www.chickasaw.net (accessed on June 12, 2011).

"Chief Joseph." *PBS.* http://www.pbs.org/weta/thewest/people/a_c/chiefjoseph.htm (accessed on August 11, 2011).

"Chief Joseph Surrenders." *The History Place.* http://www.historyplace.com/speeches/joseph.htm (accessed on August 11,2011).

Chief Leschi School. http://www.leschischools.org/ (accessed on November 2, 2011).

"Chief Seattle Speech." *Washington State Library.* http://www.synaptic.bc.ca/ejournal/wslibrry.htm (accessed on November 2, 2011).

"The Children of Changing Woman." *Peabody Museum of Archaeology and Ethnology.* http://www.peabody.harvard.edu/maria/Cwoman.html (accessed on July 15, 2011).

"The Chilula." *The Indians of the Redwoods.* http://www.cr.nps.gov/history/online_books/redw/history1c.htm (accessed on August 11, 2011).

Chinook Indian Tribe/Chinook Nation. http://www.chinooknation.org/ (accessed on November 2, 2011).

"Chinookan Family History." *Access Genealogy.* http://www.accessgenealogy.com/native/tribes/chinook/chinookanfamilyhist.htm (accessed on November 2, 2011).

"Chippewa Cree Tribe (Neiyahwahk)." *Montana Office of Indian Affairs.* http://www.tribalnations.mt.gov/chippewacree.asp (accessed on June 3, 2011).

"Chiricahua Indian History." *Access Genealogy.* http://www.accessgenealogy.com/native/tribes/apache/chiricahua.htm (accessed on July 20, 2011).

Chisolm, D. "Mi'kmaq Resource Centre," *Cape Breton University.*http://mrc.uccb.ns.ca/mikmaq.html (accessed on May 15, 2011).

"Choctaw Indian History." *Access Genealogy.* http://www.accessgenealogy.com/native/tribes/choctaw/chostawhist.htm (accessed on June 21, 2011).

"Choctaw Indian Tribe." *Native American Nations.* http://www.nanations.com/choctaw/index.htm (accessed on June 21, 2011).

Choctaw Nation of Oklahoma. http://www.choctawnation.com (accessed on June 12, 2011).

"Chumash." *Four Directions Institute.* http://www.fourdir.com/chumash.htm (accessed on December 1, 2011).

The Chumash Indians. http://www.chumashindian.com/ (accessed on August 11, 2011).

Clark, William. "Lewis and Clark: Expedition Journals." *National Geographic.* http://www.nationalgeographic.com/lewisandclark/record_tribes_020_5_1.html (accessed on June 19, 2011).

———. "Lewis and Clark: Missouri Indians." *National Geographic.* http://www.nationalgeographic.com/lewisandclark/record_tribes_012_1_9.html (accessed on June 20, 2011).

"Coast Miwok at Point Reyes." *U.S. National Park Service.* http://www.nps.gov/pore/historyculture/people_coastmiwok.htm (accessed on August 11, 2011).

"Coastal Miwok Indians." *Reed Union School District.* http://rusd.marin.k12.ca.us/belaire/ba_3rd_miwoks/coastalmiwoks/webpages/home.html(accessed on August 11, 2011).

"Comanche." *Edward S. Curtis's The North American Indian.* http://curtis.library.northwestern.edu/curtis/toc.cgi (accessed on July 4, 2011).

"Comanche Indian History." *Access Genealogy.* http://www.accessgenealogy.com/native/tribes/comanche/comanchehist.htm (accessed on July 4, 2011).

"Comanche Language." *Omniglot.* http://www.omniglot.com/writing/comanche.htm (accessed on July 4, 2011).

Comanche Nation of Oklahoma http://www.comanchenation.com/ (accessed on July 4, 2011).

"Community News." *Mississippi Band of Choctaw Indians.* http://www.choctaw.org/ (accessed on June 12, 2011).

Compton, W. J. "The Story of Ishi, the Yana Indian." *Ye Slyvan Archer.* July 1936. http://tmuss.tripod.com/shotfrompast/chief.htm (accessed on August 11, 2011).

The Confederated Salish and Kootenai Tribes. http://www.cskt.org/ (accessed on August 11, 2011).

Confederated Tribes and Bands of the Yakama Nation. http://www.yakamana-tion-nsn.gov/ (accessed on August 11, 2011).

Confederated Tribes of the Colville Reservation. http://www.colvilletribes.com/ (accessed on August 11, 2011).

Confederated Tribes of Siletz. http://ctsi.nsn.us/ (accessed on November 2, 2011).

Confederated Tribes of the Umatilla Indian Reservation. http://www.umatilla.nsn.us/ (accessed on August 11, 2011).

"Confederated Tribes of the Umatilla Indians." *Wisdom of the Elders.* http://www.wisdomoftheelders.org/program305.html (accessed on August 11, 2011).

"Confederated Tribes of the Yakama Nation." *Wisdom of the Elders.* http://www.wisdomoftheelders.org/program304.html (accessed on August 11, 2011).

"Connecting the World with Seattle's First People."*Duwamish Tribe.* http://www.duwamishtribe.org/ (accessed on November 2, 2011).

Conrad, Jim. "The Natchez Indians." *The Loess Hills of the Lower Mississipi Valley.* http://www.backyardnature.net/loess/ind_natz.htm (accessed on June 27, 2011).

Cordell, Linda. "Anasazi." *Scholastic.* http://www2.scholastic.com/browse/article.jsp?id=5042 (accessed on July 20, 2011).

"Costanoan Indian Tribe." *Access Genealogy.* http://www.accessgenealogy.com/native/tribes/costanoan/costanoanindiantribe.htm (accessed on August 11, 2011).

Costanoan Rumsen Carmel Tribe. http://costanoanrumsen.org/ (accessed on August 11, 2011).

"Costanoan Rumsen Carmel Tribe: History." *Native Web.* http://crc.nativeweb.org/history.html (accessed on August 11, 2011).

Cotton, Lee. "Powhatan Indian Lifeways." *National Park Service.* http://www.nps.gov/jame/historyculture/powhatan-indian-lifeways.htm (accessed on June 1, 2011).

Council of the Haida Nation (CHN). http://www.haidanation.ca/ (accessed on November 2, 2011).

"A Coyote's Tales—Tohono O'odham." *First People: American Indian Legends.* http://www.firstpeople.us/FP-Html-Legends/A_Coyotes_Tales-TohonoOodham.html (accessed on July 20, 2011).

"Creek Indian." *American Indian Tribe.* http://www.creekindian.com/ (accessed on June 12, 2011).

"Creek Indians." *GeorgiaInfo.* http://georgiainfo.galileo.usg.edu/creek.htm (accessed on June 12, 2011).

"Crow/Cheyenne." *Wisdom of the Elders.* http://www.wisdomoftheelders.org/program206.html (accessed on July 5, 2011).

"Crow Indian Tribe." *Access Genealogy.* http://www.accessgenealogy.com/native/tribes/crow/crowhist.htm (accessed on July 5, 2011).

Crow Tribe, Apsáalooke Nation Official Website. http://www.crowtribe.com/ (accessed on July 5, 2011).

"Culture and History." *Innu Nation.* http://www.innu.ca/index.php?option=com_content&view=article&id=8&Itemid=3&lang=en (accessed on May 19, 2011).

"Culture& History." *Aleut Corporation.* http://www.aleutcorp.com/index.php?option=com_content&view=section&layout=blog&id=6&Itemid=24 (accessed on August 15, 2011).

"Culture and History of the Skokomish Tribe." *Skokomish Tribal Nation.* http://www.skokomish.org/historyculture.htm (accessed on November 2, 2011).

Curtis, Edward S. *The North American Indian.* Vol.13. 1924. Reprint. New York: Johnson Reprint Corporation, 1970. Available online from *Northwestern University Digital Library Collections.* http://curtis.library.northwestern.edu/curtis/viewPage.cgi?showp=1&size=2&id=nai.13.book.00000192&volume=13#nav-Edward (accessed on August 11, 2011).

"Dakota Indian Tribe History." *Access Genealogy.* http://www.accessgenealogy.com/native/tribes/siouan/dakotahist.htm (accessed on July 5, 2011).

"Dakota Spirituality." *Blue Cloud Abbey.* http://www.bluecloud.org/dakotaspirituality.html (accessed on July 5, 2011).

"Dams of the Columbia Basin and Their Effects on the Native Fishery." *Center for Columbia River History.* http://www.ccrh.org/comm/river/dams6.htm (accessed on August 11, 2011).

Deans, James. "Tales from the Totems of the Hidery." *Early Canadiana Online.* http://www.canadiana.org/ECO/PageView/06053/0003?id=986858ca5fbdc633 (accessed on November 2, 2011).

Deer Lake First Nation. http://www.deerlake.firstnation.ca/ (accessed on June 5, 2011).

"Delaware Indian Chiefs." *Access Genealogy.* http://www.accessgenealogy.com/native/tribes/delaware/delawarechiefs.htm (accessed on June 8, 2011).

"Delaware Indian/Lenni Lenape." *Delaware Indians of Pennsylvania.* http://www.delawareindians.com/ (accessed on June 8, 2011).

"Delaware Indians." *Ohio Historical Society.* http://www.ohiohistorycentral.org/entry.php?rec=584 (accessed on June 2, 2011).

The Delaware Nation. http://www.delawarenation.com/ (accessed on June 2, 2011).

Delaware Tribe of Indians. http://www.delawaretribeofindians.nsn.us/ (accessed on June 2, 2011).

DelawareIndian.com. http://www.delawareindian.com/ (accessed on June 2, 2011).

Dene Cultural Institute. http://www.deneculture.org/ (accessed on June 10, 2011).

Deschenes, Bruno. "Inuit Throat-Singing." *Musical Traditions.* http://www. mustrad.org.uk/articles/inuit.htm (accessed on August 15, 2011).

"Desert Native Americans: Mohave Indians." *Mojave Desert.* http:// mojavedesert.net/mojave-indians/ (accessed on July 20, 2011).

Dodds, Lissa Guimarães. "'The Washoe People': Past and Present." *Washoe Tribe of Nevada and California.* http://www.Washoetribe.us/images/ Washoe_tribe_history_v2.pdf (accessed on August 15, 2011).

"Duwamish Indian Tribe History." *Access Genealogy.* http://www.accessgeneal-ogy.com/native/tribes/salish/duwamishhist.htm (accessed on November 2, 2011).

"The Early History and Names of the Arapaho." *Native American Nations.* http://www.nanations.com/early_arapaho.htm (accessed on July 2, 2011).

Eastern Shawnee Tribe of Oklahoma. http://estoo-nsn.gov/ (accessed on June 12, 2011).

Eck, Pam. "Hopi Indians." *Indiana University.* http://inkido.indiana.edu/ w310work/romac/hopi.htm (accessed on July 20, 2011).

Edward S. Curtis's The North American Indian. http://curtis.library.northwest-ern.edu/curtis/toc.cgi (accessed on August 11, 2011).

Elam, Earl H. "Wichita Indians." *Texas State Historical Association.* http://www. tshaonline.org/handbook/online/articles/bmw03 (accessed on June 9, 2011).

Ely Shoshone Tribe. http://elyshoshonetribe-nsn.gov/departments.html (accessed on August 15, 2011).

Etienne-Gray, Tracé. "Black Seminole Indians." *Texas State Historical Associa-tion.* http://www.tshaonline.org/handbook/online/articles/bmb18 (accessed on June 12, 2011).

Everett, Diana. "Apache Tribe of Oklahoma." *Oklahoma Historical Soci-ety.* http://digital.library.okstate.edu/encyclopedia/entries/A/AP002. html(accessed on July 15, 2011).

"Eyak, Tlingit, Haida, and Tsimshian." *Alaska Native Heritage Center Museum.* http://www.alaskanative.net/en/main_nav/education/culture_alaska/eyak/ (accessed on August 15, 2011).

Fausz, J. Frederick. "The Louisiana Expansion: The Arikara." *University of Missouri–St. Louis.* http://www.umsl.edu/continuinged/louisiana/Am_ Indians/8-Arikara/8-arikara.html (accessed on June 19, 2011).

———. "The Louisiana Expansion: The Kansa/Kaw." *University of Missouri-St. Louis.* http://www.umsl.edu/continuinged/louisiana/Am_Indians/3-Kansa_Kaw/3-kansa_kaw.html (accessed on June 17, 2011).

———. "The Louisiana Expansion: The Missouri/Missouria." *University of Missouri–St. Louis.* http://www.umsl.edu/continuinged/louisiana/Am_ Indians/2-Missouria/2-missouria.html (accessed on June 20, 2011).

— — —. "The Louisiana Expansion: The Oto(e)." *University of Missouri-St. Louis.* http://www.umsl.edu/continuinged/louisiana/Am_Indians/4-Oto/4-oto.html (accessed on June 20, 2011).

Feller, Walter. "California Indian History." *Digital Desert.* http://mojavedesert.net/california-indian-history/ (accessed on August 11, 2011).

— — —. "Mojave Desert Indians: Cahuilla Indians." *Digital-Desert.* http://mojavedesert.net/cahuilla-indians/ (accessed on August 11, 2011).

"First Nations: People of the Interior." *British Columbia Archives.* http://www.bcarchives.gov.bc.ca/exhibits/timemach/galler07/frames/int_peop.htm (accessed on August 11, 2011).

"First Peoples of Canada: Communal Hunters." *Canadian Museum of Civilization.* http://www.civilization.ca/cmc/home (accessed on June 10, 2011).

"Flathead Indians (Salish)." *National Geographic.* http://www.nationalgeographic.com/lewisandclark/record_tribes_022_12_16.html (accessed on August 11, 2011).

"Flathead Reservation." http://www.montanatribes.org/links_&_resources/tribes/Flathead_Reservation.pdf (accessed on August 11, 2011).

Flora, Stephenie. "Northwest Indians: 'The First People.'" *Oregon Pioneers.* http://www.oregonpioneers.com/indian.htm (accessed on August 15, 2011).

Forest County Potawatomi. http://www.fcpotawatomi.com/ (accessed on June 5, 2011).

Fort McDowell Yavapai Nation. http://www.ftmcdowell.org/ (accessed on July 20, 2011).

"Fort Mojave Indian Tribe." *Inter Tribal Council of Arizona, Inc.* http://www.itcaonline.com/tribes_mojave.html (accessed on July 20, 2011).

Fort Peck Tribes. http://www.fortpecktribes.org/ (accessed on June 4, 2011).

Fort Sill Apache Tribe. http://www.fortsillapache.com (accessed on July 20, 2011).

"Fort Yuma-Quechan Tribe." *Inter-Tribal Council of Arizona, Inc.* http://www.itcaonline.com/tribes_quechan.html (accessed on July 20, 2011).

Gangnier, Gary. "The History of the Innu Nation." *Central Quebec School Board.* http://www.cqsb.qc.ca/svs/434/fninnu.htm (accessed on May 24, 2011).

Gerke, Sarah Bohl. "White Mountain Apache." *Arizona State University.* http://grandcanyonhistory.clas.asu.edu/history_nativecultures_whitemountainapache.html (accessed on July 20, 2011).

"Geronimo, His Own Story: A Prisoner of War." *From Revolution to Reconstruction.* http://www.let.rug.nl/usa/B/geronimo/geroni17.htm (accessed on July 20, 2011).

"Gifting and Feasting in the Northwest Coast Potlatch." *Peabody Museum of Archaeology and Ethnology.* http://www.peabody.harvard.edu/potlatch/ (accessed on November 2, 2011).

Glenn Black Laboratory of Archaeology. "Burial Mounds." *Indiana University.* http://www.gbl.indiana.edu/abstracts/adena/mounds.html (accessed June 7, 2011).

— — —. "The Ohio Valley-Great Lakes Ethnohistory Archives: The Miami Collection." *Indiana University.* http://gbl.indiana.edu/ethnohistory/ archives/menu.html (accessed on June 7, 2011).

Glover, William B. "A History of the Caddo Indians." Formatted for the World Wide Web by Jay Salsburg. Reprinted from *The Louisiana Historical Quarterly*, 18, no. 4 (October 1935). http://ops.tamu.edu/x075bb/caddo/ Indians.html (accessed on June 12, 2011).

GoodTracks, Jimm. "These Native Ways." *Turtle Island Storytellers Network.* http://www.turtleislandstorytellers.net/tis_kansas/transcript01_jg_tracks. htm (accessed on June 20, 2011).

"Grand Village of the Natchez Indians." *Mississippi Department of Archives and History.* http://mdah.state.ms.us/hprop/gvni.html (accessed on June 27, 2011).

Great Basin Indian Archives. http://www.gbcnv.edu/gbia/index.htm (accessed on August 15, 2011).

Great Basin National Park. "Historic Tribes of the Great Basin." *National Park Service: U.S. Department of the Interior.* http://www.nps.gov/grba/histo-ryculture/historic-tribes-of-the-great-basin.htm (accessed on August 15, 2011).

Greene, Candace S. "Kiowa Drawings." *National Anthropological Archives, National Museum of Natural History.* http://www.nmnh.si.edu/naa/kiowa/ kiowa.htm (accessed on July 4, 2011).

"Haida." *The Kids' Site of Canadian Settlement, Library and Archives Canada.* http://www.collectionscanada.ca/settlement/kids/021013-2061-e.html (accessed on November 2, 2011).

"Haida Heritage Center at Qay'llnagaay." *Haida Heritage Centre.* http://www. haidaheritagecentre.com/ (accessed on November 2, 2011).

"Haida Language Program." *Sealaska Heritage Institute.* http://www.sealaska-heritage.org/programs/haida_language_program.htm (accessed on November 2, 2011).

"Haida Spirits of the Sea." *Virtual Museum of Canada.* http://www.virtualmuseum. ca/Exhibitions/Haida/nojava/english/home/index.html (accessed on November 2, 2011).

Handbook of American Indians. "Arikara Indian Tribe History." *Access Genealogy.* http://www.accessgenealogy.com/native/tribes/nations/arikara.htm (accessed on June 19, 2011).

Handbook of American Indians.. "Quapaw Indian Tribe History." *Access Genealogy.* http://www.accessgenealogy.com/native/tribes/quapaw/quapawhist. htm (accessed on June 20, 2011).

"History—Incident at Wounded Knee." *U.S. Marshals Service.* http://www. usmarshals.gov/history/wounded-knee/index.html (accessed on July 4, 2011).

"History: We Are the Anishnaabek." *The Grand Traverse Band of Ottawa and Chippewa.* http://www.gtbindians.org/history.html (accessed May 13, 2011).

"History and Culture." *Cherokee North Carolina.* http://www.cherokee-nc.com/ history_intro.php (accessed on June 12, 2011).

"A History of American Indians in California." *National Park Service.* http:// www.nps.gov/history/history/online_books/5views/5views1.htm (accessed on August 15, 2011).

"History of Northern Ute Indian, Utah." *Online Utah.* http://www.onlineutah. com/utehistorynorthern.shtml (accessed on August 15, 2011).

"History of the Confederated Tribes of the Siletz Indians." *HeeHeeIllahee RV Resort.* http://www.heeheeillahee.com/html/about_tribe_history.htm (accessed on November 2, 2011).

Hollabaugh, Mark. "Brief History of the Lakota People." *Normandale Community College.* http://faculty.normandale.edu/-physics/Hollabaugh/Lakota/ BriefHistory.htm (accessed on July 4, 2011).

Holt, Ronald L. "Paiute Indians." *State of Utah.* http://historytogo.utah.gov/ utah_chapters/american_indians/paiuteindians.html (accessed on August 15, 2011).

Holzman, Allan. "Beyond the Mesas [video]." *University of Illinois.* http://www. vimeo.com/16872541 (accessed on July 20, 2011).

— — —. "The Indian Boarding School Experience [video]." *University of Illinois.* http://www.vimeo.com/17410552 (accessed on July 20, 2011).

Hoopa Tribal Museum and San Francisco State University. http://bss.sfsu.edu/ calstudies/hupa/Hoopa.HTM (accessed on August 11, 2011).

Hoopa Valley Tribe. http://www.hoopa-nsn.gov/ (accessed on August 11, 2011).

"Hopi." *Four Directions Institute.* http://www.fourdir.com/hopi.htm (accessed on July 20, 2011).

"Hopi." *Southwest Crossroads.* http://southwestcrossroads.org/search. php?query=hopi&tab=document&doc_view=10 (accessed on July 20, 2011).

"Hopi Indian Tribal History." *Access Genealogy.* www.accessgenealogy.com/ native/tribes/hopi/hopeindianhist.htm (accessed on July 20, 2011).

"Hopi Tribe." *Inter Tribal Council of Arizona, Inc.* http://www.itcaonline.com/ tribes_hopi.html (accessed on July 20, 2011).

"Hupa." *Four Directions Institute.* http://www.fourdir.com/hupa.htm (accessed on August 11, 2011).

"Hupa Indian Tribe." *Access Genealogy.* http://www.accessgenealogy.com/native/tribes/athapascan/hupaindiantribe.htm (accessed on August 11, 2011).

Huron-Wendat Nation. http://www.wendake.com/ (accessed May 12, 2011).

Hurst, Winston. "Anasazi." *Utah History to Go: State of Utah.* http://historytogo.utah.gov/utah_chapters/american_indians/anasazi.html (accessed on July 20, 2011).

Indian Country Diaries. "Trail of Tears." *PBS.* http://www.pbs.org/indiancountry/history/trail.html (accessed on June 12, 2011).

"Indian Peoples of the Northern Great Plains." *MSU Libraries.* http://www.lib.montana.edu/epubs/nadb/ (accessed on July 1, 2011).

Indian Pueblo Cultural Center. http://www.indianpueblo.org/ (accessed on July 20, 2011).

"Indian Tribes of California." *Access Genealogy.* http://www.accessgenealogy.com/native/california/ (accessed on August 11, 2011).

"Indians of the Northwest—Plateau and Coastal." *St. Joseph School Library.* http://library.stjosephsea.org/plateau.htm (accessed on August 11, 2011).

"Innu Youth Film Project." *Kamestastin.* http://www.kamestastin.com/ (accessed on May 24, 2011).

"The Inuit." *Newfoundland and Labrador Heritage.* http://www.heritage.nf.ca/aboriginal/inuit.html (accessed on August 15, 2011).

"Jemez Pueblos." *Four Directions Institute.* http://www.fourdir.com/jemez.htm (accessed on July 20, 2011).

"Jemez Pueblo." *New Mexico Magazine.* http://www.nmmagazine.com/native_american/jemez.php (accessed on July 20, 2011).

Jicarilla Apache Nation. http://www.jicarillaonline.com/ (accessed on July 15, 2011).

Johnson, Russ. "The Mississippian Period (900 AD to 1550 AD)" *Memphis History.* http://www.memphishistory.org/Beginnings/PreMemphis/MississippianCulture/tabid/64/Default.aspx (accessed June 7, 2011).

"The Journals of the Lewis and Clark Expedition: Nez Percé." *University of Nebraska.* http://www.nationalgeographic.com/lewisandclark/record_tribes_013_12_17.html (accessed on August 11, 2011).

Jozhe, Benedict. "A Brief History of the Fort Sill Apache Tribe." *Oklahoma Historical Society.* http://digital.library.okstate.edu/Chronicles/v039/v039p427.pdf (accessed on July 20, 2011).

"Kansa (Kaw)." *Four Directions Institute.* http://www.fourdir.com/kaw.htm (accessed on June 17, 2011).

"Kanza Cultural History." *The Kaw Nation.* http://kawnation.com/?page_id=216 (accessed on June 17, 2011).

"Kansa Indian Tribe History." *Access Geneology.* http://www.accessgenealogy. com/native/tribes/siouan/kansahist.htm (accessed on June 17, 2011).

Kavanagh, Thomas W. "Comanche." *Oklahoma Historical Society.* http://digital. library.okstate.edu/encyclopedia/entries/C/CO033.html (accessed on July 4, 2011).

———. "Reading Historic Photographs: Photographers of the Pawnee." *Indiana University.* http://php.indiana.edu/~tkavanag/phothana.html (accessed on July 6, 2011).

"Kawaiisu." *Four Directions Institute.* http://www.fourdir.com/Kawaiisu.htm (accessed on August 15, 2011).

"The Kawaiisu Culture." *Digital Desert: Mojave Desert.* http://mojavedesert.net/ kawaiisu-indians/related-pages.html (accessed on August 15, 2011).

Kawaiisu Language and Cultural Center. http://www.kawaiisu.org/KLCC_ home.html (accessed on August 15, 2011).

Kawno, Kenji. "Warriors: Navajo Code Talkers." *Southwest Crossroads.* http:// southwestcrossroads.org/record.php?num=387 (accessed on July 20, 2011).

Kidwell, Clara Sue. "Choctaw." *Oklahoma Historical Society.* http://digital. library.okstate.edu/encyclopedia/entries/C/CH047.html (accessed on June 21, 2011).

"Kiowa Indian Tribe History." *Access Genealogy.* http://www.accessgenealogy. com/native/tribes/kiowa/kiowahist.htm (accessed on July 4, 2011).

"Kiowa Indian Tribe." *Kansas Genealogy.* http://www.kansasgenealogy.com/ indians/kiowa_indian_tribe.htm(accessed on July 4, 2011).

*Kiowa Tribe.*http://www.kiowatribe.org/(accessed on July 4, 2011).

Kitt Peak National Observatory. "Tohono O'odham." *Association of Universities for Research in Astronomy.* http://www.noao.edu/outreach/kptour/kpno_ tohono.html (accessed on July 20, 2011).

"Kwakiutl." *Four Directions Institute.* http://www.fourdir.com/kwakiutl.htm (accessed on November 2, 2011).

Kwakiutl Indian Band. http://www.kwakiutl.bc.ca/ (accessed on November 2, 2011).

"Lakota, Dakota, Nakota—The Great Sioux Nation." *Legends of America.* http://www.legendsofamerica.com/na-sioux.html (accessed on July 4, 2011).

"Lakota Page: The Great Sioux Nation." *Ancestry.com.* http://freepages.genealogy. rootsweb.ancestry.com/~nativeamericangen/page6.html (accessed on July 4, 2011).

"Lakota-Teton Sioux." *Wisdom of the Elders.* http://www.wisdomoftheelders. org/program203.html (accessed on July 4, 2011).

Larry, Mitchell. *The Native Blog.* http://nativeblog.typepad.com/the_pota- watomitracks_blog/potawatomi_news/index.html (accessed on June 5, 2011).

"Leschi: Last Chief of the Nisquallies." *WashingtonHistoryOnline.* http://washingtonhistoryonline.org/leschi/leschi.htm (accessed on August 15, 2011).

"Lewis & Clark: Chinook Indians." *National Geographic.* http://www.nationalgeographic.com/lewisandclark/record_tribes_083_14_3.html (accessed on November 2, 2011).

"Lewis and Clark: Crow Indians (Absaroka)." *National Geographic Society.* http://www.nationalgeographic.com/lewisandclark/record_tribes_002_19_21.html (accessed on July 5, 2011).

"Lewis and Clark: Native Americans: Chinook Indians." *PBS.* http://www.pbs.org/lewisandclark/native/chi.html (accessed on November 2, 2011).

"Lewis & Clark: Tribes: Siletz Indians." *National Geographic.* http://www.nationalgeographic.com/lewisandclark/record_tribes_090_14_8.html (accessed on November 2, 2011).

"Lewis & Clark: Yankton Sioux Indians (Nakota)." *National Geographic.* http://www.nationalgeographic.com/lewisandclark/record_tribes_019_2_8.html (accessed on June 12, 2011).

Lewis, J.D. "The Natchez Indians." *Carolina—The Native Americans.* http://www.carolana.com/Carolina/Native_Americans/native_americans_natchez.html (accessed on June 27, 2011).

Lipscomb, Carol A. "Handbook of Texas Online: Comanche Indians." *Texas State Historical Association.* http://www.tshaonline.org/handbook/online/articles/bmc72 (accessed on July 4, 2011).

"The Long Walk." *Council of Indian Nations.* http://www.nrcprograms.org/site/PageServer?pagename=cin_hist_thelongwalk (accessed on July 20, 2011).

"Luiseño." *Four Directions Institute.* http://www.fourdir.com/luiseno.htm (accessed on August 11, 2011).

"Luiseno/Cahuilla Group." *San Francisco State University.* http://bss.sfsu.edu/calstudies/nativewebpages/luiseno.html (accessed on August 11, 2011).

"Lumbee History & Culture." *Lumbee Tribe of North Carolina.*http://www.lumbeetribe.com/History_Culture/History_Culture%20Index.html(accessed on June 4, 2011).

"Métis: History & Culture." *Turtle Island Productions.* http://www.turtle-island.com/native/the-ojibway-story/metis.html (accessed on June 4, 2011).

Métis Nation of Ontario. http://www.metisnation.org/ (accessed on June 4, 2011).

MacDonald, George F. "The Haida: Children of Eagle and Raven." *Canadian Museum of Civilization.* http://www.civilization.ca/cmc/exhibitions/aborig/haida/haindexe.shtml (accessed on November 2, 2011).

"Maidu." *Four Directions Institute.* http://www.fourdir.com/maidu.htm (accessed on August 11, 2011).

"The Maidu." *The First Americans.* http://thefirstamericans.homestead.com/Maidu.html (accessed on August 11, 2011).

"Maidu People." *City of Roseville.* http://www.roseville.ca.us/parks/parks_n_facilities/facilities/maidu_indian_museum/maidu_people.asp (accessed on August 11, 2011).

Makah Cultural and Research Center. http://www.makah.com/mcrchome.html (accessed on November 2, 2011).

The Makah Nation on Washington's Olympic Peninsula. http://www.northolympic.com/makah/ (accessed on November 2, 2011).

Manning, June. "Wampanoag Living." *Martha's Vineyard Magazine.* May–June 2010. http://www.mvmagazine.com/article.php?25216 (accessed on June 9, 2011).

Mashantucket Museum and Research Center. http://www.pequotmuseum.org/ (accessed on June 1, 2011).

Mashpee Wampanoag Tribe. http://mashpeewampanoagtribe.com/ (accessed on June 1, 2011).

"Massacre at Wounded Knee, 1890." *EyeWitness to History.* http://www.eyewitnesstohistory.com/knee.htm (accessed on July 4, 2011).

"Massai, Chiricahua Apache." *Discover Southeast Arizona.* http://www.discoverseaz.com/History/Massai.html (accessed on July 20, 2011).

May, John D. "Otoe-Missouria." *Oklahoma Historical Society.* http://digital.library.okstate.edu/encyclopedia/entries/O/OT001.html (accessed on June 20, 2011).

McCollum, Timothy James. "Quapaw." *Oklahoma Historical Society.* http://digital.library.okstate.edu/encyclopedia/entries/Q/QU003.html (accessed on June 20, 2011).

— — —. "Sac and Fox." *Oklahoma Historical Society.* http://digital.library.okstate.edu/encyclopedia/entries/S/SA001.html (accessed on June 5, 2011).

McCoy, Ron. "Neosho Valley: Osage Nation." *KTWU/Channel 11.* http://ktwu.washburn.edu/journeys/scripts/1111a.html (accessed on June 12, 2011).

McManamon, F. P. "Kennewick Man." *Archaeology Program, National Park Service, U.S. Department of the Interior.* http://www.nps.gov/archeology/kennewick/index.htm (accessed on August 11, 2011).

Media Action. "Excerpt from Youth-led Interview with Phillip Esai." *Vimeo.* http://vimeo.com/15465119 (accessed on June 6, 2011).

— — —. "A Portrait of Nikolai." *Vimeo.* 2010. http://vimeo.com/14854233 (accessed on June 6, 2011).

"Menominee Culture." *Menominee Indian Tribe of Wisconsin.* http://www.mpm.edu/wirp/ICW-54.html (accessed on June 7, 2011).

"Menominee Indian Tribe of Wisconsin." *Great Lakes Inter-Tribal Council.* http://www.glitc.org/programs/pages/mtw.html (accessed on June 7, 2011).

Menominee Indian Tribe of Wisconsin. http://www.menominee-nsn.gov/ (accessed June 8, 2011).

"Menominee Oral Tradition." *Indian Country.* http://www.mpm.edu/wirp/ICW-138.html (accessed on June 7, 2011).

Mescalero Apache Reservation. www.mescaleroapache.com/ (accessed on July 15, 2011).

"Metis Communities." *Labrador Métis Nation.* http://www.labradormetis.ca/home/10 (accessed on June 4, 2011).

"Miami Indian Tribe." *Native American Nations.* http://www.nanations.com/miami/index.htm (accessed on June 7, 2011).

"Miami Indians." *Ohio History Central.* http://www.ohiohistorycentral.org/entry.php?rec=606 (accessed on June 7, 2011).

Miami Nation of Oklahoma. http://www.miamination.com/ (accessed on June 7, 2011).

Miccosukee Seminole Nation. http://www.miccosukeeseminolenation.com/ (accessed on June 12, 2011).

"Mi'kmaq Resources" *Halifax Public Libraries.* http://www.halifaxpublicli-braries.ca/research/topics/mikmaqresources.html (accessed on June 1, 2011).

Mississippi Valley Archaeology Center at the University of Wisconsin–La Crosse, "Early Cultures: Pre-European Peoples of Wisconsin: Mississippian and Oneota Traditions." *Educational Web Adventures.* http://www.uwlax.edu/mvac/preeuropeanpeople/earlycultures/mississippi_tradition.html (accessed on June 20, 2011).

"Missouri Indian Tribe History." *Access Genealogy.* http://www.accessgenealogy.com/native/tribes/siouan/missourihist.htm (accessed on June 20, 2011).

"Missouri Indians." *PBS.* http://www.pbs.org/lewisandclark/native/mis.html (accessed on June 20, 2011).

"Miwok." *Four Directions Institute.* http://www.fourdir.com/miwok.htm (accessed on August 11, 2011).

Miwok Archeological Preserve of Marin. "The Miwok People." *California State Parks.* http://www.parks.ca.gov/default.asp?page_id=22538 (accessed on August 11, 2011).

"Miwok Indian Tribe History." *Access Genealogy.* http://www.accessgeneal-ogy.com/native/california/miwokindianhist.htm (accessed on August 11, 2011).

"Modoc." *College of the Siskiyous.* http://www.siskiyous.edu/shasta/nat/mod.htm (accessed on August 11, 2011).

"Modoc." *Four Directions Institute.* http://www.fourdir.com/modoc.htm (accessed on August 11, 2011).

"Modoc Indian Chiefs and Leaders." *Access Genealogy.* (accessed on August 11, 2011). http://www.accessgenealogy.com/native/tribes/modoc/modocindianchiefs.htm

Modoc Tribe of Oklahoma. http://www.modoctribe.net/ (accessed on August 11, 2011).

"Mohave Indian Tribe History." *Access Genealogy.* http://www.accessgenealogy.com/native/tribes/mohave/mohaveindianhist.htm (accessed on July 20, 2011).

"Mohave National Preserve: Mohave Tribe: Culture." *National Park Service.* http://www.nps.gov/moja/historyculture/mojave-culture.htm (accessed on July 20, 2011).

"The Mohawk Tribe." *Mohawk Nation.* http://www.mohawktribe.com/ (accessed on June 7, 2011).

Montana Arts Council. "From the Heart and Hand: Salish Songs and Dances: Johnny Arlee, Arlee/John T., Big Crane, Pablo." *Montana Official State Website.* http://art.mt.gov/folklife/hearthand/songs.asp (accessed on August 11, 2011).

Morris, Allen. "Seminole History." *Florida Division of Historical Resources.* http://www.flheritage.com/facts/history/seminole/ (accessed on June 12, 2011).

Muscogee (Creek) Nation of Oklahoma. http://www.muscogeenation-nsn.gov/ (accessed on June 12, 2011).

Museum of the Aleutians.. http://www.aleutians.org/index.html (accessed on August 15, 2011).

Mussulman, Joseph. "Osage Indians." *The Lewis and Clark Fort Mandan Foundation.* http://lewis-clark.org/content/content-article.asp?ArticleID=2535 (accessed on June 12, 2011).

Muwekma Ohlone Tribe. http://www.muwekma.org/ (accessed on August 11, 2011).

The Myaamia Project at Miami University. http://www.myaamiaproject.com/ (accessed on June 7, 2011).

Myers, Tom. "Navajo Reservation" (video). *University of Illinois.* http://www.vimeo.com/8828354 (accessed on July 20, 2011).

Nametau Innu. "Your First Steps in the Innu Culture." *Musée Régional de la Côte-Nord.* http://www.nametauinnu.ca/en/tour (accessed on May 26, 2011).

Narragansett Indian Tribe. http://www.narragansett-tribe.org/ (accessed on June 1, 2011).

"Natchez Indian Tribe History." *Access Geneology.* http://www.accessgenealogy.com/native/tribes/natchez/natchezhist.htm (accessed on June 27, 2011).

Natchez Nation. http://www.natchez-nation.com/ (accessed on June 27, 2011).

"Natchez Stories." *Sacred Texts.* http://www.sacred-texts.com/nam/se/mtsi/#section_004 (accessed on June 27, 2011).

National Library for the Environment. "Native Americans and the Environment: Great Basin." *National Council for Science and the Environment.* http://www.cnie.org/nae/basin.html (accessed on August 15, 2011).

National Museum of American History—Smithsonian Institution. "Pueblo Resistance: We Are Here." *Mexico State Record Center and Archives.* http://www.newmexicohistory.org/filedetails.php?fileID=23042 (accessed on July 20, 2011).

National Museum of the American Indian. "Central Plains." *Smithsonian.* http://americanindian.si.edu/searchcollections/results.aspx?regid=58 (accessed on July 4, 2011).

— — —. "Prairie." *Smithsonian.* http://americanindian.si.edu/searchcollections/results.aspx?regid=60 (accessed on June 12, 2011).

— — —. "Southern Plains." *Smithsonian.* http://americanindian.si.edu/searchcollections/results.aspx?regid=61 (accessed on June 20, 2011).

"Native Americans: Osage Tribe." *University of Missouri.* http://ethemes.missouri.edu/themes/1608?locale=en (accessed on June 12, 2011).

"Navajo (Diné)." *Northern Arizona University.* http://www.cpluhna.nau.edu/People/navajo.htm (accessed on July 20, 2011).

Navajo Indian Tribes History. *Access Genealogy.* http://www.accessgenealogy.com/native/tribes/navajo/navahoindianhist.htm (accessed on July 20, 2011).

The Navajo Nation. http://www.navajo-nsn.gov/history.htm (accessed on July 31, 2007).

"Nde Nation." *Chiricahua: Apache Nation.* http://www.chiricahuaapache.org/ (accessed on July 20, 2011).

"New Hampshire's Native American Heritage." *New Hampshire State Council on the Arts.* http://www.nh.gov/folklife/learning/traditions_native_americans.htm (accessed on June 5, 2011).

"Nez Percé." *Countries and Their Culture.* http://www.everyculture.com/multi/Le-Pa/Nez-Perc.html (accessed on August 11, 2011).

"Nez Percé (Nimiipuu) Tribe." *Wisdom of the Elders.* http://www.wisdomoftheelders.org/program303.html (accessed on August 11, 2011).

"Nez Percé National Historical Park." *National Park Service.* http://www.nps.gov/nepe/ (accessed on August 11, 2011).

Nez Percé Tribe. http://www.nezperce.org/ (accessed on August 11, 2011).

"Nisqually Indian Tribe, Washington." *United States History.* http://www.u-s-history.com/pages/h1561.html (accessed on August 15, 2011).

Nisqually Land Trust. http://www.nisquallylandtrust.org (accessed on August 15, 2011).

"NOAA Arctic Theme Page." *National Oceanic and Atmospheric Administration.* http://www.arctic.noaa.gov/ (accessed on August 15, 2011).

"Nohwike Bagowa: House of Our Footprints" *White Mountain Apache Tribe Culture Center and Museum.* http://www.wmat.us/wmaculture.shtml (accessed on July 20, 2011).

"Nootka Indian Music of the Pacific North West Coast." *Smithsonian Folkways.* http://www.folkways.si.edu/albumdetails.aspx?itemid=912 (accessed on August 15, 2011).

Northern Arapaho Tribe. http://www.northernarapaho.com/ (accessed on July 2, 2011).

Northern Cheyenne Nation. www.cheyennenation.com/ (accessed on July 4, 2011).

"Northwest Coastal People." *Canada's First Peoples.* http://firstpeoplesofcanada.com/fp_groups/fp_nwc5.html (accessed on August 15, 2011).

"Nuu-chah-nulth." *Royal British Columbia Museum.* http://www.royalbcmuseum.bc.ca/Content_Files/Files/SchoolsAndKids/nuu2.pdf (accessed on August 15, 2011).

"Nuu-chah-nulth (Barkley) Community Portal." *FirstVoices.* http://www.firstvoices.ca/en/Nuu-chah-nulth (accessed on August 15, 2011).

Nuu-chah-nulth Tribal Council. http://www.nuuchahnulth.org/tribal-council/welcome.html(accessed on August 15, 2011).

"Official Site of the Miami Nation of Indians of the State of Indiana." *Miami Nation of Indians.* http://www.miamiindians.org/ (accessed on June 7, 2011).

Official Site of the Wichita and Affiliated Tribes. http://www.wichitatribe.com/ (accessed on June 9, 2011).

Official Website of the Caddo Nation. http://www.caddonation-nsn.gov/ (accessed on June 12, 2011).

Ohio History Central. "Adena Mound." *Ohio Historical Society.* http://www.ohiohistorycentral.org/entry.php?rec=2411 (accessed June 7, 2011).

"Ohkay Owingeh." *Indian Pueblo Cultural Center.* http://www.indianpueblo.org/19pueblos/ohkayowingeh.html (accessed on July 20, 2011).

*Ohlone/Costanoan Esselen Nation.*http://www.ohlonecostanoanesselennation.org/(accessed on August 11, 2011).

Oklahoma Humanities Council. "Otoe-Missouria Tribe." *Cherokee Strip Museum.* http://www.cherokee-strip-museum.org/Otoe/OM_Who.htm (accessed on June 20, 2011).

Oklahoma Indian Affairs Commission. "2011 Oklahoma Indian Nations." *Pocket Pictorial Directory.* Oklahoma City: Oklahoma Indian Affairs Commission, 2011. Available from http://www.ok.gov/oiac/documents/2011.FINAL.WEB.pdf (accessed on June 12, 2011).

The Oregon History Project. "Modoc." *Oregon Historical Society.* http://www.ohs.org/education/oregonhistory/search/dspResults.cfm?keyword=Modoc&type=&theme=&timePeriod=&region= (accessed on August 11, 2011).

"The Osage." *Fort Scott National Historic Site, National Park Service.* http://www.nps.gov/fosc/historyculture/osage.htm (accessed on June 12, 2011).

Osage Nation. http://www.osagetribe.com/ (accessed on June 12, 2011).

"Osage Indian Tribe History." *Access Genealogy.* http://www.accessgenealogy.com/native/tribes/osage/osagehist.htm (accessed on June 12, 2011).

The Otoe-Missouria Tribe. http://www.omtribe.org/ (accessed on June 20, 2011).

Ottawa Inuit Children's Centre. http://www.ottawainuitchildrens.com/eng/ (accessed on August 15, 2011).

Ottawa Tribe of Oklahoma. http://www.ottawatribe.org/history.htm (accessed May 13, 2011).

"Our History." *Makah Cultural and Research Center.* http://www.makah.com/history.html (accessed on November 2, 2011).

"Pacific Northwest Native Americans." *Social Studies School Service.* http://nativeamericans.mrdonn.org/northwest.html (accessed on August 15, 2011).

Paiute Indian Tribe of Utah. http://www.utahpaiutes.org/ (accessed on August 15, 2011).

The Pascua Yaqui Tribe. http://www.pascuayaqui-nsn.gov/ (accessed on July 20, 2011).

"The Pasqu Yaqui Connection." *Through Our Parents' Eyes: History and Culture of Southern Arizona.* http://parentseyes.arizona.edu/pascuayaquiaz/ (accessed on July 20, 2011).

"Past and Future Meet in San Juan Pueblo Solar Project." *Solar Cookers International.* http://solarcooking.org/sanjuan1.htm (accessed on July 20, 2011).

Pastore, Ralph T. "Aboriginal Peoples: Newfoundland and Labrador Heritage." *Memorial University of Newfoundland.* http://www.heritage.nf.ca/aboriginal/ (accessed on August 15, 2011).

Paul, Daniel N. "We Were Not the Savages." *First Nation History.* http://www.danielnpaul.com/index.html (accessed on June 1, 2011).

"Pawnee." *Four Directions Institute.* http://www.fourdir.com/pawnee.htm (accessed on July 6, 2011).

"Pawnee Indian Museum." *Kansas State Historical Society.* http://www.kshs.org/places/pawneeindian/history.htm (accessed on July 6, 2011).

"Pawnee Indian Tribe History." *Access Genealogy.* http://www.accessgenealogy.com/native/tribes/pawnee/pawneehist.htm (accessed on July 6, 2011).

Pawnee Nation of Oklahoma. http://www.pawneenation.org/ (accessed on July 6, 2011).

"Pecos Indian Tribe History." *Access Genealogy.* http://www.accessgenealogy.com/native/tribes/pecos/pecoshist.htm (accessed on July 20, 2011).

"Pecos National Historical Park." *Desert USA.* http://www.desertusa.com/pecos/pnpark.html (accessed on July 20, 2011).

"Pecos Pueblos." *Four Directions Institute.* http://www.fourdir.com/pecos.htm (accessed on July 20, 2011).

"People of Pecos." *National Park Service.* http://www.nps.gov/peco/historyculture/peple-of-pecos.htm (accessed on July 20, 2011).

"People of the Colorado Plateau: The Hopi." *Northern Arizona University.* http://www.cpluhna.nau.edu/People/hopi.htm (accessed on July 20, 2011).

"People of the Colorado Plateau: The Ute Indian." *Northern Arizona University.* http://cpluhna.nau.edu/People/ute_indians.htm(accessed on August 15, 2011).

"The People of the Flathead Nation."*Lake County Directory.* http://www.lakecodirect.com/archives/The_Flathead_Nation.html (accessed on August 11, 2011).

"Peoples of Alaska and Northeast Siberia." *Alaska Native Collections.* http://alaska.si.edu/cultures.asp (accessed on August 15, 2011).

"Pequot Lives: Almost Vanished." *Pequot Museum and Research Center.* http://www.pequotmuseum.org/Home/MashantucketGallery/AlmostVanished.htm (accessed June 8, 2011).

Peterson, Keith C. "Dams of the Columbia Basin and Their Effects of the Native Fishery." *Center for Columbia River History.* http://www.ccrh.org/comm/river/dams7.htm (accessed on August 11, 2011).

Peterson, Leighton C. "Tuning in to Navajo: The Role of Radio in Native Language Maintenance." *Northern Arizona University.* http://jan.ucc.nau.edu/-jar/TIL_17.html (accessed on July 20, 2011).

"Pima (AkimelO'odham)." *Four Directions Institute.* http://www.fourdir.com/pima.htm (accessed on July 20, 2011).

"Pima Indian Tribe History." *Access Genealogy.* www.accessgenealogy.com/native/tribes/pima/pimaindianhist.htm (accessed on July 20, 2011).

Pit River Indian Tribe. http://www.pitrivertribe.org/home.php (accessed on August 11, 2011).

"Pomo People: Brief History." *Native American Art.* http://www.kstrom.net/isk/art/basket/pomohist.html (accessed on August 11, 2011).

Porter, Tom. "Mohawk (Haudenosaunee) Teaching." *FourDirectionsTeachings.com.* http://www.fourdirectionsteachings.com/transcripts/mohawk.html (accessed June 7, 2011).

"Powhatan Indian Village." *Acton Public Schools: Acton-Boxborough Regional School District.* http://ab.mec.edu/jamestown/powhatan (accessed on June 1, 2011).

"Powhatan Language and the Powhatan Indian Tribe (Powatan, Powhatten, Powhattan)." *Native Languages of the Americas: Preserving and Promoting Indigenous American Indian Languages.* http://www.native-languages.org/powhatan.htm (accessed on on June 1, 2011).

"Preserving Sacred Wisdom." *Native Spirit and the Sun Dance Way.* http://www. nativespiritinfo.com/ (accessed on July 5, 2011).

"Pueblo Indian History and Resources." *Pueblo Indian.* http://www.puebloindian.com/ (accessed on July 20, 2011).

Pueblo of Acoma. http://www.puebloofacoma.org/ (accessed on July 20, 2011).

Pueblo of Jemez. http://www.jemezpueblo.org/ (accessed on July 20, 2011).

Pueblo of Zuñi. http://www.ashiwi.org/(accessed on July 20, 2011).

Puyallup Tribe of Indians. http://www.puyallup-tribe.com/ (accessed on November 2, 2011).

Quapaw Tribe of Oklahoma. http://www.quapawtribe.com/ (accessed on June 20, 2011).

"The Quapaw Tribe of Oklahoma and the Tar Creek Project." *Environmental Protection Agency.* http://www.epa.gov/oar/tribal/tribetotribe/tarcreek.html (accessed on June 20, 2011).

"Questions and Answers about the Plateau Indians." *Wellpinit School District 49 (WA).* http://www.wellpinit.wednet.edu/sal-qa/qa.php (accessed on August 11, 2011).

"Questions and Answers about the Spokane Indians." *Wellpinit School District.* http://wellpinit.org/q%2526a (accessed on August 11, 2011).

Redish, Laura, and Orrin Lewis. *Native Languages of the Americas.*http://www. native-languages.org (accessed on August 11, 2011).

"Research Starters: Anasazi and Pueblo Indians." *Scholastic.com.* http://teacher. scholastic.com/researchtools/researchstarters/native_am/ (accessed on July 20, 2011).

"The Rez We Live On"(videos). *The Confederated Salish and Kootenai Tribes.* http://therezweliveon.com/13/video.html (accessed on August 11, 2011).

The Rooms, Provincial Museum Division. "Innu Objects."*Virtual Museum Canada.* 2008. http://www.museevirtuel-virtualmuseum.ca/edu/ViewLoit Collection.do;jsessionid=3083D5EEB47F3ECDE9DA040AD0D4C956? method=preview⟨=EN&id=3210 (accessed on May 24, 2011).

Sac and Fox Nation. http://www.sacandfoxnation-nsn.gov/ (accessed on June 5, 2011).

"Sac and Fox Tribe." *Meskwaki Nation.* http://www.meskwaki.org/ (accessed on June 5, 2011).

San Carlos Apache Cultural Center. http://www.sancarlosapache.com/home.htm (accessed on July 20, 2011).

"San Carlos Apache Sunrise Dance." *World News Network.* http://wn.com/ San_Carlos_Apache_Sunrise_Dance (accessed on July 20, 2011).

"San Juan Pueblo." *New Mexico Magazine.* http://www.nmmagazine.com/ native_american/san_juan.php (accessed on July 20, 2011).

"San Juan Pueblo O'Kang." *Indian Pueblo Cultural Center.* http://www.indianpueblo. org/19pueblos/ohkayowingeh.html (accessed on July 20, 2011).

"The Sand Creek Massacre." *Last of the Independents.* http://www.lastoftheinde- pendents.com/sandcreek.htm (accessed on July 2, 2011).

"Seminole Indian Tribe History." *Access Genealogy.* http://www.accessgenealogy. com/native/tribes/seminole/seminolehist.htm (accessed on June 12, 2011).

Seminole Nation of Oklahoma. http://www.seminolenation.com/ (accessed on June 12, 2011).

Seminole Tribe of Florida. http://www.seminoletribe.com/ (accessed on June 12, 2011).

"Sharp Nose." *Native American Nations.* http://www.nanations.com/arrap/ page4.htm (accessed on July 2, 2011).

"The Shawnee in History." *The Shawnee Tribe.* http://www.shawnee-tribe.com/ history.htm (accessed on June 12, 2011).

"Shawnee Indian Tribe History." *Access Genealogy.* http://www.accessgenealogy. com/native/tennessee/shawneeindianhist.htm (accessed on June 12, 2011).

"Shawnee Indians." *Ohio Historical Society.* http://www.ohiohistorycentral.org/ entry.php?rec=631&nm=Shawnee-Indians (accessed on June 12, 2011).

Shawnee Nation, United Remnant Band. http://www.zaneshawneecaverns.net/ shawnee.shtml (accessed on June 12, 2011).

"A Short History of the Spokane Indians." *Wellpinit School District.* http://www.wellpinit.wednet.edu/shorthistory (accessed on August 11, 2011).

"Short Overview of California Indian History." *California Native American Heritage Commission.* http://www.nahc.ca.gov/califindian.html (accessed on August 15, 2011).

Sicade, Henry. "Education." *Puyallup Tribe of Indians.* http://www.puyallup-tribe. com/history/education/ (accessed on November 2, 2011).

"Simon Ortiz: Native American Poet." *The University of Texas at Arlington.* http://www.uta.edu/english/tim/poetry/so/ortizmain.htm (accessed on July 20, 2011).

Simpson, Linda. "The Kansas/Kanza/Kaw Nation." *Oklahoma Territory.* http:// www.okgenweb.org/-itkaw/Kanza2.html (accessed on June 17, 2011).

The Skokomish Tribal Nation. http://www.skokomish.org/ (accessed on Novem- ber 2, 2011).

Skopec, Eric. "What Mystery?" *Anasazi Adventure.* http://www.anasaziadventure. com/what_mystery.pdf (accessed on July 20, 2011).

Smithsonian Folkways. "Rain Dance (Zuñi)." *Smithsonian Institution.* http:// www.folkways.si.edu/TrackDetails.aspx?itemid=16680 (music track) and http://media.smithsonianfolkways.org/liner_notes/folkways/FW06510.pdf (instructions for dance). (accessed on July 20, 2011).

Snook, Debbie. "Ohio's Trail of Tears." *Wyandotte Nation of Oklahoma*, 2003. http://www.wyandotte-nation.org/culture/history/published/trail-of-tears/ (accessed May 11, 2011).

The Southern Arapaho. http://southernarapaho.org/ (accessed on July 2, 2011).

Southern Ute Indian Tribe. http://www.southern-ute.nsn.us/ (accessed on August 15, 2011).

Splawn, A. J. *Ka-mi-akin, the Last Hero of the Yakimas.* Portland, OR: Kilham Stationary and Printing, 1917. Reproduced by Washington Secretary of State. http://www.secstate.wa.gov/history/publications_detail.aspx?p=24 (accessed on August 11, 2011).

"Spokane Indian Tribe." *Access Genealogy.* http://www.accessgenealogy.com/native/tribes/salish/spokanhist.htm (accessed on August 11, 2011).

"Spokane Indian Tribe." *United States History.* http://www.u-s-history.com/pages/h1570.html (accessed on August 11, 2011).

Spokane Tribe of Indians. http://www.spokanetribe.com/ (accessed on August 11, 2011).

Sreenivasan, Hari. "'Apache 8' Follows All-Women Firefighters On and Off the Reservation." *PBS NewsHour.* http://video.pbs.org/video/2006599346/ (accessed on July 20, 2011).

Stands In Timber, John. "Cheyenne Memories." *Northern Cheyenne Nation.* http://www.cheyennenation.com/memories.html (accessed on July 4, 2011).

Stewart, Kenneth. "Kivas." *Scholastic.* http://www2.scholastic.com/browse/article.jsp?id=5052 (accessed on July 20, 2011).

"The Story of the Ute Tribe: Past, Present, and Future." *Ute Mountain Ute Tribe.* http://www.utemountainute.com/story.htm (accessed on August 15, 2011).

Sultzman, Lee. *First Nations.* http://www.tolatsga.org/sf.html (accessed on June 5, 2011).

Swan, Daniel C. "Native American Church." *Oklahoma Historical Society.* http://digital.library.okstate.edu/encyclopedia/entries/N/NA015.html (accessed on August 11, 2011).

"Taos Pueblo." *Bluffton University.* http://www.bluffton.edu/-sullivanm/taos/taos.html (accessed on July 20, 2011).

"Taos Pueblo." *New Mexico Magazine.* http://www.nmmagazine.com/native_american/taos.php (accessed on July 20, 2011).

Taos Pueblo. http://www.taospueblo.com/ (accessed on July 20, 2011).

"Taos Pueblo: A Thousand Years of Tradition." *Taos Pueblo.* http://taospueblo.com/ (accessed on July 20, 2011).

"Territorial Kansas: Kansa Indians." *University of Kansas.* http://www.territorialkansasonline.org/-imlskto/cgi-bin/index.php?SCREEN=

keyword&selected_keyword=Kansa%20Indians (accessed on June 17, 2011).

"Throat Singing." *Inuit Cultural Online Resource.* http://icor.ottawainuitchildrens. com/node/30 (accessed on August 15, 2011).

"Tlingit Tribes, Clans, and Clan Houses: Traditional Tlingit Country." *Alaska Native Knowledge Network.* http://www.ankn.uaf.edu/ANCR/Southeast/ TlingitMap/ (accessed on November 2, 2011).

"Tohono O'odham (Papago)." *Four Directions Institute.* http://www.fourdir. com/tohono_o'odham.htm (accessed on July 20, 2011).

"Totem Pole Websites." *Cathedral Grove.* http://www.cathedralgrove.eu/ text/07-Totem-Websites-3.htm (accessed on November 2, 2011).

"Trading Posts in the American Southwest." *Southwest Crossroads.* http:// southwestcrossroads.org/record.php?num=742&hl=chiricahua:: apache (accessed on July 20, 2011).

"Traditional Mi'kmaq Beliefs." *Indian Brook First Nation.* http://home.rushcomm. ca/-hsack/spirit.html (accessed on June1,2011).

"Tsmshian Songs We Love to Sing!" *Dum Baaldum.* http://www.dumbaaldum. org/html/songs.htm (accessed on August 15, 2011).

"Umatilla Indian Agency and Reservation, Oregon." *Access Genealogy.* http:// www.accessgenealogy.com/native/census/condition/umatilla_indian_ agency_reservation_oregon.htm (accessed on August 11, 2011).

"Umatilla, Walla Walla, and Cayuse." *TrailTribes.org: Traditional and Contemporary Native Culture.* http://www.trailtribes.org/umatilla/home.htm (accessed on August 11, 2011).

"Unangax & Alutiiq (Sugpiaq)." *Alaska Native Heritage Center.* http://www. alaskanative.net/en/main_nav/education/culture_alaska/unangax/ (accessed on August 15, 2011).

Unrau, William E. "Kaw (Kansa)." *Oklahoma Historical Society.* http://digital. library.okstate.edu/encyclopedia/entries/K/KA001.html (accessed on June 17, 2011).

Urban Indian Experience. "The Duwamish: Seattle's Landless Tribe." *KUOW: PRX.* http://www.prx.org/pieces/1145-urban-indian-experience-episode-1- the-duwamish(accessed on November 2, 2011).

The Ute Indian Tribe. http://www.utetribe.com/ (accessed on August 15, 2011).

"Ute Nation." *Utah Travel Industry.* http://www.utah.com/tribes/ute_main.htm (accessed on August 15, 2011).

Virtual Archaeologist. "The Like-a-Fishhook Story." *NDSU Archaeology Technologies Laboratory.* http://fishhook.ndsu.edu/home/lfstory.php (accessed on June 19, 2011).

"A Virtual Tour of California Missions." *MissionTour.* http://missiontour.org/ index.htm (accessed on August 11, 2011).

"Visiting a Maidu Bark House." *You Tube.* http://www.youtube.com/watch?v=fw5i83519mQ (accessed on August 11, 2011).

"The Wampanoag." *Boston Children's Museum.* http://www.bostonkids.org/educators/wampanoag/html/what.htm (accessed on June 1, 2011).

"Washoe." *Four Directions Institute.* http://www.fourdir.com/washoe.htm (accessed on August 15, 2011).

"Washoe Hot Springs." *National Cultural Preservation Council.* http://www.ncpc.info/projects_washoe.html (accessed on August 15, 2011).

"Washoe Indian Tribe History." *Access Genealogy.* http://www.accessgenealogy.com/native/tribes/washo/washohist.htm (accessed on August 15, 2011).

"We Shall Remain." *PBS.* http://www.pbs.org/wgbh/amex/weshallremain/ (accessed on July 20, 2011).

Weiser, Kathy. *Legends of America.* http://www.legendsofamerica.com (accessed on July 20, 2011).

"White Mountain Apache Indian Reservation." *Arizona Handbook.* http://www.arizonahandbook.com/white_mtn_apache.htm (accessed on July 20, 2011).

"White Mountain Apache Tribe." *Inter Tribal Council of Arizona.* http://www.itcaonline.com/tribes_whitemtn.html (accessed on July 20, 2011).

"White Mountain Apache Tribe: Restoring Wolves, Owls, Trout and Ecosystems" *Cooperative Conservation America.* http://www.cooperativeconservation.org/viewproject.asp?pid=136 (accessed on July 20, 2011).

"Who Were the Lipan and the Kiowa-Apaches?" *Southwest Crossroads.* http://southwestcrossroads.org/record.php?num=522&hl=chiricahua:: apache (accessed on July 20, 2011).

"Wichita." *Four Directions Institute.* http://www.fourdir.com/wichita.htm (accessed on June 9, 2011).

Wind River Indian Reservation. http://www.wind-river.org/info/communities/reservation.php (accessed on July 2, 2011).

Wind River Indian Reservation: Eastern Shoshone Tribe. http://www.easternshoshone.net/ (accessed on August 15, 2011).

WMAT: White Mountain Apache Tribe. http://wmat.us/ (accessed on July 20, 2011).

"Wounded Knee." *Last of the Independent.* http://www.lastoftheindependents.com/wounded.htm (accessed on July 4, 2011).

The Wounded Knee Museum. http://www.woundedkneemuseum.org/ (accessed on July 4, 2011).

Wyandot Nation of Anderdon. http://www.wyandotofanderdon.com/ (accessed May 13, 2011).

Wyandot Nation of Kansas. http://www.wyandot.org/ (accessed May 13, 2011).

Wyandotte Nation of Oklahoma. http://www.wyandotte-nation.org/ (accessed May 13, 2011).

"Yakima Indian Tribe History." *Access Genealogy.* http://www.accessgenealogy. com/native/tribes/yakimaindianhist.htm (accessed on August 11, 2011).

Yakama Nation Cultural Heritage Center. http://www.yakamamuseum.com/ (accessed on August 11, 2011).

"Yaqui." *Four Directions Institute.* http://www.fourdir.com/yaqui.htm (accessed on July 20, 2011).

"Yaqui and Mayo Indian Easter Ceremonies." *RimJournal.* http://www.rimjournal. com/arizyson/easter.htm (accessed on July 20, 2011).

"Yaqui Sacred Traditions." *Wisdom Traditions Institute.* http://www.wisdomtraditions. com/yaqui2.html (accessed on July 20, 2011).

"Yuma (Quechan)." *Four Directions Institute.* http://www.fourdir.com/yuma. htm (accessed on July 20, 2011).

Yuman Indian Tribe History." *Access Genealogy.* http://www.accessgenealogy. com/native/tribes/yuman/yumanfamilyhist.htm (accessed on July 20, 2011).

"The Yup'ik and Cup'ik People—Who We Are." *The Alaska Native Heritage Center Museum.* http://www.alaskanative.net/en/main_nav/education/ culture_alaska/yupik/ (accessed on August 15, 2011).

"Yup'ik Tundra Navigation." *Center for Cultural Design.* http://www.ccd.rpi. edu/Eglash/csdt/na/tunturyu/index.html (accessed on August 15, 2011).

"The Yurok." *California History Online.* http://www.californiahistoricalsociety. org/timeline/chapter2/002d.html# (accessed on August 11, 2011).

"Yurok." *Four Directions Institute.* http://www.fourdir.com/yurok.htm (accessed on August 11, 2011).

The Yurok Tribe. http://www.yuroktribe.org/ (accessed on August 11, 2011).

Zeig, Sande. *Apache 8* (film). http://www.apache8.com/ (accessed on July 20, 2011).

"Zuñi." *Northern Arizona University.* http://www.cpluhna.nau.edu/People/zuni. htm (accessed on July 20, 2011).

"Zuñi." *Southwest Crossroads.* http://southwestcrossroads.org/record. php?num=2&hl=zuni (accessed on July 20, 2011).

"Zuñi Pueblo." *New Mexico Magazine.* http://www.nmmagazine.com/native_ american/zuni.php (accessed on July 20, 2011).

"Zuñi Pueblos (Ashiwi)." *Four Directions Institute.* http://www.fourdir.com/ zuni.htm (accessed on July 20, 2011).

Index

Italics indicates volume numbers; **boldface** indicates entries and their page numbers. Chart indicates a chart; ill. indicates an illustration, and map indicates a map.

G

N

U

U•X•L Encyclopedia of Native American Tribes, 3rd Edition

X

Y